McCoubrey & White's

Textbook on

Jurisprudence

....

Fifth edition

Professor J. E. Penner

Professor of Law, University College London

Dr E. Melissaris

Senior Lecturer in Law, London School of Economics

OXFORD

UNIVERSITY PRESS

OXFORD
UNIVERSITY PRESS

Great Clarendon Street, Oxford, OX2 6DP,
United Kingdom

Oxford University Press is a department of the University of Oxford.
It furthers the University's objective of excellence in research, scholarship,
and education by publishing worldwide. Oxford is a registered trade mark of
Oxford University Press in the UK and in certain other countries

© Estate of Hilaire McCoubrey, Nigel White, James Penner, Emmanuel Melissaris 2012

The moral rights of the authors have been asserted

First published by Blackstone Press 1993
Second Edition published 1999
Third Edition published 2003
Fourth Edition published 2008

Impression: 1

Public sector information reproduced under Open Government Licence v1.0
(http://www.nationalarchives.gov.uk/doc/open-government-licence/
open-government-licence.htm)

Crown Copyright material reproduced with the permission of the
Controller, HMSO (under the terms of the Click Use licence)

British Library Cataloguing in Publication Data

Data available

Library of Congress Cataloging in Publication Data

Library of Congress Control Number: 2012941354

ISBN 978–0–19–958434–5

Printed in Great Britain by
Ashford Colour Press Ltd, Gosport, Hampshire

PREFACE

As Hilaire McCoubrey and Nigel White wrote in the third edition of this book, jurisprudence is a topic which allows us, indeed requires us, to stand back from the detail of law and consider what the significance of law is, how it operates in our day to day lives, and how it figures in the way we think about our relations to others, in particular about society and politics and the way the communities we live in are organised.

Learning jurisprudence will not make you a better lawyer in any direct way (although exercising your brain cells in any demanding way will make you a better lawyer insofar as it makes you a better thinker, better able to spot flaws in arguments, better able to think round problems, and jurisprudence will certainly hone your skills at that). But that is not why you are expected or required to study jurisprudence. As a lawyer, you should study jurisprudence as a simple matter of intellectual self-respect. If, after three years of law school, you are unable to articulate in a reasonably sophisticated way what the *significance* of your subject is, what philosophical puzzles it gives rise to, what is interesting and controversial and fascinating about it in social, political, and historical terms, then your education is, quite simply, incomplete. No one expects every student to excel in jurisprudence, any more than we would expect every student to excel in the law of contract or trusts or criminal law. But every student who claims brains sufficient to read law has sufficient grey matter to 'get' jurisprudence, and so will you.

This is intended to be a user-friendly book which provides a guide to the content, implications, and problems of the major theories. The presentation, we hope, is not over-simplified nor made needlessly obscure. Like any university-level subject, jurisprudence is largely about deepening your understanding of what might at first appear simple. Don't expect to become good at jurisprudence overnight. Probably the best way to get the subject under your skin is to talk about it with others. Bother your friends and relatives if you must. If you can explain Hart's criticism of Austin's theory by way of the 'being obliged/being under an obligation' distinction to your mother so that she understands it, then you understand it; if you can't, then you probably don't. Of course, discussing jurisprudence with your fellow students, and so teaching each other, works even better. Form a study group with others whose brains you respect, meet regularly (it does not matter where—pub, coffee shop, launderette, wherever) and discuss what you're reading at the minute. Being able to articulate your ideas is vital and *if you can say it, you can write it* (in an essay, in an exam). So get reading, and get speaking. Good luck.

J. E. Penner and E. Melissaris
11 April 2012

NEW TO THIS EDITION

(1) Substantial revisions to the material in Part I, Theories of the Nature of Law.

(2) A brand new Part II, Particular Philosophical Issues in Law with three new chapters on:
   - The nature of norms;
   - Law and governance; and
   - Law and adjudication.

(3) A brand new Part III, The Intellectual Foundations of the Liberal Social Contract Tradition, with three new chapters on the political and legal philosophy of:
   - Thomas Hobbes;
   - Immanuel Kant; and
   - John Rawls.

(4) Substantial revision of the chapters on Marxism and postmodern legal theory.

OUTLINE CONTENTS

DETAILED CONTENTS

1

What is Jurisprudence?

Introduction

The subject matter of jurisprudence is the theoretical or philosophical study of law. As you can imagine, there is much of philosophical and theoretical interest in the phenomenon of law. What are the defining or essential features of law and legal systems? Is there a moral obligation to obey the law? How do legal rules work? What are the connections between law and justice? These and other questions of this fairly abstract kind are the sort of questions that will be addressed in this book. The book is divided into four Parts: I Theories of the Nature of Law; II Particular Philosophical Issues in Law; III The Intellectual Foundations of the Liberal Social Contract Tradition in Political and Legal Philosophy; and IV Against and Beyond Liberalism.

1.1 Theories of the nature of law

As its name indicates, this Part of the book concerns itself with the various theories that have tried to identify the essential features of law and legal systems. What might such a feature be? Well, the law is typically enforced by a state which uses coercion, punishments or the threat thereof, to ensure that the law is complied with. Is it therefore true, we may ask, that the law is necessarily coercive? Some theorists have thought so, for example Kelsen, who thought that law was by definition the form of social order which applies sanctions to those who break rules. Others, such as Raz, would say no—for Raz, even a society of angels would need laws; for example, however morally stainless they might be, as drivers they would need traffic laws, rules of the road to avoid crashing into each other, just as much as we fallen creatures do.

To take another example, everyone agrees that the Nazi legal system contained some very wicked laws. Some philosophers, such as Fuller, have contended that the Nazi legal system was so wicked that it did not really count as a legal system at all, on the basis that there are minimum moral requirements which a system of state rules must possess for it to be a legal system at all. Hart, by contrast, thought this a confusion: wicked though it was, the Nazis still had a legal system; it was just a very wicked legal system, which because of its wickedness no one had any moral obligation to obey.

Now stop and think for a moment about these two examples. You almost certainly start thinking by noticing you have a gut reaction, preferring the view of one of the theorists to the other in each case. To put this slightly more elaborately, you have a 'philosophical intuition' that one view is better than the other. These intuitions are important, and you should pay attention to them. But they are never enough, of course, to conclude which side of an argument is right (if either is). The next thing you must proceed to do is to see whether you can defend your intuition by giving reasons why it is sound, reasons which anyone can assess whether they share your intuitions or not. That is when philosophy begins.

This part of jurisprudence is largely a matter of entering centuries old debates about particularly knotty issues which arise when we try to say, with rigour and precision, what the phenomenon of law is, what it amounts to, what makes it important to human societies. When we do the philosophy of law, first, if we are wise, we learn what other thinkers have said about an issue. Not only will this save us time—why re-invent the wheel, after all?—it will enrich our understanding of the problem. As is true elsewhere, often the 'key' to unlocking a difficult philosophical puzzle which has troubled people for ages is to try a different angle, re-frame the problem, question the question.

The most central question in the philosophy of law, as you will no doubt have figured out yourself, is 'What is law?'. What is the right way to describe, and in doing so describe the significance of, the law, which shows that we understand the phenomenon? This is a big question to ask, and one of the most important moves forward in our appreciation of this question was made by Hart, when he broke it down into three parts. In a sense, Hart asked why people have difficulties or are puzzled when they are asked to come up with an answer to it, and he said this was because there were three underlying issues that kept coming up but were never properly addressed. In order to answer the big question, said Hart, you must first be able to answer these three:

> How do law and legal obligation differ from, and how are they related to, orders backed by threats? How does legal obligation differ from, and how is it related to, moral obligation? What are rules, and to what extent is law an affair of rules?
>
> (H.L.A. Hart, *The Concept of Law*, 2nd ed. (Oxford: Oxford University Press, 1994), p. 13)

Identifying these questions was such a substantial move forward because these questions focus our attention on three historical strands of the philosophical theorising about law which to this day shape the subject in large part. The first—law and its relation to coercion—which is the issue in the first of our examples above, gives voice to one version of what is known as 'positivism', the idea that law is a manmade institution of political power, and as such, is the means by which the state organises its day-to-day regulation of its subjects by laying down standards backed up by the threat of sanction. The second question, reflected in the second of our examples above, draws our attention to the 'natural law' tradition, which holds, roughly, that for a legal system to count as genuinely lawful, it cannot depart too far from the dictates of morality, the source of which morality is not 'manmade', but is in some sense independent of the customs or ways of life of people, i.e. of whom it applies to. The final question is one which Hart deserves a lot of credit for noticing and for making explicit, for it is one which has tended to be neglected in legal theorising, or at least is generally approached only tangentially. As we will see, Hart, and later Raz, have probably made the most significant contribution to jurisprudence in the past century by showing how the law can be seen as a form of communal practical reason, i.e., a social institution by which people coordinate their behaviour to achieve goals they could not achieve simply by acting independently. This last question may be the one which is the most philosophically demanding for beginners, and we will attack it slowly, step by step, when we discuss Hart's and Raz's work.

Hart was the pivotal figure of the philosophy of law of the twentieth century, and this book is largely shaped around the central importance of his work. Chapters 2 and 3 explore classical natural law theory and classical positivism, which together formed the traditional philosophical landscape Hart encountered. Chapters 4 and 5 look at Hart's work. Chapter 6 looks at the main currents in legal philosophy following Hart, focussing on the work of Dworkin and Raz.

1.2 Particular philosophical issues in law

The second Part of the book follows on from the first. In the three chapters of Part II, we will look at some particular aspects of the law that have given rise to theoretical inquiry and dispute. In the short Chapter 7 we will look at the philosophical issues raised by the law's use of norms, i.e. things that require a standard of behaviour, such as orders, rules, and duties. This is a nuts and bolts chapter; although we will look at various controversies that have been occasioned by the investigation of the nature of norms, such as the debate between 'will' and 'interest' theorists of rights, and the question whether Hohfeld's analysis of legal norms in terms of fundamental 'jural' conceptions is a move forward, this is not a difficult part of the book; it is principally there to get you up to speed on the philosophical issues and vocabulary in this neck of the woods.

In the somewhat longer Chapter 8 we see how the philosophy of law meshes with political philosophy more generally; we will look at three questions: is there a *duty* on those who have the power to govern, to do so, and if so, what sort of duty is it? Secondly, for those who take up the position of governors, what gives them the *right* to rule over others. This is also sometimes framed as the question of legitimate authority. Finally, we will ask whether the subjects of the law have a general moral obligation to obey the law; interestingly, until the 1970s most theorists thought this was obviously the case, and the task was deciding how best to justify such an obligation. These days, the view is now quite the opposite, i.e. that there is no general obligation to obey all the laws of even a just legal system.

Chapter 9 is a long chapter. It deals with one of the central features of law, adjudication, and the theories attention to it has generated. Section 1 of the chapter deals with American legal realism and its sceptical challenge to the idea that judges decide cases by applying determinate legal rules. Addressing the realists, especially their rule scepticism, will involve us in some quite deep philosophical issues, taking us, for example, into the philosophical work on rule-following of Ludwig Wittgenstein. The second section of the chapter considers legal interpretivism, a theory of law originating in the work of Dworkin, and which began its life as a way of better accounting for the nature of legal argument and judicial decision-making. Finally, the chapter looks at the rule of law and the recent claim by Waldron that the values underlying adjudication deserve a more prominent place in our understanding of the value of law.

1.3 The intellectual foundations of the social contract tradition

In the third Part of the book, we will turn from legal philosophy narrowly conceived to political philosophy and its implications for law. We will focus on a particular strand within political philosophy, namely the liberal social contract tradition and three influential representatives of this strand, Thomas Hobbes, Immanuel Kant and John Rawls.

To grasp what political philosophy is about, consider the world in which we live. We all have our own views on happiness. Some are hedonists while others are more interested in their intellectual or spiritual development. We have different views on the origins of our very existence. Many believe that a supreme being created the world, while others refuse to believe anything that we are not able to grasp with the use of logic and scientific method. We also have different views on what is right and what is wrong. For some there is no such thing as 'objective morality'; we are only guided by our desires, they maintain. Others believe that there are some moral norms that transcend our experience in the here and now. Furthermore, in order for us to be able to live our lives in the way that we choose, we need to have access to and use of material resources. But not only are these resources not infinite and unlimited but they are also diminished by the minute.

How, then, can we all live together peacefully? How will it be possible for people with such different views on the very meaning and value of life, people who occupy the same space and must share the same resources, to co-exist without disagreement and competition getting the better of us? Answering this question is the central task of political philosophy. Its aim is to formulate general principles, which can provide the basis for an institutional structure, which will in turn effectively govern our co-existence and provide stability in the long run. To put it slightly differently, the objective is to justify the state and set the conditions under which it can legitimately impose coercion. How these foundational political principles are to be set is, of course, a contested issue. For some, natural law theorists for instance, political principles are objective moral principles writ large. For others the domain of the political is largely independent of morality, it is an autonomous normative order, which regulates only our lives as citizens, as members of the political community, and not our private or social existence.

It should already be pretty obvious that the foundational principles underpinning our political communities will have a direct effect both on the content and the form of the law. Say, for example, that at the foundational level it is agreed that the best way of organising our political affairs is by granting absolutely equal rights and equal shares of resources to every participant in the political community without remainder. This already means that the law will be subject to constraints as to what it may or may not expect of citizens. But its form may also be affected. For instance, it is only a legal system that meets the basic rule of law requirements of being accessible and knowable by all, clear and intelligible and so on that can serve the principle of equality. Because political philosophy sets the conditions of legitimacy of law, it may also have a direct bearing on the question of law's validity and normativity. In the previous Parts of the book we have already discussed the idea that, should the law fail to measure up to some standards of rightness, then it does not count as law at all and therefore fails to generate any duties. If this is the case, one must have a very clear view as to what are the criteria of legitimacy and this is a task for political philosophy.

Political philosophy is rich and constantly evolving and it is impossible to even begin to give a comprehensive account of all the approaches to political philosophical questions here. We will therefore narrow things down and only discuss three central moments in the development of a specific tradition of political philosophical thought, namely the liberal social contract tradition. Let us explain some preliminaries to this.

1.3.1 **What is liberalism?**

Liberal political theory starts from the fundamental assumption that the individual enjoys ontological, epistemological and normative priority. This means, first, that the individual is considered as an atomic unit, the final and irreducible level of analysis in a socially and politically relevant sense. To put it simply, communities are understood first and foremost as groups of independent individuals and as depending for their existence on the attitudes of these individuals. If this sounds like common sense, it should be placed against the background of theories according to which individuals are not self-contained and independent but simply parts of social wholes.

On the epistemological side of the idea, it is only as individuals that we can make sense of the world and our place in it. This means, among other things, that we cannot take the perspective of others when making decisions about our lives, although this is not to say that we cannot, or indeed that we ought not to, take others into account when doing so.

Finally, and perhaps most importantly, the individual enjoys normative priority in the sense that she is the ultimate source of authentication of all norms, both moral and political. There is no universal agreement amongst liberals as to how exactly the individual is the source of all value; for some it is because morality is tied up to our desires while others reduce it to our faculty of reasoning; for some what is right and wrong depends on our actual decisions in the here and now whereas for others we are constrained by norms which derive from an idealised conception of humanity even if we fail to appreciate and be motivated by these norms. Be that as it may, what is important to highlight for our purposes at this stage is that individuals are the source and the primary subject and beneficiary of moral and political norms. One thing should be emphasised though. Not all liberal political theory is individualistic in the sense that it shows disregard for the community as something valuable. But the individual is still the normative starting point.

A corollary of the centrality of the individual in liberal thought is the assumption that individuals bear two fundamental traits: we are free and we are equal. What freedom and equality exactly are is again an open question—for example, for some they are natural rights whereas for others are simply descriptions of certain empirical attributes—but the general idea is nevertheless a common locus in liberal theory. It also arguably poses the biggest challenge to it, because freedom and equality pull in opposite directions. Maximise one and you lose some of the other. Think about it: say that goods are distributed equally amongst the members of a group irrespective of desert, productivity, need and so forth. Now, if one wants to earn more for whatever reason and is prepared to work harder and so on, she will have a reasonable complaint that her freedom is being compromised, because she is not given the opportunity to pursue her own idea of the good life. Now imagine the opposite, namely a society, in which everyone is entitled to maximum freedom. It is not hard to see how equality would be compromised in such conditions if not for any other reason at least because resources are scarce and not everyone can enjoy the maximum of their desired proportion and because accidentally acquired traits would disadvantage some segments of the population. Liberal political philosophy therefore centrally asks how we can strike the right balance between freedom and equality so as not to sacrifice either. The upshot should be an arrangement in which each citizen will enjoy a private and inviolable sphere of control, in which she will be able to pursue her ideas but which will also be subject to limitations necessary for others to be afforded the same rights.

1.3.2 **What is the social contract tradition?**

Recall that the challenge for political philosophy is to justify the state by formulating general political principles of legitimacy, which make our peaceful co-existence possible and stable in the long term. And liberal political philosophy pursues this aim by reserving a central place for the individual as free and equal. However, there is disagreement within liberal political theory broadly conceived on how this aim is to be pursued, disagreement which is largely due to the different interpretation of the initial premises. For some liberal theorists, political principles and norms can be formulated in a way independent of the attitudes or acceptance of the members of the political community. A state can therefore be legitimate and, indeed, just to the extent that it treats its citizens as free and equal without being under an obligation to take into account citizens' views on how their lives in common ought to be governed.

The social contract tradition starts from the very different assumption that if we hold as true the foundational premise that we are free and equal, then we are also compelled to hold that basic political principles can only be legitimate if they are acceptable or, in an alternative view, actually accepted by everyone in the political community. That is the crux of the idea of the social contract. Political arrangements rest on an agreement, whether actual or hypothetical or a bit of both, between all members of the political community to abide by the same norms, which will govern the political aspect of their lives.

You will not be surprised to hear that, once again, there is no general consensus within the social contract tradition on a number of issues: on why we may be motivated to agree on a social contract in the first place; on the parties to the social contract and their characteristics; on the reasons for which we are under an obligation to abide by the terms of the social contract; on what the terms of the social contract will be and so on.

It is of course impossible to consider all the variations of the basic idea of the social contract in this. In this Part's three chapters we will only discuss three important steps in the long line of development of the tradition. We will start with two of the most important and influential representatives of the Enlightenment, namely Thomas Hobbes and his theory of the state in terms of the rationally motivated submission to the sovereign and Immanuel Kant and his legal and political philosophy in terms of independence from the choices of others. Finally, we will turn to the work of John Rawls, arguably the most influential political philosopher of the last century, and his theory of justice and the legitimacy of the state in contemporary conditions of pluralism.

1.4 **Against and beyond liberalism**

Most of the legal and political theories that we will have discussed in the first three Parts of the book are broadly placed in the liberal tradition. This is not to say that there are no important, and often irreconcilable, differences between them. They do, however, converge on some similar assumptions. For instance, their starting point is, more often than not, that of the individual as an atomic unit of analysis, both empirical and normative; they impute certain universal and uniform characteristics to the individual, which are independent of the latter's situatedness; they consider reason as central both to our understanding of the human condition and as the starting point in the legitimation of the state and law; they view the world in terms of the particular instantiation of universal categories.

In the final Part, we will turn to radically different ways of viewing society, politics, the state and law. These theories reject or substantially qualify such fundamental assumptions. Of course, as we shall see, each does this in its own way and they differ greatly in their conclusions. However, they do have some things in common. For instance, they display a critical attitude towards the mainstream and dominant ways of thinking about the state and law. They employ conceptions of the subject and society, which are generally premised on the particular and the material rather than the universal and the abstract. Although their aim is emancipation, and this much they share with many liberal theories, their conclusions are radical in that they often do not envisage emancipation being achieved through law or at least not through the established legal categories of the past two centuries or so.

We will begin by giving an, admittedly brief and cursory, outline of the central tenets of Marxist theory and their application to law. We will then consider feminist legal theory in its various expressions. Finally, we will look at poststructuralist and postmodern approaches to law (parts of Chapter 15 have been adapted from E. Melissaris, 'The "Other" Jurisprudence: Poststructuralism, Postmodernism and the Law' in T. Murphy (ed.) *Western Jurisprudence* (Dublin: Round Hall, 2004).

PART I
Theories of the Nature of Law

2

Natural Law

Introduction

One of the three recurrent issues framing our attempts to grasp the nature of law that Hart famously identified in *The Concept of Law* was this:

> How does legal obligation differ from, and how is it related to, moral obligation?
>
> (H. L. A. Hart, *The Concept of Law*, 2nd ed. (Oxford: Oxford University Press, 1994), p. 13)

The various ways in which law and morality are related have been a focus of enormous attention throughout the history of the philosophy of law. The first question one might obviously ask, therefore, is: what is morality? Philosophers have given many answers to that question, but a helpful starting point is provided by Gardner (J. Gardner, 'Nearly Natural Law' (2007) 52 *American Journal of Jurisprudence* 1) who points out that human beings are rational: they respond to reasons. This means that they can understand that standards of behaviour apply to them, and some of these standards of behaviour are moral standards of behaviour. What makes a standard moral, rather than a standard of another kind, such as a contingent standard such as: if you want to catch the 2:15 p.m. train to London, you should leave for the station no later than quarter to two? Very roughly, moral standards are those which have particular urgency; they prevail over one's present personal preferences. The fact that I agreed to come to dinner with you this evening means that I ought to go even if now I don't feel very much like doing so; the fact that a person has fallen and needs assistance means that I ought to come to their aid even if it means that I will be delayed in getting to the market, and so on.

The theories called 'natural law theories' place a particular emphasis on the fact that rulers, lawyers and other legal officials are subject to moral standards in the way they make and apply laws: they should do so in ways that contribute to, rather than impair, human flourishing, and it is to those theories we now turn.

2.1 Classical natural law

From the time of the ancient Greeks until the sixteenth or seventeenth centuries, there was essentially only one philosophy of law: natural law. As a term, however, 'natural law' is misleading, since originally it did not denote a theory of law at all, much less a 'natural' theory of law. Originally, 'natural law' was an idea whose purpose was to explain the nature of *morality*, not the nature of *law*. The basic idea was that man, using his reason, and possibly with the help of the revelation of the gods or God, could come to understand how he should act rightly in respect of his fellow man, and this was understood as a kind of 'higher law', a law above and superior to the laws men set for themselves. This 'higher law' morality of reason and revelation was a morality which purported to take account of man's *nature*, hence the title *natural*. And because this combination of revelation and reason laid down rules for behaviour, the word *law* seemed appropriate, hence *natural law*. Natural law, then, was principally a theory of the nature of morality in which the law was used as a model for understanding it.

Of course, part of any concern with understanding morality, understanding what it is to act morally or immorally, is a concern with the actions of rulers who lay down laws for their subjects, and so the claims of natural law as a philosophy of morality applied just as much to them as to individuals generally. So a part of natural law, obviously a very important part, explained what it was to rule and legislate and judge cases rightly; so part of natural law was the morality of 'law', narrowly construed as the laws passed by legislation and the legal system of courts, judges, and so on.

Why is natural law no longer the only game in town? In a word, the answer is *positivism*. Legal positivists, whose story we will begin to explore in the next chapter, take a variety of positions, but what links them together is the view that the law is not related to morality in the way natural lawyers believe it is. Positivists typically begin the making of their case against what they conceive to be natural law's mistaken idea that the law is necessarily connected with morality by pointing out, first, that many legal systems are wicked, and second, that what is really required by morality is controversial. As to the first point, wicked legal systems are by definition immoral, so the existence of wicked legal systems would appear to allow that there is no necessary requirement that the laws of all legal systems are moral, or that the legal systems themselves are in some sense moral, and so on. The immorality of a law seems not to affect whether it *is* a law one whit. The thrust of this observation was most graphically put by Austin, who remarked that

> The most pernicious laws...are continually enforced as laws by judicial tribunals. Suppose an act [that is] innocuous...be prohibited by the sovereign under the penalty of death; if I commit this act, I shall be tried and condemned, and if I object...that [this] is contrary to the law of God..., the Court of Justice will demonstrate the inconclusiveness of my reasoning by hanging me up, in pursuance of the law of which I have impugned the validity.
>
> (J. Austin, *The Province of Jurisprudence Determined* (London: Weidenfeld & Nicolson, 1954), p. 185)

As to the second point, examples of moral controversy are legion. For some people a woman's right to have an abortion is an essential human right, the denial of which is immoral. For others, a right to abort a foetus is tantamount to a right to murder. Yet despite this deeply divisive controversy there need be no similar controversy over what the *law* is in respect of abortion that one finds in any particular jurisdiction; moral uncertainty or controversy does not in any way entail *legal* uncertainty or controversy. Laws regarding abortion may be perfectly certain, with no controversy whatsoever about what those laws require.

What positivists conclude from these sorts of consideration is that the true nature of law is that of a kind of social technology, a social institution of some kind which works to regulate the behaviour of its subjects and resolve conflicts between them. The law has no necessary moral character. The philosophy of law, then, according to positivists, is the philosophy of a particular social institution, not a branch of moral or ethical philosophy.

It is worthwhile bearing this positivist challenge to natural law in mind as you make your way through this chapter, for there has developed a long-standing 'natural law–positivist debate'. We will see when we look at the Natural Law Revival later in this chapter and the work of Dworkin in Chapter 6 that modern natural lawyers and 'evaluative theorists' of the law generally do mount arguments, unlike the classical natural lawyers, that legal positivism is fatally misconceived. In the perspective of these theorists, natural law can be described fairly accurately as that philosophy of law which emphasises the *continuity* of law with morality, not merely that branch of moral philosophy whose aim is to describe the ways in which law can be moral or immoral. In rough terms, they argue that the law can only rightly be seen as a moral enterprise, a particular social enterprise which is by its very nature geared to do good by bringing order and justice to people living in communities.

2.1.1 The central concerns of naturalist theories

Naturalist thought covers a vast historical spectrum from the Old Testament to the present day, but in its classical forms up to the late eighteenth century certain central concerns may readily be identified. By reference to the work of the great thirteenth-century theorist St Thomas Aquinas, it has been remarked elsewhere that naturalist thought

> ...implies not that 'bad' laws cannot be made and imposed but that such laws are defective in being wrongly made and are thus limited or even entirely lacking in their claim to be obeyed as a matter of conscience. This is in fact a concern with the moral nature of the power to make laws rather than with the formal identification of State prescription.
>
> (H. McCoubrey, *The Development of Naturalist Legal Theory* (London: Croom Helm, 1987), p. xii)

Naturalist argument is thus not directed to the formal identification of positive law by courts, but to the limits of the right of governments to make laws and the implications for the degree of the obligation to obey associated with law, especially when such limits are ignored. In somewhat more modern terms, the twin pillars of naturalist argument may be said to be, on the one hand, a 'proper purposes' doctrine in law-making, and, on the other, the nature and limitations of the obligation to obey law. Austin was right: he might indeed be punished for an innocuous or even beneficial act pursuant to a valid rule of positive law recognisable as such. That observation is not contradicted by the proposition that the law concerned was improperly made, defective in the obligation it imposed, and ripe for change. The problem which naturalists must address is, of course, that of the limits of their argument. Jeremy Bentham stated the dangers in 1776 in an attack upon the 'Introduction' to Sir William Blackstone's *Commentaries*. He wrote of naturalism that

> ...the natural tendency of such doctrine is to impel a man, by the force of conscience, to rise up in arms against any law whatever that he happens not to like.
>
> (J. Bentham, *A Fragment on Government* (Oxford: Basil Blackwell, 1948), p. 93)

Naturalist argument in fact goes to some length to avoid any such counsel of anarchy and, although classical arguments were set down in eras remote from our own, their basic concerns are in very many respects thoroughly 'modern'. For this reason they continue to merit close attention.

2.2 Classical Greco-Roman natural law

For the present purpose the most important contributions to classical Hellenistic legal theory were made by Plato (c. 427–347 BC) and Aristotle (384–322 BC). The latter was the pupil of the former, who had, in turn, been taught by Socrates. Their views differed in certain important respects and this difference was to be reflected also in much later developments in legal theory. Both were, however, generally rationalist in their approach in that they considered 'good' and 'bad' laws, and the appropriate reactions to them, to be discoverable by human reason through the process of rational reflection.

2.2.1 Platonic anti-legalism

In the *Republic,* Plato set out a model for the perfect society, which he founded not upon a rule of laws but upon a form of 'benevolent dictatorship' through the government of 'philosopher kings'. Such rulers were to be trained through a rigorous, if less than wholly practical, education and would then proceed upon the rationally perceived dictates of ultimate virtue. Their rule would thus not be encumbered by legal forms but moulded by wisdom and accepted through the very evidence of its excellence. Law as such was conceded little or no role, being considered a crudely inflexible means of transmitting the requirements of virtuous reason. The viability of this programme must be doubted in practice and many have urged that the argument of the *Republic* should not be taken as a practically intended manifesto. Trevor J. Saunders remarks that

> It makes much better sense to think of the *Republic* as an extreme statement, designed to shock, of the consequences of an uncompromising application of certain political principles—in fact, as an unattainable ideal.
>
> (T. J. Saunders, 'Introduction' in Plato, *Laws* (Harmondsworth: Penguin, 1975), p. 28)

Plato did in fact undertake some attempts to give rulers philosophical training, notably in the case of Dionysius II of Syracuse, who, although he respected Plato, showed little evident aptitude for idealised philosopher-kingship.

A distant political parallel may here be drawn between Platonism and Confucian thought. Confucius (K'ung-Fu-tzu, 551–479 BC) also taught that rulers should mould their conduct to a perceived virtue and thereby acquire for their rule the 'mandate of heaven' and emphasised example and the dictates of li (rites), rather than the coercive demands of fa (positive law). He commented upon the legendary ruler Yao that

> Sublime, indeed was he. 'There is no greatness like the greatness of heaven', yet Yao could copy it.
>
> (Confucius, *Analects*, 8.19, transl. A. Waley (London: Unwin Hyman, 1988))

The Confucian scholar Mencius (Meng K'e) wrote later that

> ...only the benevolent man is fit to be in high position. For a cruel man to be in high position is for him to disseminate his wickedness among the people.
>
> (Mencius, *Mencius*, transl. D. C. Lau (Harmondsworth: Penguin, 1970), 4A, 1)

There is here more than a slight echo of the Platonic philosopher-king, the more so when it is borne in mind that when, some time after Confucius's death, Confucianism was adopted as the official ideology of Imperial China by the Han dynasty, law was relegated to a subordinate position as a means for the punishment of malefactors, rather than for the guidance of the well-intentioned. Confucius himself had disparaged law as a means of dispute resolution, remarking that

> I could try a civil suit as well as anyone. But better still to bring it about that there were no civil suits!
>
> (Confucius, *Analects*, 12.13, transl. A. Waley)

Official Confucianism was, however, compromised by a number of other influences which introduced more than a slight element of harsh reality to Imperial Chinese government.

Plato himself advanced a more practical model in his later work, *The Laws*, which purports to set out a code for the fictional Athenian colony of Magnesia. As a means of virtuous instruction, a legal code was obviously seen by Plato as a second best in comparison with the rule of the elusive philosopher-king. Nonetheless the laws are advanced as a form of regulation which, although authoritarian, should not be tyrannical, indeed they are presented as being as much didactic as coercive. Plato urges therefore that laws should not only compel but also persuade, commenting that

> ...no legislator ever seems to have noticed that in spite of its being open to them to use two methods..., compulsion and persuasion..., they...never mix in persuasion with force when they brew their laws.... It seems obvious...[that the reason for the legislator giving a] persuasive address was to make the person to whom he promulgated his law...[have a] greater readiness to learn.
>
> (Plato, *Laws*, 722–3, transl. T. J. Saunders, revised reprint (Harmondsworth: Penguin, 1976), pp. 184–5)

The laws are then considered a vehicle not only for coercive control but also for education in virtue. It is thus presumed that the laws themselves will be 'good', in inculcating a rationally perceived model of virtuous living, which leads to the question of the appropriate response when the laws are not in fact so designed or administered.

2.2.2 Plato and the obligation to obey

Plato considered this question at length, in the context of the trial and execution of his own teacher Socrates (469–399 BC), in the works which have been collected and published in English as *The Last Days of Socrates*. The teaching of Socrates was offensive in a number of respects to the Athenian establishment of the day and he was eventually charged with impiety and corruption of youth—in effect sedition—and brought to trial. He was convicted and condemned to death but execution was delayed upon ritual grounds during the ceremony of the 'mission to Delos', with the implication that if Socrates, a well-known philosopher, were to escape and flee into exile he would at once relieve Athens of the irritation of his teaching and the odium of bringing about his death. In *The Last Days of Socrates*, Plato purports to present statements and conversations of Socrates relating to law and the duty of obedience. In fact he is setting out developed 'Socratic' arguments upon these points in the form of a monologue and three dialogues in the setting of Socrates' trial and execution. Two sections are of immediate interest: the *Apology*, which is an idealised representation of Socrates' contentions before the Athenian tribunal, and the *Crito*, which is represented as a dialogue between Crito and Socrates, who is imprisoned and awaiting execution, upon the arguments for escape which Socrates rejects in an analysis of the nature and extent of the duty to obey positive law. Both sections deal explicitly with the problem of obligation in relation to a 'bad' law, or a law 'badly' administered.

In the *Apology*, Socrates is represented as arguing that the State has no right to demand that a person commit evil, and where this is in fact demanded the only honourable course is refusal. He gives as an example an order given to him and others during the oligarchic rule of the '30 tyrants' to arrest Leon of Salamis in order that he might be unjustly executed. Socrates alone refused and argued that had not the '30 tyrants' then been overthrown he would himself have been put to death (Plato, *Apology*, 31D–33B, transl. H. Tredennick, in *The Last Days of Socrates*, revised reprint (Harmondsworth: Penguin, 1969), p. 65). One may argue about the formal status of particular instructions by the State (see A. D. Woozley, *Law and Obedience. The Arguments of Plato's Crito* (London: Duckworth, 1979), pp. 55–8), but it would seem clear that Socrates denies the right of the State to command injustice and it is difficult to imagine that the formal context of the command would be sufficient to create such a 'right'. Socrates does not, however, deny that the State can in practice wreak injustice—Leon of Salamis was, after all, executed. The point of the argument is made clear by Socrates's statement after his own condemnation that

> ...the difficulty is not so much to escape death; the real difficulty is to escape from doing wrong.... When I leave this court I shall go away condemned...to death, but [my accusers] will go away convicted by Truth herself of depravity and wickedness.
>
> (Plato, *Apology*, 38A–39D, transl. H. Tredennick, in *The Last Days of Socrates*, p. 73)

If, upon Socrates's argument in the *Apology*, there can be no ethical obligation to do wrong at the behest of the State, a clear distinction is drawn between such a case and the obligation which arises where the State, through its law, does not command wrong of an individual but actually does wrong to him or her; that is to say, where the individual is not sought to be made an actor in 'legal' wrongdoing, but is the victim thereof. This is the subject of the dialogue in the *Crito*.

In the *Crito* three grounds for an obligation to comply with the law are set out in the course of an argument presented as a hypothetical discussion between Socrates and the personified laws of Athens. These arguments have a considerable social-contractarian element and may be seen, in some respects, as precursors of seventeenth and eighteenth-century thought and, indeed, of certain modern theories. The first is an overtly paternalist argument, making a clear comparison between the relationship of parent and child and that of State and citizen (Plato, *Crito*, 50E–51C, transl. H. Tredennick, in *The Last Days of Socrates*, p. 91). In essence, the individual is argued to have an obligation to obey arising from gratitude for the law maintaining a system in which he or she has chosen to reside, thereby acknowledging its authority. This argument falls somewhat oddly upon modern ears, but there is also advanced a more general social-contractarian argument founded upon voluntary residence in a State. As the personified laws are made to contend

> ...whoever ... stays [in the State]..., seeing the way in which we decide our cases in court and the other ways in which we manage our city, we say he has thereby, by his act of staying, agreed with us that he will do what we demand of him.
>
> (Plato, *Crito*, 51D–E, transl. A. D. Woozley, in A. D. Woozley, *Law and Obedience. The Arguments of Plato's Crito* (London: Duckworth, 1979), p. 152)

This is a frequently encountered form of argument in favour of an obligation to obey the law. It rests upon the assumption that the individual is free to depart to some other State, and legal system, but having not done so and continued to take the benefits of the system in question, he or she is properly taken to have accepted an obligation of obedience. The most severe form of argument in this part of the *Crito* is that by disobeying, in Socrates' case by escaping, an individual attempts to destroy both the law and the social fabric which it supports and which—by remaining in the State—that individual must be taken to have accepted whilst it was of benefit to her or him. Thus the personified laws of Athens are made to ask Socrates straightforwardly

> Do you intend anything else by this [disobedience]...than to destroy both...the laws and the entire city—at least as far as you can? Or do you think it possible for that city to exist and not be overthrown in which the decisions of the courts...are set aside and made ineffective [by private citizens]?
>
> (Plato, *Crito*, 50B, transl. A. D. Woozley, in A. D. Woozley, *Law and Obedience. The Arguments of Plato's Crito*, p. 150)

This is, of course, closely paralleled by Bentham's denunciation of the tendencies of naturalist argument in general, to which reference was made above.

These arguments leave open to the individual residing in a State of whose laws he or she does not approve only three permissible options. These are (a) to persuade the State to amend the law or laws in question; (b) to move to some other, and more acceptably governed, State; or (c) to remain in the territory and obey (Plato, *Crito*, 51D–52A). In short, options of persuasion, departure, or obedience. The departure referred to is one admitted by the State and not an illegal 'escape' such as *Crito* is made to urge upon Socrates.

Such conclusions rest upon two important assumptions about the nature of the State in question. It is first assumed that some form of 'persuasion', whether by personal contention or through participation in a political process, is possible. Second, it is presumed that 'legitimate' departure to some other State is possible. The first condition will certainly not be met by undemocratic States. The second will, in any modern setting, present greater difficulties than Socrates would have encountered in moving to some other neighbouring small City-State. Whether or not Socrates' arguments for obedience are weakened or even vitiated by the absence of these conditions is not specified in the text of the *Crito*. It would seem, however, curious to argue that the potential victim of genocide, for example, in the Third Reich, who can manifestly neither persuade nor depart, should therefore submit willingly to slaughter.

There is an apparent inconsistency in the argument for disobedience found in the *Apology* and that for obedience found in the *Crito* (this is explored in A. D. Woozley, *Law and Obedience. The Arguments of Plato's Crito*, pp. 17–27). However, it is arguable that this may be resolved by drawing the distinction between a duty to do no wrong to others and a duty to accept an unjust infliction pursuant to an obligation already accepted. Plato's argument denies the right of the State to command evildoing, but it also denies the right of an individual to refuse submission when wrongful acts are commanded by the law to be done to him or her, subject, perhaps, to the availability of the options of persuasion and (prior) departure. We will return to the obligation to obey the law in Chapter 8.

2.2.3 The teleological analysis of Aristotle

Although Plato emphasised the importance of the didactic element of positive law, he ultimately considered humankind to be perversely inclined and in need of authoritarian guidance from a philosopher-king or, at least, an enlightened legislator who, by reason of superior wisdom and rigorous training, had a privileged insight into the true nature of virtue. By contrast, Aristotle taught that human beings have an inherent potential for good, the achievement of which it is the proper function of the State to facilitate. In this he saw properly conceived laws as a better instrument for the inculcation of virtue than any realistically probable form of autocratic or oligarchic rule.

This idea of the proper purpose of law derives from a teleological analysis of the human condition. Aristotelian teleology teaches that all things have a potential for development specific to their nature, the achievement of which is its particular 'good'. Thus, the 'good' of an acorn is to develop into an oak tree. Anything which assists this process is 'good' for the acorn; anything which is a hindrance thereto is 'bad' for it. The case of humankind is, of course, more complex, primarily by reason of the attribute of rationality which confers powers of choice, which may be exercised for good or ill. In the *Politics*, Aristotle argued that one of the products of reason is the nature of the human being as a *politikon zo⁻on* (Aristotle, *Politics*, 1253a.7), a 'political animal', a creature fit for life in society, the highest and most complex form of which is the City-State, or *Polis*. A 'good' law is then one which enables its subjects, as social creatures, to achieve their maximum potential appropriate development and in this, as for Plato, there is clearly a large element of moral education. The legislators who are to draft such laws will clearly require extensive training, much in the manner of their Platonic counterparts, even if the substance of perceived virtue is much more accessible in the Aristotelian model.

Interestingly, in the *Nichomachean Ethics*, Aristotle appears to concede the existence of a morality higher than that embodied in 'good' laws, which we will see is reflected in Aquinas, ideas of natural law. This is expressed as a distinction between universal justice and that embodied in particular provisions. Aristotle indicates that this is not a different order of justice but an equitable standard, which the law itself should reflect but which may also be used to correct difficulties that may arise from the unfairness of particular applications of rules which are 'good' as general provisions. Thus it is stated in the *Nichomachean Ethics* that

...equity, although just, and better than a kind of justice, is not better than absolute justice only than the error due to generalisation....it is a rectification of law in so far as law is defective on account of its generality.

(Aristotle, *Ethics*, transl. J. A. K. Thomson, revised H. Tredennick (Harmondsworth: Penguin, 1976), p. 200)

The question of obligation and the associated problem of the 'bad' law is little considered by Aristotle, which is not, perhaps, surprising in a work primarily concerned with the identification of the 'proper' uses of law and legislative power. In the Aristotelian scheme, however, it would seem that the citizens were to be educated in the constitutional structures of their State whatever its moral qualities, leaving, in case of bad, or badly administered laws, only the resorts admitted by the arguments advanced by Plato through Socrates.

We must also remember that to modern eyes, some of the seeming curiosities of Platonic and Aristotelian analysis arise from the political context in which they were advanced. The ancient Greek City-States were, by modern standards, extremely small political units, which were yet further reduced, for present purposes, when it is borne in mind that the politically enfranchised citizen body constituted a relatively small proportion of the total population. In such contexts, arguments of individual persuasion and relatively free departure to a more congenial State have more practical merit than they might in a large modern democracy, to say nothing of a modern totalitarian State.

2.2.4 Cicero's natural law: universal and rational

Confrontation with problems of scale and diversity of traditions within larger political groupings were forced upon the ancient world by the massive military expansion undertaken by Alexander of Macedon, Alexander the Great, whose tutor had been Aristotle, and the subsequent rise of the Roman Empire. One fruit of these developments was the rise of Stoic philosophy, which taught that there is a rationally observable higher order, a cosmic reason, which may be appreciated by all people, not just a privileged 'civilised' few, and that 'good' local laws made by any particular State should conform to this wisdom in order to guarantee, or establish, the natural and rational order of human social life.

The apparent universalism of this was the foundation for the work of the most important pre-Christian Roman legal theorist, Cicero (106–43 BC), whose statement of natural law was the first systematically to distinguish between morality conceived as a 'higher law' appreciable universally through the faculty of reason and an earthly, positive law, which could fail to accord with it. It is also to Cicero that we owe the term *lex naturae*, or natural law, as a term for this higher law.

According to Cicero, at the level of positive enactment, the law, termed the *lex vulgus*, was essentially an exercise of political power that might or might not be appropriate in terms of the advancement of its proper purposes. As in earlier theories, in their different ways, understanding of such 'proper purposes' was to be derived from insight into a higher rationality insofar as it relates to the human condition. For Cicero, such cosmic reason, the *lex caelestis*, was a divine law but one accessible in its relevant parts to the human mind, through rational insight and enquiry. Such perceptions were then considered 'natural law', the *lex naturae*, and it is this which Cicero advances as the proper model for the making of laws (Cicero, *De Legibus*, 1.56).

It was, significantly, accepted that the *lex naturae* might find different applications in the practical circumstances of different peoples, leaving, nonetheless, a common structure of basic principle. In Roman practice this idea found expression, rather literally, in the concept of a *ius gentium*, thought to be a body of legal principles common to all peoples, as compared with the *ius civile*, which was the particular law of a given State, especially of the Roman Empire. The moral quality and claims of all the practical variants would, however, rest upon concordance with the *lex naturae*.

The *lex vulgus* might, of course, in all too many cases be, in varying degrees, questionable upon this evaluation. For Cicero, as for other classical writers, the judgement thus made was an assessment of quality which might have important implications for individual action but would not compromise the claim of the *lex vulgus* to any formal status as positive law.

In many ways this final phase of development of classical Graeco-Roman legal theory was readily adaptable to the revolution in thought which followed inevitably from the adoption of Christianity as the official religion of the Roman Empire by the Emperor Constantine the Great in AD 312. This policy change necessitated a fusion between the apparently very different Christian and Graeco-Roman traditions of jurisprudence, which continues, directly and indirectly, to have a marked influence today.

2.3 The Christian impact: Augustine and Aquinas

Classical natural law theory underwent a revolution in the western philosophical tradition under the impact of Christian theologian philosophers, the most important of whom were Augustine and Aquinas. It is important to realise that similar religious foundations for philosophical reflection on the nature of law can be found in the Judaic and Islamic traditions of jurisprudence, so a brief look at those is warranted.

The ancient Judaic tradition of jurisprudence appears to be much more absolute in its claims than any of the Hellenistic approaches. The law stated in the Pentateuch, the first five books of the Old Testament, is not represented as some higher standard by reference to which the quality of positive legal enactments might be evaluated. The written law, the Torah, is represented straightforwardly as a statement of substantive law authorised by the will of God stated to Moses on Mount Sinai (Exodus 20:1 to 21). A very detailed legal code is set out in Exodus 21:1 to 22:17. The law set out in the Old Testament was not, of course, wholly static; it represents the developing needs of a people engaged in the extended processes of settlement and urbanisation. It is important also to notice that, whilst the moral authority of this law is attributed to divine origin, it is not represented merely as an external or arbitrary imposition but, on the contrary, as a prescription offered to, and accepted by, the people. In Exodus 24:3 we are told (in the Authorised Version) that

> ...the people answered with one voice, and said, All the words which the Lord hath said we will do.

The argument is thus, in effect, that an 'offer' was made by God and 'accepted' by the people, leading to an analysis which might, with many qualifications, be described as a form of 'social contract' with God.

This is, however, quite different from the Platonic contractarian argument considered above in two vital respects. First, the higher law is accepted once and for all as a conscious submission to authority. Secondly, the higher law is not seen merely as a standard of evaluation, but as a concrete divine prescription, violation of which would constitute an abomination. It is clear from various incidents recounted in the Old Testament that disaster was considered potentially to follow both for those enacting abominable human laws in defiance of the Torah and also for those obeying them. It may be added in parenthesis that an attempt is made in Judaic jurisprudence to circumvent the inherent inflexibility of holy laws—divine prescription can hardly be subject to revision—through the use of the body of scholarly interpretation in the Halacha. This is said, ingeniously if not wholly satisfactorily, to have the same authority as the Torah, because a right interpretation is, by definition, inseparable from the original proposition to which it relates. (Judaic jurisprudence undergoes significant change in a Christian context, by reference, in particular, to the doctrine of grace, but this falls beyond the remit of the present discussion.)

Islamic jurisprudence is not, as western natural law theory is, a theory of law upon the basis of which comparisons and evaluations may be made about the law's substance. On the contrary, Islamic law, the *Shari'ah,* in the Muslim concept quite simply *is* the law. In this sense, Islamic jurisprudence should not strictly be seen as either 'natural law' or 'positivist' in character since these categories have little real meaning in a Muslim context. However, whilst this is true in principle, the reality is, inevitably, somewhat more complex. In practice, Islamic States, and multi-cultural States in which Islam is the dominant faith tradition, do have 'secular' law-making institutions and indeed do so by necessity. The *Shari'ah* lays down both highly specific rules and broad principles and the latter at least require implementation in given, and mutable, social circumstances, which may differ in a number of regards from those which obtained in the lifetime of the Prophet.

To take an obvious example, the *Shari'ah* makes no direct provision for the regulation of modern vehicular traffic and by reason of historical fact could not have done so. Basic principles of social responsibility within the law, however, indicate clearly what sort of measures are required and these can be translated into specific rules by a 'secular' legislative process. In many Islamic States there will be one or another form of Religious Council which advises the government upon the *Shariat* rectitude of its 'secular' legislation. Such constitutional mechanisms come close at least to certain notions found in historical Christian natural law, for example, that the Church had the power to confer legitimacy on, or withdraw legitimacy from, secular authorities in their conduct as legislators (and otherwise).

The *Shari'ah* is considered a holy law revealed by Allah through the Prophet Muhammad. The matter of divine origin is fundamental to Islamic jurisprudence and the bedrock and primary source of Islamic law is the text of the *Qu'ran* received by the Prophet between the ages of 41 and 63 over a period of 22 years, two months and 22 days. The *Qu'ranic* texts, of course, required and still require interpretation and application and in these processes lie much of the Islamic 'science' of jurisprudence. One possible source of confusion is immediately obviated in that only the classical Arabic text is accepted as authentically the *Qu'ran*—translations are permissible but are not in themselves authoritative, and are thus not in any way conceived as alternatives to or variations of *Qu'ranic* norms but rather as parts of the process of *Tafsir*—interpretation and clarification.

The accepted hierarchy and significance of non-*Qu'ranic* sources was established by one of the greatest of early Islamic jurists, Muhammad ibn-Idris ash-Shafi'i, to whom much credit is due for the systematisation of 'scientific' Islamic jurisprudence. The most important of the sources of the *Shari'ah* beyond the *Qu'ran* itself is treated in effect as a supplementary, but not alternative, primary source and is the *Sunnah*—the life and teaching of the Prophet. The secondary interpretative sources are then *Ijma*—the consensus of the Muslim community, *Qiyas*—understanding by analogy, and *Ijtahad*—understanding by personal reasoning, which supposedly ended with the early 'closing of the gates of *ijtahad*' but may possibly have reopened in the thirteenth or fourteenth centuries AH (i.e. nineteenth century AD).

In the present context it is important to note that the interaction, especially of the various secondary sources, may be seen as a means of solving one of the fundamental problems of any system of religious law. The point at which the law is received is necessarily in some fixed historical era and whilst general principles may hold good for all time, detailed applications will need to be considered in the light of social changes, which will almost certainly become more radical as the time of accepted revelation becomes more remote. This is not a problem unique to Islam, but is found in one way or another in most faiths, certainly all those with significant normative content.

The processes of jurisprudential adaptation in the context of Christianity will be considered below; those adopted within Islamic jurisprudence are different, but continuities are also apparent. Islam shares with other religions the need both to conserve the purity of foundational doctrine whilst also finding effective application in sometimes radically changing historical circumstances. This was exacerbated in the case of Islam by the early 'closure of the gates of *ijtahad*' (human interpretative development) which sought, in theory if not quite in practice, to set the law in a definitive interpretation for all time. More recently, the need has in fact been felt for an increase in the moulding of application to changing circumstances, which has led in some sense to a reopening of *ijtahad*. N. J. Coulson remarks of this that

> These recent developments have given to Islamic law a new historical perspective. *Shar'ia* [*Shari'ah*] doctrine, which grew to maturity in the first three centuries of Islam and which then remained essentially static for a period of ten centuries, appears now in the course of further evolution.
>
> (N. J. Coulson, 'Islamic Law' in J. Duncan and M. Derrett, *An Introduction to Legal Systems* (London: Sweet & Maxwell), 1968, p. 54 at p. 55)

Christianity's change in AD 312 from intermittently persecuted sect to official religion rendered imperative an accommodation between the moral teaching and tradition of the Church and the secular institutions of the Empire by which it had now been embraced. This initiated a process which was completed only in the High Middle Ages, long after the fall of the Roman Empire in the West. The conclusions reached formed the basis of Western legal theory until the upheavals of the sixteenth and seventeenth centuries and retain an important, if less overt, influence even up to the present time.

The early stage of the process of fusion is best represented in the work of St Augustine of Hippo, and the later, medieval, phase by that of St Thomas Aquinas. The distinction between the two theories rests in part upon the classical models with which they worked. At the time of St Augustine the works of Aristotle had been lost, so he adopted an approach of Christian Platonism. When Aquinas wrote, many of the works of Aristotle had been rediscovered, allowing in a number of respects a more subtle Christian adaption of classical theory.

2.3.1 Christian Platonism: St Augustine of Hippo

St Augustine (345–430 AD), the Bishop of Hippo near Carthage in North Africa, had, before his conversion to Christianity, been a teacher of rhetoric in Milan and was therefore well qualified to attempt the reconciliation of Christian and Hellenistic thought.

In his greatest work, *De Civitate Dei* (*The City of God*), St Augustine portrayed the human condition as torn between the attractions of good and evil, with the perfect state being one of voluntary submission to the will of God, which is here functionally equivalent to the ideal Platonic republic's acting in accordance with the higher understanding of the philosopher-king. The will of God is then seen as the highest law, the *lex aeterna* (eternal law), for all people, playing something of the role of Stoic cosmic reason. Positive law, the *lex temporalis*, is for St Augustine relegated to an even less honoured place than its equivalent had been for Plato. It is presented as a means for the coercive discouragement of vice, which represents the abuse of freedom of will through bad choices. For the right-choosing people who act in accordance with the relevant and knowable aspects of the *lex aeterna*, positive law is not relevant.

This opens the broad question of laws which are not 'good' in the Augustinian scheme of things, those which encourage or even command vicious conduct. It is here that certain statements of St Augustine, taken well out of context, have served to fuel the naturalist–positivist debate. The best known of these statements is the seemingly dramatic assertion that 'lex iniusta non est lex'—an unjust law is no law (*De Libero Arbitrio*, 1.5.33; an accessible version of this work will be found in St Augustine, *On the Free Choice of the Will*, transl. A. S. Benjamin and L. H. Hackstaff (Indianapolis, Ind: Bobbs-Merrill, 1964)). The idea that a State cannot in practice make and enforce unjust regulations would be absurd as a matter of observation, without need for theoretical analysis, and this was certainly no less the case in St Augustine's day than at present. What St Augustine actually meant is shown by the statement that nothing which is just is to be found in positive law (*lex temporalis*), which has not been derived from eternal law (*lex aeterna*) (St Augustine, *De Libero Arbitrio*, 1.6.50). Thus, an unjust law is one which does not concord with the higher (divine) reason and which is thus conceived, or directed, for an improper purpose. A positive law so devised might, of course, be coercively enforced but could not be argued to have any moral force, especially in forcing vice (sin) upon the virtuous. The argument, in short, relates to the moral obligation attaching to law, rather than the ability of a State actually to do wrong through its laws.

Augustine considered that the authority of governments rested not upon their coercive power but upon the purposive propriety of their actions. In *De Civitate Dei* unjust governments are equated with criminal gangs. Citing Cicero, Augustine describes a pirate condemned to death by Alexander the Great who, when asked by Alexander how he dared to be a pirate, replied that whilst Alexander had a vast navy and was called an Emperor, he had just one ship and was denounced as a pirate (St Augustine, *De Civitate Dei*, 4.5.4).

As pointed out above, St Augustine imposed upon the idea of law a very narrow definition of terms according to which positive law (but not eternal law) is limited to the role of coercive discouragement of vice (sin); essentially the territory mapped by the criminal law. Other roles are more or less arbitrarily excluded from the positive–legal sphere. Such a limitation is by no means an exclusively Augustinian phenomenon— indeed, treating criminal law as the entirety of law, or at least as the central core of law, is a costly theoretical error which has happened time and again in the history of legal philosophy—but the theory of whoever falls prey to it labours under its distorting effect, whether applied to Roman, medieval, or modern legal systems, in all of which positive law manifestly serves, well or otherwise, much broader functions. This weakness in the Augustinian analysis was avoided in the much later Thomist (referring to St Thomas Aquinas) analysis of law.

2.3.2 Christian Aristotelianism: St Thomas Aquinas

Although in his great work, the *Summa Theologica*, St Thomas Aquinas (1225–74) refers to St Augustine with great respect, the analysis of positive law which is advanced in it differs dramatically from the Augustinian model. The impact on Aquinas of the works of Aristotle, which had been rediscovered by the thirteenth century, is obvious. Like Aristotle, and unlike St Augustine, Aquinas considered that positive law plays a proper and 'natural' part in the political and social life of human beings, which is not constrained or defined by a sole concern with sin. In the introduction to the volume of the *Summa Theologiae* (*Summa Theologica*) dealing primarily with questions of law, the Dominican editors state that

> The subject [law] is...freed from a current Augustinism which stressed the minatory role of law.... [Aquinas] brings out the potestas directiva, relegating the potestas coactiva to a secondary office of positive law, and one not called for if citizens are truly lawful. In brief, law has a dignity greater than that of a remedy propter peccatum.
>
> (St Thomas Aquinas, *Summa Theologiae*, general ed. T. Gilby (London: Blackfriars with Eyre and Spottiswoode, 1966), vol. 28, 1a2ae, 90–7, Introduction, pp. xxi–xxii)

In the Thomist analysis, therefore, law may take its current coercive elements from the fact of vice, but the punishment of vice is not its only or primary aim; it is also admitted to have the capacity to set out guidance for 'good' living in the community, irrespective of vice as such.

The Thomist definition of 'law' (all law, not just positive law) is worth pausing over. It is stated that law

> ...nihil est aliud quaedam rationis ordinatio ad bonum commune, ab eo qui curam communitatis habet, promulgata.
>
> (St Thomas Aquinas, *Summa Theologica*, 1a2ae, 90.4)

That is to say that 'law' is nothing but a rational regulation for the good of the community, made by the person(s) having powers of government, and promulgated.

Notice that there are both 'natural law' and 'positivist' elements in this definition. Starting with the latter, the last two requirements, essentially enactment and promulgation by a sovereign, frame the law as a social phenomenon, the product of the public exercise of a political power, and would not look out of place in the least in the work of Jeremy Bentham. (These requirements of sovereignty and promulgation are in fact extended by Aquinas to the eternal law (*lex aeterna*), the will of God, in particular as it relates to human actions, as well as to human positive law-making.)

The first two elements of the Thomist definition, rationality and intent for the good of the community, are the 'natural law' components. Both of these requirements relate directly to the Thomist notion of the 'good law'. Such a law must be rational because, it is presumed, virtue is derived from reason, here, ultimately, the reason of God in the *lex aeterna*. It must also be directed to the good of the community, or the 'common good', rather than for the particular benefit of a specific person, such as the legislator. Obviously, a provision for the common good will benefit particular individuals. The law of contract is a convenience for individuals desiring to enter into contractual relations, but it is expressed generally and embraces all who may, individually, find themselves in the given situation. As to the general nature of 'goodness' for this purpose, Aquinas essentially adopts the teleological analysis of Aristotle. F.C. Coplestone remarks that

> ...moral law is for [Aquinas]...one of the ways in which creatures are directed towards their several ends. He sees the moral life in the general setting of the providential government of creatures.... the moral law...is a special case of the general principle that all finite things move towards their ends by the development of their potentialities.
>
> (F. C. Coplestone, *Aquinas* (Harmondsworth: Penguin, 1955), pp. 119–20)

Assuming the existence of the higher rationality of the *lex aeterna* governing the potential for 'good' of human beings, the next obvious question is the means by which it can be known. In the Thomist scheme, ultimate reason is accessible to human beings through two principal media. These are (a) the *lex divina* (divine law), which is presented essentially as scriptural revelation; and (b) the *lex naturalis* (natural law), which is the fruit of rational human observation of an order which itself, by definition, rests upon the *lex aeterna*. Human positive law, the *lex humana*, will be 'good' insofar as it rests upon these foundations and 'bad' in so far as it does not.

For Aquinas, very clearly, a provision of positive law which facilitates or serves a teleologically good purpose will be binding upon the consciences of those to whom it is addressed, irrespective of their enforcement by agencies of the State. Many laws are, after all, recognised as having a force far beyond their potential for coercive enforcement. The reason that the overwhelming majority of people do not commit murder is not fear of arrest but recognition that murder is wrong. Indeed, that recognition clearly antedates the legal rule. In Thomist terms the rule is founded, in this case, upon indications of both the *lex divina* and *lex naturalis*. Any viable society must place strict limits upon interpersonal violence, although these may vary somewhat, otherwise it will inevitably tear itself apart.

Aquinas was, perhaps, the first natural law theorist to appreciate the issue of laws which are not *required* by the *lex divina* or *lex natura*, but are laws which should be complied with nonetheless, into which category we might place many of the 'conventional' laws, such as the rules of the road, or the formalities associated with conveyancing. Aquinas distinguished between laws arising by *specificatio* and *determinatio*, i.e. between laws specified by the divine or natural law, such as the law against murder, and laws which might rationally have been laid down differently, such as the rule laying down which side of the road to drive on; the latter are fixed or determined in one form or another by practical reason guided by the limits set by the divine and natural laws. There remains, however, the problem of the bad law.

For Aquinas, a provision of positive law might be bad in two ways; it might contravene the *lex divina*, and would then be abominable, or it might be humanly 'unfair'. It might, of course, be both. The basic Thomist reaction to bad laws merits quotation and is that

> ...lex tyrannica cum non sit secundum rationem non est simpliciter lex sed magis est quaedam perversitas legis. (A tyrannical law made contrary to reason is not straightforwardly a law but rather a perversion of law.)
>
> (St Thomas Aquinas, *Summa Theologica*, 1a2ae, 92.114)

In this context it should be noted that 'tyranny' refers to lack, or abuse, of sovereign authority, but not necessarily with the modern connotation of cruelty. In the Thomist scheme the obligation to obey such a perverted law will rest upon the nature of its error. If it is actually contrary to the higher reason of the *lex aeterna* there can be no moral obligation to obey attached to it. If, on the other hand, it is badly conceived and humanly unfair, the extent of any moral obligation to obey would depend on the circumstances. The practical examples offered here by Aquinas are not particularly helpful in that they relate principally to exceptions of necessity where in a particular case obedience would be manifestly inappropriate and official dispensation cannot be sought. In the more general context of bad law Aquinas argues that the moral obligation to obey fails in the case of a humanly bad law unless greater 'scandal' would result from disobedience (St Thomas Aquinas, *Summa Theologica*, 1a2ae, 96.4; also 2a2ae, 104.6). The point is spelt out by Aquinas in *De Regimine Principum* (*Of the Government of Princes*), in which it is urged that some degree of unjust government should be tolerated for fear of bringing on a worse state of things by rebellion or disobedience, but that there are limits to this. Tarquinius Superbus, the last king of ancient Rome, and the Emperor Domitian are cited as examples of properly deposed tyrants (St Thomas Aquinas, *De Regimine Principum*, 6.44).

The essential point is that governmental authority has a moral base which may be weakened or lost through abuse of power. This must, again, emphatically be distinguished from any idea that an unjust government cannot coercively impose its laws: the argument relates to its right to do so and the quality of the moral obligation to obey, if any, which will result from such an attempt. The idea of government as a morally defined activity is, of course, far from being limited to the theories of medieval European scholasticism. In responding to the question of the permissibility of tyrannicide, the Confucian scholar Mencius (Meng K'e) stated in an ancient Chinese context that

> A man who mutilates benevolence is a mutilator, while one who cripples rightness is a crippler. He who [does such things is] . . . an 'outcast'. I have indeed heard of the punishment of the 'outcast [King] Tchou', but I have not heard of any regicide.
>
> (Mencius, *Mencius*, 1.B.8, transl. D. C. Lau (Harmondsworth: Penguin, 1970), p. 68)

Despite the vast differences of context, the functional parallel is obvious. The essential concern of the argument, the limit of moral authority, as compared with the coercive capacity of government, recurs in every historical context. The insights of the Thomist analysis of law have much to say of modern abuse of positive law, once the appropriate cultural transitions have been undertaken.

2.3.3 The standing of classical natural law theory

As we have seen, classical natural law theory, broadly understood to encompass its Graeco-Roman and Christian variations, is directed to the quality and propriety of lawmaking, and to the obligation to obey positive laws which fail to adhere to the higher law by which they are to be judged. So conceived, it escapes the charge made against it by the early positivist theorists that it breached the distinction between 'is' and 'ought', descriptive and normative, propositions by claiming that only good law is 'law'. No such claim is made by the theories here considered.

A more difficult question is whether classical natural law provides a sufficient theoretical base for analysing the processes and results of making and administering positive law from a moral perspective. While any student of jurisprudence has much to learn by the questions posed and the answers given in the natural law traditions, as we shall now see, modern natural law theorists have laboured to bring moral analysis to law in quite different ways.

2.4 **The natural law revival: Fuller and Finnis**

In Anglo-American jurisprudence and much of the spectrum of common law legal thought, classical natural law ideas were, from the middle of the nineteenth century onwards, largely overshadowed by the varieties of positivist legal theory. This also happened in other jurisdictions, although to varying degrees. The reasons for this were various and related to the general culture of the period as well as to matters of a specifically jurisprudential nature, but undoubtedly one of the factors was the rise of the modern State, which began to regulate society in more and more ways largely through legislation.

Issues concerning the relation between law and morality became particularly relevant in the earlier part of the twentieth century, most particularly in the 1930s, as the emergence of modern totalitarian States, of a variety of ideological colourings, posed moral and ethical questions about the operation of law which, if hardly new, had emerged in varied and stark forms. This was the case in different ways in the fascist States and in the former USSR under the Stalin dictatorship. The questions were rendered both practically and ethically unavoidable when the full scope of legal abuse under the Nazi Third Reich in Germany between 1933 and 1945 was unambiguously exposed in the aftermath of its defeat. These concerns raised doubts about the adequacy or relevance of positivist legal theories, which focus upon the descriptive analysis of legal systems, not their moral adequacy or inadequacy. In short, how can an analysis concerned essentially with what law 'is' deal with the problem of a law which, upon civilised criteria, manifestly 'ought not' to be as it 'is', or 'was'? Positivism does not strictly deny the importance of the moral, ethical, or even political quality of law, but the relegation of these issues to a realm beyond jurisprudence increasingly seemed to exclude matters from consideration which were not peripheral but central to the operation of law in the modern world. The result was a revival of interest in natural law jurisprudence and this has had a marked effect upon modern developments in theory from the middle of the twentieth century to the present time.

A number of theories have been developed in the context of modern naturalism, but two merit particular attention. These are, in chronological order, the 'procedural naturalism' advanced by Lon L. Fuller and the theory of 'natural rights' advanced by John Finnis.

2.5 **Fuller's procedural natural law**

Lon L. Fuller, professor of general jurisprudence at Harvard University from 1948 to 1972, was immediately concerned with the problems raised by the totalitarian abuse of law in the 1930s and 1940s and advanced a theory of law which he categorised as 'procedural naturalism' in an effort to set out the minimal requirements for a recognisable 'legal system'. The basis for this analysis was the perceived weakness of law in the Third Reich and the extent to which it could realistically have been considered to have been 'law' in any meaningful sense. It is possible to debate in some detail whether the Third Reich actually was a *Rechtsstaat,* one governed by the 'rule of law'. Fuller himself specifically debated this issue with H. L. A. Hart (see 5.4.1).

However, the theory which Fuller advanced was not specifically tied to the question of the use of law in the Third Reich, but sought to make a much more general point about the nature and functions of a legal system. As its usual description suggests, Fuller's theory was not founded upon the substantive content of legal provisions but upon the procedural structure of a legal system. It is open to some question whether this approach is correctly termed a 'natural law' theory (for discussion of this see 7.1.4); it cannot, however, be denied that the analysis raises issues of profound importance for the understanding of law.

In *The Morality of Law*, Fuller addresses the problem of the interface between law and morality with particular regard to the fact that in the general legal theory of the time,

> There is little recognition...of a much larger problem, that of clarifying the directions of human effort essential to maintain any system of law, even one whose ultimate objectives may be regarded as mistaken or evil.
>
> (Lon L. Fuller, *The Morality of Law*, rev. ed. (New Haven, Conn: Yale University Press, 1969), p. 4)

Consideration of this larger issue forms the bulk of the work, but as a preliminary to this Fuller analysed the nature of the morality to which law is to be related. At this basic level too he considered contemporary jurisprudential debate to have become confused and, thus, urgently to require clarification.

2.5.1 Moralities of aspiration and of duty

Fuller considered that debate upon the morality of law had become confused in part through a failure adequately to distinguish between two levels of morality, which he defined as moralities of 'aspiration' and of 'duty'. Fuller states the distinction between the two moralities in terms of the level of the demand imposed:

> The morality of aspiration...is the morality of the Good Life, of excellence, of the fullest realisation of human powers.... Where the morality of aspiration starts at the top of human achievement, the morality of duty starts at the bottom. It lays down the basic rules without which an ordered society is impossible, or without which an ordered society directed toward certain specific goals must fail of its mark.
>
> (*The Morality of Law*, pp. 5–6)

The essential difference is indicated by Fuller's choice of terms. The morality of 'aspiration' is a goal of excellence, or even perfection, closely related, as Fuller points out, to the Platonic ideal. It is in a sense a maximum goal. The morality of 'duty' on the other hand is a minimum standard which must be attained before the enterprise can be recognised to have the identity which it claims at all. One may aspire to excellence but the standard of 'duty' is the minimum required for a viable social order so that failure to achieve it is not merely, in some sense or to some degree, a lapse but is actually a wrong.

Fuller contends that the division between these two moralities is not a gulf separating polar extremes, but a point upon a graduated scale. Thus

> ...we may conveniently imagine a...scale...which begins...with the most obvious demands of social living and extends upward to the highest reaches of human aspiration. Somewhere along this scale there is an invisible pointer that marks the dividing line where the pressure of duty leaves off and the challenge of excellence begins.
>
> (*The Morality of Law*, pp. 9–10)

Fuller argues that, wherever that pointer might be fixed, the appropriate standard of evaluation in the analysis of law, in terms of its claim to be 'law', is one of 'duty' rather than 'aspiration'. This relates partly to a view of the basic function of law. It is implicit in Fuller's analysis that it is not the business of law to prescribe for excellence but rather to ensure the minimum baseline from which development towards excellence might move.

To express the point in somewhat different terms, insofar as law cannot make people 'good' but rather establish a base for the inhibition of 'badness' from which a good life may develop, this rather minimalist moral analysis of the comparative standard for law may be accepted. It does not, however, state the limits of the moral questions which may be asked about law. Beyond the establishment of the base for a viable society, it does not seem unreasonable to suggest that law may also facilitate, or hinder, aspiration towards higher social conditions, even accepting the validity of the distinction between 'aspiration' and 'duty'. This indeed figures prominently amongst the concerns of some of the classical natural law theories considered above. The analysis of moral criteria and their relationship with law advanced by Fuller is important in itself but also to a large extent informs the nature of his general legal theory. Ultimately this goes to the root of the question, which may be raised upon the claim of the theory fully to fit into the natural law category.

2.5.2 The criteria of law-making

The major part of Fuller's argument concerns the essential requirements for the making of recognisably 'legal' norms within the context of a 'morality of duty'. He commences this analysis by considering the reign of a hypothetical king called Rex. Rex is a hereditary monarch succeeding to a well-established dynasty with, unfortunately, a lamentable record in matters legal. The attempts of the well-intentioned but incompetent Rex to improve matters are then used as a hypothetical model of the ways in which the enterprise of law-making might be rendered ineffectual or, indeed, vitiated altogether.

The subject of this analysis is termed by Fuller 'the morality that makes law possible' (Lon L. Fuller, *The Morality of Law*, ch. 2). The product is essentially a set of minimum criteria for recognisable legislative, or other 'legal', activity, which Fuller expresses in the form of eight negative criteria which would, to varying extents, individually and cumulatively indicate failure in law-making. Some of these negative criteria require further comment, but the list may usefully be set out as such. The more or less fatal defects are set out by Fuller as 'eight ways to fail to make law' (*The Morality of Law*, pp. 33–41). The summarised list (see *The Morality of Law*, p. 39) is:

  (a) failure to establish rules at all, leading to absolute uncertainty;

  (b) failure to make rules public to those required to observe them;

  (c) improper use of retroactive law-making;

  (d) failure to make comprehensible rules;

  (e) making rules which contradict each other;

  (f) making rules which impose requirements with which compliance is impossible;

  (g) changing rules so frequently that the required conduct becomes wholly unclear;

  (h) discontinuity between the stated content of rules and their administration in practice.

Any of these would manifestly pose a problem, whether all would be absolutely fatal defects in an endeavour to make law raises somewhat more complex questions. A system which failed to make rules at all would clearly be only very dubiously a recognisable legal system. Similarly, a rule with which compliance would be impossible might be recognised by a court as law (indeed, there are examples of such rules being applied), but, equally, they would be, and have been, of very dubious quality indeed. An obvious example would be a law penalising people on the basis of an inherent quality such as their racial identity. The Nuremberg race laws of the Nazi Third Reich which in practice, if not quite in form, made it illegal to be Jewish, were an especially stark example of precisely this.

Some of the listed defects would, whilst being objectionable in general, not necessarily be unacceptable in all cases. Retroactivity would be a good example. One might reasonably consider that for a law to be made retroactively so as to cure a failure in the existing law would not only be unobjectionable but highly desirable. Fuller counsels against this as a general conclusion, citing the Roehm purge of 1934 under the Third Reich as a warning instance. Hitler had come to consider the SA faction led by Roehm as a threat to his position and therefore descended upon the group at one of their meetings and ordered the summary shooting of some hundred persons. Subsequently a retroactive decree was enacted converting these murders into lawful 'executions', informed by Hitler's claim that he himself was the 'supreme court' of the German *Volk* (see *The Morality of Law,* pp. 54–5).

This seems a rather curious example with which to illustrate the point. In the first place it may be questioned whether the Third Reich was a *Rechtsstaat,* a State ruled by law, at all, a question of which Fuller was well aware (see 5.4.1). Second, this use of law to validate a patently political purge which was wholly devoid of legal process is subject to so many other objections, even in terms of Fuller's procedural criteria, that the question of 'retroactive cure' seems at most a peripheral issue. There are, of course, numerous objections to retroactive legislation, or judicial precedents, and Fuller gives a number of examples. One may nonetheless suggest that if a law which is reasonable in itself failed to take account of some situation in which people are greatly and improperly prejudiced by its application, then retroactive relief for those people would seem justifiable. The important point to be emphasised is the element of 'relief' which should also require that the action does not unfairly prejudice other people who relied upon the law as it stood. Such instances may be rare, may indeed be hoped to be so, but the possibility should not be ignored.

Similarly, complex arguments may be raised about the practical implications of a number of Fuller's negative criteria. It may, however, be accepted that most of them most of the time would be severely deleterious in their effects and that a 'legal system' subject to all of them would hardly be recognisable as such. Beyond this, however, there arises the vital question of the practical operation and impact of the procedural criteria.

In particular it must be asked to what extent failure in relation to the negative criteria will vitiate the claim of a purported 'legal system' to be such. Is failure in all eight required before this point is reached, or will failure in just one suffice? The answer would seem to be that this is not truly an 'eight-point test' with some 'passmark' which a candidate legal system must attain. It would seem that all the negative criteria represent defects but that these are cumulative in effect. A system which at all times failed in all eight regards would clearly be entirely unacceptable. A system which failed occasionally in one or two would not.

2.5.3 **Procedural morality and the substance of laws**

An equally important question arises in the relation of Fuller's procedural morality to
the substantive content of laws. For Fuller the negative criteria which he sets out reflect
an 'inner morality' of law, that is to say 'the morality that makes law possible' (the
heading of Chapter 2 of *The Morality of Law*). This is throughout a procedural morality
which is concerned with the capacity of a system to produce norms which are recognisably 'legal' at all. The possibility of procedurally adequate enactment of substantively
iniquitous laws is to a large extent ignored. Fuller himself remarks

> In presenting my analysis of the law's internal morality I have insisted that it is, over a
> wide range of issues, indifferent toward the substantive aims of law and is ready to serve
> a variety of such aims with equal efficacy.
>
> (Lon L. Fuller, *The Morality of Law*, p. 153)

It would indeed be expected that a procedural morality might admit and encompass a
broad range of substantive enactments. The analysis would be open to criticism were it
not so. This still, however, leaves open the problem of procedurally adequate iniquity.

 What if, for example, in a totalitarian State it were to be enacted that any person who
expressed disagreement with any publicly stated opinion of the dictator upon any matter would, from the date of the enactment, be shot; further, that this rule contradicts
no other rule and is then applied rigorously and to the letter at all times. The 'law' is a
rule, it is public, not retroactive, comprehensible, not contradicted by other rules, not
impossible to obey, not subject to change, and applied exactly as it is stated. In short,
it satisfies perfectly Fuller's procedural criteria but is still profoundly objectionable as
a use of law according to many of the classical natural law theories. It might well, for
example, from the viewpoint of the Thomist analysis be considered classically a 'tyrannical' law and thus a perversion or abuse of law (*perversitas legis*, see 2.3.2).

 Fuller claimed that procedural naturalism to some extent set up barriers to the imposition of substantive iniquity. He remarks expressly that

> ...I treated what I have called the internal morality of law as itself presenting a variety of
> natural law. It is, however, a procedural or institutional kind of natural law, though...it
> affects and limits the substantive aims that can be achieved through law.
>
> (*The Morality of Law*, p. 184)

Some forms of substantive iniquity clearly could not be imposed in a manner compliant with Fuller's procedural criteria, but it would seem an exaggerated claim to suggest
that 'good' procedures preclude 'bad' law. Fuller does not actually make such a claim.
Indeed, the basic distinction between the moralities of 'aspiration' and of 'duty' from
which he commences his argument tend against any such proposition. The limits of the
substantive impact of a procedural morality are suggested in Fuller's comment that

> ...an acceptance of this [internal] morality is a necessary, though not a sufficient con-
> dition for the realisation of justice,...this morality is itself violated when an attempt
> is made to express blind hatreds through legal rules, and...the specific morality of law
> articulates...a view of man's nature that is indispensable to law and morality alike.
>
> (*The Morality of Law*, p. 168)

In response to this one must ask why it would be procedurally impossible to express 'blind hatreds' through 'law'—many States seem to have achieved this feat with ease—unless, of course, a substantive morality is to be smuggled into the procedural criteria.

In addressing this issue Fuller is very critical of Hart's 'minimum content of natural law' (see 5.4.3) and starts from the proposition that, whereas the morality of duty is a requirement, the morality of aspiration is a source of 'counsel' only. He does, however, admit one 'imperious' tenet of substantive natural law in the maintenance of 'channels of communication' between people, and peoples (*The Morality of Law*, p. 186). Insofar as this rather minimalist conception seems to imply a recognition of common humanity, it may be accepted as an essential tenet of natural law. However, it is hardly sufficient. In the light of Fuller's criticism of Hart it is perhaps curious that his very limited substantive naturalism seems to be appended to his procedural model as a rather awkward addition. It certainly fails to answer Hart's central objection to Fuller's claim to have discerned an inner morality of law, which is that his eight principles are really principles of *effectiveness*, not of morality. We could equally, said Hart, construct an inner morality of poisoning: use tasteless, odourless poisons, use poisons that are difficult to detect in the victim's body, and so on (H. L. A. Hart, *Essays in Jurisprudence and Philosophy*, ch. 16).

Ultimately it may be suggested that an attempt to absorb a substantive naturalism into a procedural argument is yet another instance of the inappropriate extension of a concept into areas well beyond its proper remit. Beyond this there arises the question of whether Fuller's approach is truly to be considered 'naturalist' at all.

2.5.4 Is procedural natural law actually a natural law theory?

Fuller clearly considered his procedural criteria to represent an 'internal morality' of law and properly to be categorised as a natural law analysis (see *The Morality of Law*, p. 184). His theory was also evidently a response to the inadequacies of strict positivism as a vehicle for the consideration of the abuse of law by twentieth-century totalitarian regimes. The procedural emphasis of the analysis, however, raises some doubt as to the strength of its naturalist claims.

Fuller criticises the essentially amoral stance of positivist theory, arguing that it omits any concept of 'reciprocity' between the citizen and the State, by which is meant an idea that recognition and compliance on the part of the citizen goes hand in hand with defined expectations of the State, default in which would be in some sense wrongful. This idea of legitimate expectation by the subjects of law, as compared with the mere identification of rules, is significant. It may, indeed, be accepted as distinguishing the central arguments of Fuller from those of Hart, subject to the latter's 'minimum content of natural law'.

Ultimately, however, the procedural naturalism advanced by Fuller is less purposive than its author claims and the issues of the proper use of law which are central to classical naturalism are largely ignored in the analysis. It has been suggested elsewhere that

> ...Fuller may fairly be said to have contributed an interesting and important critique of positivist formalism from a quasi-naturalist viewpoint but his theory must none the less be considered somewhat peripheral from the viewpoint of the mainstream of naturalist thought.
>
> (H. McCoubrey, *The Development of Naturalist Legal Theory* (London: Croom Helm, 1987), p. 179)

In its significant divergence from mainstream naturalist concerns, Fuller's theory would perhaps be more appropriately categorised as an anti-positivist analysis than as a naturalist theory *stricto sensu*.

2.6 John Finnis and the theory of natural rights

Unlike Fuller's concept of procedural natural law the theory of 'natural rights' advanced by John Finnis falls unequivocally into the category of 'natural law' theory. Indeed, in presenting his case Finnis places considerable emphasis upon the analysis advanced by St Thomas Aquinas (see 2.3.2).

Finnis' contribution to modern natural law jurisprudence may be argued to be important in two quite different ways. It is not unique in its broadly Thomist base, but its development from that base is both innovative and distinctive in a manner different from modern restatements of Thomism such as that advanced by John C. H. Wu (see J.C.H. Wu, *The Fountain of Justice* (London: Sheed and Ward, 1959)). Finnis' core concern with the theory of rights sets the classical naturalist concern with the moral or ethical and purposive nature of law into a modern discourse of 'rights' which is firmly rooted in fundamental preoccupations of the modern legal and political world. Secondly, Finnis' theory moves away from the still essentially formal concerns of post-positivist analyses, such as that of Fuller, and adds a modern natural law voice to jurisprudential debate. This serves the interest of a diversification of the range of analyses which may be seen as a prerequisite for the adequate address of the broad issues arising from the operation of law in the modern world.

2.6.1 Finnis' defence of naturalism

Finnis commences his analysis with a defence of naturalist jurisprudence from the conventional criticism that it somehow violates the distinction between descriptive and normative, 'is' and 'ought', propositions classically set out by David Hume. Finnis addresses this basic issue in the form in which it is pressed by Julius Stone, and offers a decisive response to the standard positivist critique.

> Have the natural lawyers shown that they can derive ethical norms from facts?...the answer can be brisk: They have not, nor do they need to, nor did the classical exponents of the theory dream of attempting any such derivation.
>
> (J. M. Finnis, *Natural Law and Natural Rights* (Oxford: Clarendon Press, 1980), p. 33, referring to J. Stone, *Human Law and Human Justice* (London: Stevens and Sons, 1965), p. 212)

Finnis contends that classical naturalist argument does not improperly derive 'ought' propositions from the simple observation of human conduct, a descriptive 'is' proposition. He argues instead that people understand their individual aspirations and nature from an 'internal' perspective and that from this there may be extrapolated an understanding of the 'good life' for humanity in general. Thus a general 'good' may be derived from particular experiences or appreciations of 'good', which is not to say that what people in fact want they always 'ought' to have. To take a very crude example, the self-perceived 'good' of a serial killer is manifestly incompatible with the 'good' of other people and cannot, thus, form any part of the general human 'good'. In contrast, an individual's wish for personal security can be something of general application and thus symptomatic of such general human 'good'. Finnis explains this form of derivation of the concept of 'good', by reference to St Thomas Aquinas.

> The basic forms of good grasped by practical understanding are what is good for human beings with the nature they have. Aquinas considers that practical reasoning begins...by experiencing one's nature...from the inside, in the form of one's inclinations....by a simple act of noninferential understanding one grasps that the object of the inclination...is an instance of a general form of good, for oneself (and others like one).
>
> (*Natural Law and Natural Rights*, p. 34)

As an analysis of the derivation of human 'good' this has much to commend it since such 'good' necessarily relates to human nature, without making any assumption that what people 'want' is necessarily what 'ought' to be.

A somewhat distinct point may, however, be made here. Positive law sets out basic prescriptions for the conduct of human society and in so doing it may reasonably be argued that it ought to serve the needs which arise from human nature. If that nature were different, so too, no doubt, would be human expectations of law, assuming such an institution to be relevant to the hypothetical circumstances. Human nature as it is cannot, according to Hume's basic dictum, found an 'ought', i.e., the fact that people are that way does not necessarily mean that they ought to be so. The 'is' of law is not the same as the 'is' of human nature and granted that law operates in human society there is no breach of Hume's argument in stating that what law is ought to conform to requirements dictated by what human nature is. The issue is one of the relation of legal function to the external parameter of human need. If this is accepted one can then proceed to Finnis' essential contentions regarding the determination of what need, or needs, law is to serve.

2.6.2 The basic goods

In order to determine what are the basic goods which human beings, by reason of their nature, value, Finnis advances certain generalisations about human societies which lead to a model of what things most people in most societies may be considered to think important. Finnis argues that despite the very considerable cultural diversity of human societies, there are certain basic concerns which are preponderantly found in a survey of the literature of anthropological investigations. On the basis of these general concerns Finnis sets out a model of seven 'basic forms of human good'. These are:

(a) Life, meaning not merely existence but also the capacity for development of potential. Within the category of life and its preservation Finnis includes procreation.

(b) Knowledge, not only as a means to an end but as a good in its own right, which improves life quality.

(c) Play, in essence the capacity for recreational experience and enjoyment.

(d) Aesthetic experience, in some ways related to play but not necessarily so—this is broadly a capacity to experience and relate to some perception of beauty.

(e) Sociability or friendship, occurring at various levels but commonly accepted as a 'good' aspect of social life. One might add that this 'good' would seem to be an essential aspect of human conduct as social creatures, *politikon zōon* as Aristotle put it.

(f) Practical reasonableness, essentially the capacity to shape one's conduct and attitudes according to some 'intelligent and reasonable' thought process.

(g) Religion, which is not limited to, although it clearly includes, religion in the formal sense of faith and practices centred upon some sense of the divine. The reference here is to a sense of the responsibility of human beings to some greater order than that of their own individuality.

These goods are set out concisely (see *Natural Law and Natural Rights*, pp. 86–9). A number of important questions may be asked both about this list and its particular components.

The first and most obvious question is the claim of the list to be comprehensive. Might not other goods be set out and listed? Finnis argues that

> ...there are countless objectives and forms of good. But...these...will be found, on analysis, to be ways or combinations of ways of pursuing (not always sensibly) and realising (not always successfully) one of the seven basic forms of good, or some combination of them.
>
> (*Natural Law and Natural Rights*, p. 90)

One of the great obstacles to any satisfactory compilation of lists of goods, or indeed rights in a general context, lies in the lurking danger of cultural specificity. What is accepted as appropriate in one culture may well not be in another. The basic goods advanced by Finnis are categoric rather than specific in form and might obviously find particular application in a variety of ways.

A more complex question, perhaps, arises when it is asked how choices are to be made as between basic goods should any two or more of them prove incompatible in a given situation. Each good is advanced by Finnis as fundamental and of equal importance with each of the others: there is no hierarchic ranking amongst them.

In order to determine how the goods are to be applied as criteria of evaluation in the context of the operation of a real society it is obviously necessary to set up a structured scheme of assessment. This is done through the medium of tests of 'practical reasonableness' which may provide guidance as to what, in practice, is to be considered right or wrong in applying the basic goods.

2.6.3 The tests of practical reasonableness

The basic aim of the tests of practical reasonableness is related by Finnis to the broad methodology of classical naturalist thought in relating moral and ethical criteria to action and consequences. Thus

> ...[these] requirements...express the 'natural law method' of working out the (moral) 'natural law' from the first (pre-moral) 'principles of natural law'.... [This concerns] the sorts of reasons why (and thus the ways in which) there are things that morally ought (not) to be done.
>
> (*Natural Law and Natural Rights*, p. 103)

The actual tests which Finnis sets out (*Natural Law and Natural Rights*, pp. 103–26) are:

(a) A coherent life plan, meaning a set of 'harmonious' intentions and commitments by reference to which one intends to arrange one's life.

(b) No arbitrary preferences are to be made amongst values, that is to say that a person may not individually choose to aspire to a particular good but that confers no entitlement to regard that good as devalued, for example, in reference to the wishes of others.

(c) There must be no arbitrary preferences amongst persons. This requires little comment in a modern context. The test would manifestly exclude, for example, the varieties of irrational discrimination upon bases of race, gender, or other such criteria.

(d) Proper senses of both 'detachment' and 'commitment', meaning, in effect, a sufficient degree of flexibility to respond appropriately to changes in one's own circumstances and to the changing needs of others.

(e) The significance of efficiency within reasonable limits, meaning that the efficient pursuit of goals, and avoidance of harm, is a real factor in the application of moral considerations but it cannot be treated in itself as a supreme or central principle. Taken beyond its proper limits, indeed, the pursuit of efficiency for its own sake may become both irrational and immoral.

(f) Respect for every basic value in every act, meaning ultimately that no choice should be made which directly contravenes any 'basic good'.

(g) Consideration for the common good. Finnis treats this as more or less obvious, and, indeed, such a requirement would seem inseparable from an assessment of moral relations within a social context.

(h) People should follow the dictates of their conscience, even if that conscience is, unbeknown to the actor, in error. Finnis, following Aquinas, argues that a wrong conscience should be respected as an aspect of the full personhood of the individual concerned, since in contravening its dictates that person would, in his or her own terms, act irrationally or immorally. One must conclude, however, that the second, third, and eighth tests, at least, would seem to set some limits to this. A person who felt 'conscientiously' committed to participate in genocide could hardly on that basis be admitted to do so.

Finnis argues that the tests of practical reasonableness in combination with the basic goods represent the structure of a 'natural law' analysis.

This model is indeed much more clearly a mainstream natural law argument than, for example, the procedural natural law advanced by Lon L. Fuller. Finnis argues also that the combination of the basic goods and the tests of practical reasonableness would enable a society to obviate gross injustice and that they also provide a model of basic rights.

2.6.4 From natural law to natural rights

The generation of absolute rights from the practical morality embodied in his naturalist analysis is based by Finnis upon the proposition of practical reasonableness that

> ...it is always unreasonable to choose directly against any basic value, whether in oneself or in one's fellow human beings....Correlative to the exceptionless duties entailed by this requirement are...exceptionless...human claim-rights.
>
> (*Natural Law and Natural Rights*, p. 225)

The argument is thus essentially that it will always be wrong to make a choice directly contravening any of the basic goods and that the duty to respect these goods thus generates human rights to which there can be no exceptions.

The rights which are thus derived from the basic goods (*Natural Law and Natural Rights*, p. 225) are:

(a) not to be deprived of life as a direct means to an end;

(b) not to be deceived in the course of factual communication;

(c) not to be condemned upon charges which are known to be false;

(d) not to be denied procreative capacity; and

(e) to be accorded 'respectful consideration' in any assessment of the common good.

There have been, and are, numerous assessments of the rights and their nature in various international treaties, such as the 1948 Universal Declaration of Human Rights, and in a variety of academic treatments of the theory of rights, such as the rights thesis advanced by Ronald Dworkin (see Chapter 6). All such endeavours, including that of Finnis, raise a variety of questions, according to their particular context. Lists of rights are inevitably specific expressions of more general principles and it might be argued that they are not truly autonomous but simply reflections of a moral or ethical climate in given situations. Those situations may, of course, change and threats may be posed to areas of life not formerly considered; this in turn may generate senses of new rights deriving from the basic moral climate. It may not be the case that all rights are concerned with defence of perceived entitlements from harm, but it may strongly be argued that the phrase, 'I have a right to...' would come most naturally where someone seeks to deny the proposition.

One may readily accept that Finnis' 'exceptionless claim rights' are properly derived from their given context and are in themselves by and large unexceptionable. It would, however, be rash to take them as an exhaustive list or even one which leaves no questions open. The exceptionless claim-right not to be deprived of life as a means to an end may be considered as a particularly stark example. A person in Finnis' scheme may of course choose to undertake actions which place his or her own life at risk, for example, in attempting to rescue another person from danger. Can people be required so to act? If the 'claim-rights' are 'exceptionless', presumably they may not. Here, however, one encounters the always difficult interface between individual and community expectations. To avoid the military examples, one might consider a small community faced by an uncontrolled forest fire. Fighting the fire may well be a life-threatening activity for the fire-fighters (i.e., potentially all the physically fit persons in the community), not fighting the fire may also be life-threatening (for everyone in the community). The answer here lies in the criteria of practical reasonableness but its discernment may well present considerable difficulties in some cases.

2.6.5 The obligation to obey in Finnis' theory

Finnis' analysis of the obligation to obey law is in many ways more subtle than the approach adopted in many theories of law. He identifies four types of obligation which may be associated with law. These are: sanction-based obligation, 'intra-systemic' formal obligation, moral obligation, and a distinct 'collateral' moral obligation (see *Natural Law and Natural Rights,* p. 354). The first three may broadly be seen, respectively, in the classical positivism of Bentham and Austin (see Chapter 3), the later positivism of H. L. A. Hart (see Chapter 5), and in the spectrum of natural law theories.

In a direct comment upon the views of John Austin, Finnis remarks that the dismissal of some of these senses to other disciplines or even, as for John Austin, their denunciation as 'nonsense' is an 'unsound jurisprudential method' (see *Natural Law and Natural Rights*, p. 354). In this Finnis is surely correct. It may be argued very strongly that the idea of 'obligation' which is associated with law is not a singular phenomenon but, rather, a combination of different obligatory factors which have been variously explored by different schools of jurisprudence. The coercive, formal and moral elements in the obligatory characteristic of law may readily be seen. Jurisprudence has suffered, it may be argued, from trying to choose between these elements. It is not one but all of them in combination which will define the issue of legal obligation.

Finnis' division between moral and 'collateral' moral obligation is interesting. In effect he suggests that in disobeying a law, even a bad law, a person places at risk the whole legal system and that there may therefore be a 'collateral' moral obligation to obey such a law, notwithstanding its immorality, because of the damaging incidental effects of disobedience (see *Natural Law and Natural Rights*, pp. 361–2). This may be questioned insofar as the question of collateral damage can be seen as part of the question of moral obligation in general (see, for example, the Socratic argument in Plato's *Crito*, analysed in 2.2.2). The internal morality of law, in contrast, is bound up in its formal dimension, which necessarily supposes the uniform obligation, subject to any explicit or implicit formal exceptions, to obey the law. This is perhaps a quibble, but it may be suggested that the tripartite categorisation of legal obligation into coercive, formal, and moral elements has much to commend it. Finnis doubts the value of the coercive element, in the light of its predictive uncertainty. It may, however, still be suggested that coercion remains an element in the equation, even if not a perfectly satisfactory one.

Finnis sets out the reasoning of the good citizen, based upon practical reasonableness, in relation to the duty to obey as a three-stage process (*Natural Law and Natural Rights*, p. 316). The stages are:

(a) The common good demands compliance with law.

(b) Where conduct is stipulated by law compliance can only be rendered by observing such conduct.

(c) Therefore the conduct so stipulated as obligatory must be performed.

The first stage will generally be assumed, leaving only the second and third stages open to discussion in a given case. However, in appropriate circumstances, the first stage may be reclaimed allowing choices to be made amongst variously 'moral' but universally 'valid' (in a formal sense) legal provisions.

There is for Finnis, as for St Thomas Aquinas (see 2.3.2), a 'weighting' in favour of obedience in most cases. Thus

> ...the reasons that justify the vast legal effort to render the law...impervious to discretionary assessments...are reasons that also justify us in asserting that the moral obligation to conform to legal obligations is relatively weighty.
>
> (*Natural Law and Natural Rights*, p. 319)

The 'justification' is of course precisely the uniformity of law as a general public prescription.

2.6.6 The importance of Finnis' theory

The theory of law advanced by Finnis is clearly one that fits centrally into the spectrum of natural law thought. It relates closely at many points to the thinking of St Thomas Aquinas, but also offers an original approach which speaks very clearly to the modern age. This is particularly the case in its analysis of essential naturalist issues in terms of a modern discourse of rights. This is a highly significant contribution to the modern natural law revival, not as an abolition or denial of other schools of jurisprudence, but rather as a redress of an imbalance which existed in conventional jurisprudence from the middle of the nineteenth century to the latter part of the twentieth century.

FURTHER READING

Aquinas, Thomas, Saint, *Selected Political Writings*, transl. J. G. Dawson, ed. Oxford: Basil Blackwell, 1954.

Aquinas, Thomas, Saint, *Summa Theologiae (Summa Theologica)*, 1a2ae. 90–97, Dominican ed. (London: Eyre and Spottiswoode, 1966).

Augustine of Hippo, Saint, *On the Free Choice of the Will*, transl. A.S. Benjamin and H. Hackstaff (Indianapolis, Ind: Bobbs Merill, 1979).

Beyleveld, D. and Brownsword, R., *Law as a Moral Judgment* (London: Sweet & Maxwell, 1986).

Cicero, *On the Commonwealth and On the Laws,* transl. J.E.G. Zetsel (Cambridge: Cambridge University Press, 1999).

Coulson, N.J., *A History of Islamic Law* (Edinburgh: Edinburgh University Press, 1964).

Coulson, N.J., *Conflicts and Tensions in Islamic Jurisprudence* (Chicago: University of Chicago Press, 1969).

D'Entrèves, A.P., *Natural Law*, rev. ed. (London: Hutchinson, 1970).

Epstein, R., 'The Not So Minimum Content of Natural Law' (2005) 25 *Oxford Journal of Legal Studies* 219.

Finnis, J.M., *Natural Law and Natural Rights* (Oxford: Clarendon Press, 1980).

Fuller, Lon L., *The Morality of Law,* rev. ed. (New Haven, Conn: Yale University Press, 1969).

Fuller, Lon, L., 'Positivism and fidelity to law: a reply to Professor Hart' (1957–58) 71 *Harv L Rev* 630.

Gardner, J., 'Nearly Natural Law' (2007) 52 *American Journal of Jurisprudence* 1.

George, R., (ed.), *Natural Law Theory: Contemporary Essays* (Oxford: Clarendon Press, 1992).

George, R., *In Defence of Natural Law* (Oxford: Clarendon Press, 1999).

Hart, H.L.A., *Essays in Jurisprudence and Philosophy* (Oxford: Clarendon Press, 1983) ch. 16.

Hobbes, T., *Leviathan*, ed. C. B. Macpherson (Harmondsworth: Penguin, 1968).

MacCormick, N., 'Natural law reconsidered' (1981) 1 *Oxford J Legal Stud* 99.

McCoubrey, H., *The Development of Naturalist Legal Theory* (London: Croom Helm, 1987).

Penner, J., Schiff, D., and Nobles, R. (eds), *Jurisprudence and Legal Theory: Commentary and Materials* (Oxford: Oxford University Press, 2002), ch. 2.

Plato, *The Laws*, transl. T. J. Saunders, rev. reprint (Harmondsworth: Penguin, 1976).

Shiner, R., *Norm and Nature* (Oxford: Clarendon Press, 1992).

Woozley, A. D., *Law and Obedience: The Arguments of Plato's Crito* (London: Duckworth, 1979).

3

Classical Legal Positivism:
Bentham, Austin, and Kelsen

Introduction

Positivist theories of law may briefly be described as those which understand the law to be a particular sort of social ordering, a certain kind of social technology by which individuals who live together can coordinate their behaviour and resolve disputes. Whilst positivists would not deny that the creation of functioning legal systems has been a cultural achievement that has delivered many benefits, they would deny that the simple existence of a functioning legal system stands as a moral advance in relation to any other sort of social ordering regardless of the circumstances. It may be the case that the sort of order and dispute resolution provided by law is superior to any other available means in advancing the morally worthwhile goals of a community in certain circumstances, but if this is so it is an empirical matter, not a conceptual truth about the nature of law.

The foregoing might be called the positivist thesis about the nature of a *legal system*. But another positivist thesis, as set out by Gardner, is the following.

> In any legal system, whether a given norm is legally valid, and hence whether it forms part of the law of that system, depends on its sources, not its merits.
>
> (J. Gardner, 'Legal Positivism: 5½ Myths' (2001) 46 *American Journal of Jurisprudence* 199)

This might be called the positivist thesis about the *sources of law*; the idea here is that the law is man-made, either by judges or legislatures or collectively by custom. If it is not made, it is not law. The merits (whether moral, or aesthetic, or economic) of any particular norm, any particular rule or standard or right or duty that might make it a good norm for a legal system to adopt, do not thereby make it a norm of the system. Contrariwise, a norm of the legal system is not expunged from the system simply because of its merits, or more plausibly, its demerits. Bentham, Austin, and Kelsen are all examples of positivists adhering to these two theses.

3.1 Bentham's concept of jurisprudence

The founder of classical English positivist legal theory was Jeremy Bentham (1748–1832), whose ideas were later developed, some would say not entirely fortunately, by his disciple, John Austin (1790–1859). Bentham set out to counter what he considered to be the errors of the conventional jurisprudence of his time, which was of a quasi-natural law type. In part he objected to a debased conventional natural law, which actually bore little resemblance to classical natural law theory. He took particular exception to Sir William Blackstone's uncritical account of the English constitution, making unsubstantiated appeals to natural rights in support of given practices, in the Introduction to his *Commentaries on the Laws of England*. Bentham also had a strong political objection to natural rights doctrine, the correctness of which was later confirmed for him by the events of the French Revolution. Bentham summed up this concern in the complaint that

> ... the natural tendency of such [natural rights] doctrine is to impel a [person] ..., by the force of conscience, to rise up in arms against any law whatever that he happens not to like. What sort of government it is that can consist with such a disposition, I must leave our Author [i.e., Blackstone] to inform us.
>
> (J. Bentham, *A Fragment on Government* (Oxford: Basil Blackwell, 1967), ch. 4, para. 19)

This was to a considerable extent a misapprehension of the claims of natural law theories, but a genuine difficulty in the conventional jurisprudence which Bentham attacked.

Beyond this Bentham attacked natural law upon philosophical grounds. In some ways Bentham stood in a tradition of increasing 'secularisation' in legal theory which can be traced at least to the seventeenth century, for example, in the work of Thomas Hobbes (1588–1679). Bentham's immediate philosophical inspiration, however, lay in the distinction between 'is' and 'ought', descriptive and normative, as exposed by David Hume. Hume wrote that

> In every system of morality ... I am surpriz'd to find, that instead of the usual [association] ... of propositions, is, and is not, I meet with no proposition that is not connected with an ought, or an ought not. ... as this ... expresses some new relation or affirmation, 'tis necessary that it shou'd be observ'd and explain'd; ... for what seems altogether inconceivable [is], how this new relation can be a deduction from others, which are entirely different from it.
>
> (D. Hume, *A Treatise of Human Nature,* ed. L. A. Selby-Bigge and P. H. Nidditch (Oxford: OUP, 1978), 3.1.1)

In other words, it does not follow from the fact that a thing or condition 'is' that it 'ought' so to be. Whether the classical natural lawyers discussed in the last chapter really fall foul of this criticism is to be doubted, but the conventional quasi-natural law ideas attacked by Bentham were much more open to it.

In any event, Bentham's broad aim was to establish a scientific jurisprudence which would clearly distinguish between the descriptive and the normative and deal with each upon its own appropriate level without confusion. To this end he made a division between 'expositorial' and 'censorial' branches of jurisprudence. Of these, Bentham stated succinctly that

> To the province of the Expositor it belongs to explain to us what ... the law is: to that of the Censor, to observe what he thinks it ought to be.
>
> (*A Fragment on Government,* Preface, para. 13)

In short, the existing state of the law should be considered without reference to intrusive moral or ethical criteria of identification, though thereafter, but only thereafter, its quality and any necessary improvements may be considered as a separate issue. Bentham had in fact a broad interest in law reform and made numerous suggestions for changes in legal substance and application, both in England and abroad. His best-known scheme for an 'ideal' prison—the Panopticon—was ultimately rejected in the United Kingdom, but was followed to a small extent in the United States. On the level of theory, Bentham's censorial jurisprudence is by no means without interest, but it is the expositorial jurisprudence which Bentham and Austin developed in their command theory of law which has left the greatest mark on Anglo-American legal theory.

3.2 Bentham and Austin's command theory of law

Bentham's definition of law is commonly summarised as 'the command of a sovereign backed by a sanction', although this is in fact an unduly simplified expression of his model. Bentham himself defined 'a law', and the singularity is important, as

> ...an assemblage of signs declarative of a volition conceived or adopted by the *sovereign* in a state, concerning the conduct to be observed...by...persons, who...are or are supposed to be subject to his power: such volition trusting for its accomplishment to the expectation of certain events...the prospect of which it is intended should act as a motive upon those whose conduct is in question.
>
> (J. Bentham, *Of Laws in General,* ed. H. L. A. Hart (London: Athlone Press, 1970), ch. 1, para. 1)

We see here the elements of:

(a) 'command'—the will conceived by the sovereign is manifestly imperative;

(b) 'sovereignty'; and

(c) 'sanction', in the attachment of motivations to compliance in the form of anticipated consequences.

The relationships and the detail of these elements are manifestly more complex than the bald summary would seem to suggest. On first sight this definition is obvious. Law, whether statute or case, is never suggestive but always imperative in its expression. It is also clearly made either by government or by institutions acting under the authority of government. Compliance and failure of compliance are clearly attended by consequences which urge compliance.

The principal difficulty of the Benthamite and Austinian concept of 'command' lies in the literality with which the concept is taken. Despite their acknowledgement that a 'sovereign' may be a body of persons rather than a single autocrat— indeed, the nineteenth-century English legal sovereign was clearly a collective body—Bentham and Austin seem to have become entrapped in a discourse of personal imperation. In part this followed from the expository nature of their jurisprudential enterprise in that a description of fact is not necessarily a very adequate vehicle for the analysis of a process. In the context of English law, and up to a point other common law systems, with equivalents in other legal systems, two particular problems arise in the interpretation of 'command' in the personalised form advanced in classical positivism. Laws commanded by long-dead members of the sovereign Crown in Parliament continue to be law, although apparently not commanded by the current sovereign. Further, some species of laws may be made upon a delegated basis by subsidiary bodies, such as local authorities, acting within their appointed competences (i.e., *intra vires*) and, through the system of binding precedent (*stare decisis*) by judges. Bentham explained these phenomena as acts of 'adoption' and tacit command. Such adoption was argued to take either of two forms: 'susception', when the mandate in question has already been issued, and 'pre-adoption', when it has not already been issued. Susception thus applies to the laws of former sovereigns and consists essentially of not repealing them and may, on the same basis, apply to prior acts of subsidiary bodies. Pre-adoption can only apply to the future acts of subsidiary bodies, consisting essentially of authorisation, since pre-adoption of the acts of a future sovereign would, on any analysis, be nugatory. At the extreme, Bentham went much further in arguing that any transaction or claim to authority enforceable at law was a command of the sovereign by adoption. In a famous passage he remarked that

> Not a cook is bid to dress a dinner, a nurse to feed a child, ... an officer to drive the enemy from a post, but it is by [the sovereign's] orders.
>
> (*Of Laws in General*, ch. 2, para. 6)

The diversity of these examples, and others omitted, demonstrates the peculiarity of the proposition. The officer's orders rely upon a structure of superior authority and military law which ultimately derive from sovereign authorisation and, as Bentham interpreted the situation, the sovereign 'adopts' each successive level of 'command' by not countermanding it. Military orders, perhaps, fit reasonably well with a 'command' theory, but the cook and the nurse, in more modern language we should perhaps refer more generally to 'employees', fit much more oddly into this scheme. It is true that a contract of employment may ultimately be enforced through legal proceedings, but to ascribe the arrangement itself upon this basis to sovereign command seems a contorted and needless nicety of interpretation. This is a point that emerges more clearly perhaps in the context of the application of 'sanctions' to facilitative laws such as provision for contract.

The idea of tacit, or adoptive, command has been much attacked, not least within the positivist tradition. H. L. A. Hart remarks that

> The incoherence of the theory ... may be seen most clearly in its incapacity to explain why the courts of the present day should distinguish between a Victorian statute which has not been repealed as still law, and one which was repealed under Edward VII as no longer law. Plainly ... the courts ... use ... a criterion [of legal identification] ... which embraces past as well as present legislative operations.
>
> (H. L. A. Hart, *The Concept of Law* (Oxford: Clarendon Press, 1961), p. 63)

In short, legislation is a process the products of which are identified according to criteria of recognition without need for 'adoption' by the personnel of a given time. These criteria include, of course, due authority, but this is not quite the same thing as a requirement for command by a presently extant individual or body. The idea of adoption of contracts and other similar arrangements, founded upon the notion that to permit is to command, seems to involve even more clearly a distortion of language. In general, a permission is not a command: 'You may' is not synonymous with 'You must'.

It would seem to be that in avoiding one set of fictions Bentham fell into another. The discourse of imperation becomes distorting when it is followed too literally and too simple a model is imposed upon actually rather complex processes of authorisation. It is undeniable that laws are imperatively expressed and are in their effects both prescriptive and normative, but it does not follow from this that all laws are simply orders. Many laws are facilitative; for example, a contract or a will may only be made by following the instructions set out by law, but it hardly follows that one performing a contract or making a will does so at the *command* of the sovereign, even if the instrument does eventually fall to be interpreted by a court.

Turning to the issue of the character of the sovereign who issues the commands, in view of his philosophical starting point it is not surprising that Bentham was anxious in his definition of 'sovereignty' to avoid any suggestion of a right to rule. True to his expository intention, he was concerned simply to describe the fact of rulership. Thus he defined a 'sovereign' as

> ...any person or assemblage of persons to whose will a whole political community are (no matter on what account) supposed to be in a disposition to pay obedience: and that in preference to the will of any other person.
>
> (*Of Laws in General,* ch. 2, para. 1)

Several things are noteworthy about this definition. Its basis is a factual, or supposed, habit of obedience on the part of those subject to the sovereign, and it is the fact rather than the cause which is important. The quality of the sovereignty is unimportant and the habit of obedience might arise from any cause from coercively induced fear through to moral admiration; most likely it will combine a wide range of elements in varying degrees. The final clause, the preferential habit of obedience, refers obviously to the primacy of the sovereign, as compared with any subordinate power. Austin expressed this more strongly by insisting upon not only a positive mark of sovereignty (obedience by others) but also a negative mark

> That [sovereign] is *not* in a habit of obedience to a determinate human superior.
>
> (*The Province of Jurisprudence Determined,* p. 194)

Austin's point is seemingly obvious in that a person or entity which is meaningfully sovereign is surely not subject to any other sovereign. The addition of this negative mark can, however, be argued to be unduly restrictive in the light of the political realities even of the nineteenth century, and much more so of the twentieth and twenty-first centuries.

Neither Bentham nor any other positivist has denied that a sovereign body might, indeed undoubtedly will, be subject to political and practical limitations in the exercise of power. The sensitive questions arise rather in relation to the imposition of formal or legal limitations upon sovereign power. Austin dismissed this notion outright, stating that

> ...it follows from...the nature of sovereignty and independent political society, that the power...of a sovereign...in its...sovereign capacity, is incapable of *legal* limitation. A...sovereign...bound by a legal duty, [would be]...subject to a higher or superior sovereign [and]...[s]upreme power limited by positive law, is a flat contradiction in terms.
>
> (*The Province of Jurisprudence Determined,* p. 254)

Constitutional laws which seek to limit sovereign power are seen as mere 'guides', a form of 'positive morality' which does not fall within the category of 'laws properly so-called' from this point of view. On Austin's logic this would be unavoidable, because it is clearly absurd for a body to command itself, and a still greater absurdity appears when the question of the attachment of sanctions to such law is addressed. Bentham, on the other hand, took a somewhat more flexible approach. He admitted limitations upon the exercise of sovereign power through a 'transcendent' law amounting to a self-denying ordinance by the sovereign and through a limitation of the 'habit of obedience'. The first of these was termed an 'express convention' and defined as:

> ...the case where one state, has, upon terms, submitted itself to the government of another: or where the governing bodies of a number of states agree to take directions in certain specified cases, from some body or other that is distinct from all of them.
>
> (*A Fragment on Government,* ch. 4, para. 23, n. 1)

Upon a Benthamite analysis, the instruments establishing the European Communities would thus be express conventions in this sense. Bentham's account of such express conventions suggests that he considers them an enshrinement of a limitation of the habit of obedience. H. L. A. Hart remarks that

> ...in his [Bentham's] view the importance of an express convention in limiting the authority of a supreme legislature was derivative from what he takes to be the fundamental fact of the subjects' limited habitual obedience.
>
> (H. L. A. Hart, *Essays on Bentham* (Oxford: Clarendon Press, 1982), p. 231)

Such express conventions would be by their nature inter-State; for reasons set out below the term 'international' is perhaps in this context to be avoided. Bentham also admitted, however, the possibility of some limitations of sovereign power within a State. Bentham was willing to admit, reluctantly and with distaste, formal and 'legal' limitations upon prima facie sovereign power, in the form of laws *in principem,* which is to say laws directed to the sovereign (by the sovereign) as compared with more normal laws *in populum* (directed to the sovereign's subjects). In a 'command theory' such laws are profoundly problematic. How can a sovereign (or any other body) meaningfully 'command' itself or, indeed, its *ex hypothesi* unlimited 'successors'? Bentham gives a complex explanation of these 'laws *in principem'* which he terms *pacta regalia,* stating that

> When a reigning sovereign then in the tenor of his laws engages for himself and for his successors he does two distinguishable things. By an expression of will which has its own conduct for its objects, he enters himself into a covenant: by an expression of will which has the conduct of his successors for its object, he addresses to them a recommendatory mandate.
>
> (*Of Laws in General,* ch. 4, para. 16)

Bentham was unwilling generally to admit that such *pacta regalia* would truly equate with 'laws' in the normal sense and considered that they would be maintained only by 'auxiliary sanctions' such as political or religious pressure. Where they actually were maintained by courts of law he considered that sovereignty must be held to be shared between the political leadership and the courts, which would evidently be the

Benthamite analysis of the United States' constitution, a situation which, however, he felt to be highly undesirable in the light of his disapprobation of judicial incursions upon sovereign action.

The Benthamite and Austinian analyses of limitations upon sovereignty, formal and otherwise, involve a number of devices which appear, and to some extent are, markedly contorted. Much of this may be argued to have been unnecessary in that the problem derives not from anything fundamental to the approach adopted but from the insistence upon a misleading personal analogy for sovereignty. Bentham and Austin were fully aware of the corporate nature of the British sovereign, and yet the personal language ('he' and 'his') is both noteworthy and significant. Clearly, for an individual meaningfully to command him or herself is difficult and to issue binding instructions to another individual who will occupy the same place is similarly problematic. The analogy is, however, dubious in that the sovereignty, whether individual, group, autocratic, totalitarian or democratic, is in one way or another the expression of a process which is at once the head and part of a legal order. This lack of distinction between authoritative process and pure imperation is perhaps the great lacuna in their analysis, one addressed in the revised positivism advanced by H. L. A. Hart.

3.3 The attachment of sanctions

Bentham states that

> Nature has placed mankind under the governance of two sovereign masters, *pain* and *pleasure*.
>
> (J. Bentham, *An Introduction to the Principles of Morals and Legislation,* ed. J. H. Burns and H. L. A. Hart (London: Methuen, 1982), ch. 1, para. 1)

This is the fundamental basis of the principle of utility upon which Bentham founded his 'censorial jurisprudence', but in the context of 'sanctions' the idea is that the 'obligation' to obey law consists simply of the anticipation (primarily the fear) of consequences attached to non-compliance, or, to a lesser extent, of consequences following from compliance. The motive for obedience to law, meaning the factors upon which it relies to secure its intended effects rather than the general, and much more variously derived, 'habit of obedience' to the sovereign, thus becomes in Bentham's terms

> …the expectations of so many lots of pain and pleasure, as connected in a particular manner in the way of causality with the actions with reference to which they are termed *motives*. When it is in the shape of pleasure…they may be termed *alluring* motives: when in the shape of pain, *coercive* [motives].
>
> (*Of Laws in General,* ch. 11, para. 1)

Bentham actually admitted that there may be several types of motivation for compliance with law, including 'physical', 'political', 'moral', and 'religious' sanctions, but the apparent concession to a 'naturalist' form of analysis is misleading. Neither Bentham nor Austin ever denied the existence of factors affecting law beyond their defined 'province of jurisprudence'. Within that province, however, it is clear that Bentham envisages only a political sanction, one imposed by the sovereign, as a definitive characteristic of 'law'.

There are several points to be noticed in Bentham's basic statement upon the motivation for compliance with law. The first is that this is a probabilistic concept of obligation. There can be no absolute certainty that a given sanction will be effective in a given case. The person who gets away with an illegal act has patently evaded the applicable sanction and, indeed, the obligation to obey has failed in this situation. The motivation acts through the expectation of entailed consequences rather than through the certainty of them. Secondly, the motivating consequence, the 'sanction', is connected in a particular manner by way of causality with the action, or forbearance, to which it is directed. The unpleasant, or pleasant, consequence is not the product of a random association but is itself an imposition by the sovereign. Clearly, under Bentham's basic definition it is a part of 'a law' and as such 'legal' in nature. Finally Bentham admits two forms of sanction: coercive (i.e., negative) sanctions, which threaten an unpleasant consequence for disobedience and, with less emphasis, 'alluring' sanctions, which promise a beneficial consequence in case of compliance. Provisions supported by an 'alluring sanction' were termed by Bentham 'praemiary laws' and were clearly considered to be the exception rather than the rule.

Austin was not prepared to make this concession and followed the logic of a discourse of 'sanctions' to its apparent ultimate conclusion. He stated

> It is the power and the purpose of inflicting eventual *evil,* and *not* the power and the purpose of imparting eventual *good,* which gives to the expression of a wish the name of a *command.*
>
> (*The Province of Jurisprudence Determined*, p. 17)

In fairness to Austin, it is important to consider this seemingly inflexible statement in its proper context. Although Austin here expressly disagreed with Bentham, he conceded that a promised 'reward' might well be a motive for compliance. His point was rather that if 'law' is to be categorised as 'command', then the associated sanction can only be negative in nature. In short, orders do not derive their particular quality from promises of benefit (even though these may be offered) but from, at least, an implicit threat of coercion. Within the immediate logic of a command theory this is not as negligible an argument as has sometimes been suggested. The problem is the extension of this logic to aspects of the law where it clearly fails to fit. Illustrative examples are not hard to find. The legal requisites for the making of a will have been set out by legislation from the Wills Act 1837 onwards and failure to satisfy these requirements may lead to the failure of the will. This, on Austin's analysis, is the negative sanction, the fear of failure, which motivates compliance on the part of a testator. Such logic may certainly be imposed on the process but it may clearly be seen to be an imposition. The aim of the testator is to ensure the posthumous disposition of his or her property in a particular way. If the formalities are not correctly observed, who is 'punished'? Certainly not the testator, at least from any viewpoint of earthly relevance. The primary 'victims' are surely the 'innocent' beneficiaries. A more credible analysis would seem to be that the formalities of testamentation are essentially a set of 'instructions' for the attainment of a given objective, in this case the disposal of property after death in accordance with one's wishes. In a similar way, the instructions accompanying self-assembly furniture are, one hopes, an accurate guide to the assembly of the piece concerned. If the person assembling, for example, a chair, does not correctly follow the instructions and, when sat upon, the chair falls apart, this might be considered a 'penalty' for failing to follow the instructions. It would, however, more realistically be considered a natural, if unfortunate, result of incompetence and a failure to gain an anticipated 'reward'.

The distortion of usage imposed by Austin's insistence upon a narrow 'command' model, ironically inspired precisely by a desire to avoid distortion of descriptive language, discloses Austin's failure to expose the facilitative side of the law. The legal power to make a will is facilitative; it enables a convenient and socially necessary process to be performed; it entails a guarantee that the State will, by virtue of its authority, enable the will thus expressed to be implemented. A person who fails to observe the formalities is not truly punished, or punished at all, but rather fails effectively to take advantage of the recognised facility offered. At all events, the sanctions element of the classical command theory emphasises its 'social realist attitude' towards law-making as a power relation, defined, if not entirely characterised, by the potential for the application of coercive force.

3.4 Kelsen's pure theory of law

Hans Kelsen (1881–1973) unequivocally distinguished, in Benthamite terminology, his expositorial 'pure theory of law' from censorial jurisprudence.

> The pure theory of law is a theory of positive law. As a theory it is exclusively concerned with the accurate definition of its subject-matter. It endeavours to answer the question, What is the law? but not the question, What ought it to be? It is a science and not a politics of law.
>
> (H. Kelsen, 'The pure theory of law', transl. C. H. Wilson (1934) 50 *LQR* 474 at p. 477)

This is manifestly a positivist agenda, both in its emphasis upon what law 'is' and in its claims to 'scientific' analysis. However, the theory cannot simply be equated with the English positivist tradition associated with Bentham and Austin, for Kelsen's pure theory was advanced in a different context and was to a significant extent influenced by rather different considerations from those which shaped the English positivist tradition. Kelsen's work originated in the intellectual climate of post-1918 Vienna. This was a period of dramatic change. The dismemberment of the Austro-Hungarian Empire after the First World War and the transition from imperial centre to the capital of a much reduced republic enhanced a critical 'scientific' tradition which already had deep roots in pre-war Austria, seen, for example, in the psycho-analytical work of Sigmund Freud. Both the strengths and the weaknesses of this general tradition may be seen to advantage in Kelsen's legal theory.

Like all positivists Kelsen was concerned with what law 'is', but he was not directly concerned with the substantive norms of any particular legal system. His interest was instead in the nature of the building blocks out of which a legal system, any legal system, is constructed. The model which he advanced is one of a hierarchy of norms, each of which is validated by a preceding norm until, finally, an ultimate source of authorisation is reached in a basic norm termed the *Grundnorm*. This model is essentially abstract and Kelsen never suggested that actual legal systems are expressly formulated in this way. Rather, Kelsen suggests, this is how a legal system, whatever its mode of expression, actually works.

Kelsen termed his legal theory 'pure', implying some lack of contamination. By this he meant that the theory excluded from consideration all factors which could not be regarded as of the essence of 'law'. These included a wide range of considerations which other schools of jurisprudence incorporate in their models of law and its operation, for some of which Kelsen manifested an unmistakable contempt. This endeavour to establish a pure theory rested upon a concept of knowledge which owed much to the work of Immanuel Kant (1724–1804).

3.4.1 **Pure theory and the Kantian theory of knowledge**

Immanuel Kant argued that in acquiring knowledge human beings impose a framework of categorisations upon their impressions of the world beyond themselves. The impressions thus processed in the cause of understanding therefore have imposed upon them a structure which is not necessarily inherent in the objective phenomena observed. In other words, the nature of the human perceptual and cognitive faculties contributes to the shape of our concepts, and thus the way in which we think about the world. Two of the best examples of this are our concepts of space and time, which we find it impossible to 'think outside of'. It should be emphasised that this is not to assert a condition of error or falsity, it is simply to advance an analysis of the ways in which the world impinges upon us are tracked, processed, and structured into forms of understanding acceptable to human mentality.

In what can only be described as a bold move, Kelsen claims to have set out a similar formal conceptual structure through which the nature of law and legal systems may be known, even though this structure may be far removed from the overt substance of any given legal system. Thus, for Kelsen, although jurisprudence is to be considered a science in the sense that it aims to discover the facts about our concept of law, it should not be treated as a natural science, which is concerned with the observation of facts and analysis of causal relations. Instead, Kelsenian jurisprudence seeks to discover a logical structure underlying the objective reality of our concept of law.

The pure theory is a science of norms, one concerned with 'ought' propositions and not the study of factually descriptive 'is' propositions. Lest it be thought that there is here a conflict with the claimed positivism of Kelsen's theory, it should be emphasised that these are not, for example, the moral or ethical 'oughts' with which naturalist theories are concerned. The point is rather that law is by its nature normative: it is concerned precisely with what people 'ought', or 'ought not', to do. Of course, people do not always actually do what they ought to, or, indeed, always avoid doing what they ought not to do. For Kelsen legal norms take the general form that if condition x applies then consequence y ought to follow. The effect of such a norm is essentially to validate, i.e., render 'legal', the actions or decisions which in any given case comprise consequence y. Again, it must be stressed that this is a model of how the law works and not a description of how it is stated. In English law the Town and Country Planning Act 1990 does not, quite, state that 'if development is undertaken without planning permission, then an enforcement notice ought to be served upon the developer'. There is a certain degree of local planning authority discretion in this respect. The process is seen by Kelsen as one of authorisation. Thus the local planning authority is authorised by the summary norm stated above to serve enforcement notices in appropriate cases, but not, of course, in inappropriate ones.

How compelling is Kelsen's 'Kantian' approach to theorising the law? Two difficulties might immediately be noticed. First, it is one thing for Kant to argue that our concepts of 'space' and 'time' are more or less unshiftable constraints upon our ability to conceive the world, unshiftable in the sense that they seem more or less 'hard-wired' in us, as aspects of our fundamental way of seeing the world we cannot sensibly transcend. It is quite another to say the same thing about the concept of law, in respect of which it is easy to observe shifting historical and cultural understandings. In the second place, Kelsen ties his idea of law to the normative (rather than causal) relation that if x then y ought to follow, where y is a sanction; so Kelsen embraces a sanction theory of law, and so his theory raises the same sort of worries as Bentham and Austin's command ('orders backed by threats') theory of law.

3.4.2 The meaning of 'purity'

Kelsen's theory is represented to be 'pure' in the sense that it carefully excludes from consideration all factors and issues which can be considered not to be strictly 'legal'. These include all the moral, ethical, sociological, and political factors and values which are commonly advanced in explanation or pleaded in justification of law. Kelsen explained that

> The pure theory of law...establishes the law as a specific system independent even of the moral law. It does this not...by defining the legal norm...as an imperative, but as an hypothetical judgment expressing a specific relationship between a conditioning circumstance and a conditioned consequence.
>
> ('The pure theory of law', transl. C. H. Wilson (1934) 50 *LQR* 474 at pp. 484–5)

Such 'conditioned circumstances' arising in the application of positive law are not, of course, denied to have moral, political, or sociological effects, but their analysis is relegated to disciplines other than that of jurisprudence.

The purity of Kelsen's theory inevitably, and intentionally, distances it from real legal systems. The model is a blueprint for the operation of legal systems in general rather than any particular legal system. The logic behind the purity of the model is clear enough, but it must be asked whether such an attempt to isolate the essence of 'law' from all other factually associated factors may not tend to distort the analysis.

There is a further, more serious problem, however. As Hart pointed out (H. L. A. Hart, 'Kelsen Visited', *UCLA Law Review*, 10 (1962–63), 709), Kelsen's theory is too pure. By requiring all laws to be understood as 'if x then y ought to occur' conditional norms, and prohibiting inquiry into the different sorts of reasons for laws, Kelsen's theory is unable to distinguish between a tax and a fine. Consider: if I earn £10,000, then I ought to pay HMRC £2,000; if I park on double yellow lines and am ticketed, I ought to pay £20 to the local authority. According to Kelsen's theory, there can only be one way to understand the requirement to pay both the £2,000 and the £20, as a sanction. But a tax is not a sanction—the purpose of income tax is not to punish me for earning income, and the government does not want the income tax to *dissuade* people from earning income in the way that a fine for parking on double yellow lines is meant to dissuade people from illegal parking, for if it did that then the government's revenue would fall. Kelsen's theory, being structurally blind to a distinction that anyone familiar with the law recognises, simply fails to capture an important aspect of the way the law works, a failing common amongst sanction theories of law.

3.4.3 **The hierarchy of norms**

The Kelsenian model of a legal system is one of a hierarchy of norms in which each norm is validated by a prior norm until the point of origin of legal authority is reached with the basic norm, the *Grundnorm*. In order to comprehend this system it is necessary to appreciate the nature of the norms in question and the function of the hierarchic relationship existing between them. Both these questions raise a number of important, and in some ways problematic, issues.

3.4.3.1 The structure of norms

The nature of the norms which form the Kelsenian hierarchy is determined by the intended purity of the analysis. The pure theory excludes not only moral, political, and sociological values but also ideas of the purpose, in the sense of legislative or judicial intention, of law; we have just seen how this can give rise to a problem, in the inability of the Kelsenian to distinguish a tax from a fine. Such ideas are considered by Kelsen to rest upon, for example, political or sociological values. The pure theory is concerned with the active function of legal norms, that is to say, how they actually work. Interpreting norms should be left to moralists, politicians, and sociologists.

As we have seen, according to Kelsen the key function of law in this sense is one of coercion. He argued that all legal norms are concerned with force, either with a response to unilateral use of force, for its suppression, or in the threatened or actual use of legal force to secure compliance with lawful orders and directions. The second category, of course, embraces the first insofar as, for example, a tortfeasor or criminal may be confronted with legal force in order to terminate the wrongful conduct in question. Thus the normative formula—if condition x is satisfied then consequence y ought to follow—will take the concrete form that if the specified situation occurs then the stated sanction ought to be applied.

The emphasis upon coercion resonates strongly with the Benthamite/Austinian concept of law as the 'command of a sovereign backed by a sanction'. There is a significant difference, however, in that Bentham and Austin saw the application of sanctions as a predictive element accounting for the working of legal obligation. Kelsen's norms, in contrast, are not supposed to be factually predictive. It is simply being stated that a sanction ought to be applied in a given case, not that it actually will be applied. The difference is fundamental and rests ultimately upon the Humean dichotomy between descriptive, 'is', and normative, 'ought', propositions.

It is a further noteworthy feature of the system that the legal norms are the province of officials, not the citizens. For Kelsen, a primary norm, i.e. that which regulates the conduct of citizens, stipulates the power of an official to apply a sanction where a citizen commits what Kelsen calls a 'delict'. But there is no imposition of a *duty* not to commit the delict on the citizen; rather, the citizen is merely liable to suffer the sanction in case he does.

The Kelsenian norm, therefore, states the conditions for the application of sanctions, always bearing in mind that these are hypothetical norms concerned with the way in which positive law acts, rather than with the forms in which it may be stated. In effect, the norms are summaries of authorisations admitting the taking of given action in response to the occurrence of given events. Within the Kelsenian model the next, and vital, question is that of the relationship between the norms and the manner of their validation.

3.4.3.2 Validation in the hierarchy of norms

The Kelsenian norms are not represented as being equal in status. Their relationship is vertical, rather than horizontal. Kelsen stated that

> The legal order is not a system of coordinated norms of equal level, but a hierarchy of different levels of legal norms. Its unity is brought about by ... the fact that the validity of a norm, created according to another norm, rests on that other norm, whose creation in turn, is determined by a third one.
>
> (H. Kelsen, *Pure Theory of Law,* transl. M. Knight (Berkeley, Calif: University of California Press, 1967), pp. 221–2)

Thus, upon the Kelsenian model, the norm that if the judge hearing a case orders the payment of damages by the defendant then damages ought to be levied (under coercion if need be), follows from the prior norm that, if the conduct of a defendant falls within the stated category then the judge ought to make an award of damages, and so on up to a legislative enactment or (in a common law system) an original judicial precedent. Behind this, ultimately, there lurks the *Grundnorm* itself. Such a linear example is a little simplified in that, although a line of norms may be traced from the *Grundnorm* through legislation down to the enforcement of a particular judgment, there will in practice be several lines of norms involved. They will include norms of judicial appointment leading to the conclusion that if the judge has been duly appointed to office then judgments made within the scope of his or her authority ought to be enforced.

The structure of these norms is also dynamic rather than static. It is not the substantive content of norms which is here in question but the manner of their authorisation, and such authorisations clearly include the possibility of authorised changes.

The formal nature of Kelsen's analysis of the hierarchy of norms is striking. The quality of a judgment, or even of legislation, is irrelevant. All that matters is that an unbroken chain of normative authorisation 'validates' the final decision or action, whatever that may be. All of this supposes an existing and stable legal order, but some means must be found to identify what, in a given case, that order actually is. In Kelsen's theory the answer to that question is found in the basic norm termed the *Grundnorm*.

3.4.3.3 The *Grundnorm*

The *Grundnorm* (or 'basic norm') is the starting point of any chain of legal norms, the apex of a normative pyramid which, through a long line of connections, authorises the decisions and actions taken in the system at ground level, i.e., in the determination of particular issues and cases. What then is the *Grundnorm*? According to Kelsen

> ...the basic norm...must be formulated as follows: Coercive acts sought to be performed under the conditions and in the manner which the historically first constitution, and the norms created according to it, prescribe.
>
> (In short: One ought to behave as the constitution prescribes.) *(Pure Theory of Law,* transl. M. Knight, pp. 200–1)

A number of points arise from this definition. Most obviously it must be asked whether the *Grundnorm* is identical with the 'constitution' and why the 'historically first' constitution should be selected, rather than that which is currently operative.

In terms of professional legal discourse it would be tempting to identify the *Grundnorm* with the constitution, especially in a State such as the United States which, unlike the

United Kingdom, has a written constitutional document. This would not, however, be correct because the constitution itself is a norm, the effect of which might crudely be summarised in the form: if a decision or an action is constitutional then it ought to be permitted. The *Grundnorm* operates one step further back and does not define the constitution, but instead validates it. It is, in short, the presupposition of the validity of the constitution, or the constitutional order, of the State in question, without which the whole legal edifice dependent upon it must crumble. In the pure Kelsenian concept no assumptions are made about the substance of the constitution and certainly not that it should be democratic or involve any balance of powers or any other such concepts. A constitution to the effect that 'if the autocrat gives an order, then it ought to be enforced' would be sufficient for this purpose, apart from the all too evident difficulties in attempting to found a functioning legal system upon such a minimalist basis.

It is worth pausing here to note that the theory of the *Grundnorm* completes Kelsen's 'Kantian' concept of law. Kelsen's claim is that our concept of law is logically structured in two ways: first, the law is a normative order, where a norm is understood to be a conditional permission to impose a sanction; secondly, via the *Grundnorm*, the law is made up of norms whose validity ultimately derives from an historical moment establishing a constitutional order.

The reference to a 'historically first' constitution involves a chain of constitutional validations in which constitutional evolution, through processes of amendment or other procedures not involving a revolutionary discontinuity, lead back to a first accepted constitution. The 'historical first' is thus the starting point of the current constitutional order and not necessarily whatever arrangement originally obtained in the country concerned. From this point of view the historically first English constitution would be the Revolutionary settlement of 1689 and not the arrangements of William the Conqueror, or Edward the Confessor. In the United States it would be the independence constitution and not the arrangement of colonial government under George III. The Kelsenian first constitution is thus the product either of revolutionary discontinuity or (highly unlikely in the modern world) of a truly first writing upon a political blank slate.

Which constitution is operative in a given country at a given time is a matter to be determined by reference to effectiveness, i.e., what constitution is actually applied. From this it would seem to follow that the *Grundnorm* cannot in Kelsen's terms truly be considered 'pure'. Effectiveness in the end rests upon all the moral, ethical, political, and sociological factors which are carefully excluded from the pure theory, and yet this is the means by which the *Grundnorm,* the fountain-head of the system, is to be identified. This paradox is, however, more apparent than real. The *Grundnorm* is the assumption of the validity of the constitution and not its particular identity. The relation of the *Grundnorm* to the criterion of 'effectiveness' is simply the point at which Kelsen's hypothetical hierarchy of norms attaches to reality. Once it has been determined, through the test of effectiveness, what constitution is being assumed to be valid in a given State, the Kelsenian analysis begins to be applied to the actual substance of a real legal system. The point of contact is vitally important but it is essentially extrinsic to the pure theory itself. The doctrine of effectiveness does, however, raise a controversial issue. This arises from the treatment of a change of *Grundnorm* through a revolutionary discontinuity, that is to say when the line from a historically first constitution is broken and a new primary historical foundation is laid.

3.4.3.4 The problem of revolutionary transition and lawful decolonisation

Where a revolutionary change takes place, breaking the chain of continuity from the historically first constitution then in place, the substantive, although not the hypothetical, effect of the *Grundnorm* in the given situation will change. In short, the practical efficacy of the new order will lead to the *Grundnorm* authorising a revised chain of norms. So, while people sometimes refer to the *Grundnorm* changing when there is a revolution, this is not, strictly speaking, correct; rather, the legal order imposed by the revolutionary government now serves the role of the 'first historical constitution' that must be obeyed.

Kelsen has been criticised for omitting from his analysis of a discontinuous change in a legal order any consideration of political or moral evaluation of the revolutionary, or indeed pre-revolutionary, regime. J. W. Harris remarks that

> Surely, it has been argued, lawyers take other things into account—such as the justice of the revolutionary cause, or the approval or disapproval of the populace—not just the fact of enforcement? Whether Kelsen, or his critics, correctly describe what lawyers do in such contexts is an issue of history.
>
> (J. W. Harris, *Legal Philosophies* (London: Butterworths, 1980), p. 71)

The essence of this question seems to be one of context, as so often in issues of jurisprudence. It must be remembered that revolutionary regimes do not approach legal institutions as suppliants seeking their approval. A legal order of some sort will no doubt be required, but if the existing institutions are unwilling to validate the new regime, they will, by one means or another, certainly be replaced by another which is more compliant.

The main stumbling-block here is the question of what exactly is meant by 'effectiveness'. The Kelsenian view of revolutionary change has from time to time been judicially considered. In a case arising from the unilateral declaration of independence by the Smith regime in Rhodesia (now Zimbabwe) in 1965, *Madzimbamuto* v *Lardner Burke* (1968) 2 SA 284, it was suggested that the effectiveness of a revolutionary regime rests to a very significant extent upon the willingness of the judiciary to implement its decrees. In relation to this and other cases, in which the Kelsenian issue of effectiveness has been judicially considered, R. W. M. Dias comments that

> ...it may well be that...pronouncements [of the illegality of a revolutionary regime] will nearly always be retrospective, since judges sitting under the power of a regime may have little alternative but to accept it as legal; those who refuse will be replaced, or their judgments will be nullified.
>
> (R. W. M. Dias, *Jurisprudence*, 5th ed. (London: Butterworths, 1985), p. 366)

They may have 'alternatives' but they will almost certainly be profoundly unpleasant. Certainly no revolutionary regime has ever given up the power it has seized simply because the judges disapprove of it. Interestingly, the Supreme Court of Pakistan rejected the Kelsenian model in *Jilani* v *Government of Punjab* PLD 1972 SC 670, overruling a pro-Kelsenian view taken in 1958 at a time when an 'illegal' regime was in fact in power.

Lawyers and others may, of course, criticise the new order and might even resist it, with whatever long-term success or failure. This, however, relates to moral, ethical, political, and sociological considerations which are, *ex hypothesi*, excluded from the pure theory. Kelsen should not be understood to deny the existence or even the effect of such considerations; they are indeed inherent in the concept of 'efficacy', since successful resistance will, of course, render a system inefficacious whether by revolution or counter-revolution. Kelsen, however, relegates consideration of these issues to disciplines other than that of jurisprudence. The problem this relegation creates, however, is similar to the one his purity causes when it prevents a recognition within his theory of the difference between a tax and a fine (see 3.4.2). If the only thing which a system of coercion requires to attract the application of the *Grundnorm* is effectiveness, so that any effective coercive regime is a legal order, then the theory would appear to be unable even to conceive of an illegal or unlawful (however temporary) regime. It may be that there really is no difference between an 'unlawful' and a 'lawful' regime; perhaps effectiveness is really all. But if that is the case then the *Grundnorm* seems to lack the quality of normativity. After all, one should have no sense that one *ought* to follow the dictates of any regime which just happens to be effective, however tyrannical it might be. One may be forced to do so as a practical matter, but 'ought' does not come into it. Kelsen insisted to the end that 'might did not make right' and that whilst effectiveness was a necessary condition for the *Grundnorm* to apply to a normative order, it was not sufficient. However he never identified the further factor, which, together with effectiveness, rendered a regime legitimate in the sense of its attracting the imprimatur of the *Grundnorm*.

If anything, the problems with making sense of the *Grundnorm* are worse when it comes to lawful decolonisation, for example, the many cases in which sovereignty was transferred by Act of Parliament to newly independent former colonies, as in the case of Canada, Australia, India, and so on. In these cases there is no discontinuity of authority (of norm authorisation), and yet the result is the creation of a new 'first' historic constitution, in the sense that henceforward the constitution of the newly independent country itself has the imprimatur of the *Grundnorm* in that it is the country's new independent constitution which must be obeyed, not the UK Parliament.

3.4.4 The role of public international law in pure theory

Thus far the *Grundnorm* has been treated as the basic element of national, or municipal law, which functionally it essentially remains throughout Kelsen's thought. However, in his later writings Kelsen considered the relation between public international and national, or municipal law and was led to postulate an international *Grundnorm* ranking prior to the municipal *Grundnorm* that applies to validate the constitutions of particular States. If this move is taken to be central rather than peripheral to Kelsenian jurisprudence, then it has the potential substantially to affect the role of the *Grundnorm* when viewed from a national perspective.

The nature of public international law and its relation to municipal law have been considered problematic by a number of legal theorists. The English positivist tradition tends to take a dismissive view of the international legal order. John Austin, speaking at a time when international law was institutionally much less developed than is now the case, relegated the system to the sphere of 'positive morality'. Kelsen, ultimately, took a radically different view which led him in part to reassess the nature of his *Grundnorm* and to move it into the 'international' sphere.

3.4.4.1 Monism, dualism, and the *Grundnorm*

There are two broad views which can be taken of the relation between international law and municipal law. They may be considered essentially separate systems in which the external obligations of a State (under international law) have only a political relation to its use of internal law-making powers within the national system. Thus, a State which, through its municipal law, is violating international law will be in breach of external obligations and may be made the object of sanctions. The offending municipal law will, however, be 'law' until, or rather unless, the State is forced, through sanctions or other pressures, to change it. This, crudely, is the 'dualist' view. Alternatively, it may be argued that there is only one legal order which comprises both international and municipal law, and any municipal law which violates international obligations or norms will, to a greater or lesser extent, be thereby invalidated. This, again crudely, is the 'monist' position. For a variety of reasons Kelsen ultimately took up a monist view.

The principal reason was his view that valid legal orders should not conflict, and that if States were part of an international legal order, which they may generally be considered to be, then international and municipal law should be considered as part of a unified, monist system. From a Kelsenian viewpoint it follows from this proposition that international law must have a *Grundnorm*. Kelsen also took it that since the international system was the overall unity, its *Grundnorm* must rank prior to the municipal *Grundnorm* and thus be the ultimate source of authority for municipal systems also. It may be argued that this question is somewhat removed from the realities of both international and municipal law. States do have international legal obligations which do impinge upon the organisation of their municipal law. Sometimes at least quasi-monist doctrines may be found in municipal law, but the wholesale implausibility of the entire picture must be noticed. The Kelsenian theory of law is one of the dynamic authorisation of norms; is it really to be contended that most Parliamentary legislation, for example, is authorised by the British consititution, which is authorised by a customary norm of international law? If so, what becomes of the continuity of the British constitutional order? A Kelsenian might claim that at one point in the more or less recent past the municipal *Grundnorm* was superceded by the international one, but if that were so, one would expect there to be some 'revolutionary' moment when this occurred which can be identified; but that seems extremely unlikely given the incremental nature of international law development.

Furthermore, in international law, perhaps even more than in municipal law, matters of morality, ethics, and politics are in practice inseparable from the working of the legal order. As we shall now see, the possibly distorting implications of the assumptions of the pure theory become very acute in the case of the *Grundnorm* of public international law.

3.4.4.2 The *Grundnorm* of public international law

In endeavouring to postulate an international *Grundnorm*, Kelsen followed a similar process of tracing to that which led from the particular municipal decision back to the municipal *Grundnorm*. If here the point of concretised application is a decision of the International Court, or presumably of other international bodies such as, for example, the United Nations Security Council, then a chain of authorisation may be followed. The chain will lead back to one of the sources of public international law, as set out in art. 38 of the Statute of the International Court of Justice; that is to say, in brief summary, treaties, international custom, recognised general principles of law and, as 'subsidiary' sources, judicial decisions and academic writings. Kelsen contends that treaties, customs, etc. all relate back to an essential requirement that States ought to conduct themselves in accordance with the custom established amongst them, which includes the doctrine of *pacta sunt servanda* (agreements are to be observed), which is the fundamental basis of treaty obligations. This norm of custom is then, for Kelsen, what the international *Grundnorm* validates (see H. Kelsen, *General Theory of Law and State*, transl. A. Wedberg (Cambridge, Mass: Harvard University Press, 1949), pp. 369–70).

If there must indeed be an international *Grundnorm*, Kelsen's description of it is not, perhaps, unreasonable. However, the attempt to force international law into pure theory does seem, to say the least, to betoken an element of that desire for inappropriate comprehensiveness of analysis which is one of the weaknesses of much jurisprudence. For the character of the international *Grundnorm* has nothing like the historical character of the original municipal *Grundnorm*, in the same way that custom, as a source of law or norms, has nothing like the historical character of a constitution-founding revolution. In 3.4.3.4 we saw that Kelsen's theory seemed to indicate that the normative force of the *Grundnorm* was apparently attracted by any effective regime. However misguided this might be, the idea at least operates: whether a regime is effective is at least a matter of fact about which one can be more or less certain; when the facts indicate it is, the *Grundnorm* kicks in and (this is the implausible part) Kelsen now believes it becomes a normative legal order which we ought to obey. But the case is very different with a custom. The question whether a practice is a custom, i.e. a practice which is *binding*, is not a matter of fact in the same way: a custom *is* binding, at least in part, because people come to *believe* it is binding. But if, before something can be a custom, it must already attract this sort of normative allegiance (i.e. people believe it is binding on them), then there is no work for the *Grundnorm* to do. The function of the *Grundnorm*, after all, is part of our conceptual outlook on the world that tells us that something is binding; i.e. it represents our belief that the law is binding. But if something is a custom, it is already believed to be binding.

3.5 The significance of classical positivist theories

Whilst there are significant differences between the Benthamite/Austinian and Kelsenian forms of postivism, their common deficiencies arguably outweigh their distinct merits. The average person on the street, if asked to describe what their idea of law was, would probably describe something like a coercive order, of rules laid down by a political superior and backed by sanctions. But, as we shall see when we discuss Hart's criticisms of such theories in the next chapter, while such a view seems to come to people easily, it also tends to come apart under a little scrutiny. Both the Benthamite/ Austinian and the Kelsenian theories suffer from this scrutiny, and for essentially the same reasons; first, that sanction theories of law misdescribe the law (not all laws are orders backed by threats or conditional permissions to impose sanctions) and secondly, they misconceive the way in which the law is binding, for they do not properly describe what it means for the law to be *authoritative*, i.e for the law to act as an authority in respect of our conduct, rather than simply a power able to enforce its will by threat of punishment.

FURTHER READING

Austin, J., *The Province of Jurisprudence Determined* (London: Weidenfeld & Nicolson, 1955).

Bentham, J., *A Fragment on Government* (Oxford: Basil Blackwell, 1967).

Bentham, J., *Of Laws in General*, ed. H. L. A. Hart (London: Athlone Press, 1970).

Duxbury, N., 'Kelsen's Endgame' (2008) 67 *Cambridge Law Journal* 51.

Harris, J. W., 'When and why does the *Grundnorm* change?' [1971] *CLJ* 103.

Hart, H. L. A., *The Concept of Law* (Oxford: Clarendon Press, 1961), chs 2, 3, and 4.

Hart, H. L. A., *Essays on Bentham* (Oxford: Clarendon Press, 1982).

Finnis, J., 'Revolutions and Continuity of Law' in A. W. B. Simpson (ed.), *Oxford Essays in Jurisprudence*, 2nd Series (Oxford: Clarendon Press, 1973).

Kelsen, H., 'The pure theory of law', transl. C. H. Wilson (1934) 50 *LQR* 474 and (1935) 51 *LQR* 517.

Kelsen, H., *General Theory of Law and State,* transl. A. Wedberg (Cambridge, Mass: Harvard University Press, 1949).

Kelsen, H., *Pure Theory of Law,* transl. M. Knight (Berkeley, Calif: University of California Press, 1967).

Kelsen, H., 'Professor Stone and the Pure Theory of Law' (1965) 17 *Stanford Law Review* 1130.

Moles, R. N., *Definition and Rule in Legal Theory* (Oxford: Basil Blackwell, 1987), chs 1 and 2.

Morrison, W., *John Austin* (London: Edward Arnold, 1982).

Paulson, S., 'The Neo-Kantian Dimension of Kelsen's Pure Theory of Law' (1992) 12 *Oxford Journal of Legal Studies* 311.

Paulson S. and Paulson, B., *Normativity and Norms: Critical Perspectives on Kelsenian Themes* (Oxford: Clarendon Press, 1998).

Penner, J., Schiff, D., and Nobles, R (eds), *Jurisprudence and Legal Theory: Commentary and Materials* (Oxford: Oxford University Press, 2002), chs 3 and 5.

Postema, G. J., *Bentham and the Common Law Tradition* (Oxford: Clarendon Press, 1986), chs 5 and 7.

Raz, J., *The Authority of Law* (Oxford: Clarendon Press, 1979), ch. 7.

Raz, J., *The Concept of a Legal System,* 2nd ed. (Oxford: Clarendon Press, 1980), pp. 93–120.

Tur, R. and Twining, W., *Essays on Kelsen* (Oxford: Clarendon Press, 1986).

4

Hart: The Critical Project

Introduction

The command theories of law advanced by Bentham, Austin, and Kelsen (see Chapter 3) are subject to a number of difficulties when presented as a complete description of the operation of positive law. The legal theory of H. L. A. Hart was founded upon a critique of the classical command model, taking Austin's work as his target, which led to a revised 'positivist analysis' founded not upon a combination of command and force (or sanction), but upon the combination and operation of rules in a 'legal system'. Hart commences from the basic proposition that

> The most prominent general feature of law at all times and places is that its existence means that certain kinds of human conduct are no longer optional, but in some sense obligatory.
>
> (H. L. A. Hart, *The Concept of Law* (Oxford: Clarendon Press, 1961), p. 6)

The key words are, of course, 'in some sense' and Hart denies that the classical positivist models of law, as implicitly coercive expressions of political power, sufficiently account for the character of law as an obligation-imposing social phenomenon. In saying so however, Hart did not oscillate to the other end of a positivist–natural law spectrum. He also argued that an equation of the obligatory characteristic of positive law with moral obligation is equally inadequate; natural law theory (see Chapter 2) must equally be rejected on the ground that it insufficiently distinguishes the particular character of legal obligation. Hart expressed the goal of his theory as

> ...an improved analysis of the distinctive structure of a municipal legal system and a better understanding of the resemblances and differences between law, coercion, and morality, as types of social phenomena.
>
> (*The Concept of Law*, p. 17)

This 'improved' analysis is essentially a revised positivism which is presented as building upon the 'failure' of classical positivism but which stands in its own right as a distinct account of the jurisprudential character of positive law.

Probably the most significant ways in which Hart's positivism differed from its classical positivist predecessors were first, his insistence upon paying attention to the way in which the law operated as a system of rules of various kinds, and second, his emphasis on the facilitative, rather than the coercive, function of the law.

4.1 **Hart's methodology**

Hart studied philosophy before training and practicing as a lawyer, and returned to teach philosophy at Oxford before his election to the Chair of Jurisprudence. Because of this, Hart was philosophically competent in a way that was unusual for jurisprudents, and it showed in the philosophical quality of his ideas, and the precision and clarity with which he expressed them. One of the issues that confronts any reader of *The Concept of Law* is the philosophical methods he employed. In the preface to the book Hart famously described the character of the work as follows:

> The lawyer will regard the book as an essay in analytical jurisprudence, for it is concerned with the clarification of the general framework of legal thought, rather than with the criticism of law or legal policy.... Notwithstanding its concern with analysis the book may also be regarded as an essay in descriptive sociology; for the suggestion that inquiries into the meaning of words merely throw light on words is false. Many important distinctions, which are not immediately obvious, between types of social situation or relationships may best be brought to light by an examination of the standard uses of the relevant expressions and of the way in which these depend on a social context, itself often left unstated. In this field of study it is particularly true that we may use, as Professor J. L. Austin said, 'a sharpened awareness of words to sharpen our perception of the phenomena'.
>
> (*The Concept of Law*, p. vi)

Three claims about the work are made in this passage. The first is that the work is a work of analysis, or is analytical; that is, Hart is concerned to clarify our understanding of what the law *is*. He is not concerned here with what Bentham would call *censorial* jurisprudence, criticism of the law, or advancing legal policies. This analytic project is captured by the very title of the book, *The Concept of Law*; the goal is to explicate our concept of law, i.e. what our idea of law is.

The second is the first statement after the ellipsis in the quotation, that the work is also a work of 'descriptive' sociology. This particular passage has been the source of much puzzlement by readers over the years. The book does not look very much like a work of sociology. Indeed, if we think of sociology as an *empirical* social science, then *The Concept of Law* utterly fails as a work of sociology because it neither presents, nor analyses, any empirical data whatsoever. But it is clear that Hart cannot mean 'sociology' in this sense, for this claim is explained by Hart in the next part of the sentence by the assertion that philosophical analysis, an inquiry into the meaning of words, throws light on more than just the meaning of words, but can point out actual differences in the real world, between one social situation or relationship and another. This assertion is the third claim.

Citing Austin, Hart claims that by attending to *linguistic* distinctions we may reveal truths about the phenomena these words refer to. At the time Hart wrote *The Concept of Law*, 'linguistic' philosophy in various forms was at the height of its popularity. The central claim of 'linguistic' philosophers was that by looking at the structure of human language we might resolve age-old philosophical puzzles. One variant of this approach was taken by Wittgenstein (who taught at Cambridge until his death in 1951) in his later work, of whose work Hart was aware. In very rough terms, one might say that Wittgenstein argued that the grammar of natural languages sets traps; it allows us to ask baffling 'philosophical questions' which are in reality a form of nonsense. For example, because the word 'number' or 'five' functions as a noun, grammatically it is perfectly correct English to ask, 'Where are numbers?' Thus using nouns to refer to numbers leads us to treat numbers as objects (since objects are also referred to with nouns), and then, since objects exist in time and space, to ask the philosophical non-sense question, 'Where do numbers exist?'. Wittgenstein captured the essence of this claim with the slogan: 'Philosophical problems arise when language *goes on holiday.*' (L. Wittgenstein, *Philosophical Investigations*, 2nd ed., transl. G. E. M. Anscombe (Oxford: Basil Blackwell, 1958), para. 38.) Wittgenstein argued that the role of the philosopher was akin to that of a therapist; the job of the philosopher was to untangle these linguistic webs so that we could avoid falling into philosophical error. Hart preferred the linguistic philosophy of J. L. Austin (nb: *not* John Austin, the classical positivist of Chapter 3), which acquired the name 'ordinary language philosophy'. Austin's claim was compellingly simple. Human beings interact with the world, and acquire knowledge of it by so doing. Humans also communicate with each other about the world, predominantly in natural languages such as English. If our communications with each other are going to work, our languages had better map onto the world pretty accurately. When I ask you to shut the door, the effectiveness of this utterance will largely turn on whether the words 'shut', 'door' actually *refer*, i.e. actually frame a request which can be carried out. Assuming, therefore, that because language by and large works in this way, when we wish to investigate a phenomenon philosophically, it makes sense to examine the way we talk about it, for the way we talk about it will reflect tacit or implicit knowledge we have about it. In particular, we draw upon our linguistic intuitions. Probably the most famous instance in *The Concept of Law* is the difference between 'being obliged' and 'being under an obligation'. Our linguistic intuition is this—when ordered to hand over our money to a gunman, we might say that we are 'obliged' to do so, by the force of circumstances, but we would not say that we were 'under an obligation' to do so. By attending to our linguistic intuition here, we see that our different willingness to use these two expressions distinguishes two different social situations; thus by attending to language, we reveal something about the world.

In view of the clear connection Hart sees between 'descriptive sociology' and ordinary language philosophy and which he explicitly expresses in this passage, it is a mistake to pull Hart's philosophical method in *The Concept of Law* into two, possibly warring, elements, 'sociology' versus 'linguistic philosophy'. Rather, Hart simply claimed that his philosophical analysis, paying attention to language in the way he did, mapped onto reality, in this case social reality, which makes sense since the law is a social phenomenon.

4.2 Hart's gunman and the critique of command theory

Hart commences from a very simple instance of a coercive order, that made by an armed bank robber, the 'gunman', to a bank clerk to hand over money upon immediate pain of being shot (*The Concept of Law*, p. 19). This example parallels the reference by St Augustine of Hippo, in a very different naturalist context (see Chapter 2), to a captured pirate brought before Alexander the Great. When asked how he dared to rob ships at sea, the pirate replied that he had only one ship and was condemned as a pirate, whereas Alexander had many and was acclaimed an Emperor, making the point that power as such does not confer legitimacy (St Augustine, *De Civitate Dei*, 4.5.4). Hart's point is narrower and is simply that the bank robber has no *authority* over the clerk. The obvious contrast is with a tax demand made pursuant to law by HMRC or an equivalent agency. This too is superficially a demand with menaces but, although defaulters are certainly threatened with penalties, the demand is made with authority. Further, the obligation to pay is general to all relevant persons in receipt of taxable income and exists whether or not enforcement is immediately practical. Upon this basis Hart makes a clear distinction between the situations of 'being obliged' and being 'under obligation', the former involving the actual or predictable application of compulsion, the latter involving a concept of duty whether or not any sanction can reasonably be expected to be applied.

Hart emphasises the obligation element and he argues that the command model, however it may be elaborated or distorted, cannot adequately account for this in the complex structures of a real society. In the concluding summary of his critique of command theory Hart lists four principal defects in the analysis (*The Concept of Law*, p. 77). These are:

(a) Law, even a criminal statute, is, notably unlike the coercive demands of a gunman, addressed generally rather than to a particular person, and applies even to those enacting it.

(b) Some laws do not impose duties but rather create powers, whether public or private, for example, delegated legislative authority or the capacity to initiate legal relations, and these cannot readily be forced into a model of coercive orders. Hart's showing that every legal system contains power-conferring rules as well as duty-imposing rules, and his showing that the former cannot sensibly be re-cast as variations on the latter, is, perhaps, Hart's greatest contribution to our understanding of the nature of law, for so much turns on it. In the first place, it emphasises a feature of the law which command, or 'orders backed by threats', theories utterly neglect: the way in which the law *facilitates* the coordination of behaviour, allowing people to act together (for example by making binding agreements, or licensing the use of their property, or empowering representatives to pass legislation) in ways which they could not otherwise do. Second, it forces us to re-think our naïve views of the law as just a coercive enforcer; it makes us realise the positive way in which the law can contribute to human flourishing, thereby explaining the natural law claims about the morally valuable quality of the law but from a positivist point of view.

(c) Not all legal rules emerge from a command process at all, an obvious example being those deriving from custom. It may be added here that Hart has, of course, dismissed any Benthamite explanation in terms of a tacit command evidenced by enforcement in the courts as a rationalising distortion.

(d) The idea of unlimited sovereignty which is free of all legal constraint fails to take account of the continuity of law, which is an obvious feature of a modern legal system, without reference, again, to a distorted explanation of tacit command. As Hart showed, the notion of sovereignty is itself one which turns on the application of certain rules, rules which provide for the legislative capability of the sovereign, and rules which provide for the orderly succession of power. The prince succeeds to the throne on the death of his father not because he immediately establishes a new habit of obedience amongst the population—habits are not formed in an instant—but because the rules of succession provide that he does.

Hart emphasises that these failures are not incidental but fundamental, in that the basic components of command theory are incapable of any combination which will give an account of what he argues to be the essential feature of law, the application of duty-imposing and power-conferring rules forming a system so as to provide a means for the regulation of social life. Thus he states that

> What is most needed as a corrective to the model of coercive orders or rules, is a fresh conception of legislation as the introduction or modification of general standards of behaviour to be followed by the society generally.
>
> (*The Concept of Law*, p. 43)

4.3 Hart and moral analyses of positive law

The relationship between law and morality, or more accurately between legal validity and moral quality, has posed major questions for jurisprudence over the centuries. The moral criteria for the evaluation of positive law and the implications of their application are the particular concern of natural law theories (see Chapter 2) but have at various times troubled positivists also. Debate in this context has taken a variety of forms. There has been some concern with the role, if any, which moral criteria of evaluation, or identification, ought to be permitted. This question arose with particular urgency in the early part of the twentieth century in the particular context of totalitarian abuses of positive law, notably in the Nazi Third Reich and in the former USSR under Stalin. There has also arisen the question of the extent to which positive law may properly be used to enforce moral propositions for their own sake. H. L. A. Hart has made very significant contributions to both of these areas of contention from a positivist perspective.

4.3.1 Abuse of law: the debate between Hart and Fuller

The oppressive or tyrannical use of positive law by a variety of political regimes has not, unfortunately, been confined to any particular historical era. However, the use of law and the legal system in the Nazi Third Reich undoubtedly raised the issue in a very stark and extreme form. Whether or not the Third Reich was a *Rechtsstaat*, in effect a State subject to the rule of law, is a question which raises a number of fundamental jurisprudential issues. After the Second World War and the collapse of the Third Reich through military defeat, an immediate practical problem was faced in the question of the rectification of specific decisions embodying abuses of legal process under the former regime. In this context a major debate took place between H. L. A. Hart and the natural lawyer Lon L. Fuller upon the question of the validity of some or all Nazi laws and legal decisions.

The immediate focus of the debate was one of the so-called 'grudge cases' reconsidered in 1950 (an account of the case is given in H. O. Pappe, 'On the validity of judicial decisions in the Nazi era' (1960) 23 *MLR* 60). Grudge cases were broadly those in which persons living under Nazi jurisdiction had made use of oppressive laws and procedures for the settlement of personal grudges or ambitions.

The first defendant had in 1944 wished to eliminate her husband, a German soldier, and had to this end reported to the authorities critical remarks which he had made about Hitler whilst on leave from the army. He was charged under laws of 20 December 1934 and 17 August 1938 with making statements critical of the Reich and potentially impairing its defence. He was convicted and condemned to death but was 'reprieved' and sent to the Eastern front. In the event he survived, and after the war his wife and the judge who had tried his case were brought to trial upon charges under the 1871 German Criminal Code, para. 239, relating to unlawful deprivation of liberty. The post-war (West) German court found the judge to be not guilty because the decision had been made under a then existing, albeit oppressive and cruel, law. The woman who had reported the victim was, however, found guilty because she had acted from personal malice in a way which was contrary to conscience and thought to be immoral at the time. The court expressly stated that its decision was not founded upon any idea that the laws under which the victim had in 1944 been convicted were invalid on moral grounds.

Regrettably, the argument between Hart and Fuller was founded upon a brief and misleading report of the case ((1950–51) 64 *Harv L Rev* 1005), which seemed to give the impression that the postwar court had decided that the laws in question were formally invalidated by their immoral substance. For this reason the debate between Hart and Fuller concentrated upon this issue, which, as we have seen, forms no essential part of classical natural law theory (see Chapter 2) and ignored some of the more interesting issues arising from the postwar treatment of grudge cases.

Hart's argument (see H. L. A. Hart, 'Positivism and the separation of law and morals' (1958) 71 *Harv L Rev* 593) was broadly that the laws made in Nazi Germany, however oppressive or immoral, were validly made by the recognised law-making institutions at the time and therefore must be considered to have been 'law'. Hart admitted that the actions of grudge informers may well have deserved punishment, but concluded that it would be better in the particular circumstances to enact straightforwardly retrospective penal legislation than to rely upon an invalidating effect of immorality. Fuller on the other hand (Lon L. Fuller, 'Positivism and fidelity to law: a reply to Professor Hart' (1958) 71 *Harv L Rev* 630), argued that the formalistic conception of the duty to obey law embodied in positivism attempts to isolate legal obligation from all other forms of obligation was awry. In the post-Nazi context, judges, according to Fuller, had no choice but to consider moral questions in their attempt to rebuild a viable legal order.

 (As a footnote, in a subsequent decision upon very similar facts—an account may be found in H. O. Pappe, 'On the validity of judicial decisions in the Nazi era' (1960) 23 *MLR* 260 at p. 264—the defendant in the postwar trial was charged with unlawful deprivation of liberty and attempted homicide. After an initial acquittal the case went to the West German Federal Supreme Court, which quashed the decision and referred the case back to the lower court. The Supreme Court made two fundamentally significant points. First, if the wartime proceedings were improper then the presiding judge was as guilty as the informer who had initiated them. Secondly, there was no need to consider the validity of the Nazi laws in question since even upon their face they had not been correctly applied. The law concerned 'public' statements, and if this meant anything at all it must imply a distinction between those and 'private' statements, which would surely include the conversation between spouses here in question. Secondly, even if this point were not well taken, the court had a broad sentencing discretion and to apply the death penalty (later commuted) in a case of this type amounted to a culpable abdication of responsibility. Thus, the wartime proceedings had been procedurally improper and both the defendant and the judge had a case to answer. The defendant had had, through malicious misuse of process to encompass injury, the *mens rea* of crime which found its *actus reus* in the improper proceedings to which she was an accessory. This line of argument has surely much to commend it in that it relies upon procedural abuses for the resolution of the 'formal' question and these are far from hard to find in Nazi jurisprudence.)

4.3.2 **The enforcement of morality: Hart and Devlin**

The use of positive law to enforce moral propositions for their own sake has at various times been a source of controversy. In 1859 John Stuart Mill argued that society has no 'right' to enforce its moral perceptions where their violation would not cause objectively perceptible 'harm' to others (see J. S. Mill, *On Liberty,* ed. G. Himmelfarb (Harmondsworth: Penguin, 1974)). He argued that, in the absence of 'harm', diversity is a positive factor in society which is dangerously inhibited by 'moral' repression. This issue endures in modern debate (see, for example, Stuart Hampshire, 'Public and private morality', in *Public and Private Morality,* ed. Stuart Hampshire (Cambridge: Cambridge University Press, 1978)). There remained, however, the difficult question of what precisely constitutes 'harm' for this purpose. Mill's proposition was questioned by Sir James Fitzjames Stephen (J. F. Stephen, *Liberty, Equality, Fraternity* (London: Smith Elgard and Co., 1874)), who argued that society could not safely be precluded from enforcing its morality at 'need', even if it should not always do so.

Hart and Devlin's 'debate' resulted from the publication of the Wolfenden Report *(Report of the Committee on Homosexual Offences and Prostitution* (Cmnd 247) (London: HMSO, 1957)), which recommended that male homosexuality between consenting adults and prostitution, subject to protection of minors, should not be criminal (female homosexuality was anyway not criminal). This recommendation was followed in due course. In his 1958 Maccabean Lecture on Jurisprudence, Lord Devlin took exception not to the Committee's conclusion, but to the form of supporting argument it adopted (see P. Devlin (Baron Devlin) *The Enforcement of Morals* (London: Oxford University Press, 1965), especially chs 1 and 6). This was essentially an application of the Millsian 'harm principle', arguing that there are private areas of morality into which the law should not intrude. In response to this Devlin contended broadly that society rests upon the base of a shared morality which is in itself a 'seamless web' and which can be legally defended exactly as society may be defended from subversive action *(The Enforcement of Morals,* pp. 13–14). Like Sir James Fitzjames Stephen before him, Lord Devlin did not argue that society should always enforce all aspects of its moral code, but he did urge that society must always be able to defend itself against a threat to its moral structure felt to be intolerable.

For Devlin the 'morality' in question is a 'jury-box' morality, that of the average 'right-minded' citizen *(The Enforcement of Morals,* p. 15). Devlin admits the obvious potential tension between private inclinations and the 'public' demands of a society and suggests three basic principles in attaining a balance between them. These are: (a) maximum freedom compatible with social integrity; (b) the law should, however, be slow to change its 'moral' stance lest the moral social base be subverted; and (c) privacy should to the greatest possible extent be respected.

This position is in some respects stronger than Hart allowed or represented. It is, however, subject to at least two major questions. There is an obvious danger in relying on a simple 'popular' morality as a basis for legal intervention which might simply lead to persecution of the unpopular. Beyond this, Devlin's argument for moral enforcement actually rests upon an analogy with 'subversion', in particular with treason, which is surely a refined form of the 'harm' principle.

In response to Lord Devlin's argument, Hart defended a staunchly liberal position (see H. L. A. Hart, *Law, Liberty and Morality* (London: Oxford University Press, 1963)). He criticises a tradition of 'judicial moralism' *(Law, Liberty and Morality,* p. 7), citing the early remark of Lord Mansfield in *Jones* v *Randall* (1774) Lofft 383, at p. 385, that

> Whatever is *contra bonos mores est decorum,* the principles of our law prohibit, and the King's court as the general censor and guardian of the public manners, is bound to restrain and punish.

He cites *Shaw v Director of Public Prosecutions* [1962] AC 220 as an example of the same principle. There, a charge of 'conspiracy to corrupt public morals' had been upheld in a case involving publication of what amounted to a directory of prostitutes. In more recent times, some of the views expressed by the Court of Appeal in *R v Brown* [1992] QB 491, a case involving charges of assault in relation to consensual acts of homosexual sado-masochism, seem to proceed from a somewhat similar base of moral disapprobation as such.

Hart proceeded to distinguish between 'moderate' and 'extreme' varieties of the moral thesis, suggesting that Stephen represented the latter and Devlin the former. He identified moderation with emphasis upon the value of morality as a 'social cement' and extremism with the enforcement of morality as an end in itself. It must, however, be doubted whether Stephen could fairly thus be categorised as 'extreme'. Hart's central criticism of Devlin's position is, however, much more soundly based. He attacks the populist model of morality partly upon the basis of the importance of minority rights. Thus

> The central mistake is a failure to distinguish the acceptable principle that political power is best entrusted to the majority from the unacceptable claim that what the majority do with that power is beyond criticism and must never be resisted.
>
> (*Law, Liberty and Morality*, p. 79)

Devlin did not actually quite claim this. However, the question of the morality to be enforced is a serious one and the peril suggested by Hart does seem to lurk within the model of popular morality.

Finally, Hart recognises the need for enhanced legal protection of those who are too young, too ill, or otherwise hindered from fully voluntary decision-making to protect themselves effectively. This is not, however, a moral argument as such, merely an admission of a special application of a harm principle. In particular, Hart denies, with Mill, any right to protection from being shocked.

There is clearly a major distinction between the foundations of Hart's and Devlin's arguments upon this issue. However, one may reasonably ask in how many cases the practical applications of moderate moralism and Hart's qualified liberalism would diverge in any large measure.

4.3.3 Hart's minimum content of natural law

Neither Hart nor any other mainstream positivist denies that important moral questions may be asked about positive law and its application. However, insofar as positivism claims to be able to supply a comprehensive account of law, the impact of moral questions upon the assessment of 'law' quality needs to be addressed. In particular, whether or not any classical natural lawyer has held the position that a law needs to meet a minimal level of moral acceptability to be *legally* valid, such a position is held in various degrees by modern theorists. Hart seeks to avoid what he perceives as the errors found in the adoption of moral criteria of legal validity, while at the same time acknowledging what he calls a 'minimum content of natural law', which comprises those necessary norms of social interaction which, while reflecting moral or 'natural law' considerations, are necessary for any system of law to be minimally *effective* as a legal system. He states that

> ...some very obvious generalizations—indeed truisms—concerning human nature..., show that as long as these hold good, there are certain rules of conduct which any social organisation must contain if it is to be viable. Such rules do in fact constitute a common element in the law and convention morality of all societies [which distinguish them] as different forms of social control.
>
> (*The Concept of Law*, p. 188)

It would be difficult to dissent very strongly from this proposition. In most, if not all, countries fundamental moral norms are enshrined in law, for example, as basic criminal taboos. The proscription of murder is an obvious example and it would, indeed, be difficult to imagine a viable society in which murder was compulsory rather than forbidden. It may be added that many such provisions not only seek to penalise deviance but, equally importantly, to reaffirm the moral base of the social order. This point leads back to some extent to Lord Devlin's argument upon the enforcement of morality through law (see 4.3.2).

Hart's 'minimum content of natural law' rests, as Hart puts it, upon

> The general...argument...that without such a content laws and morals could not forward the minimum purpose of survival which men have in associating with each other.
>
> (*The Concept of Law*, p. 189)

Hart suggests five 'truisms' which underlie the content of any viable set of legal rules. These are:

(a) Human vulnerability, which dictates the proscription of the major crimes of violence.

(b) Approximate equality, meaning that although human beings have different capacities no person is so overwhelmingly powerful as to be able to sustain permanent dominance by individual effort. Thus, there is a need for a 'system of mutual forbearance and compromise which is the base of both legal and moral obligation' (*The Concept of Law*, p. 191).

(c) Limited altruism, which makes rules of mutual forbearance necessary to secure a balance between altruistic and selfish inclinations in a social pattern of life.

(d) Limited resources, which, since necessities are not infinitely available and can be won only through labour, demands some system of entitlement to property.

(e) Limited understanding and strength of will, which tempt individuals into deviant or antisocial conduct for short-term personal gain and render sanctions necessary. Hart is, however, careful to make clear that these sanctions are not the source of obligation but merely a defence against atypical deviance.

The significance which Hart attributes to the satisfaction of these basic requirements is considerable. He states that

> If the system is fair and caters genuinely for the vital interests of all those from whom it demands obedience, it may...retain [their] allegiance...for most of the time, and will accordingly be stable. [But]...a narrow and exclusive system run in the interests of the dominant group...may be made continually more repressive and unstable with the latent threat of upheaval.
>
> (*The Concept of Law*, p. 197)

This is essentially a practical argument to the effect that laws which fail to serve their basic social function(s) will ultimately cease to be viable and will, in one way or another, be displaced. In this way Hart's claim that there is a minimal content of natural law in all functioning systems is misleading; it is not an endorsement of natural law to any extent. Rather, it is what might be called an 'error theory' for the natural law intuition that the law is to some extent essentially morally good because of the way that it contributes to human flourishing. His claim is that for a *viable* order regulating human society, certain sorts of rules are essential; it is a matter of effectiveness or viability, not moral goodness.

FURTHER READING

Devlin, P., *The Enforcement of Morals* (London: Oxford University Press, 1965).

Fuller, Lon L., 'Positivism and fidelity to law: a reply to Professor Hart' (1958) 71 *Harv L Rev* 630.

Hart, H. L. A., 'Positivism and the separation of law and morals' (1958) 71 *Harv L Rev* 593; also in Dworkin, R. M. (ed.), *The Philosophy of Law* (London: Oxford University Press, 1977), ch. 1.

Hart, H. L. A., *The Concept of Law* (Oxford: Clarendon Press, 1961).

Hart, H. L. A., *Law, Liberty and Morality* (London: Oxford University Press, 1963).

MacCormick, N., *H. L. A. Hart* (London: Edward Arnold, 1981).

Moles, R. N., *Definition and Rule in Legal Theory* (Oxford: Basil Blackwell, 1987), chs 3 and 8.

Penner, J., Schiff, D., and Nobles, R. (eds), *Jurisprudence and Legal Theory: Commentary and Materials* (Oxford: Oxford University Press, 2002), ch. 4.

5

Hart's Theory of Law

Introduction

In the last chapter we looked at Hart's criticisms of classical positivist theory and certain moralist claims about the law. Now we turn to Hart's construction of a better theory, in particular in contrast to the theory set out by Austin.

5.1 The importance of rules

The existence and the interaction of rules are fundamental to Hart's legal theory and appear to be obviously the substance of law. Whether one considers statutes, case decisions, or even customary law—from s. 57(1) of the Town and Country Planning Act 1990 ('Subject to the following provisions of this section, planning permission is required for the carrying out of any development of land') to the rule in *Rylands* v *Fletcher* (1868) LR 3 HL 330 (dealing with the liability of those who accumulate dangerous things upon land which are liable to do damage and which escape and in fact cause damage)—the law appears to consist of rules.

The rules form a normative regulatory structure which exists as a system, rather than as a pattern of discrete commands. They apply to anyone in the relevant situation, for example, considering the development of land or accumulating dangerous things upon it. They are also not temporally limited in operation. *Rylands* v *Fletcher* was decided by judges who are no longer capable of wielding a judicial authority, which itself derived from the authority of a Crown in Parliament comprising persons now dead. Seen in this light the importance of rules as a basic building block of law can hardly be doubted, although a number of modern theorists cast doubt upon the exclusive importance of rules in the structure of law. A prominent example is found in the work of Ronald Dworkin (see Chapter 6), who contends that law consists not only of rules but also of policies and principles, most especially the latter, which come into play in discerning the 'right answer' in 'hard cases' to which the naked rules afford no clear outcome. Dworkin nonetheless concedes the importance of Hart's analysis of rules (R. M. Dworkin, *Taking Rights Seriously* (London: Duckworth, 1977), p. 20).

The underlying theme of Hart's analysis of law as rules may be suggested to be precisely that concept of law-making as a facilitative process which, as has already been discussed in the last chapter, was the major weakness of classical positivism as a complete explanation of positive law in operation.

5.2 **Obligation and the internal aspect of rules**

Legal rules are not optional prescriptions; they create obligations which are characteristic in type. Hart distinguishes the 'obligation' associated with positive law from mere convergent habit and also from any psychological experience of 'feeling bound'. He argues that not all rules are necessarily obligation-imposing, but that those which are so are distinguished by one primary and two subsidiary characteristics (see *The Concept of Law*, pp. 84–5). The primary characteristic is one of 'seriousness of social pressure' for conformity. The two subsidiary characteristics are, first, that the rule is thought to be important because it maintains some significant element of social life and, secondly, that the conduct required may conflict with the wishes of the person(s) to whom the rule applies. The combination of these factors is suggested to inform the meaning of statements about 'obligation' in social context. Thus, the obligatory characteristic of positive law may be taken to involve rules requiring patterns of conduct, which are not necessarily those desired by those subject to them, which support some perceived plank of social relations and which are the subject of significant pressure for conformity.

This analysis informs Hart's idea of an 'internal aspect' of rules. He states that

> What is necessary is that there should be a critical reflective attitude to certain patterns of behaviour as a common standard, and that this should display itself in criticism (including self-criticism), demands for conformity, and in acknowledgements that such criticisms and demands are justified, all of which find their characteristic expression in the normative terminology of...'right' and 'wrong'.
>
> (*The Concept of Law*, p. 56)

The 'critical reflective attitude' manifests itself in acceptance of the existence of rules constituting in themselves a justification for criticism of deviant conduct. Thus whilst from an 'external' viewpoint one might be able to predict the consequences of given action or inaction, and even to live satisfactorily in the society concerned, one would lack understanding of a vital element in the operation of the prescription. As Hart expresses it

> ...the external point of view, which limits itself to the observable regularities of behaviour, cannot reproduce...the way in which the rules function...in the lives of those who normally are the majority of society....For them the violation of a rule is not merely a basis for the prediction that a hostile reaction will follow but a *reason* for hostility.
>
> (*The Concept of Law*, p. 88)

This model of 'obligation', which is claimed to be distinct from the classical positivist emphasis upon a coercive 'obliging' and from the naturalist emphasis upon moral aspiration, raises a number of important questions.

Although Hart does not use the term, the method of analysis which he adopts has, as MacCormick points out, a distinct *hermeneutic* element (N. MacCormick, *H. L. A. Hart* (London: Edward Arnold, 1981), in particular at pp. 38 and 59). Hermeneutic method has antique roots, most particularly, although not only, in Protestant approaches to Biblical exegesis, but is primarily concerned with the interpretation and understanding of the language of texts and materials viewed in their contextual continuity. Applied to understanding a phenomenon such as law, the hermeneutic approach requires us to appreciate that what a social phenomenon *is* is determined in part by what the participants in the phenomenon *think it is*, or to put this another way: you cannot understand social practices like law, or chess or marriage or opera for that matter, unless you understand what the participants think they are up to. Chess is a game with rules and a point; it is not simply moving interestingly shaped objects around a board to make pretty patterns.

The extraordinary contortions necessary to display the command theory as a 'complete' account have been considered above (see Chapters 3 and 4). Hart's 'rules of obligation' are not made subject to distortions upon such a scale, partly because they are not deployed over so wide a front. Hart admits the possible role of coercive sanctions as a subsidiary obliging agency in relation to law. What he does not appear to consider, oddly from a hermeneutic viewpoint, is that whilst his categories of 'being obliged' and being 'under obligation' are different, their significance for legal theory may vary according to the context in which they are considered.

There are, of course, a considerable range of possible analyses of the obligatory characteristic of law beyond the one proposed by Hart. Naturalist analysis emphasises moral criteria of evaluation (see Chapter 2), some 'Scandinavian realist' theories stress the psychological experience of 'feeling bound'. From a rather different perspective Marxist analyses tend to treat concepts of legal obligation as artificial constructs which conceal different, and not necessarily beneficial, agendas (see Chapter 13). Without claiming that all disagreements can thus be reasoned out of existence, it would seem reasonable to argue that legal obligation is by its nature a many-sided phenomenon, each aspect of which must be analysed and distinguished in its own right, without selective exclusion.

However, the existence of alternative approaches to a particular phenomenon should not be taken to devalue a theory within its proper context. The particular context appropriate to Hart's rules model is ultimately made obvious by his analysis of the nature of a legal system.

5.3 The union of primary and secondary rules

The idea of rules imposing obligations is not held out by Hart as a sufficient basis for the establishment of a legal system. Hart argues that such primary duty-imposing rules cannot, at any level of organisation beyond the extremely simple, exist satisfactorily in isolation. He sets out three principal defects which would exist in a society which sought normative regulation through primary rules alone. These are:

(a) The primary rules may be 'uncertain' in application, that is to say that no procedures would exist for their interpretation and the determination of their scope where this was not intrinsically clear.

(b) The rules would be 'static', with the only mechanism for change being the very slow processes of developing customary practice.

(c) The application of such rules will be 'inefficient' granted the lack of mechanisms for the resolution of disputes and the determination and enforcement of remedies and punishments.

Hart argues that these difficulties are resolved by the addition of 'secondary rules', which

> ...specify the ways in which the primary rules may be conclusively ascertained, introduced, eliminated, varied, and the fact of their violation conclusively determined.
>
> (*The Concept of Law*, p. 92)

The three types of secondary rule which meet these three defects of a structure of primary rules alone are described by Hart as the 'rule of recognition', 'rules of change', and 'rules of adjudication'. The first affirms the claim of purported rules to command institutional support; it is, in short, a criterion of identification of valid rules of the system. In most legal systems there will not be one simple rule of recognition operating as a criterion of identification for legal rules but, rather, a more or less complex structure of rules which will collectively perform the function of identification. Such rules, which may both define and limit legislative capacity within a given system, may also be suggested to solve the problem of constitutional limitations upon sovereign power (see 4.2), which was a cause of difficulty for both Bentham and Austin.

The second kind of secondary rule is related to the first in that it provides a mechanism whereby new rules may be introduced and old rules may be changed or abolished. The third kind is obvious in its functions both in its most formal context in law courts and in lesser adjudicatory bodies acting under formal authority.

Hart contends that a 'legal system' properly so called is the product of the combination, or 'union', of these two types of rule. The rule of recognition, as the criterion of identification, is fundamental to the system, but the form and function of 'secondary rules' in general raise a number of important issues.

A peripheral consideration arises from Hart's legal anthropology. Hart gives as the type of a society governed by primary rules alone

> ...primitive communities...where the only means of social control is that general attitude of the group towards its own standard modes of behaviour in terms of which we have characterised rules of obligation.
>
> (*The Concept of Law*, p. 89)

In practice the identification of 'standard modes of behaviour' indicates the existence of some form of 'secondary rule' mechanism. It may also be thought that qualities of stasis, in the sense of inhibiting rigidity, and uncertainty would to a large extent be mutually exclusive. However, Hart suggests that such 'primitive' societies, lacking developed secondary rules would be 'pre-legal', since they appear to lack the institutional base and rules necessary for a recognisable 'legal system'.

In practice there is good reason to think that many so-called 'primitive' societies have sophisticated means of identifying, interpreting, and applying their social norms. Modern legal-anthropological thought would certainly not necessarily concur with a dismissal of the 'legal' usages of 'primitive', meaning not high-technology, societies. Simon Roberts remarks that

> While there may be some room for argument as to what constitutes legislative and adjudicative organs, or centrally organised sanctions, Hart appears simply wrong [in arguing that societies without such institutions are difficult to imagine beyond the

very smallest scale]: many societies *have* existed without them and [legal anthropology examines] how order is secured in such societies.

(S. Roberts, *Order and Dispute: An Introduction to Legal Anthropology* (Harmondsworth: Penguin, 1979), p. 25)

The key words here are perhaps 'what constitutes' the legal-systemic institutions in any given case. Anthropological scholarship tends to suggest that the relevant tests are not so much institutional as functional, i.e., how are tasks performed appropriately in their given context, not what institutional similarities with advanced systems can be discerned. The doubt which may reasonably be cast upon the anthropological base of the description of the need for secondary rules does not, however, deny the importance of the case being made in relation to the operation of modern municipal legal systems.

Within such legal systems the operation of secondary rules will, as Hart suggests, be much more complex than a simple categorisation of them might seem to suggest. It has already been suggested that rules of recognition act in a much more complex fashion than a simple single rule. Similar points may be made about other types of secondary rule.

Power-conferring 'rules of change' may operate at a variety of levels in government and other public administration, but may also be argued to operate in the 'private' sector. Making a will or entering into a contract alters the legal position of the parties concerned and may be seen as a creation of a form of local legal regime for them. Hart refers to the work of Hans Kelsen (see Chapter 3) in support of a quasi-legislative analysis of the creation of, for example, contractual relations (see *The Concept of Law*, p. 94), and this type of thought is more familiar in civilian jurisdictions than in the common law tradition. However, this extension of the idea of rules of change appears to go too far. Whilst the legal power to make a will or enter into a contract does allow one to create legal rights and duties and powers that did not exist prior to the exercise of the power, this does not amount to a power to add new laws to the system; not all legal powers are secondary powers to change the law, and to the extent Hart said otherwise, he was simply mistaken.

Rules of adjudication can also be seen to involve a large and complex body of procedural provision, but may extend into many much less formal areas of dispute resolution than litigation.

It is important to see how the rules of recognition, change, and adjudication interact and work together. In order to address the defects that exist in the state of nature, an authority to change the rules, to administer the rules, and to identify the rules is required. But these functions depend upon each other. It is no use for an authority to create new rules if these are not recognised, so the rule of change and the rule of recognition are intimately linked. Indeed, Raz has claimed that the essential function of the rule of recognition is to identify law-creating acts, i.e. acts of legislation (see Joseph Raz, 'Dworkin: A New Link in the Chain' (1986) 74 *California Law Review* 1103). This is not quite right. The rules of recognition may also recognise law-creating facts; custom is recognised as a source of law in many legal systems, but customs are not the product of individual acts, but of the fact that a social norm has been adhered to over time and accepted as binding by those involved. Similarly, whilst laying down rules and recognising them as rules of the system is a worthwhile endeavour in itself—for the rules can be used by subjects to guide their behaviour—rules also function as guides to the resolution of disputes, so rules of adjudication that empower authorities like courts to apply the rules and address cases where they have been breached are generally also found; in most systems, those who have the power and the duty to recognise the rules are also the ones with the power and duty to apply them, i.e. judges. Finally, the resolution of disputes is a contentious business, and the positive law so far recognised by the rule of recognition may not determine the dispute; in many legal systems, common law systems being the most obvious example, the rules of adjudication not only empower judges to determine disputes but to develop the law, making new rules to meet novel cases, and setting precedents for other courts to follow. So the rules of change and the rules of adjudication are clearly linked in some jurisdictions.

Although Hart refers to the secondary rules as remedies for the defects of stasis, inefficiency, and uncertainty that characterise the primitive society with only primary rules, the secondary rules *address* these defects; they do not *cure* them. There is a tension between a world of rules considered abstractly and the operation of rules in the real world. Considered abstractly, rules of change allow an authority to cure any defect in the rules because they become out of date. But does the institution of rules of change mean that there will actually be no problems of out of date rules in actual legal systems? Of course not. Think of the inefficiencies of legal development by judicial precedent, the difficulties in achieving statutory law reform, and so on. Consider also the problem of inefficiency and the rules of adjudication. Is it really possible that any system of rules could be perfectly efficiently administered given that it is humans who will have the powers to apply the rules? Are all criminals caught? Are there never any errors in the application of rules? Finally, consider the rule of recognition. How could it possibly cure, i.e. eradicate, uncertainty in the law? The rule of recognition tells judges that they must apply the rules found in statutes, cases, and so on, but not to apply the rules found in the Bible. But that does not mean there is no uncertainty about what the rules in statutes and cases are or how they should be applied. For all kinds of reasons, from vagueness in the language of statutory rules to the inability to foresee how a rule will work in all possible situations to which it may apply, there will be uncertainty in the law. The rule of recognition would have to work magic to cure those sorts of uncertainty. So it is a mistake to think that there is a flaw in the rule of recognition, or the idea of a rule of recognition, because rules of recognition do not guarantee that there will be a clear legal answer to resolve every legal dispute.

Besides Hart's emphasis on the internal aspect of legal obligation, the model of law as a system is perhaps Hart's most important contribution to legal theory and it undoubtedly deals far better than command theories with a number of issues. There are, however, a number of points which remain open to question. These primarily focus upon the crucial questions of validation, interpretation, and application which lie at the heart of a legal system.

5.4 The rule of recognition

The establishment of a critical reflective standard is an important aspect of the attachment of obligation to law, but it is not necessarily a uniquely legal phenomenon and Hart does not claim it to be so. In order to find a foundation for the legal rules which are to be understood internally it is evidently necessary to discover a criterion by reference to which those rules which are legal can be identified. In short, what is the way in which we distinguish legal rules from other social rules, such as the rules of games or the rules of etiquette? The problem is that identified by Hart as 'uncertainty' and the solution offered is the 'rule of recognition'.

Hart illustrates the operation of such a rule by reference to the very simple legal and political context of a hypothetical Rex dynasty. Rex I is presented as an autocratic monarch originally established in power more or less by force who, after suppression of early resistance, is in practice generally obeyed. Rex I is thus, in effect, a crowned gunman who has established power in a political society without any necessary connotation that obedience is right, although some of the aspects of early Rexite government might be considered in some basic sense legal. If, however, Rex I dies and, in Hart's example, is succeeded by his eldest son Rex II, who continues to be obeyed, a very simple rule of male primogeniture (succession by eldest son) would seem to have developed as a criterion of legislative authority. That is to say that Rex II has legislative capacity not, or not only, because he originally wielded effective force but because a rule confers a formal legislative authority upon him. In the simple system of the Rex dynasty this rule will then establish a critical reflective standard according to which the word of Rex II, and Rex III, will be law. It is noteworthy that, after the initial establishment in power of Rex I, this is not a system that relies upon a Benthamite *realpolitik* but upon a form of right to rule which Bentham and Austin were unable to account for. Note also, however, that this is not a moral but a formal, legal right to rule; whether Rex I, Rex II, or Rex III are in any way good rulers is not at this point relevant.

The rule of recognition established by the hypothetical Rex dynasty is as simple as can be imagined, involving nothing more than the proposition that the person who is the eldest child of the previous autocrat inherits legislative capacity. In reality, even in an autocratic monarchy or dictatorship, rules of recognition are, generally, considerably more complex than this. The model of such rules also solves the problem of constitutional law which proved so difficult to incorporate in Bentham and Austin's command theory. With the appreciation of legislative capacity as a feature of an authorised system comes the idea that the identifying rule can both define and limit, without any question of sovereignty as such arising. The rule of recognition is, in Hart's terms, clearly a 'secondary rule', but it is in very significant ways quite unlike any other such rules.

Legislative and other legal decision-making powers are validated by rules, and subordinate powers, such as that of a local authority to make by-laws, rest upon some statutory authorisation. However, the proposition that in the United Kingdom the Crown in Parliament possesses legislative authority represents the end of this line of reasoning. As Hart puts it

> ...we have reached a rule which, like the intermediate statutory order and statute, provides criteria for the assessment of the validity of other rules; but it is also unlike them in that there is no rule providing criteria for the assessment of its own legal validity.
>
> (*The Concept of Law*, p. 104)

The rule of recognition is thus an 'ultimate rule'. It is a criterion of validity which cannot itself be validated since validity is an internal statement made within a system, the functioning of which depends upon the supposition of the rule of recognition itself. The question is not one of validation but whether the particular rule is accepted by the courts or not.

The rule of recognition in Hart's model has an obvious and close relationship with the *Grundnorm* in Hans Kelsen's pure theory (see 3.4.3.3). The *Grundnorm* in Kelsen's theory is the foundation of a hierarchy of norms each of which is validated by a prior norm until, finally, the *Grundnorm* itself is reached. This is validated by no other norm and is essentially the root assumption of the existence of the legal system. In both

Hart's and Kelsen's theories the basic rule or norm may reasonably be taken as the point at which the legal theory plugs into political reality. As Hart also pointed out, the practical acceptance of a given rule of recognition as the ultimate criterion of validity for a legal system must involve consideration of a number of 'external' factors (*The Concept of Law*, pp. 147–54). Indeed, the fountain of internality cannot itself derive 'internally'. N. E. Simmonds remarks that

> The significance of [propositions about legal validity] can only be clarified by reference to [a] ... context ... involving the ascription of authority to certain sources of norms.... legal discourse is linked to law as a fact without itself being reducible to factual, descriptive discourse.
>
> (N. E. Simmonds, 'Practice and validity' [1979] *CLJ* 361 at p. 364)

Considering the case where judicial decision alters the rule of recognition, Hart said

> The truth may be that, when courts settle previously unenvisaged questions concerning the most fundamental constitutional rules, they *get* their authority to decide them after the questions have arisen and the decision has been given. Here all that succeeds is success. It is conceivable that the constitutional question at issue may divide society too fundamentally to permit of its judicial decision. The issues in South Africa concerning the entrenched clauses of the South Africa Act, 1909, at one time threatened to be too divisive for legal settlement. But where less vital social issues are concerned, a very surprising piece of judicial law-making concerning the very sources of law may be calmly 'swallowed'.
>
> (*The Concept of Law*, p. 153)

In a very general sense the 'rule of recognition' may be taken as the means whereby the divide between factual, descriptive and 'legal' discourse is bridged. One way of thinking about this is in terms of the 'current political settlement'. States do more than make law, of course, but law-making is one of their chief activities, and so one very important element of the political or constitutional settlement in any country is the power of institutions to make law. The rule of recognition recognising as it does the valid sources of law-making (Parliament, the courts, the EU, etc.) thus reflects the political settlement at any one time along this law-making dimension.

Once established, such an authorising rule may, of course, fail or be changed by various forms of political discontinuity, including such a minor change as the judicial manipulation by the courts of the rules of precedent, under which one court is bound to recognise the decisions of its own or other courts as binding upon it. This point may also reasonably be considered in the context of the seventeenth-century crisis in English, and United Kingdom, constitutional development.

The political, economic, and religious conflicts which fuelled the Civil War led to the overthrow and execution of Charles I and, after various political shifts, to the installation of Oliver Cromwell as Lord Protector in 1653. Cromwell may be taken, in very much more complex circumstances, as a rough equivalent of Rex I (he was in fact offered, but declined, the throne on several occasions). His son, Richard Cromwell followed him as Lord Protector but, unlike Rex II, proved unable to sustain the position in the face of political uncertainties and the ambitions of a variety of warlords and was overthrown in May 1659. In what is now a somewhat antique text, G. M. Trevelyan makes the telling point that

> Oliver [Cromwell]...had striven ever more earnestly, if not successfully, towards constitutional growth. But the generals...each [strove]...to realize by force his own personal ambition, or some visionary reign of Christ. In its last stage the military rule contained no power of evolution or principle of settlement.
>
> (G. M. Trevelyan, *England under the Stuarts* (1904), (London: Methuen, 1965), p. 314)

The 'rule' establishing the Puritan 'Commonwealth' thus failed and in 1660 the 'Restoration' of Charles II took place upon the initiative of General Monk with the agreement of a 'free Parliament'. The situation restored was, however, hardly that once claimed by Charles I and was in a number of respects clearly 'upon terms', despite the Royalist pretence that no legally significant interregnum had occurred between 1649 and 1660.

The constitutionally decisive move occurred with the Glorious Revolution of 1688. At that time James II was overthrown and a body claiming 'Parliamentary' status and comprising peers and MPs, although they had not been duly summoned to sit in Parliamentary session, invited James's daughter Mary and her husband William, Prince of Orange, jointly to assume the throne as William III and Mary II. This invitation was expressly upon limiting terms recited in the 1688 Declaration of Right and the 1689 Bill of Rights, and in a number of respects these measures represented the decisive shift of power from monarch to Parliament and the foundation of the subsequent model of the Crown in Parliament. In these events there may be discerned a complex shifting of 'rules' conferring legislative authority in a manner quite consistent with Hart's analysis.

5.5 Legal systems and the importance of officials

The standpoint of officials of the legal system is of crucial importance in Hart's model of a legal system. The point is made plainly in his statement that

> There are...two minimum conditions necessary and sufficient for the existence of a legal system.... rules of behaviour which are valid according to...criteria of validity must be generally obeyed, and...its rules of recognition...and its rules of change and adjudication must be effectively accepted as common public standards of official behaviour by its officials.
>
> (*The Concept of Law*, p. 113)

As Hart then adds, this is

> ...a Janus-faced statement looking both towards obedience by ordinary citizens and to the acceptance by officials of secondary rules as critical common standards of official behaviour.
>
> (*The Concept of Law*, p. 113)

He thus contends essentially that whereas 'primary rules' are addressed to all citizens, including officials in their personal capacities, 'secondary rules' are primarily contrived for official rather than 'private' consumption. The basis for this argument is partly that the necessity for a detailed understanding of the system and its criteria of validity is largely confined to those who in practice operate it, which is to say officials. It would perhaps be more accurate to refer to those who are 'officially' engaged within the legal system, including judges and the practising legal profession, as well as those who are 'officials' in the narrower context of current linguistic usage. In any event the 'Janus-faced' analysis of the 'official' and 'general' understanding of rules poses important issues.

It may first be said that as a matter of fact it is clearly the case that lawyers in particular, but also a variety of other 'officials', will have a more detailed and technical familiarity with what Hart terms 'secondary rules' than will most people. This is to say no more than that, in medical equivalence, a doctor would be expected to have a more technical view of the patient's condition than the patient, which is not to say that the latter will not be aware of being ill. Hart's proposition is, admittedly, not that the general public are actually unaware of secondary rules; it is merely that their need for detailed awareness is not the same as that of officials. Another way of putting this is in terms of the dependency of lay subjects' acceptance of the law upon the acceptance of officials. The special importance of officials accepting the secondary rules of the legal system is that if they do not, it is not clear how the citizens could; if the officials are not playing the game, then it is not clear that any game is being played at all, thus there is nothing for the citizens to accept. Even accepting this point, it might still seem that general public awareness plays a more vital role in the operation of law than Hart concedes.

The overwhelming proportion of daily legal activity proceeds without any need for official intervention. The average person will undertake a number of legal transactions on most days, for example, entering into contracts for the purchase of goods or services. Statistically, the likelihood of any of these being considered by a court is so vanishingly small as to be discountable, but there will, nonetheless, be a consciousness to some extent that a potentially justiciable obligation is being created. By the same token a failure by someone to do a promised favour might be rude and might occasion resentment, but it would hardly raise thoughts of litigation. Such practical judgements require all participants in the legal system, not just specialist officials, to have some critical consciousness of its criteria and application, even if the latter do have a more detailed knowledge. Brendan Edgeworth remarks that

> One is presented... with the professional's world-view as the yardstick of reality. But all levels of society produce, apply and interpret 'the law', and its social existence cannot be identified in totality without examining the entire range of hermeneutical forms associated with it.
>
> (B. Edgeworth, 'Legal positivism and the philosophy of language: a critique of H. L. A. Hart's "descriptive sociology"' (1986) 6 *LS* 115 at p. 138)

H. L. A. Hart's pre-eminent contribution to legal theory is the understanding of law as a facilitative system of rules, and the obligation with which he is concerned is that which is recognisable according to the formal criteria adopted within the system. In cases of doubt or dispute the question can only effectively be determined by a court and in this context the formal cognition of judges and officials is decisive. The argument, in short, properly addresses not understanding as such, but authoritative understanding. Viewed in this light the official emphasis is comprehensible, but any implication that general public understanding, at some level, is somehow an optional extra, discounts a major practical aspect of law in operation.

This raises a final issue regarding what officials and lay subjects of the law 'accept'. Hart suggests that what is required for a viable legal system is that officials accept the secondary rules, in particular the rule of recognition, and that the lay subjects accept the primary rules. But this may seem rather artificial. Grant Lamond (in a yet unpublished paper, 'The Rule of Recognition as Customary Law') has recently proposed that what officials accept is not the rule of recognition, but rather *the legal system itself*. What does is mean to say one 'accepts the legal system'? The idea would be that the rule officials accept is a rule requiring them to apply all the rules of the legal system, including of course the rules that authorise its legislatures, courts, and enforcement agencies, irrespective of what the system's rule of recognition is or has been. Call this rule the 'rule of law'. The rule of recognition is clearly related to the rule of law, because the laws the rule of law requires officials to apply derive from the sources identified by past and current rules of recognition.

Now, you may ask—what is the difference between accepting such a 'rule of law' and accepting a 'rule of recognition', since in practice they would amount to the same thing. At any one time, the rules that one must apply by accepting the rule of law are the identical set of laws that one must apply if one accepts the rule of recognition, since the rule of recognition determines what that set of laws is. But thinking this way would be a mistake. Compare: to love human beings might entail that I love featherless bipeds, since the set of human beings is identical with the set of featherless bipeds. But this does not mean that to love human beings is to love them *because* they are featherless bipeds. The same lesson applies here. When we talk about someone's acceptance of something and want to know what he accepts and *why* he accepts it, how he conceives of what he accepts (the 'description under which' he accepts it), is vital to grasp. And different reasons apply to accepting the body of laws that make up a legal system from those that apply to accepting a rule of recognition, that is, accepting the sources of law from which that body of laws springs.

In the first place, notice that legal systems have continuity even though the rule of recognition (i.e. the valid sources of law) undergoes changes. Laws typically remain valid even though their source has been abolished. Ancient statutes may be valid, Privy Council decisions on appeals from Australia are still valid in Australia although the Privy Council is no longer a source of law in Australia, and so on. Legal systems, i.e. all the valid standards of law in the system, maintain their identity even though the valid sources change. This point really is nothing more than an application of the view that the identity of a legal system can be construed dynamically, not merely momentarily, and that acceptance of a legal system as a dynamic entity whose individual laws are ever-changing is the mode of acceptance which makes sense. No one accepts only a momentary legal system, re-adjusting their acceptance from moment to moment, day to day.

How do the reasons for accepting a legal system differ from those given for accepting the sources of laws? We might accept Parliament as a source of laws because the law-making institution of a representative democracy is a legitimate source of legislation. Or a staunch republican might deprecate Parliamentary legislation because of the involvement of the Queen and the House of Lords. Or we might say that appellate courts are an acceptable source of law because senior judges have an expertise in solving co-ordination problems the solutions to which must be sensitive to moral considerations. All of these reasons may be false, but they are the sort of reasons people would give and do give in explaining their acceptance of the sources of law. Regarding the actual rules of the system that have been produced over time by its sources, different considerations apply. However impeccable the sources, if the standards of the system are incoherent or significantly unjust or ineffective, that is a reason for not accepting the legal system, and contrariwise, their coherence, justice, and effectiveness are reasons for accepting the legal system despite its having been created by less than impeccable sources.

Furthermore, there is what might be called a 'faute de mieux' issue here. In the case of accepting a legal system, the acceptance turns largely on there being no presently available better alternative. No one thinks that the regime of Saddam Hussein deserved high marks as a source of law, but that did not mean that there was not official and citizen acceptance of the legal system itself, in particular all the mundane standards of the legal system, traffic rules, contract, tort and property law, and so on. Presumably this acceptance was not a happy one, and one assumes that the acceptance there owed largely to the fact that there was no acceptable alternative immediately available. Perhaps people were mistaken in bestowing their acceptance; perhaps lawlessness is better than a very degraded lawfulness. The point is that this reason for acceptance, which is surely very common over the history of legal systems, has nothing to do with reasons concerning the merit or demerit of the sources that produced the standards.

So it makes sense to say that one accepts a legal system, including of course its secondary rules, without accepting the legal system *because* of its secondary rules, and one can accept a legal system, again including its secondary rules, even if one believes the secondary rules are seriously defective.

If all of this is right, the obligation that citizens accept is that of complying with the body of laws, i.e. the standards which are applied and enforced by the institutions identified through their practice as the 'legitimate' legal authorities. For officials, the acceptance is likely to be richer, for although there may be exceptions, most officials *consent* to being officials, whereas most lay subjects do not fall under the sway of their legal jurisdictions by consent. So for officials, their acceptance of rule of law is also to accept that serving as an official of the system is, to put it very colloquially, an OK thing to do.

5.6 Public international law in Hart's theory

Over many years theorists and international lawyers have debated the status of international law, which centres upon the theorist's doubt that public international law has, or has had, sufficient institutions, such as courts, legislatures, and so on, realistically to be considered 'law'. Hart framed this doubt by saying

> The absence of these institutions means that the rules for States resemble that simple form of social structure, consisting only of primary rules of obligation, which...we are accustomed to contrast with a developed legal system.
>
> (*The Concept of Law*, p. 209)

This refers back to an anthropological argument which has been suggested above to be doubtful (see 5.3), but it also refers to a conventional, if again doubtful, comparison between public international and 'primitive' law. This is not, however, the basic thrust of Hart's argument. His concern is rather with the 'binding' or obligatory effect of public international law. Hart argues that whilst the command theory fits international law no better than municipal law, the contention that public international law is no more than a form of moral claim does not fit either the usage or discourse of international law. In the end, however, he is constrained to deny that the public international legal system possesses any true rule of recognition which provides general criteria of validity for its rules. He finally notes the argument that some multilateral treaties may bind States which are not expressly party to them and, thus, have a form of 'legislative' effect. This, Hart concedes, may be an element of a nascent rule of recognition. He suggests, therefore, that

> ... international law is at present in a stage of transition towards acceptance of this and other forms which would bring it nearer in structure to a municipal system.
>
> (*The Concept of Law*, p. 231)

He adds that although at present the analogy between public international and municipal law may be one of content rather than form

> ... no other social rules are so close to municipal law as those of international law.
>
> (*The Concept of Law*, p. 231)

This is an ambivalent position to take and it would appear that public international law fits a little awkwardly into Hart's analysis of legal systems. Quite clearly the standard statement of the sources of public international law, for the purposes of the International Court of Justice, in art. 38 of the Statute of the Court, is not a rule of recognition for Hart's purposes, although the language used implies an assumption of the existence of some such rule. The later form of Kelsenian pure theory (see 3.4.4) takes a reverse position to that of Hart and accepts international law as the foundation for the existence of municipal law systems. It is not necessary to go to quite such lengths, however, to wonder whether Hart's doubts about the status of public international law create a difficulty for his theory which might easily be avoided.

The problem appears essentially to be one of institutional comparison, in much the same form as that which arises in the context of Hart's legal anthropology. Quite obviously the formal structure and context of application of the norms of public international law are significantly different from those of municipal law. If, however, a functional analysis is adopted, examining not institutional similarities or divergences, but the purpose and operation of norms in the municipal and international norms in their respective contexts, a much stronger case may be made out for the 'legal' nature of the latter. This, perhaps, tips the balance of argument in that it may be contended that public international law is not in a state of transition to something more like a municipal legal system as Hart suggests (*The Concept of Law*, p. 231) but, rather, performs the same function differently but appropriately in the context of a different type of community, that of nations.

5.7 The significance of Hart's theory

Hart was the most important legal philosopher of the twentieth century. It is difficult to understate the influence of *The Concept of Law* on the jurisprudential debate, and even more difficult to identify each of the novel insights and arguments which fill the book from start to finish. It is possible, however, to isolate a central theme, and that is a picture of law in which the law can be understood to make a 'positive', facilitative contribution to our lives, rather that the largely 'negative' picture of law peddled by positivists like Bentham, Austin, and Kelsen, a law defined in terms of coercion and sanction. Two features of Hart's philosophy of law stand out in this regard.

The first is the way Hart made it clear that the attitude of the participants of the law was essential for understanding the nature of the law, in a way that no future theorist can ignore. Hart was the first theorist who fully accepted, and integrated into his work, the hermeneutic point that what a social institution like the law is, depends (in part) upon what the participants *think* it is. If the subjects of the law did not distinguish between being obliged and being under an obligation, or if they thought of the law as nothing more than coercion, then the law would simply not be the social institution it is, any more than chess would be a game if the participants thought the point was to arrange these oddly shaped pieces into interesting patterns on a chequerboard.

The second lies in Hart's recognition of the secondary rules, rules which so many theorists have either missed, misdescribed, or avoided. One can only speculate about the cause of this, but one reason is surely that Hart was just a very clever philosopher, who was able to frame questions meticulously, and assess candidate answers with a discernment that his predecessors lacked. At all events, until the role of secondary rules is recognised, the myriad ways in which the law can be used as a technique for allowing people to achieve goals they could not otherwise—which allow them to create things like traffic codes and rules of commerce and deal with crime fairly, systematically, and justly rather than with revenge, feud, or vendetta— until these functions of the law are recognised, then our picture of it is both wrong and unnecessarily bleak.

Besides changing analytical philosophy of law forever, there is no doubt that this positive image of the law also contributed to the modern revival of natural law theory through the work of its most important living proponent, John Finnis (see 2.6). Finnis explicitly builds on the work of Hart by insisting that the law is even more beneficial than Hart let on; it is not simply *a* means of achieving social goals, but should be understood to be *the* central social manifestation of the moral enterprise of creating the conditions for human flourishing. In this way, the revival of natural law theorising, in which Hart was only tangentially interested, owes its greatest debt to Hart's work.

FURTHER READING

Dworkin, R. M., *Taking Rights Seriously* (London: Duckworth, 1977), chs 2 and 3.

Green, L., 'General Jurisprudence: A 25th Anniversary Essay' (2005) 25 *Oxford Journal of Legal Studies* 565.

Hart, H. L. A., *The Concept of Law* (Oxford: Clarendon Press, 1961).

Kramer, M., 'The Rule of Misrecognition in the Hart of Jurisprudence' (1988) 8 *Oxford Journal of Legal Studies* 401.

Lacey, N., *A Life of HLA Hart: The Nightmare and the Noble Dream* (Oxford: Oxford University Press, 2004).

MacCormick, N., *H. L. A. Hart* (London: Edward Arnold, 1981).

MacCormick, N., *Rhetoric and the Rule of Law: A Theory of Legal Reasoning* (Oxford: Oxford University Press, 2005).

Penner, J., Schiff, D., and Nobles, R. (eds), *Jurisprudence and Legal Theory: Commentary and Materials* (Oxford: Oxford University Press, 2002), ch. 4.

Simpson, A., *Legal Theory and Legal History* (London: Hambledon, 1987), 359–82.

6

Post-Hart Analytical Philosophy of Law:
Dworkin and Raz

Introduction

Ronald Dworkin succeeded H. L. A. Hart to the chair of jurisprudence at Oxford University. His theories are largely built on criticisms of Hart, in particular what he perceived as the 'positivist' elements of Hart's theory of law. By contrast, Joe Raz is undoubtedly Hart's most important intellectual heir. Not only has Raz developed many of Hart's ideas, in particular Hart's recognition of the authoritative character of law, but he has also devoted much writing to defending Hart's insights, particularly from Dworkin's onslaughts. It is therefore appropriate that their work is looked at together, for it is very much intertwined.

6.1 An overview of Dworkin's philosophy of law

Ronald Dworkin's theory of law can be regarded as an extended development of, if not a new form of, natural law theory, an explicitly 'moral' theory of law, a theory which is explicitly framed as an opponent to positivism, and in particular the positivism of Hart.

Dworkin's first attack on Hart, launched in the 1960s, can be called his 'rules and principles' critique of Hart's positivism. Here, Dworkin argued that Hart's positivism failed because the rule of recognition could only identify legal rules, but failed to identify what Dworkin called legal 'principles', which had a significant place in judges' reasoning.

In the 1970s Dworkin produced his first really general theory of the law and judicial reasoning, in particular in his famous paper, 'Hard Cases' (R. M. Dworkin, 'Hard Cases' (1975) 88 *Harvard LR* 1057). In this paper, Dworkin set out the claims that have characterised his work ever since: that judges do not have any significant discretion in deciding cases where the law is uncertain, that there is always a right legal answer to a legal question, and that judges are theorists in the sense that they must decide cases in the spirit of philosophers working to develop a fully comprehensive theory of political morality. This last claim is personified in the figure of 'Hercules', a judge with unlimited intelligence, knowledge, and time to think, whose methods of decision-making serve, for Dworkin, as an idealised model of what judges actually do when they decide 'hard cases', that is cases where the law is unsettled.

The last substantive stage in the development of his theory came in 1986 when Dworkin published *Law's Empire* (R. M. Dworkin, *Law's Empire* (London: Fontana)). In this book, Dworkin tweaked the character of his theory by changing Hercules from a moral-political philosopher into a kind of literary or artistic critic; now, a judge was to decide hard cases not so much by developing and applying a philosophical theory of justice but was to decide so as to frame the law in its best light, to make of the law the best it could be. Perhaps more importantly, in this stage of his work Dworkin made explicit two of his most controversial claims: (1) he claimed that the work of lawyers and judges, that is the legal work of preparing legal arguments and deciding cases, is a kind of less abstract jurisprudence, and that jurisprudence is a kind of legal reasoning, but at a more abstract level; in short, legal reasoning is continuous with jurisprudence; (2) he claimed that there was no such thing as a purely descriptive philosophy of law, of the kind Hart purported to pursue; every legal theory necessarily depended, whether explicitly or implicitly, on judgements about what the law or a legal system ought to be.

In more recent years, Dworkin has appeared to move away from the 'literary' or aesthetic reading of Hercules and the job of jurisprudence, and the more straightforward images of jurisprudence as a branch of moral and political philosophy have re-emerged, and so we will mostly look at his theory in that guise.

6.2 An overview of Raz's philosophy of law

Owing to his work on the nature of authority it is possible to claim that Joseph Raz is one of the most important political philosophers of the late twentieth and early twenty-first centuries. In fact, while Raz began his philosophical work very much in the tradition of Hart's philosophy of law, much of his work is only tangentially related to the law, falling squarely in the realm of political philosophy.

Two aspects of Raz's work are of greatest importance to his philosophy of law: his theory of practical reason and norms, and his related analysis of authority.

Taking practical reason and norms first, Raz was concerned to show the way in which norms like rules and rights operate in our practical reasoning. We reason practically when we reason about what to do. Normally, we choose to act by looking at the various reasons there are for acting one way rather than another, and choose based on the balance of reasons. Raz famously explained that rules enter into our practical reasoning as *exclusionary* reasons. When there is a rule, such as the rule we must stop if the light is red, the rule requires us to act in a certain way, excluding our deciding to act on the balance of reasons (on our own judgement about whether to proceed on the basis of whether the junction is busy, what other cars or pedestrians are doing, and so on). By explaining norms such as rules and rights in this way, Raz developed Hart's project of showing how the law can serve as a technique for solving social problems and achieving goals we could not achieve otherwise; in short, Raz explained the law as a device or technique of collective or communal practical reason.

As to authority, it is difficult to overstate Raz's contribution in this area, for Raz seems to have found a solution to the central problem of authority that had for centuries eluded the grasp of political philosophers, which is the question whether it is ever rational to comply with an authority. We will look at this in some detail below, but obviously to the extent that the law is authoritative, a claim central to Hart's theory of law, then the legitimacy of the law turns on whether an authority can be legitimate, and part of that legitimacy turns on whether it is rational to obey an authority.

6.3 Dworkin and Raz on rules and principles

6.3.1 Can the rule of recognition account for principles? Dworkin's challenge

> I want to make a general attack on positivism, and I shall use H. L. A. Hart's version as a target.... My strategy will be organised around the fact that when lawyers reason or dispute about legal rights and obligations, particularly in those hard cases when our problems with these concepts seem most acute, they make use of standards that do not function as rules, but operate differently as principles, policies, and other sorts of standards. Positivism, I shall argue, is a model of and for a system of rules, and its central notion of a single fundamental test for law forces us to miss the important roles of these standards that are not rules.
>
> (R. M. Dworkin, *Taking Rights Seriously* (London: Duckworth, 1977), p. 22)

One aspect of Hart's theory examined in the course of Chapter 5 was his analysis of the judicial function (see H. L. A. Hart, *The Concept of Law* (Oxford: Clarendon Press, 1961), ch. 7), although it is also implicit in his basic notion of law, being a type of social rule. Hart states that in the majority of cases the rules will be clear. However, they will, at some point, become indeterminate and unclear, because they have what Hart calls an 'open texture', a defect inherent in any use of language.

We can take the simple example of a local by-law that prohibits 'vehicles' from entering public parks. In the absence of a list of vehicles, which, even if provided, would be incomplete, it would be unclear whether the by-law prohibited motorised wheelchairs, roller-skates, or skateboards. At this margin of uncertainty Hart states that judges or officials must use their discretion in deciding whether a particular case comes within the rule or not. In exercising this discretion, the judge or official will look to the purposes or the social consequences of adopting a certain interpretation of the rule, for example, the competing policy arguments that, on the one hand, the park is a place of peace and quiet, which would necessitate a wide interpretation of the by-law to include the controversial cases within the prohibition (with the exception of wheelchairs), and on the other hand, the contention that the park is a place of recreation and enjoyment, which would lead to the by-law being interpreted restrictively so as to allow roller-skates and skateboards.

Dworkin argues against this approach, which allows for the judge or official to make a policy decision not based on law in hard or unclear cases. According to Dworkin, in a hard or unclear case the judge does not revert to policy and act as a law-maker; rather, he applies legal principles to produce an answer based on law. If true, this severely undermines Hart's theory. By seeing law solely as a system of rules, Hart fails to take account of an important part of law, its general principles. In particular, the rule of recognition can only identify rules, but it cannot identify these principles.

Dworkin gives us an example of a legal principle in the case of *Riggs* v *Palmer* (1889) 22 NE 188, in which a New York court had to decide whether a murderer could inherit under the will of the grandfather he had murdered. The court held that the relevant statutes literally gave the property of the deceased to the murderer. But then the court reasoned (at p. 190)

> ...all laws as well as all contracts may be controlled in their operation and effect by general, fundamental maxims of the common law. No one shall be permitted to profit by his own fraud, or to take advantage of his own wrong, or to found any claim upon his own iniquity, or to acquire property by his own crime.

So denying the murderer his inheritance.

Standards such as 'no man may profit from his own wrong' have, according to Dworkin, relative weight when considered judicially, and so help to determine the case in favour of one of the parties when the rules have run out. He is suggesting that, in unclear cases, the judges do not have complete discretion to make new law; instead they fall back on legal principles to make a decision based on existing law (meaning rules and principles). It is worth noting, however, that in *Riggs* v *Palmer* the rules were clear: the murderer should have inherited, and the legal principle in fact overruled the rule. It may be inferred that Dworkin is giving legal principles another role. As well as acting as the cement of the law, filling in its gaps and loopholes, they are also used to prevent injustices which would arise out of a simple application of the rules. Hart himself says that rather than relying on the judges using policy to deal with unclear cases, most 'mature' legal systems lean towards certainty and predictability by stretching the rules to deal with unclear cases. However, Hart admits that the more rules are stretched the more their application becomes artificial, leading to cases of injustice (*The Concept of Law*, pp. 126–7). If the legal system is seen as being comprised of both rules and overarching principles, then it is possible to avoid such injustices.

However, if Dworkin's controversial choice of examples to illustrate the basic components of his theory is ignored, it will be seen that the main thrust of his argument is that rules, whether precedents or statutes, are applicable in 'an all or nothing fashion' and so there may be cases, particularly hard ones, which are not covered by rules, or if there are rules they are unclear. In a common law system it is quite possible for each party to a case to be able to marshal an equally impressive set of precedents in their favour. Positivists like Hart state that when there are such hard cases in the law, judges either have the power to make new law or, as is more likely, they stretch one line of precedents to cover the case in preference to the other line of argument. Given that they have a choice, it could be argued that the reason for choosing one line of precedents over another is based not on law but on non-legal factors such as considerations of what the judges think is best for society. In this sense they act as a sort of deputy law-maker. Dworkin states that such a role belongs to the legislature, not to the judges, not least because judges have not been democratically elected for such a job.

Dworkin is arguing that in all cases, including in hard cases, judges are always constrained by the law. He paints a picture of a gapless legal universe where in every adjudication there are legal rules and standards which the judge is obliged to follow, although he does have discretion in the weak sense of weighing the standards set him by authority. What Dworkin denies is that judges have discretion in the strong sense to decide cases without being bound by precedent or statute.

6.3.2 Does Dworkin accurately describe the role of principles in law? Raz's reply

6.3.2.1 Raz on norms

The picture of practical reasoning which Raz constructs aims to show how norms, i.e. standards for behaviour, such as rules, rationally contribute to practical reasoning, deciding what to do. The law as a whole is, on these terms, an institution of communal practical reason, for the rules of law, its procedures, and its decisions in cases all aim to guide people to do certain things rather than others.

The central idea in Raz's picture of the way that norms contribute to practical reason is that of the 'exclusionary' reason. In the normal case when we reason what to do, say, deciding what to have for dinner, we act rationally if we decide on the balance of reasons. Framing this choice will be all sorts of norms. We should not, for example, choose to eat the neighbours. The norms that set standards on our behaviour, and thus limiting our (legitimate) choices are 'exclusionary' reasons. These reasons are 'exclusionary' in the sense that they exclude our acting on any weighing up of the balance of reasons we might undertake with regard to that possible choice. So, the moral norm that we are not to kill and eat the neighbours is understood to deny us the right to decide for ourselves whether to eat them by weighing up the various factors that would apply to the case (Are the neighbours annoying? Might they be tasty? Would it be wrong to kill them?).

The use of exclusionary reasons as a technique or device of practical reason is employed in countless contexts, in committee decisions, judicial decisions, Parliamentary legislation, and so on. Exclusionary reasons provide a means to allocate the *deliberative* and *executive* phases of practical reason to different occasions or different people or both. The 'deliberative' phase of practical reason occurs when a decision-maker considers and weighs the reasons that bear on the issue; this deliberative phase obviously comes to an end when a decision is made as to what to do. The 'executive' phase is acting on the basis of that decision.

Consider, as an example, the procedures of a body like a student law society, deciding how much to subsidise tickets to its summer ball. In the deliberative phase various issues will be considered, such as how much money the society has, what other projects the money could be spent on, how much a subsidised ticket price will attract students, and so on. A proposal is then put, and the society decides on a subsidy, perhaps by majority vote. This decision ends the deliberative phase of the practical reasoning process. Now we pass to the executive phase: the various officers of the society organising the ball must now treat the issue of the subsidy as decided, and implement the society's decision. They must treat the society's decision as an *exclusionary* reason governing their behaviour; they must not reconsider all the factors that went into the decision and then act on what they themselves would decide. If they did that, the society's decision would have been pointless, for it would not, practically speaking, have decided anything.

Exclusionary reasons work in the same way in respect of judicial decisions. Lawyers for the parties are entitled to make representations to the judge, but once the judge decides, the deliberative phase is over, and the parties must then act on what the judge orders, taking his decision as an exclusionary reason. If the parties were free to act on what they thought was the right result in law, it would defeat the whole purpose of bringing the dispute to court. Similarly, when Parliament passes a law following debate, the law must henceforward be taken as an exclusionary reason for action by the subjects of the law.

This analysis of practical reasons and norms develops Hart's positive project of showing how the law operates as an institution of communal practical reason. The separation of the deliberative and executive phases of practical reason and the issuing of exclusionary reasons provides for the coordination of behaviour by different people who share general goals and values but where it is unlikely that this coordination can be achieved by people acting on their own assessment of all the relevant facts.

6.3.2.2 The use of rules and principles as a matter of legal policy

Applying his theory of practical reason and norms, Raz outlines the following distinction between rules and principles: rules are more or less specific standards which are highly exclusionary, whereas principles are more or less abstract and broad standards which, rather than excluding a decision-maker's use of his own judgement, positively invite it, though at the same time setting some exclusionary limits on it.

Raz points out that positivists have never denied the existence of legal principles. Whether the law relies upon principles or rules to order an area of doctrine is a matter of legal policy. For example, in many common law jurisdictions sentencing of criminal offenders was largely guided by principles of sentencing, though through rules the law placed upper (and sometimes lower) bounds on the sentence that could be pronounced. Similarly, bills of rights typically rely on broad statements of rights, guaranteeing the right to freedom of speech, for example. In other areas of the law, such as tax law, the law is very much made up of rules, sometimes very intricate rules. In short, rules and principles are the results of different normative techniques.

This characterisation of principles turns Dworkin's claim that the existence of legal principles shows that judges have no discretion on its head. According to this view, the existence of legal principles, far from showing that judges have no true discretion, are the best evidence that judges do have discretion. Where the principles are ones which guide judges when they decide a case where the rules conflict, or the rules would operate unjustly, the principles reflect judges' powers (if the system is one in which precedents must be followed) to make new law.

6.4 Dworkin's theory of law: the rights thesis, the right answer thesis, and law as integrity

6.4.1 The rights thesis

Dworkin's theory of the judicial process is based on the distinction between rights (principles) and policies (goals).

> Arguments of policy justify a...decision by showing that the decision advances or protects some collective goal of the community as a whole. The argument in favour of a subsidy for aircraft manufacturers, that the subsidy will protect national defence, is an argument of policy. Arguments of principle justify a...decision by showing that the decision respects or secures some individual or group right. The argument in favour of anti-discrimination statutes, that a minority has a right to equal respect and concern, is an argument of principle.
>
> (*Taking Rights Seriously*, p. 82)

6.4.1.1 Objections to judicial decision-making on policy grounds

Dworkin's main contention is that judges do not have the discretion to decide unclear cases by reference to policy, and that in fact they decide them on the basis of principles. He raises two objections to those who would argue for judicial decision-making on policy grounds. First, judges are not elected to make policy decisions. Secondly, judges would be applying retroactive law if they made their decisions on policy grounds, whereas a principled decision means that the judge is upholding rights and duties that already exist (*Taking Rights Seriously*, p. 84; *A Matter of Principle*, pp. 18–23).

It is difficult to know quite what to make of the first argument, in particular in a legal system like that of the United Kingdom, where even following the passage of the Human Rights Act 1998 judges are regarded as having fairly limited ability to develop the law. Positivists, in general, simply do not share Dworkin's concerns about the democratic legitimacy of judges developing the law where the law is unsettled or the application of the rules would work significant injustice. The positivist would say that where, as in most common law countries at least, judges have the power to make law in this gap-filling, interstitial way, everyone both recognises that judges have this power and accepts it as an ineradicable part of the system, since it would be inconvenient, to say the least, to have to send all cases of unsettled law back to the legislature for 'democratic' resolution. Disallowing judges from resolving disputes where the law was not perfectly clear would also undoubtedly cause a great deal of injustice, on the principle that justice delayed is justice denied.

The concern for democratic legitimacy is obviously more compelling in the United States in view of the power the Constitution gives to the Supreme Court to determine the contours of the law touching very controversial moral and political issues, such as the right to abortion, on the basis that such matters are matters of constitutionally guaranteed rights. Indeed, the debate over appointments to the Supreme Court typically takes the form of an evaluation of the relative merits of 'conservative' and 'liberal' judges, and one might well be concerned that this reflects an entrenched belief that, contrary to Dworkin's claims, the Supreme Court often acts as a legislature.

Dworkin's second argument goes to the issue of the unfairness of retroactive law. It is based on the concept accepted in most legal systems that law is meant as a guide to human behaviour. If judges, on occasion simply made the law instead of applying settled law, they would be failing to allow people to act in accordance with already established rules. Individuals would be unable to plan their affairs to keep within the bounds of what is legally acceptable if there was a possibility that a judge might decide to extend a law or a line of precedents to cover marginal cases. This appears a powerful argument although, if judges were making new law in only a small number of cases, it could be argued that their decisions would not significantly undermine the ideal of certainty in the law. Furthermore, if judges occasionally decide to extend the law in marginal or hard cases, they are simply bringing certain activities clearly within the law when before they were seen as being within the margins of what was legally acceptable. It could be argued that if individuals use law as a guide, they should order their affairs so that they are operating not at the margins of legality but clearly within the parameters set by the law. Finally, in many of the hard cases that Dworkin is concentrating on, a litigant is hardly likely to know that the weight of rules and principles will be in his or her favour until the judgment is actually given. Thus even with a principled decision, that is, a decision entirely based on a judge's reasoning from existing law, taking no policy factors into account, the litigant seems to be no better off than if subjected to a retroactive, policy-based decision. Either way, the litigant's rights or duties are not known until judgment.

6.4.1.2 Entrenched rights

Dworkin describes policies as collective goals which encourage trade-offs of benefits and burdens within a community in order to produce some overall benefit for the community as a whole, for example, the drive for economic efficiency. Principles and individuated rights, such as the very general right to equal concern and respect, the right to freedom of speech, or the right to recover damages for emotional loss in negligence claims, may be sacrificed to the collective welfare by the legislature but not by the judiciary (*Taking Rights Seriously*, pp. 90–6).

If this was the extent of his theory, it would seem to be very limited, and certainly could not be described as a theory going beyond the judicial process, because it would not protect rights against legislative interference. His argument that the judiciary acts as the protector of individual's rights would be hollow if the government of the day could simply take those rights away by a policy decision embodied in legislation. However, Dworkin's theory has a wider political import and as part of this he argues that rights cannot simply be overridden by governments using simple utilitarian calculations of what is best for the community or on what he calls 'consequentialist' grounds.

> But those Constitutional rights that we call fundamental like the right of free speech, are supposed to represent rights against the Government in the strong sense....If citizens have a...right of free speech, then governments would do wrong to repeal the First Amendment [of the American Constitution] that guarantees it, even if they were persuaded that the majority would be better off if speech were curtailed.
>
> I must not overstate the point. Someone who claims that the citizens have a right against the Government need not go so far as to say that the State is never justified in overriding that right. He might say, for example, that although citizens have a right to free speech, the Government may override that right when necessary to protect the rights of others, or to prevent a catastrophe, or even to obtain a clear and major public benefit (though if he acknowledged this last as a possible justification he would be treating the right in question as not among the most important or fundamental). What he cannot do is to say that the Government is justified in overriding a right on the minimal grounds that would be sufficient if no such right existed. He cannot say that the Government is entitled to act on no more than a judgment that its act is likely to produce, overall, a benefit to the community. That admission would make his claim of a right pointless, and would show him to be using some sense of 'right' other than the strong sense necessary to give his claim the political importance it is normally taken to have (*Taking Rights Seriously*, pp. 191–2).

Dworkin's theory involves more than simply judicial protection of established rights, but also has the wider dimension of entrenching certain rights, whether they be against the government, such as the right to free speech, or between individuals, such as the right to recover damages for negligence. His theory is designed to give special place to rights as 'trumps' over general utilitarian justifications throughout the legal process, not merely in hard cases. He deals with hard cases by saying that they can only be decided on the basis of existing rights not policies, for the simple fact that to allow policy-making by the judiciary in these marginal cases would undermine his thesis that judges are the protectors of rights.

Rights, whether they be derived from legal rules, or from more general legal principles, protect individuals from political decisions, even if those decisions would improve collective goals. The more concrete or institutional a right is, the more dramatic the general collective justification will have to be if it is to be defeated, whereas a more abstract right might be defeated by a more marginal collective justification.

It follows that in order to make this theory applicable to legal systems, it is necessary not only to be able to identify what rights an individual has against the government and against other individuals, but also to be able to identify the degree to which each right is entrenched within a given legal system. The more entrenched or institutionalised a right is, the less a government is able to enact legislation which undermines that right. Dworkin provides a general distinction between abstract or background rights and institutional or concrete rights.

> Any adequate theory will distinguish…between background rights, which are rights that provide a justification for political decisions by society in the abstract, and institutional rights, that provide a justification for a decision by some particular and specified political institution.
>
> (*Taking Rights Seriously*, p. 93)

An abstract right is a

> …general political aim the statement of which does not indicate how that general aim is to be weighed or compromised in particular circumstances against other political aims.
>
> (*Taking Rights Seriously*, p. 93)

For example, the British right to free speech was not, prior to 1998, a concrete right contained in any constitutional provision and it was overridden on collective policy grounds, such as preventing terrorist organisations from having the 'oxygen of publicity' by prohibiting media reporting of their statements, which was the purpose of the British government's 1988 ban on reporting a number of organisations, both legal and illegal, operating mainly in Northern Ireland, introduced by the Home Secretary (Parliamentary Debates (Hansard), Commons, 6th ser., vol. 138 (1987–88), cols 885–95). See further, *R* v *Secretary of State for the Home Department, ex parte Brind* [1991] 1 AC 696. In addition, it is unclear how such abstract rights are to be weighed against other background individuated rights such as the right to privacy. The European Court of Human Rights is now making what were once abstract rights more concrete, preventing them from being easily set aside for policy reasons and weighing up the relative merits of each right against each other. Thus there is a gradual concretisation of abstract rights in the United Kingdom through the European Convention on Human Rights (213 UNTS 221, ratified by the United Kingdom in 1951, entered into force in September 1953), although it is true to say that the proper incorporation of the treaty into UK law allows, our courts to institutionalise rights rather than relying, under the Human Rights Act 1998, on the European Court's jurisprudence, not to mention the savings in time and money for litigants who want to take advantage of the European Convention.

'Concrete' or institutional rights are more precisely defined aims and, at their most concrete, grant individual rights before institutions such as the courts. Dworkin gives the rather obscure hypothetical example of a concrete right derived from the more general right of freedom of expression (*Taking Rights Seriously*, pp. 93–4). A court, in deciding whether to uphold the right of a newspaper to publish secret defence plans, would weigh the newspaper's right to freedom of expression against the competing rights of the soldiers to security. The newspaper's concrete right to publish weighs more heavily than the rights of the soldiers in this particular instance because it is supported by the background right of freedom of expression, provided that the publication does not threaten the lives of individual soldiers.

6.4.1.3 The consequentialist theory of rights

In the example just looked at, namely, a dispute between a newspaper and the rights of soldiers to security, it could be strongly argued that the court is not balancing the competing rights of the newspaper against those of the soldiers. In reality the court will balance the newspaper's rights to publish against the policy argument that the interests of society are best served by maintaining secrecy as far as issues of national defence are concerned. In Dworkin's hypothetical example the court upholds the newspaper's rights, but it is more common in England for the courts to uphold the government's claims that defence documents should be kept secret in the public interest (J. A. G. Griffiths, *The Politics of the Judiciary*, 4th ed. (London: Fontana, 1991), p. 281). If the court decides in favour of secrecy it is surely doing so on the basis of a policy decision, not on the basis that it is protecting the rights of soldiers, although that may be a consideration in its overall policy decision.

Dworkin attempts to deflect this argument by advising us not to confuse arguments of principle and arguments of policy with a different distinction between consequentialist and non-consequentialist theories of rights (*Taking Rights Seriously*, p. 307). A court may in fact consider the consequences of its decision in the light of its effect on future litigants' rights. In other words the court may take account of wider issues only when looking at rights. In the defence cases, Dworkin is arguing that the courts are simply balancing the alleged rights of the litigants before them against the wider rights of individuals potentially affected by their decisions. This is what Dworkin means by a consequentialist theory of rights. He claims that his theory encompasses such an approach and is not simply concerned with upholding the rights of litigants who appear before courts. This approach means that the court may decide to protect the rights of individuals even though they are not before the court, and have not had representations on their behalf heard by the court.

Dworkin briefly discusses the case of *D* v *National Society for the Prevention of Cruelty to Children* [1978] AC 171 (*Taking Rights Seriously*, pp. 308–9) as an illustration of this point. The National Society for the Prevention of Cruelty to Children (NSPCC) is an independent body which receives and investigates complaints from members of the public about cases of ill-treatment or neglect of children. The society received a complaint from an informant about the treatment of a 14-month-old girl, and an NSPCC inspector called at the parents' home. The mother subsequently brought an action against the society for damages for personal injuries alleged to have resulted from the society's negligence in failing properly to investigate the complaint and the manner and circumstances of the inspector's call, which she said had caused her severe and continuing shock. The society denied negligence and applied for an order that there should be no disclosure of any documents which revealed or might reveal the identity of the complainant, on the grounds, inter alia, that the proper performance by the society of its duties required that the absolute confidentiality of information should be preserved, that if disclosure were ordered in the mother's action, its sources of information would dry up and that would be contrary to the public interest.

Now this appears to be a straight fight between the claimant's right to damages if she had proved negligence and the defendants' argument of public policy that the protection of children would be jeopardised if the claimant had access to information necessary for her action. However, Dworkin seems to suggest that, in fact, all the court was doing was undertaking a consequentialist examination of rights. In other words, it was balancing the claimant's right on the one hand against the competing rights of children in general on the other. In deciding in favour of the society the court came down in favour of the argument that disclosure could jeopardise the protection of children from abuse in future cases, not for any policy reason but because the rights of children weighed more heavily than the right of the claimant in this particular case.

However, an examination of the House of Lords' judgment in this case reveals scant evidence that the judges felt it necessary to find against the claimant on the ground that to uphold her right would have undue consequences for the protection of children's rights in the future. The House seemed more concerned with balancing the claimant's alleged right with the argument of public policy that disclosure would not be for the benefit of the community, and the policy argument prevailed. For example, Lord Edmund-Davies said, at p. 245

> ...where (i) a confidential relationship exists...and (ii) disclosure would be in breach of some ethical or social value involving the public interest, the court has a discretion to uphold a refusal to disclose relevant evidence provided it considers that, on balance, the public interest would be better served by excluding such evidence.

Dworkin has criticised other theories for not reflecting the actual judicial decision-making process, in that if actual decisions are examined judges do not decide cases on grounds of policy. That may be so in the majority of cases, yet in *D v National Society for the Prevention of Cruelty to Children* and in other hard cases, judges are clearly deciding cases on policy grounds and it appears to be Dworkin who is alleging that this is merely a cover for rights-based arguments. It is not sufficient to argue that a court, when talking about 'discretion' and 'public interest', really means that it is weighing up competing rights. It may be that judges reason on the basis of rights most of the time, but in the hard cases they do reason and have reasoned on policy grounds. Judges appear to believe that they have the discretion to make law in these cases.

6.4.2 The right answer thesis

Dworkin's view of judicial precedent is that judges agree that earlier decisions have gravitational force or weight. The legislature may make decisions inconsistent with earlier ones but a judge rarely has this independence, because he will always try to connect his decision with past decisions. It is because policy decisions may be inconsistent and are not individuated that a judge, when defining the particular gravitational force of a precedent must take into account only the arguments of principle that justify that precedent, ignoring arguments of policy (*Taking Rights Seriously*, pp. 110–23; *Law's Empire*, pp. 23–9, pp. 238–50). In effect judges are always looking back to precedents or statutes to justify their decisions, whilst the legislature, in formulating policy and enacting it in the form of legislation, is forward-looking. Furthermore, in looking back, the judge only looks for principles (and rules) not, for instance, at the policy that may have generated a particular piece of legislation.

Dworkin seems to admit that in practice this approach will not necessarily produce consistency in judicial decision-making, with the result that in the same case, different judges would come up with a different answer even though they were seeking the answer only in rules and principles. However, he does contend that in theory there is only one single 'right' answer to all legal questions. Unfortunately, it appears that only one person could achieve this answer every time; that person is Hercules, Dworkin's mythical judge, 'a lawyer of superhuman skill, learning, patience and acumen' (*Taking Rights Seriously*, p. 105).

> [Hercules] must construct a scheme of abstract and concrete principles that provides a coherent justification for all common law precedents and, so far as these are to be justified on principle, constitutional and statutory provisions as well.
>
> (*Taking Rights Seriously*, pp. 116–17)

The one right answer thesis has caused great debate amongst legal theorists (see, for example, A. C. Hutchinson and J. N. Wakefield, 'A hard look at "hard cases": the nightmare of a noble dreamer' (1982) 2 *Oxford J Legal Stud* 86), but the controversy is to a certain extent overblown. When Hercules is constructing his scheme of abstract and concrete principles, presumably any idea that contributes to his scheme counts as a reason, a *legal* reason, for deciding the case one way rather than another. This makes it more likely that Dworkin's 'right answer thesis', that there will always be law to determine a hard case, is correct. At the same time, however, the thesis appears much less radical. There will almost always be some reasons to decide a case one way rather than another, and the more those reasons count as legal reasons, the more law there is to determine an answer to a case. Given that apparently all a reason has to do to be a legal reason is to form part of a sensible theoretical accounting of the law, it would seem that most reasons relevant to deciding a case on any ground whatsoever count as legal reasons. Of course this way of looking at things generates its own problem, which is that is seems massively to expand what counts as part of the law, and this strain makes the theory seem less plausible.

6.4.3 **Law as integrity**

In *Law's Empire* Dworkin set out the most complete version of his theory of law, which he called 'law as integrity'. He stated that any judge, Hercules again being the ideal, must be able to justify his decision in any case, but particularly in a contentious hard case, by constructing a theory of the law's rules and principles into which his decision fits, and which shows the law 'in its best light'. Again, following along with the rights thesis, the judge's theory must be a theory of principle, not policy. What is it for a theory to succeed in showing the law in its best light? A theory will be tested in two dimensions, fit and substance. (Although Dworkin used different terms in the book to characterise the second dimension, it is conventional to refer to it as 'substance'.) 'Fit' means fit with what is accepted as settled law. This is one reason for the name of the theory as 'law as integrity'. A person with integrity is one whose current views are in keeping with his past views in large measure: a person whose views change with the weather shows no integrity, and neither would a body of law that did so. In this way, the dimension of fit ensures that the law of any jurisdiction is true to its past. 'Substance' refers to concordance with substantive political morality. To show the law in its best light, then, is to try to construct a theory of the law which fits the settled law as well as it can, while at the same time interpreting the law so as best to accord with morality, in particular with the moral virtue justice.

6.4.3.1 Integrity in practice

Law's Empire commences with a discussion of several illustrative cases, one of which is the negligence case of *McLoughlin v O'Brian* [1983] 1 AC 410, which Dworkin uses to support his theory of law as integrity. The case concerned the question of whether the claimant could recover damages for emotional injuries suffered away from the scene of a car crash in which her family had been injured as a result of the defendant's negligence.

The Court of Appeal [1981] QB 599 recognised that, although the defendant owed the claimant a duty of care and that her emotional injuries were reasonably foreseeable, her 'right' to recover was limited on the policy ground that liability for negligence had to stop somewhere. The House of Lords reversed that decision. Several of their lordships admitted that the policy consideration that such a precedent could open the floodgates of litigation, as taken into account by the Court of Appeal, may, in very grave circumstances, be sufficient to distinguish a line of precedent and so justify a judge's refusal to extend the principle of those cases to larger areas of liability. But such arguments must be sufficiently grave, which they were not in this case (see, for example, Lord Edmund-Davies [1983] 1 AC 410 at pp. 426–9).

Lord Scarman, on the other hand, went further, saying that once the claimant had established her right to recover, no argument of policy could take it away. Any adverse effects on the community should be dealt with by the legislature (at pp. 429–31).

Lord Scarman's judgment does correspond closely to Dworkin's approach. Nevertheless, only Lord Scarman's judgment seems to accord with Dworkin's theory; the rest of the judges seemed to believe that the judiciary could take account of policy arguments and in certain circumstances, they, not the legislature, could use them to deny a right. Although Dworkin admits that on occasions policy grounds can be used to overrule a right, that, according to Dworkin, can only be done by the legislature and not by the judges as the majority in *McLoughlin* v *O'Brian* seem to suggest. Dworkin uses the case because Lord Scarman seems to embody Hercules to a certain extent, yet overall the vast majority of judges in both the Court of Appeal and the House of Lords seemed willing to balance policy considerations against a set of precedents containing the right to recover damages for emotional injuries caused by negligence. Again Dworkin's choice of examples tends to illustrate that his theory is not descriptive of what judges actually do and that, if anything, he is describing the approach of a minority of the judiciary.

6.4.3.2 Fit and substance: incommensurable?

Finnis argues that fit and substance will not serve together as criteria which determine which judge's theory puts the law in the best light, because fit and substance are incommensurable values; that is, they are not values of the same kind that can be measured on the same scale.

> Hercules himself, no matter how superhuman, could not justifiably claim unique correctness for his answer to a hard case (as lawyers in sophisticated legal systems use that term). For in such a case, a claim to have found the right answer is senseless, in much the same way as it is senseless to claim to have identified the English novel which meets the two criteria 'shortest and most romantic' (or 'funniest and best', or 'most English and most profound'). Two incommensurable criteria of judgment are proposed—in Dworkin's theory, 'fit' (with past political decisions) and 'justifiability' (inherent substantive moral soundness). A hard case is hard (not merely novel) when not only is there more than one answer which violates no applicable rule, but the answers thus available are ranked in different orders along each of the available criteria of evaluation: brevity, humour, Englishness, fit (integrity), romance, inherent 'quality', profundity, inherent 'justifiability' and so forth.
>
> (J. Finnis, 'On Reason and Authority in *Law's Empire*' (1987) 6 *Law and Philosophy* 357)

Finnis argues that faced with the task of assessing a 'best' theory, which must be considered in light of incommensurable values, one can only conscientiously bear in mind all the relevant variables and *choose*.

This is a difficult criticism to assess. While it raises a genuine issue, it is not clear whether it should be taken as a criticism so much of 'law as integrity' as the right answer thesis (see 6.4.2), i.e. whether it undermines the cogency of justifying decisions in terms of fit and substance, or whether it undermines the belief that justifying decisions in this way will serve to indicate a single best answer.

6.4.3.3 Raz's critique

Raz points out that in all versions of his theory, Dworkin has distinguished between what is more or less settled law, to which the criterion of fit applies in 'law as integrity', and substantive moral considerations, which play some role in determining the boundaries of the legal. In early versions, one might have said that the total law consisted of the settled law and all the principles that theoretically cohered with the settled law; the law included all its coherent theoretical implications. However, this was an inherently conservative view of the law. Critics pointed out that this theory would seem to indicate that a judge in apartheid South Africa should decide a hard case in keeping with the principles of apartheid, on the basis that these principles best cohered with the settled law of the time. Perhaps partly in response to this worry, law as integrity seemed to grant more weight to substantial justice, so that one could frame the law in its best possible light; thus, for example, even pre-apartheid South African law embodied certain principles of fairness and justice, and presumably a judge could decide a hard case by drawing upon and extending these, rather than depending upon apartheid principles, as the former would clearly show South African law in its best light.

However, it is not clear that Dworkin's theory ever escapes the need for something like the rule of recognition to determine what the established law is, i.e. some standard criteria which more or less certainly identifies the settled law. And so long as Dworkin intends to maintain a distinction between what is required under the law and what is required by morality unfettered by law, then this need remains (see Joseph Raz, 'Dworkin: A New Link in the Chain' (1986) 74 *California Law Review* 1103).

6.5 Are lawyers moral philosophers?

One of Dworkin's more interesting claims is that the sort of project Hart proposed to undertake, a philosophical investigation of the law which did not make any claims about the moral value of the law, is impossible. Dworkin claims that any 'external', merely descriptive approach to legal theory is doomed to fail, because any proper theory of a social practice in which the participants are themselves interpreters of their practice will require the theorist to become a full, interpreting participant in order that he or she may fully capture the nature of that practice. The theorist as participant will not only describe the practice, but will also evaluate it, that is, judge its moral merit; one's moral outlook on the practice will shape every aspect of one's descriptive claims about it.

Moreover, doing jurisprudence, as a way of participating in interpreting legal practices, is only doing at a more abstract level what lawyers and judges do everyday. In the same way that judges and lawyers bring to bear their substantial commitments about justice, equality, and so forth to bear when they make arguments and render decisions, so must a legal theorist bring to bear his own substantial moral and political views when he theorises about the nature of law.

> General theories of law . . . must be abstract because they aim to interpret the main point and structure of legal practice, not some particular part or department of it. But for all their abstraction, they are constructive interpretations: they try to show legal practice

as a whole in its best light, to achieve equilibrium between legal practice as they find it and the best justification of that practice. So no firm line divides jurisprudence from adjudication or any other aspect of legal practice. Legal philosophers debate about the general part, the interpretive foundation any legal argument must have. We may turn that coin over. Any practical legal argument, no matter how detailed and limited, assumes the kind of abstract foundation jurisprudence offers, and when rival foundations compete, a legal argument assumes one and rejects others. So any judge's opinion is itself a piece of legal philosophy, even when the philosophy is hidden and the visible argument is dominated by citation and lists of facts. Jurisprudence is the general part of adjudication, silent prologue to any decision at law.

(Dworkin, *Law's Empire*, p. 90)

6.5.1 Are lawyers philosophers?

Is it true that lawyers are legal philosophers and vice versa? This seems a doubtful claim to make, if only because we seem to be able to distinguish between engaging in a practice and thinking about it, say theorising about it. We engage in all sorts of practices that require thoughtful attention, from chess to cricket to cooking to arithmetic, but thoughtfully attending to them does not seem to entail at all that we are developing a theory of each of these practices at the same time willy nilly. It would seem to be nonsense to say that having played cricket I have unknowingly been formulating or criticising theories of cricket all along, or that by speaking English I have been critically assessing Chomsky's linguistic theory. Dworkin's claim must be that true though this may be of these sorts of practices, it is different with 'interpretive' or 'theoretical' practices. By practising law, I have indeed unknowingly engaged Hart and Dworkin, adopted Razian views, or decided that natural law is sound but it is not obvious what it is about the practice of law that makes it special in this respect.

It is also well to remember that constructing theories is inherently a conscious activity, an activity in its own right. Theorising about an activity, for example, the practice of law, would seem to be an activity in itself, distinct from engaging in that activity, and this is true even if that activity is itself theoretical, as law may well be. After all, philosophy is a philosophical practice if anything is, but philosophers are not for that reason always philosophising about philosophy when they do philosophy.

6.5.2 Is descriptive philosophy of law possible?

Hart famously drew attention to the character of the law as a social practice to show that participants took the 'internal' point of view of the practice. He argued that legal theorists must take this into account in their theories, and in so doing, he himself tried to show how law was a normative practice, an 'affair' of rules. For Hart, however, paying attention to these considerations did not detract in the least from the descriptive nature of the project.

It is true that…the descriptive legal theorist must understand what it is to adopt the internal point of view and in that limited sense must be able to put himself in the place of an insider; but this is not to accept the law or share or endorse the insider's internal point of view or in any other way to surrender his descriptive stance.

(H. L. A. Hart, *The Concept of Law*, 2nd ed. (Oxford: Clarendon Press, 1994), p. 242)

Intuitively, there seems no reason to doubt this, which is not to say that a theory is not evaluative in any way. It is to say that in order to describe a practice, one need not make the same *kind* of evaluations about the practice as its participants do. There are certain kinds of values which all theories must take into account; epistemic values, i.e. the values by which we judge theories to be significant and true, such as comprehensiveness (accounting for lots of data), simplicity, elegance, productivity, and so on (see Brian Leiter, 'Beyond the Hart/Dworkin Debate: The Methodology Problem in Jurisprudence' (2003) 48 *American Journal of Jurisprudence* 17). Furthermore, someone describing the practice evaluates the practice in the sense of selecting for examination those aspects of the practice that seem to contribute most to acquiring knowledge of or understanding it, given his historical, philosophical, and sociological interests in it. The justification of a particular theory about the nature of the law 'is tied to an evaluative judgment about the relative importance of various features of social organisations, and these reflect our moral and intellectual concerns' (Joseph Raz, *Ethics in the Public Domain* (Oxford: Clarendon Press, 1994), p. 193). These concerns, however, and thus these evaluative choices, will be those of the describer, not those of the participants.

The view also leads to a certain kind of absurdity. For example, it would appear that on this view the comparative study of religions is impossible. As a theorist of more than one religion, one would have to take the position of a participant in both, subscribing to the values of both (seeing each in its best light, of course), with the result that any comparative consideration of the two would be a kind of joining of two sets of values; comparative study of religions would necessarily collapse into a kind of ecumenism, which seems absurd.

6.6 Raz and the authority of law

The *paradox of authority* can be framed in the following way: if an authority tells you to do or to believe something, and this is indeed the right thing to do or believe, then you should do it or believe it simply because *it is* the right thing to do or believe; the authority's saying so adds nothing. And if the authority tells you to do or to believe something, and this is in fact the wrong thing to do or believe, then you should not do it or believe it, simply because it is the *wrong* thing to do or believe; in such a case you should refuse to do or believe what the authority says. The result is that authority seems to make no difference in any case: if the authority tells you the right thing, it is redundant, for what is right is right independently of anything the authority says, and if the authority tells you the wrong thing, then you should not listen to it. It is never *rational* to follow an authority's guidance.

There may be a second order justification for complying with a political authority, which is not that a political authority is likely to lay down good laws; this Hobbesian justification of authority is that a world without any political authority, the state of nature in which each man is at war with each other, is worse even than living under the authority of a tyrant, so long as the tyrant does not engage in the wanton murder of his subjects.

Raz's theory aims to avoid both these ways of thinking about authority, i.e. that following an authority's guidance is inherently irrational, or that the only justification of authority is the idea that the monopolisation of force under an authority is better than the alternative of anarchy.

6.6.1 **Raz's theory of authority**

Raz begins his exploration of authority by considering the theoretical authority, a person who is an authority in respect of some kind of knowledge, like a medical doctor. The medical doctor has an expert's understanding of the facts about your condition that you do not. It would seem perfectly rational for you to listen to the doctor and believe what he says about your condition. Indeed, it would be *irrational* not to do so: by listening to him you are serving your interests by learning what is wrong with you and how to deal with it. To ignore the doctor would be equivalent to ignoring what a medical textbook, which summarises centuries of laborious investigations by many people, says. Thus, if you are to act rationally in the case of your illness, you will have to rely on knowledge and understanding which you cannot acquire all by yourself (or at least it cannot be done in most cases because of constraints of time, intelligence, and so on). In this way, listening to the authority *serves your interests* in the only way your interests can be served, and to take advantage of the authority in this way is perfectly rational.

This is the *service* conception of authority, which Raz capitalises on to explain the rationality of following *practical* authorities like the law. For if the authority serves the interests of those people subject to it by solving a problem that they are not able or likely to solve without the authority then it is obviously not irrational for them to follow that authority, and this is so even if the authority sometimes gets it wrong, so long as it is likely to get it right more often than they are themselves.

A doctor *mediates* between you and the facts which medical science has revealed and which indicate how to handle your illness—the doctor does not give you a short lesson in medicine, revealing all those facts to you (though a good doctor tells you what is wrong with you and gives you some idea of the nature of your condition), but gives you a prescription. In a similar way, a legislature considers all the reasons that apply in deciding, say, whether or not, wills should be formalised by being written, signed, and attested by two witnesses, and then passes a law one way or another, which everyone must now follow.

This is the essence of what Raz calls the 'normal justification thesis' for an authority: an authority is justified as such, i.e. is a legitimate authority to which you should listen, when it actually serves you by mediating between you and the reasons that apply to you in this helpful way: an authority is justifiably an authority for you when you are more likely to act correctly on the balance of reasons that apply to you if you follow the directives of the authority than if you were to act on your own assessment of the balance of reasons.

6.6.2 **The authority of law**

For Raz, the law's most important role as an authority lies in its ability to solve coordination problems, broadly conceived. The most obvious sort of example is that of our need of a convention as to which side of the road to drive on; neither the right nor the left is more obviously the right choice, and no general and sustained convention may have arisen in practice. By instituting a directive to drive on the left, the law provides a reason to act which makes a crucial practical difference, for (if the authority is effective) the authority's directive will provide a reason for action which did not previously exist, compliance with which will solve the coordination problem.

To take another, less obvious example, individuals may on the balance of reasons that apply to them have a moral obligation to contribute money for the provision of public goods in their community, and by providing a means (a taxing and spending agency with associated directives governing how its subjects deal with the agency) the authority can provide an institutional means of doing so. They will be better able to meet their obligations by this means than if everyone was left up to himself to decide how much he should contribute, how he should do so, and so on.

This analysis works even in respect to matters which seem very far from the setting of standards to solve coordination problems. Consider, for example, the criminal law. The injunction not to murder is not a standard that solves any coordination problem; it is a moral prohibition that applies to everyone regardless of the behaviour of others, or of the individual's expectations of the behaviour of others. But the law does more than simply enforce pre-existing, independently valid moral norms of this kind. The exact extent, scope, and justification of these norms is controversial and uncertain. While the law, to be legitimate, must by and large reflect the moral considerations which underpin these moral norms, the law can and does serve as an authority which solves a coordination problem by specifying in more or less certain terms legal norms which reflect these moral ones. Further, the law specifies more or less certain remedies or punishments for their breach, and enforces compliance with these norms to deal with those subjects of the law who would otherwise disregard these moral norms. By instituting a criminal justice system, the law creates a better way of dealing with crime, i.e. dealing with criminals in a just, fair, and certain manner, than would leaving it all to self-help, for example, revenge, feud, vendetta. The 'coordination' problem the criminal justice system addresses is the problem or goal of coordinating a community's response to crime so as to deal with it in the best way possible.

To refer back to Hart, authorities, through the use of the powers conferred by secondary rules, are able to create means of dealing with problems of uncertainty, stasis, and inefficiency that would arise in their absence.

6.6.3 Raz's critique of Dworkin's theory and soft positivism

Raz claims that all legal systems claim to be authorities, in the sense that all legal systems *require* compliance with their edicts, and all claim that they do so legitimately. Of course, it is another matter entirely whether a legal system is actually legitimate. But to be a possible legal system at all, a legal system must be able to lay down rules or orders in a way which can be taken as authoritative directions, and Raz argues that this undermines Dworkin's legal theory as well as the theoretical position known as 'soft positivism'.

Soft positivism forms a sort of 'half-way' house between Dworkin's theory of law and traditional modern positivism. As we have seen, Dworkin claims that in order to determine whether a law is valid, particularly in hard cases, will require assessing the moral quality of it in light of a defensible moral-political theory of the law of that jurisdiction. A traditional positivist, a 'hard' positivist, replies that the law is determined by something like a rule of recognition, which identifies the law on the basis of social facts such as whether Parliament passed an Act containing the law, or whether a judge relied upon it in deciding a case which binds as a precedent. The soft positivist argues that though a legal system *need not* incorporate within its rule of recognition any moral criteria for legal validity, it may do so. So, for example, if a bill of rights introduces a requirement of fair procedure, the soft positivist would accept that what the law is depends on what the morality of fairness requires.

Raz's difficulty with both Dworkin's theory and with soft positivism is that requiring moral investigation to determine the content of the law is incompatible with the law's serving as an authority. As a practical authority, the law must tell its subjects in more or less certain terms what they are required to do. It is not serving their interests as an authority if it just sends them off on a research project. It does you no good whatsoever for an authority to tell you: 'Do the right thing!'. Of course you want to do that, which is why you have come to the authority in the first place; what you want the authority to do is tell you what the right thing is, whether it is how to create a will or how to be relieved of flu.

To put the point more precisely, to be effective at all authorities must 'mediate' between the reasons which apply to their subject's case and the subject himself. The medical authority stands between the facts of medicine and his patient and serves the patient by telling him what to do without making him do a degree in medicine. Similarly, the law is not an effective authority if does not tell its subjects how to act in more or less straightforward terms, but rather tells the subject to figure it out himself taking into consideration all the relevant facts and moral considerations. Doing that is like giving them no guidance at all and whatever you might call a 'legal system' which gave no guidance or only useless guidance of this kind, you could not call it an authority. For Raz, the one thing that is true about law is that it does claim the authority to tell you what to do. Therefore, Raz holds that whenever judges are entitled to decide a case or formulate a rule on the basis of moral considerations, they are creating new law, not applying law that already exists, because the only thing that already exists in such a case are the various moral considerations that anyone would look at to decide how to act.

This point reminds us of Raz's distinction between the deliberative and executive stages of practical reason. The function of authorities is to carry out the deliberation for the authorities' subjects and produce rules or other standards which the subjects then execute. In this respect, legal rules are decisions. They are the decisions of legal authorities which result from their deliberations. For a legal standard to exist, the law must have decided to guide its subjects to act in one way rather than another. Telling the subjects to do the deliberation themselves is to make no decision at all, or rather, it is to abdicate authority in that area of human activity, which of course the law does in many areas of human life. The law, for example, refuses to regulate how many Christmas presents you should give.

It is important to note that nothing Raz says here undermines the legitimacy of courts exercising their discretion to resolve disputes where the law is unsettled or indeterminate. But when they act in this way, they are not following the law but deciding the case, in part, for non-legal reasons. The claim that courts act this way is just Hart's claim that courts exercise a discretion when there are gaps in the law. And it is well to recall that the legislature and the courts rely on this, and defer making up their minds and laying down determinative guidance in an area; instead, they produce broad or vague directions and leave it to the courts, or to later courts, to give workable guidance on a case-by-case basis.

Dworkin's reply is perfectly in keeping with his own idea of the law: he argues that Raz's concept of authority is too narrow, and fails to encompass the perfectly sensible view that even such a broad directive as 'act honestly and fairly' can be authoritative, in that the recipient of such a directive can alter his behaviour in an attempt to conform with it, and consider that whether he has or has not complied with the directive will turn on whether he has actually acted honestly and fairly, whatever those two standards actually require (Ronald Dworkin, 'Thirty Years On: A Review of Jules Coleman, *The Practice of Principle*' (2002) 115 *Harvard LR* 1655).

6.7 The impact of the work of Dworkin and Raz

It is difficult to imagine the philosophy of law over the past 40 years without these two towering figures. For those whose ultimate interest is in the way in which the law can be and is moral, Dworkin has consistently provided the most interesting and novel arguments for the proposition that one essential determinant of legal validity is moral validity. If anything, Dworkin has become firmer in recent years in pressing his view that morality is an essential determinant of legal validity. In his most recent work, Dworkin would treat jurisprudence or legal theory as a branch of moral philosophy, in effect arguing that the philosophy of law should be regarded as a philosophy of institutionalised justice (Ronald Dworkin, *Justice in Robes* (Cambridge, Mass: Harvard University Press, 2006), ch. 1). By contrast, for his part, Raz, building on the work of Hart, has anchored the positivist enterprise on probably the only unshakeable foundation, a sound theory of authority and practical reason. It falls to the twenty-first century to learn whose work better stands the test of time.

FURTHER READING

Cohen, M., (ed.), *Ronald Dworkin and Contemporary Jurisprudence* (London: Duckworth, 1984).

Coleman, J., *The Practice of Principle* (Oxford: Oxford University Press, 2001).

Dickson, J., 'Is the Rule of Recognition Really a Conventional Rule?' (2007) 27 *Oxford Journal of Legal Studies* 373.

Dworkin, R., *Law's Empire* (London: Fontana, 1986).

Dworkin, R., 'Hart's Postscript and the Character of Legal Philosophy' (2004) 24 *Oxford Journal of Legal Studies* 1.

Dworkin, R., *Justice in Robes* (Cambridge, Mass.: Harvard University Press, 2006).

Green, L., 'Three Themes from Raz' (2005) 25 *Oxford Journal of Legal Studies* 505.

Hart, H. L. A., 'American jurisprudence through English eyes: the nightmare and the noble dream' (1977) 11 *Ga L Rev* 969.

Hart, H. L. A., *The Concept of Law*, 2nd ed. (Oxford: Clarendon Press, 1994), pp. 238–76.

Leiter, B., 'Beyond the Hart/Dworkin debate: the methodology problem in jurisprudence' (2003) 48 *American Journal of Jurisprudence* 17.

Lyons, D. B., 'Principles, positivism, and legal theory' (1977) 87 *Yale LJ* 415.

Marmor, A., 'Legal positivism: Still descriptive and morally neutral' (2005) 26 *Oxford Journal of Legal Studies* 683.

Marmor, A., 'How Law is Like Chess' (2006) 12 *Legal Theory* 347.

Patterson, D., 'Dworkin and the Semantics of Legal and Political Concepts' (2006) 26 *Oxford Journal of Legal Studies* 545.

Penner, J., Schiff, D., and Nobles, R., (eds), *Jurisprudence and Legal Theory: Commentary and Materials* (Oxford: Oxford University Press, 2002), chs 8, 9, 10.

Raz, J., *The Authority of Law* (Oxford: Clarendon Press, 1979).

Raz, J., *The Morality of Freedom* (Oxford: Clarendon Press, 1986), chs 2, 3, and 4.

Raz, J., *Ethics in the Public Domain* (Oxford: Clarendon Press, 1994), chs 8 and 9.

Raz, J., *Practical Reasons and Norms* (Oxford: Oxford University Press, 1999).

Raz, J., 'Incorporation by Law' (2004) 10 *Legal Theory* 1.

Raz, J., 'Dworkin: A New Link in the Chain' (1986) 74 *California Law Review* 1103.

Soper, E. P., 'Legal theory and the obligation of the judge: the Hart/Dworkin dispute' (1977) 75 *Mich L Rev* 473.

PART II

Particular Philosophical Issues in Law

7

The Building Blocks of Law: Norms and their Nature

Introduction

In moral and legal philosophy, the word 'norm' refers to those things that require a standard of behaviour. The most obvious example is a rule: a rule requires a certain standard of behaviour, i.e. that you follow or comply with the rule. But on this view rights and duties are norms as well. My right to bodily security requires a standard of behaviour from you, i.e. that you do not physically interfere with my person. This example illustrates the *correlativity* of rights with duties: where I have a right it is standardly the case that someone else has a duty which reflects that right. So in the example just given, my right to bodily security correlates with your duty not to interfere with me physically. 'Normative' is the associated adjective, meaning 'pertaining to norms' but in particular it often means 'standard-setting'. Thus a normative regime is a regime which sets standards for some groups of people.

Try to avoid using the word 'normative' when you mean 'moral'. Morality is normative, of course, because morality requires standards of behaviour of us. But the world of the normative is much bigger than the world of the moral. Games have rules, and are thus normative; so also is any rule governed activity: long division, etiquette, and the grammar of natural languages, like English. Too often people confuse the normative with the moral, legal philosophers at times included.

7.1 Norms as exclusionary reasons

The best account of norms we have is the result of the work of Joseph Raz, in particular his books *Practical Reason and Norms* (Oxford: Oxford University Press, 1990) and *The Morality of Freedom* (Oxford: Clarendon Press, 1986). Central to his explanation is the idea of an exclusionary reason, which we have already encountered (see 6.2). To recapitulate: to reason practically is to reason about what one should do; normally, what one should do is determined on the balance of reasons. If I am hungry and wish to eat, I have to decide what to do. I may choose to go to one restaurant rather than another based on a host of reasons that apply to the case: how good the food is, how expensive the meals are, how far away the restaurants are from where I am, how much time I have, whether I am on a diet, and so on. However, there are other sorts of reasons which are sometimes called *peremptory*, or exclusionary. These reasons exclude my acting inconsistently with them, irrespective of how I would balance the reasons if I were free to comply with them or not. In the moral realm, these are the reasons which make moral demands upon us. I have moral obligations to keep my side of agreements I enter into, not to assault or kill others, not to interfere with the property of others, to take care of my children should I have any.

On this view, norms such as rules, rights and duties have the significance they do because of the way they enter into our practical reasoning as exclusionary reasons. The rule that I must stop at red lights is the rule that it is because, to the extent I follow it, I am not free to decide on each occasion when I pull up to a junction to proceed or not as I think fit. I must stop at red lights. Notice that I am not required by the rule not to *think* about whether the rule is a good one in general, or whether on this particular occasion it is doing any good (consider the case of stopping at a red light on a deserted road on a clear day when there is no other traffic about). The rule requires that I take it to be an exclusionary reason that applies to *my behaviour*. I must follow the rule, not intellectually be in favour of it. Notice also that there is nothing in this explanation of rules that requires rules to be *absolute*. There may be exceptions, understood in advance (for example, the right of emergency vehicles to run red lights), or which arise in an unanticipated fashion (I am fleeing in my car from Martians).

7.1.1 The genesis and generation of norms

Norms exist, or come to exist, in different ways. There is a debate in moral philosophy about how moral norms come to exist; some philosophers believe that moral norms apply universally to all humans, and have done so since humans have been around, simply in virtue of aspects of our human nature (our ability to feel pain and pleasure, our ability to act freely, or for other reasons). Others believe that moral norms are much more changeable and contextual; what is morally the correct thing to do turns on matters of history and culture; on this view, what morality demands is something like that which custom demands; if this is right, moral norms arise and pass away and not all people in all times and places are subject to the same moral demands. So norms, moral norms, can plausibly come into being in two ways; with the genesis of human beings to which they (it is argued) essentially apply, or with the genesis of various human cultures.

But they may also come into being in two other ways: (1) by the exercise of moral powers to create norms; and (2) by 'operation of morality' (in parity with the idea 'by operation of law'.

As to (1), by agreeing to meet for dinner we create corresponding moral obligations and rights that each of us will turn up for dinner. We thus have a 'moral power' to create new rights and duties by agreement. The parallels with our legal power to enter into contracts are obvious.

As to (2), if I accidently bump into you, knocking you over, I will have a moral obligation to help you up and apologise for my clumsiness. The parallels here with the law are also obvious; if I run you down with my car you will, by operation of law, acquire a power to bring an action against me for damages, and I, correspondingly, will be liable to be made a defendant in such an action by you.

In both these cases we have looked at the way that an individual's behaviour can give rise to new norms, but obviously the generation of norms is not restricted to these cases. The power of the legislature is an obvious further case of a power to create legal norms, as is the power of a judge to make orders against a defendant, or establish a rule with precedential force.

7.2 The variety of norms

Norms are of different general kinds. Here we will just examine the main ones which are essential for understanding legal systems. The important feature of these norms to notice is the way in which they operate as exclusionary reasons.

7.2.1 **Rules and orders**

Rules and orders are clear examples of norms which are found throughout the law. Although the distinction between them is somewhat vague, rules are usually conceived of as general directives that apply to more than one instance, such as the law requiring drivers to stop at red lights. Their normative function is clear; drivers who follow the rule are not entitled to decide on the balance of reasons whether they should stop at a red light; the rule excludes acting on this sort of deliberation; rather, they simply must stop at red lights. Orders, by contrast, are 'one-off' norms that guide the behaviours of one or a defined set of persons on one occasion, as, for example, a judge's order to a defendant to pay the plaintiff £1,000, or a lieutenant's order to his troops to attack an enemy position. Recall that one of Hart's criticisms of command theories of law (Chapter 4) was that this appeared to characterise modern legal systems as systems of orders, rather than systems of rules.

7.2.1.1 Rules as reasons and the 'practice theory' of rules

According to Hart, genuine rules, like the rule that drivers must stop at red lights, can be distinguished from mere behavioural regularities, such as one's habit of eating dinner at eight o'clock, by the attitudes of the individuals involved. We regard rules as reasons for our behaviour, reasons which prevail over mere matters of personal convenience or our current desires. Furthermore, there is social pressure to conform with rules, and we criticise people for breaking them, whereas no such similar pressure or criticism attends a failure to eat dinner at eight. So, Hart reasoned, rules can be identified as 'practices' of a particular kind, practices which are attended by social pressure to conform and criticism when people deviate. Unfortunately, this 'practice' theory of rules is quite flawed.

The most devastating counter-example was provided by Geoffrey Warnock.

> Consider the situation of a spectator of a cricket match, ignorant of the game, and trying to work out what rules the players are following. He will find for instance that, when six balls have been bowled from one end, the players regularly move round and six balls are then bowled from the other end; deviations from this, he will observe, are adversely criticised. He will probably also find that, when a fast bowler is replaced with a slow one, some persons who were previously stationed quite close to the batsman are moved further away, some, probably, a lot further away; and he will find that, if this is not done, there is adverse criticism. But if he concludes that, in so acting, the players are following rules, he will of course be right in the first case, and wrong in the second. There is *no* rule that a slow bowler should not operate with exactly the same field setting as a fast one; this is indeed scarcely ever done, and it would nearly always be regarded as wrong to do it, that is because, quite independently of the rules, it is something that there is nearly always good reason not to do.
>
> (Geoffrey Warnock, *The Object of Morality*, pp. 45–6, quoted in J. Raz, *Practical Reason and Norms* (Oxford: Oxford University Press, 1990), p. 56)

Hart's account does not distinguish between rules, exclusionary reasons, and practices which *on the generally accepted balance of reasons* are almost always the right thing to do. The practice theory also fails to account for rules which are not practised. There are some rules of law which we hope are never actually followed, such as rules punishing individuals for murder or genocide. We hope they are never practised because we hope there is never an occasion for applying them, but even if they were never applied they would still be rules of the legal system. Finally, the fact that people engage in a practice is not, without more, a reason, much less an exclusionary reason, for anyone to engage in it or carry on engaging in it; it may be in a case when there is a reason to do as everyone else does, for example, drive on the left, but that is not the general case.

Raz's explanation of rules in terms of exclusionary reasons is much better. In particular, it makes better sense of rules which have been clearly created for a purpose, as is the case with legislation. Legislated rules are the result of *decisions* taken following a process of deliberation. Only if the decision is taken seriously, i.e. the rule treated as an exclusionary reason by those to whom it is meant to apply, is there any point in legislating. Legislation creating rules is perceived both by the legislators and the subject of the law as the intended creation of an exclusionary reason.

The reason for raising Hart's practice theory of rules is not to undermine his general theory of law as the union of primary and secondary rules. Hart simply had a defective theory of rules. Plug in a sound theory of rules, and the theoretical advances Hart made in our understanding of law still stand.

7.2.2 **Duties**

The normativity of duties as exclusionary reasons is obvious. The imposition of duties by duty-imposing rules is one of the standard techniques of the law for regulating the behaviour of its subjects. Notice that duties can correlate to rights, or can be imposed simply by rules for a host of reasons. The duty to comply with your contractual obligations correlates exactly with the other party's right that you do so. But other duties we have under the law are not clearly associated with any particular rights. For example, duties under the road traffic laws can, in one sense, be thought of as correlating with the rights of other road users not to be injured, in part reflecting an interest in road safety, but these duties can also be justified in part as an element of reasonable schemes to facilitate traffic flow (consider in particular parking regulations). The facilitation of traffic flow is in everyone's interests, but we do not organise our thinking on this issue in terms of the public's or any particular person's 'right' to a working road network.

7.2.3 **Powers**

A power is a normative capacity or ability to create, alter, or abolish the norms (rights, rules, duties, or other powers) that would otherwise apply to oneself or others. A legislature has the power to make new laws, or amend or abolish old ones. A judge has the power to hear and decide cases and issue orders. Individuals have the power to enter into contracts, to licence the use of their property, and so on. Unlike rights, which can be rights to a continuing state of affairs, such as the right to be free from physical interference, powers are always powers to do something; powers are exercised. The main normative importance of powers is that they identify actions which the law specifically makes effective to make positive changes in the norms that apply. They provide a facility for altering the constellation of norms that would otherwise apply. They are normative in the sense of exclusionary reasons in two ways. For the powerholder, the requirements for the proper exercise of the power guides the behaviour when the powerholder wishes to use it; for example, to make a will the law requires that the will be signed and attested. For both the powerholder and others affected, the effective exercise of the power guides their behaviour because there are now new norms in place which serve as exclusionary reasons. It is important to notice that powers and duties may interact. A person may have a duty to exercise a power, as under a contract of sale of land; on the day of completion, the vendor is under a duty to exercise his power to transfer title to the purchaser.

7.2.4 **Rights**

Rights are norms expressed from the perspective of, and in terms of the interests of, the individual. It is possible in some cases to translate a norm framed in terms of a right into a rule: for example, the right to life is easily treated as equivalent to a rule prohibiting killing. Similarly, rights correlate with duties, so one could similarly frame the norm as a duty not to kill. Even so, formulating a norm in terms of a right makes sense. It often allows for simpler descriptions of the way a particular norm guides behaviour but because rights are typically framed in terms of the interests of individuals that are at stake. Unlike rules or duties, rights typically name the interest or value which is the reason why the right exists, as in the right to life or free speech or to be paid £10 for services rendered under a specific contract. As exclusionary reasons, rights guide the behaviour not of the rightholder but of the correlative dutybearer(s). Your right to life is an exclusionary reason for me not to kill you. As we have said, rights correlate with duties. If I have a right, then someone must be under a duty to guide their behaviour in some respect of the interest the right names. Thus my right to life entails that others are under a duty to take into account my interest in life, at least by not taking it. Notice that because rights tend merely to name an interest, they rarely specify on their face the exact contours of the right–duty relationship which defines what the right really amounts to. The right to education could mean one of two very different things. It could mean that there is a duty on others not to prevent you from getting an education, for example, denying you admission to university because of your sex or religion. On the other hand it could mean much more, comprising not only this 'negative' duty but also a 'positive' duty upon the state to provide free education.

7.2.4.1 Rights *in rem*, rights *in personam*; general and specific rights

'*In rem*' and '*in personam*' are originally Roman law phrases which distinguish rights relating to tangible things, like land and chattels, and rights that relate to specific individuals. General rights are those which everyone has by virtue of their humanity or citizenship within a jurisdiction, for example the right not to be killed or the right to vote; general rights need not be exceptionless: in jurisdictions with a death penalty, a person may lose their right to life, and children are not allowed to vote. Special rights are those which arise for other reasons, such as rights under a contract, which only specific individuals have. The distinctions are quite intuitive, though stating them in precise terms is difficult; they are best illustrated by examples:

(a) A general right *in rem*: a right to bodily security is general, obviously, for everyone has such a right, and a right *in rem* because everyone is bound not to interfere with my right to bodily security.

(b) A special right *in rem*: a property right in a tangible, whether in land or a chattel. The right is special as only the owner has (or co-owners have) the right, but *in rem* because the right binds everyone: everyone is bound not to interfere with the owner's right to immediate, exclusive possession.

(c) A general right *in personam*: a right to the care of one's parents. This is the tricky category, for we normally think of rights *in personam*, like rights under a contract, or those arising by operation of law when you negligently injure someone, as coming into existence because a transaction of some kind has taken place between the people involved, in which case the right would be special. But a right to the care of one's parents works: it is general as all children acquire it on birth, and it is *in personam* as it is only one's parents who have the correlative duty. (Notice that a right to the love of one's children cannot be a general right *in personam*—whilst *in personam*, it is not general—not everyone has children.) Another example is the right to vote. It is less general than the first example, because children do not have it, but all citizens of full age do. And it is a right *in personam* because the correlative duty binds only those officials who are in charge of conducting elections. (Note: these rights are defeasible, because one or both of one's parents may be dead, or because, in the past, one might have been elevated to the House of Lords. But that does not mean they are not general.)

(d) A special right *in personam*: contractual rights is the obvious example here.

7.2.4.2 The 'choice' or 'will' versus the 'interest' theory of rights

Under the 'choice' or 'will' theory of rights (of which Hart was a proponent), a legal right does not exist just because someone is guaranteed a benefit under the law. All true rights are coupled with powers, powers to enforce the right, or waive the right, or both. This power to exercise the right by way of enforcement or extinguish the right by way of waiver is the 'choice' or 'will' element of the right. The theory does have some intuitive resonance. We do speak of 'exercising our rights', and it does seem to explain examples such as the position of third party beneficiaries under a contract at common law (although the Contract (Rights of Third Party) Act 1999 alters the situation somewhat). At common law, third parties may benefit from the performance of a contract, but are not regarded as having any right to enforce the contract, nor any right to their benefit under it, even though the benefit arises through the performance of a legal duty by a contracting party. The choice or will theory purports to explain this by distinguishing legal benefits from legal rights on the basis that the latter are enforceable and waivable at the choice of the bearer.

According to the interest theory, a person is the bearer of a right whenever an interest of his or hers is protected by the imposition of a duty on another or others. Thus a right exists when both (1) an important interest is at stake, and (2) there is some appropriate relation between the interest bearer and another or others such that the latter are under a duty to serve, or protect, or not act so as to harm, that interest. On this theory, a right is waivable when it is in the interest of the bearer that it should be, and this makes sense because it is not always the case that an individual's overall interest is served by having each of the interests in respect of which he or she has a right enforced on every occasion. On the other hand, some interests, like the right to life, are not waivable for it is never in the bearer's overall interests for it to be waived.

Most theorists favour the interest theory. As MacCormick famously pointed out, some of the most important legal rights, like the right to life, are unwaivable.

> We are all accustomed to talking and thinking about some rights as 'inalienable'. But if the will theory is correct, the more they are inalienable, the less they are rights.
>
> (N. MacCormick, 'Rights in Legislation' in P. M. S. Hacker and J. Raz (eds), *Law, Morality and Society* (Oxford: Clarendon Press, 1977))

The will theory also cannot account for the rights of those who cannot enforce their rights on their own behalf, such as children, or animals (if animals have rights). The position of the third party beneficiary under a contract is explained by the interest theory in this way; at common law, only the interests of the parties to the contract were regarded as important. A contracting party, A, could enforce a contract with the result that a third party, B, benefited, but the contract was regarded as being enforced for A's interest (including A's interest in seeing B benefited), but not for B's interest. B's benefit was just a side-effect of A's interest being enforced, and so B was not regarded as having any rights under the contract.

It should be emphasised that just because the interest theory appears to be a better analysis of our concept of a right, that the choice or will theory says nothing of importance: it does. It emphasises the extent to which having a right is normally taken to be in 'normative control' of one's situation. As we shall see in the next section, this is an important aspect of rights even when they are not coupled with powers of enforcement or waiver.

7.2.4.3 A right to do wrong?

As we saw above, rights can be of many different kinds. In this section we need to focus on the difference between claim rights, and rights to liberties. A claim right correlates with a duty upon another person to do something, say a duty to pay one £10 under a contract. By contrast, a liberty right is a right that correlates with a duty another has not to do something, for example interfering with one's person or property, or interfering with one's freedom of religion or assembly. Roughly, these duties protect one's interest in doing what one wants with one's own, one's body or property, or engaging in some activity, worship or organising a union or club. As we saw in 7.2.4, rights are normative in providing an exclusionary reason for their correlative duty-bearers. Rights to liberties can be normative in another way. They can be seen to establish a standard for the behaviour of the rightholder, which can guide his behaviour and by which he can be judged. Because rights are instituted to protect the interests of individuals, they entitle individuals to act in reference to their own interests. In particular, they entitle (though they do not require) individuals to decide to act solely on the basis of their own interests, rather than on a more general balance of reasons which takes into account the interests of others. This is particularly clear in the case of legal rights. On the balance of reasons, it might be immoral for you to drink yourself into a stupor every evening, but despite that you have the legal right to do so, in the sense that to stop you from doing so another individual, either a private individual or an officer of the state, would have to violate your rights, for example, by taking away your alcohol, or physically restraining you.

It is in this sense that exercising your rights can appear to be selfish or at least self-centred, and it also explains the idea of having a 'right to do wrong'. In this sense, the normative impact of the institution of rights to liberties is to lower the standard by which people must act, and would otherwise be judged, from that of acting on the whole balance of reasons, to acting only on the balance of reasons that affect their own interests as they see fit. This position may be perfectly justifiable of course, for it gives effect to the value of individual autonomy. But it also shows why standing upon your rights can at times suggest selfishness, as well as showing the disquiet we might feel with a 'rights culture', in which political discourse is shaped by demands framed in terms of individual rights; it can suggest that the law and politics should be seen as a negotiation between individuals looking out only for their self-interests, rather than as an exercise in collective practical reasons in which the interests, including the shared interests, of all are given due consideration.

7.3 The Hohfeldian characterisation of legal norms

Hohfeld famously described legal norms according to a scheme of what he called 'jural correlations' and 'jural opposites'. He was concerned to expose and provide a cure for the way in which, he believed, lawyers, judges, and legal scholars used the word 'right' to mean different things, which he believed led to much confusion. He aimed to show that there were four different meanings for 'right': claim right, power, liberty, and immunity. These must be shown to correlate with their 'jural opposites', which he called duties, liabilities, 'no-rights', and disabilities. Thus if I have a claim right to be paid £10, then someone else must have a correlative duty to pay me £10; if I have a power to transfer my property, then someone else must have a correlative liability to have it transferred to them (i.e. there must be someone whose legal rights or duties change when I exercise my power, in this case by acquiring title from me); if I have a liberty to smoke—Hohfeld idiosyncratically calls it a 'privilege', but no one else does, so I do not—then someone else must correlatively have 'no right' that I do not smoke; finally, if I have an immunity, say from prosecution because of my diplomatic status, then someone else, presumably somebody like the Crown Prosecution Service, has the correlative disability to prosecute me. In the diagram of these basic legal conceptions (see Figure 7.1), 'correlations' run horizontally, whereas 'oppositions' or 'contradictions' run diagonally.

As Hohfeld noticed, all the items in the left hand column are sometimes spoken of as rights: one might have a right to be paid £10, a right to transfer one's property, a right to smoke, and a right not to be prosecuted. All of these, however, correlate with very different 'jural opposites'.

The system has some peculiar features, features which conflict with normal uses of these words made by lawyers and lay subjects of the law.

First of all, notice that liberties cannot correlate with any duties upon anyone else; on the Hohfeldian analysis it is an error to say that my right to assemble correlates with your duty not to break up my meetings. Rather, it correlates with your 'no-right' that I do not assemble; this awkward terminology is adapted from the notion that my liberty to assemble exists because you have no right that I do not. And here's where Hohfeld's notion of jural opposites comes to the fore. A no-right is the opposite of a right, and a liberty the opposite of a duty, because if you do not have no right that I do not assemble, then you do have a right that I do not assemble, and if I have no liberty to assemble,

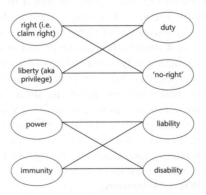

Figure 7.1 Hohfeld's jural relations

then I must have a duty not to assemble. The same working of correlatives and opposites applies *mutatis mutandis* to the second square of jural relations.

Secondly, the use of liability as a correlative of power is awkward. Normally we regard liabilities as things not to have; it sounds odd to say that I have a liability to receive birthday presents from well-wishers.

7.3.1 Problems with Hohfeld's analysis

There are three main difficulties with Hohfeld's analysis. (There are others; Hohfeld has a particularly odd understanding of rights *in rem*; for discussion see J. E. Penner, *The Idea of Property in Law* (Oxford: Clarendon Press, 1997), pp. 23–31; J. E. Penner, 'Hohfeldian Use Rights in Property' in Harris (ed.), *Property Problems: From Genes to Pension Funds* (London: Kluwer, 1997), p. 164). In the first place, the point of Hohfeld's analysis is to clarify the different normative relations that can exist and to provide a systematic set of terms which can be used to avoid confusion. In this respect the system can probably be regarded as a failure. Almost no one in law or legal philosophy regularly or consistently employs Hohfeldian terminology, for several reasons. First of all, the system is very counter-intuitive and fiendishly difficult to operate correctly. For example, we regularly pair rights to do something (liberties on Hohfeld's scheme) with duties on others not to interfere with us when we do that thing; but as we have just seen this is impermissible on Hohfeld's scheme, for liberties cannot correlate with duties. In 'Some Professorial Fallacies About Rights' ((1972–73) 4 *Adelaide LR* 377), John Finnis, whilst arguing that Hohfeldian analysis can be illuminating, also shows in various ways why people are prone to get into a muddle when using it.

The second major problem is simply that it is not clear whether the analysis delivers a true representation of legal norms. The fact that it is so counter-intuitive and is typically applied in a mistaken fashion strongly suggests that Hohfeld's analysis is more like a dogma, a re-ordering of our beliefs about rights rather than a more precise description of them. Consider, for example, whether Hohfeld's prohibition on a liberty right correlating with a duty makes sense on the 'interest' theory of rights, described above? On the interest theory, my right to speak freely protects my interest in free speech, and correlates with your duty not to interfere with me when I speak. On the Hohfeldian scheme, we would have to declare this correlation of a liberty right and a duty a mistake. We would instead have to explain first that the primary jural conception that applies when I have the liberty to speak is that others have no right that I do not. But one may well wonder what the point is of looking first to the interest of others in my speech when the interest protected is my interest in speaking without interference.

The third failing has to do with Hohfeld's dogma that all legal jural 'conceptions' must be found as part of a pair, i.e. there must be a jural relation between individual subjects of the law. This would seem to leave no room for rights, duties, or powers *arising by operation of law*.

Some norms arise by operation of law, that is, the law regards certain norms as arising purely on the basis of certain facts. If you beat someone up you will, by operation of law, be liable to action for damages to compensate for the harm you caused. More precisely, upon your committing a trespass to the person, your victim will acquire by operation of law a power to bring an action against you, and you will be liable to be brought into court if your victim exercises that power. The two of you will then, by operation of law, be subject to the regime of rights, duties, and powers under the rules of civil procedure. You will also be liable to an order to pay damages if you are found liable. Tortious and criminal liability are the classic examples of norms arising by operation of law, though there are many others (constructive trusts, estoppels, loss of rights through passage of time by limitation acts, a duty to report income to HMRC in the year it was earned if you earned income, and on and on). The problem with the Hohfeldian analysis is that these operations of law must be re-cast as the exercise of powers by some individual. So, for example, to take the assault case again, on Hohfeldian analysis it would appear that you must be regarded as having a power to endow your victim with a right to sue you for damages. Or consider another case from the law of trusts. If you innocently receive trust property transferred to you in breach of trust, you will not be personally liable to account to the beneficiaries for your innocent expenditure of the funds. But if you then learn that the property was trust property, from that point on you will be liable to dig into your own pocket to reimburse the beneficiaries if you then go on to spend or consume the trust property, for you are no longer innocent of the source of the property. Your new liability to account to, or reimburse, the beneficiaries, arises by operation of law on your coming to know the facts. But from the Hohfeldian perspective, we must analyse this situation as one where every other individual in the world (for anyone might come into the knowledge about the breach of trust and tell you about it) has a power to make you liable, and correspondingly you would have a liability vis-à-vis each of them. Even more weirdly, you might find out about the breach all by yourself, and this would seem to require an illicit Hohfeldian case whereby you had a power over yourself, and a corresponding liability. These results would seem to be crazy.

It is just a mistake to equate the operations of law with the exercise of powers. The law confers powers on people in order to facilitate various things the law regards as worthwhile. The law does not give rights to sue a tortfeasor for the reason that this would be a good technique by which tortfeasors could transfer money to their victims. Thus you do not have a power to endow someone with a claim to money damages by running them down with your car, and it would be perverse to look at running someone down as a novel way of conferring a benefit on them. You have a duty not to run people down, and their right to bring an action against you is *remedial*, to provide for their compensation. The inability to make sense of this distinction indicates a serious deficiency in the analysis.

FURTHER READING

Finnis, J., 'Some Professorial Fallacies About Rights' (1972–73) 4 *Adelaide LR* 377.

Hohfeld ,W., *Fundamental Legal Conceptions as Applied in Judicial Reasoning*, W. W. Cook, ed. (New Haven: Yale University Press, 1923) (originally published in (1913) 23 *Yale LJ* 16 and (1917) 26 *Yale LJ* 710).

MacCormick, N., 'Rights in Legislation' in P. M. S. Hacker and J. Raz (eds), *Law, Morality and Society* (Oxford: Clarendon Press, 1977).

Penner, J. E., 'The Analysis of Rights' (1997) 10 *Ratio Juris* 300–15.

Penner, J. E., 'The Elements of a Normative System' in *The Idea of Property in Law* (Oxford: Clarendon Press, 1997), ch. 2, pp 7–31.

Penner, J., Schiff, D., and Nobles, R. (eds), *Jurisprudence and Legal Theory: Commentary and Materials* (Oxford: Oxford University Press, 2002), chs. 13 and 14.

Raz, J., *The Morality of Freedom* (Oxford: Clarendon Press, 1986).

Raz, J., *Practical Reason and Norms* (Oxford: Oxford University Press, 1990).

8

···

Governing and Obedience

Introduction

The law is one form of authoritative governance and dispute resolution. In this chapter we look at three aspects of authoritative governance which have been regarded as central to the question of authority in moral and political philosophy: the moral duty to govern, the moral right to rule, and the moral obligations of subjects of an authority to obey its directives.

8.1 The duty to govern

In *Natural Law and Natural Rights*, John Finnis takes up a subject, the duty or the responsibility to govern, which has received much less attention than the right to rule and the duty to obey. He introduces the point in this way:

> Authority (and thus the *responsibility* of governing) in a community is to be exercised by those who can in fact effectively settle co-ordination problems for that community. This principle is not the last word on the requirements of practical reasonableness in locating authority; but it is the first and most fundamental. (Italics in the original.)
>
> (J. Finnis, *Natural Law and Natural Rights* (Oxford: Clarendon Press, 1980), p. 246)

Finnis' approach to the problem goes roughly like this: in any large and complex community, there will be a need for rules providing for the cooperation and coordination of individuals for the community to act *as a community*, so that its members survive and flourish, and have a reasonable chance at realising the 'basic goods' of humans (2.6.2); but history shows us that these rules are unlikely to arise through custom; rather, they are typically imposed by an authority who manages to get the bulk of the population to take its say-so as law. Because those in a position to fulfil the moral obligations of practical reasonableness have those obligations (think of the Spiderman principle, 'with great power comes great responsibility'), those who are capable of taking charge and instituting a system of rules for cooperation and the coordination of behaviour have both the right, and the duty, to govern. Leslie Green remarks

> It is important to grasp how radical Finnis's version of this idea is. Others have suggested that effectiveness is a *necessary* condition for justified political authority. If authority's role is to secure some valued end, be it justice or finality in social ordering, then it is bound to count against a putative authority that it lacks any capacity to do so. It may be

that in 1745 the Young Pretender still had the best right to the British Crown; but it is certain that after the disaster at Culloden the political claims of the Jacobites became a fantasy shrouded in tartan. Few legal philosophers (and fewer courts) would now doubt that. What is striking is not only that Finnis regards effectiveness as in such ways necessary for justified authority but that he also regards it as defeasibly sufficient: 'the sheer fact of effectiveness is presumptively (not indefeasibly) *decisive*.' Indeed, a casual reader may be shocked by Finnis's repeated insistence that raw power plays a pivotal role in both the right to rule and the duty to govern. It sounds uncomfortably close to the claim that might makes right—and that is not the sort of thing we expect to hear from a natural lawyer. (Italics in the original.)

(L. Green, 'The Duty to Govern' (2007) 13 *Legal Theory* 165 at p. 169, quoting Finnis, *Natural Law and Natural Rights,* p. 247)

There are two things to notice immediately: in the first place, might gives one the presumptive, i.e. defeasible right and duty to govern, but as this formulation indicates, with the right comes the duty to comply with the dictates of practical reasonableness. Recall that one of the principles of practical reasonableness (2.6.3) is 'Respect for every basic value in every act, meaning ultimately that no choice should be made which directly contravenes any "basic good".' Thus might does not entitle one to pursue evil; it is not a right to tyrannise or exploit. In the second place, the right and duty is a duty to *govern*; it is one thing to take authority because one can exercise effective force so as to institute a regime of rules; it is quite another to *maintain* that authority on a proper footing. Governmental authorities that cannot maintain their authority because they make such a mess of governing will lose that authority. Furthermore, regarding the individuals who stand as the executive, the legislators, and the judges, there must be put in place workable rules for the transmission of authority and succession to offices.

Green argues that Finnis' theory of the right and duty to govern is a kind of *necessity* argument: according to Finnis, a community of any size and complexity *needs* law, and thus law-makers and law appliers. But if this is so, it would seem to place a restriction upon the duty and the right to govern. Whilst it may be true that any community of sufficient size and complexity needs certain framework laws, such as rules that allow the society to deal with cases of serious crime, to establish basic human rights, to set up a workable regime of property rights and economic transactions, modern States clearly do not limit themselves to making rules of this kind. And if that is so, then the *duty* to govern and the *right* to govern may not have the same scope: the right to govern would appear to be greater. That is, we appear to accept that once having established authority by attending to the necessary framework rules, a State is in some way *entitled*, i.e. has the right, to do more, whether in terms of legislation or by way of raising funds through taxation and spending the money to provide goods of various kinds to its subjects.

Green makes a further observation, which might actually be an objection to the particulars of Finnis' theory. Finnis seems to assume that it is possible to identify the obvious areas where cooperation and the coordination of individuals is required, and the duty of the authority is to select from various regimes of rules to fill that need. But in consideration of this Green says the following

Common knowledge of our circumstances cannot simply be assumed. One of the hardest tasks in law and politics is to get people to understand the need for cooperation, especially when it is very complex or involves people unlike or remote from themselves. Two sorts of error are common. First, there may be a need for cooperation that is not adequately felt. Managing climate change poses a coordination problem in Finnis's sense if anything does, and maintaining the planet as a viable habitat for *Homo sapiens* is as clear an example of a humanly necessary task as we have. Any nation or group that could come close to providing an effective solution, or even steps toward an effective procedure *leading* to a solution, would have a powerful obligation to do so. But some people, owing to ignorance, self-deception, or wilful blindness, do not see that this is a task calling for cooperation of an unprecedented kind. The second type of error involves deeply felt coordinative 'needs' that are in fact illusory. In some societies there is a felt need to organise the ritual cutting or amputation of parts of children's genitals without anything that could possibly count as their consent or that would be a morally adequate substitute for it. It would be much better if that 'need' were *not* felt (which is *not* to say that others are thereby authorised to eliminate it). (Italics in the original.)

('The Duty to Govern', p. 177)

So whilst Finnis' theory has clearly raised a vital issue for our understanding the relationship between law and governance, it would seem that there may be more work to be done to address all the issues it raises.

Finally, Green argues that paying attention to the duty to govern raises an important issue about the role of consent in legitimate governance. As we shall see (8.2), the idea that an authority is legitimate is not generally regarded as a sound theoretical foundation for the authority of modern states. But Green draws our attention to the fact that by and large the governors themselves, the officials of the system, do in fact generally consent to taking on their positions of power. This, argues Green, illuminates our commonsense view that it would be the abdication of a government's responsibility if it delegated its core duties to others, say, to take Green's example, the UK Parliament delegating its sovereign powers to the Disney Corporation. Green concludes

Even if it is false that every subject has promised to obey, it may yet be true that many have become rulers because *they* have promised (or otherwise committed themselves) to undertake the task of governance. Surely one reason we think fundamental delegations of the duty to govern are wrong is that we have nominated, elected, and appointed people with the intention that *they* should govern and that we have done so because they have deliberately put themselves in the way of being nominated, elected, and appointed to govern. (Italics in the original.)

('The Duty to Govern', p. 184)

8.2 The right to rule

The issue of the right to rule concerns the question of an authority's moral legitimacy, which is, as we shall see, closely related to its power to issue binding directives to its subjects. Another way of putting the issue is to ask, 'What are the grounds of genuine authority?'. As with the nature of norms, we will draw again heavily on the work of Joseph Raz, so it is useful to review his work on norms in 6.3.2.1, 6.6, and 7.1.

As we have seen in 6.6, Raz posits his famous 'normal justification thesis' (NJT) as the standard basis upon which a subject of an authority acts reasonably in following the directives of an authority. At first glance, then, it would appear that any authority which fulfils the NJT, has a morally legitimate 'right to rule', for the directives of such an authority will, if followed by its subjects, be acting to serve its subjects' interests by better allowing them to comply with the (morally salient) reasons that would apply to them in any case. In this section we will look at some recent challenges to Raz's theory of authority and the right to rule, and see whether they undermine it. (In the rest of this section I draw on the yet unpublished work of, and conversations with, Miguel Lopez-Lorenzo.)

8.2.1 The 'procedure objection'

What I shall call the 'procedure objection' to Raz's theory of authority is as follows: Raz's theory fails to account for our intuitions that there is more to authority or legitimacy than whether or not the directives of authorities provide sound guidance to their subjects; we also care about *how* those directives were issued: the same directive issued by an autocrat does not have the same legitimacy as it would if it had been made by way of a democratic institution. The procedures of law-making are relevant to determining an authority's legitimacy, and they are not taken into account by the NJT; therefore, the NJY is at best a partial explanation for the conditions of legitimate authority. Indeed, it is clearly possible to hold the view that procedure matters more than the output, that is, that fairness in decision-making is more important than whether the directive decided upon is a good one or not. On this view, the principal purpose of an authority is to provide procedures that mediate the conflicts between different stakeholders and provide a common framework for decision-making, and its legitimacy is to be measured by the moral evaluation of those procedures.

Raz's own reply to this objection is, with respect, not very persuasive. He says

> Some people believe that one has a duty to obey anyone who is elected by the majority. Again, that is no problem for the service conception. If that is so it simply shows that the conditions of the service conception are met regarding anyone who is so elected.
>
> (J. Raz, 'The Problem of Authority: Revisiting the Service Conception' (2006) 90 *Minnesota Law Review* 1003 at p. 31)

The problem with this reply is that it is hard to see how it meets the objection. If one may have a duty to comply with a particular authority's procedures because of the moral quality of those procedures, then one has to accept that those procedures can and most likely will result in directives that fail to fulfil the NJT. If that is so, then the authority's directives will not serve the interests of its subjects if they follow them. But the ability of an authority to serve the interests of its subjects through the issuance of authoritative directives is just the service conception's explanation of authority. This is not to deny that on Raz's account procedures are irrelevant to the question of whether the NJT is satisfied—it might well be the case that the adoption of certain procedures (such as the rules of natural justice) make it more likely that an authority will fulfil the NJT, and if so that is a reason to adopt them. But this is an empirical matter. What makes the procedure objection the objection that it is, is its claim that the moral legitimacy of procedures is a conceptual feature of our notion of a legitimate authority, and Raz's attempt to accommodate that would appear to contradict the central claim of the service conception.

There is, however, a better reply, which is simply to distinguish between the legitimacy of institutions and the bindingness of their directives, and say that the service conception concerns the latter, not the former. The idea here is simple; the service conception responds to the question whether it is rational for someone to comply with the directives of an authority, and according to the NJT, this is so when the directive, if followed, will better allow the person to comply with reason. But the fact that an authority's directives comply with the NJT does not mean that the authority is legitimate or deserves respect, just that its directives ought to be complied with. Consider: Saddam Hussein's regime might have been despicable, so not legitimate to say the least, but that was no justification for running red lights in Baghdad, or violating any other particular rule of law. Or consider Gerald Ford's pardon of Richard Nixon for any crimes he may have committed relating to the Watergate Hotel break-in; the pardon was valid and seen as such—Nixon was relieved of any criminal liability and no US prosecutor could possibly have thought otherwise—but the fact of the pardon's legal validity did not bestow any legitimacy on Gerald Ford's decision. Validity is different from legitimacy. (Which is not to deny that they can enter into relationships of dependence—an exercise of a power to issue a directive may be invalid because it is illegitimate (for example, a court order made where a principle of natural justice was not observed) and a purported exercise of power may be illegitimate because not validly exercised—it is just that they do not always do so.) It may be that in many cases in the real world we will be faced with having to trade-off the legitimacy of an authority against the validity of its directives; we might, for example, put up with some stupid directives that capture the imagination of the majority in a representative democracy because we prize the legitimacy of democratic decision-making. So be it. It is hard to see, however, how the existence of this predicament undermines the service conception of authority.

There is one further consideration here. If Raz's reply to the procedure objection is correct it would appear to drive a wedge between epistemic (6.1) and practical authorities; one of the strengths of the service conception is that it applies the same basic analysis to authorities about what we should believe and authorities about what we should do. But the procedure issue is relevant only to the legitimacy of practical authorities. What clearly matters in the case of epistemic authorities is whether they allow us better access to the truth, not the procedures by which they arrived at it. Democratic decision-making cuts no ice in the scientific community; indeed, herd behaviour and groupthink are well-recognised as dangers to determining the truth.

8.2.2 **Darwall's objection**

This objection comes from Stephen Darwall, who proposes a 'second-personal' account of authority. According to Darwall, in every case of practical authority, the subject of the authority must owe an obligation to the authority to obey its directives. He uses as an example the case of a combined epistemic/practical authority, an expert cook, and a novice wishing to prepare a meal properly. Although the expert cook is an epistemic authority, and the novice has good reason to follow the directions the expert cook provides, still, the expert cook has no authority *over* the novice. By this Darwall means to indicate that the novice has no obligation to the expert cook to follow their directions. Darwall concludes on the basis of this sort of example that an essential feature of practical authority is that the subjects of the authority owe the authority itself an obligation to comply with its directives, and this means that the service conception is at best only a partial explanation of authority.

Raz's most considered answer to the objection (found at J. Raz, 'On Respect, Authority, and Neutrality: A Response' (2010) 120 *Ethics* 279 at pp. 300–1) is that we need to distinguish between the epistemic and practical aspects of an expert's authority. Take again the case of the expert cook; *if* the novice wishes to cook well, they will follow the directions of the expert, but as to *whether* the novice should cook any dish at all, the expert cook is not an authority, practical or otherwise, for the novice (normally) knows better than anyone else whether investing his or her time in learning to cook, pleasing friends or not with his or her dishes, and many other considerations lead on the balance of reasons to proceeding to follow the expert cook's directions. On this matter the expert cook simply has no epistemic or practical authority.

There is another reply to Darwall's objection, which is that it is utterly misconceived, at least in the case of the law. The reply is that it is plainly false to say that in general the subjects of the law owe an obligation to Parliament, or the courts, to comply with their legal duties. Whilst legislatures may create rights and impose duties, and courts adjudicate conflicts and determine the rights and duties of the litigants, the duties the subjects of the law owe are typically owed to each other; the duties one finds in the law of tort, contract, property, and crime, are duties owed to other subjects of the law, not to Parliament or the courts. Thus an authority's power to issue directives is not typically exercised so as to create duties owed to the authority itself. Raz suggests that this sort of confusion might arise from the fact that legal authorities typically (though not necessarily) also have a power to impose punishments in the case of *some* breaches of duty. But even as regards this right of the State to deal with breaches of duties we see that Darwall's theory appears deficient. Consider the civil law. Whilst legal authorities issue directives providing remedies for breaches of duty, these overwhelmingly provide for secondary obligations owed by the wrongdoer to their victims, not to Parliament or the courts.

8.3 The duty to obey

Until fairly recently, it was assumed that for the State and the law to function, it was necessary that subjects of the law had a prima facie moral obligation to obey the law. The philosophical problem this posed was how such a moral obligation should be explained and justified. This seems to be the starting point taken by, as we have seen, Plato (2.2.2) and much more recently, Finnis (2.6.5). By prima facie obligation is meant one that is *defeasible*. So, for example, whilst one might have a moral obligation to obey the laws, this is not absolute. If a law was passed requiring parents to kill their first-born sons, the general moral obligation to obey the law in this instance would be defeated, for to comply with such a wicked law would be straightforwardly and outrageously immoral.

A host of different considerations have been proposed as a ground for this general obligation. The notion of consent was here, as elsewhere (see later Part III) brought into play. Could it be said that subjects of the law, in consenting to authority, thereby undertook the moral obligation to obey? The problems with this sort of justification are well known. In the first place, there simply has been no consent to undertake such an obligation by the vast majority of the subjects of the law in the overwhelming majority of legal jurisdictions. It is sometimes said that a notional consent can do the trick; the idea is that a subject may be bound if it would have been a reasonable thing to do to consent, not whether there is any actual consent. But this sort of argument really dispenses with consent rather than depending upon it: if an undertaking to obey all the laws would *not* have been a reasonable thing to consent to, then even actual consent could not *justify* the obligation, and if it would have been a reasonable thing to consent to, then actual consent does not matter. On this 'notional' kind of consent, genuine actual consent is doing no work. On the basis of these sorts of considerations most theorists regard consent as an unlikely ground for the obligation to obey.

Another argument for the existence of the duty is based upon notions of fair play. It has been suggested that those who take the benefits of a legal system should share the burden of complying with its laws. Sometimes this sort of argument is framed as fair play between State and citizen, and sometimes as between citizens themselves. The latter view is obviously more plausible, and there is a sense that someone who would insist upon their own legal rights but seek to shirk duties that go along with respecting the rights of others is playing those others for 'suckers'. But this sort of argument does not really get at the actual problem. The obligation we are seeking to justify is a general (though defeasible) moral obligation to obey every law of the system just because it is a law of the system. Moral obligations of fair play and not treating other people as suckers are general moral obligations in their own right; complying with them does not begin to justify complying with every rule that forms part of whatever body of laws is laid down by an authority. Indeed, complying with some laws will undoubtedly work *unfairness* between subjects of the law (think of various tax regimes), and others will allow or even encourage individuals to treat others like suckers (think of financial services law, advertising regulations, and contract law generally).

Another approach, one which, as we have seen, Finnis (2.6.5) endorses, is to argue that violations of the law set an example to others; seeing someone failing to comply with the law will encourage disobedience, causing harm to the legal system, and making it less effective, and therefore less able to promote the social welfare. As the foundation for a general duty to obey the law, this looks hopeless. In the first place, contrary to the assumptions underlying the argument, certain cases of disobedience may shock people and stir them to greater levels of obedience. But assuming the sight of others obeying would lead to more disobedience, it is simply the case that many acts of disobedience, say fiddling your tax return, or smoking cannabis in the privacy of your home, would never be detected, so could hardly cause harm to the system by serving as examples of bad behaviour. So, remembering that the duty sought to be defended is a *general* one, applying to each and every law on each and every occasion for its observance, this sort of consideration does not seem capable of doing the job.

For the foregoing reasons, theorists such as M. B. E. Smith and Joseph Raz argue that there is no general though defeasible moral obligation to obey the law. Raz argues in analogy with friendship, that certain people may have a general moral obligation to obey the law. In the same way that being someone's friend creates special, expressive reasons to act in certain ways (for example an exclusionary reason, i.e. duty, not to betray a friend), people who respect and are more or less deeply committed to their communities may come under a general obligation to obey the law as an expression of that respect and commitment. But that would not ground a general obligation to obey on everyone.

Raz argues that the absence of a general obligation to obey the law does not lead to the following paradox, which can be framed in terms of a question: how can a good State, with a right to rule, i.e. a legitimate authority, have that right to rule if it is not also the case that its subjects have a general duty to comply with its directives? Aren't the right to rule and the duty to obey two sides of the same coin?

Raz's solution to the paradox, if it is one, is subtle. He makes his case by drawing upon and re-casting the distinction between laws which address wrongs which are *mala in se*, acts that are morally wrong in themselves, such as murder, and those which address wrongs that are *mala prohibita*, wrongs which depend for their wrongfulness just on the fact they have been made the subject of regulation, such as parking offences. These latter cases Raz regards as cases where the rules are created so as to provide a scheme of social coordination. Raz then asks: even in a good State whose laws properly address acts *mala in se* such as murder and whose social coordination rules coordinate the behaviour of the subjects in a fair and efficient manner to enhance social welfare, such as road traffic, do the subjects of such a State have a general obligation to obey the law? Raz says 'no'. The gist of his answer is this: in the case of laws governing acts that are *mala in se*, one has a moral obligation not to murder, steal, rape, and so on, whether the law prohibits them or not. Where the law provides *prudential* reasons to comply with these moral duties, such as the punishments that will follow their breach, it gives people who are insufficiently motivated by their free-standing moral obligation not to do these things additional reasons to fulfil their duties. But prudential reasons of this kind do not amount to moral reasons. So the moral obligation here is the free-standing moral obligation not to commit such acts, and so there is no ground for a general duty to comply with the law in this area. As regards coordination rules, the point is a little different. Raz uses the example of whether one has an obligation not to pollute a river. If everyone is polluting, one has no obligation not to pollute the river oneself, unless by one's example one might initiate a practice of keeping the river clean. On the other hand, if the river is unpolluted and people generally refrain from polluting it then one has a moral reason not to pollute it oneself. So the moral obligation here depends upon the fact of social coordination. Where there is coordination to keep the river clean, the very fact of that coordination (plus the fact that clean rivers are preferable to polluted ones) gives one a reason not to pollute, a reason that would be absent if the coordination were absent. Now consider a law prohibiting pollution of the river. Raz denies that such a rule creates an obligation to obey it. What matters is whether the law works so that people do indeed coordinate their behaviour to keep the river clean.

> It matters not at all to one's moral reasoning whether the practice of keeping the rivers clean is sanctioned by law, is maintained by exhortations and propaganda undertaken by enthusiastic individuals, or whether it grew up entirely spontaneously. It is the existence of the practice that matters not (except in special circumstances) its origins or surrounding circumstances. On the other hand, suppose that the law requires keeping the rivers clean but that nobody obeys and the rivers have turned into public sewers. The moral reasons for not throwing refuse into them that we have been considering do not exist in such circumstances notwithstanding the legal requirement not to do so.
>
> (J. Raz, *The Authority of Law*, 2nd ed. (Oxford: Oxford University Press, 2009), p. 249)

So the law, if efficacious, can *result* in one's having a moral obligation to coordinate one's behaviour with others, but this does not give rise to an obligation to obey every law whose purpose is to instil coordination; it is the fact of the social coordination itself which gives one moral reasons to join in.

FURTHER READING

Darwall, S., 'Authority and Reasons: Exclusionary and Second Personal' (2010) 120 *Ethics* 257.

Finnis, J., *Natural Law and Natural Rights* (Oxford: Clarendon Press, 1980), pp. 245–52.

Green, L., 'The Duty to Govern' (2007) 13 *Legal Theory* 165.

Hershovitz, S., 'The Role of Authority' (2010) 11(7) *Philosophers' Imprint*.

Raz, J., *The Morality of Freedom* (Oxford: Clarendon Press, 1986).

Raz, J., *Practical Reason and Norms* (Oxford: Oxford University Press, 1990).

Raz, J., *The Authority of Law*, 2nd ed. (Oxford: Oxford University Press, 2009), chs 12–15.

Raz, J., 'On Respect, Authority, and Neutrality: A Response' (2010) 120 *Ethics* 279.

Smith, M., 'Is There a *Prima Facie* Obligation to Obey the Law?' (1972–73) 82 *Yale Law Journal* 950.

9

Law and Adjudication

Introduction

One of the central features of any legal system are institutions, typically courts, for the resolution of conflicts. The nature of adjudication, and what it tells about the nature of law, are therefore important topics in the philosophy of law. The literature in this area is vast; here we will concentrate on three important claims about law which rely heavily on a characterisation of adjudication. The first derives from a loose jurisprudential movement in the United States in the first part of the last century, called 'Legal Realism'. Some realists claimed, on the basis of a certain scepticism about the way legal rules constrained judges to decide a case one way or the other, that judges had much more discretion to decide cases based on their overall impression of the justice of the case than is conventionally accepted. We will examine these claims, and then look at the important contribution by the philosopher Ludwig Wittgenstein, which meshes quite nicely with critiques of the legal realist's rule scepticism. Next we will look at 'legal interpretivism'. This is a theory of law, of which Dworkin's 'law as integrity' is the most famous example, which draws much of its attraction from the way in which it characterises legal discourse, in particular legal argumentation before the courts. Finally, we will consider the relation between the rule of law and adjudication, and what this says about the nature of law.

9.1 The American legal realist challenge to the determinacy of legal rules

American legal realism had its origins in a reaction to 'formalism', a view of the nature of law probably most exuberantly propounded by the Harvard law teacher Christopher Columbus Langdell, who argued that legal reasoning was akin to a science, in which the underlying logic of legal doctrine was discovered by those who had mastered its techniques. Thus a judge reaching a decision in a case where the law was in dispute need never consider what the effects of a rule were, or in any way be concerned with whether it was moral or not; nor was there any room for a judge to develop the law by laying down new rules; proper consideration of the legal doctrine and the principles underlying resolved any and every issue. One might well respond 'get real'; and this is precisely what the realists did—their use of the term 'realism' simply indicated that they intended to be realistic about legal indeterminacy and the way judges decided cases.

The main concern of the realist movement was the desire to discover how judicial decisions were reached in reality, which involved a playing down of the role of established rules, or the 'law in books', to discover the other factors that contributed towards a judicial decision, in order to discover the 'law in action'. Once the realists had deciphered the factors that led to judicial decisions, both non-legal and legal, they were concerned with the prediction of future decisions. The realists were adamant that only when the 'law in action' was properly understood could a more accurate prediction of judicial decisions be made. In addition, they were of the opinion that judicial decision-making would be more amenable to the needs of society if judges were more open about the non-legal factors which had influenced their decisions, instead of instinctively trying to submerge them behind the façade of syllogistic legal reasoning.

From this brief synopsis, it can be seen that the realists were radical but they were certainly not revolutionary, unlike some of their successors. They were concerned with improving the legal system and they saw that this must emerge out of their criticism of the courts. The realist approach was certainly court-centred and the rule sceptics, who constituted the bulk of the movement, mainly concentrated on the discovery of what the real rules were. However, the fact sceptics could be said to have a more fundamental critique of the established system by not only doubting the value of simply relying on the paper rules, but also doubting the adequacy of the courts as fact-finding institutions. As will be seen, such scepticism leaves little room for the improvement of the judicial system because it casts doubt on its value as a dispute-resolving mechanism, which after all is arguably one of the more important functions of a legal system.

9.1.1 Varieties of realist fact scepticism and rule scepticism

9.1.1.1 Oliver Wendell Holmes

Mr Justice Holmes of the United States Supreme Court was in many ways the founder of the American realist movement—he certainly generated the most iconic realist quotations, of which the first two given below are the most famous. He had a pragmatic approach to judicial decision-making, including a scepticism of the ability of general rules to provide the solution to particular cases.

> General propositions do not determine concrete cases...I always say in conference that no case can be settled by general propositions, that I will admit any general proposition you like and decide the case either way.
>
> (O. W. Holmes cited in W. E. Rumble, *American Legal Realism: Skepticism, Reform and the Judicial Process* (Ithaca, NY: Cornell University Press, 1968), pp. 39–40. Rumble's analysis is followed to a great extent in this chapter.)

In addition to being a rule sceptic, Holmes was at the forefront of recognising the role of extra-legal factors in judicial decision-making

> ...the life of the law has not been logic, it has been experience. The felt necessities of the time, the prevalent moral and political theories, intuitions of public policy, avowed or unconscious, even the prejudices which judges share with their fellow men, have had a good deal more to do than the syllogism in determining the rules by which men should be governed.
>
> In substance the growth of the law is legislative...The very considerations which judges most rarely mention, and always with an apology, are the secret root from which the law draws all the juices of life. I mean, of course, considerations of what is expedient for the community concerned.
>
> (M. Lerner (ed.), *The Mind and Faith of Justice Holmes: His Speeches, Essays, Letters, and Judicial Opinions* (New York: Random House, 1943), pp. 51–4)

Holmes was convinced that the judiciary plays a legislative role. Indeed, he saw it as the essence of judicial decision-making, not simply something they do in cases where the law was unsettled. While recognising that there are many non-legal factors which influence the law—Holmes mentioned morality, politics, and prejudices—he saw 'policy' as the most fundamental element, though judges were somewhat abashed in their use of it. He advocated that the judiciary should become more open in their use of policy so that there was no longer the need to peer behind the precedents and false mechanical reasoning to see what was really going on.

Furthermore, Holmes introduced a putative predictive approach to the law. For Holmes, law, or more correctly a legal duty, was simply a prediction that if a person behaved in a certain way he would be punished. This was looking at law from the perspective of the 'bad man'

> ...if we take the view of our friend the bad man we shall find that he does not care two straws for the axioms or deductions, but that he does want to know what the Massachusetts or English courts are likely to do in fact. I am much of his mind. The prophecies of what the courts will do in fact, and nothing more pretentious, are what I mean by the law.
>
> (O. W. Holmes, 'The path of the law' (1897) 10 *Harv L Rev* 457, pp. 460–1)

For Holmes and the other realists the notions of legal duty and legal right were not to be answered by fruitless searches for the source of obligation, whether legal or moral, but by means of a simple predictive exercise. For most realists this was simply a prediction of how the courts would react to particular behaviour

> ...when I talk of the law I talk as a cynic. I don't care a damn if twenty professors tell me that a decision is not law if I know that the courts will enforce it.
>
> (O. W. Holmes cited in M. D. Howe (ed.), *Holmes-Laski Letters: The Correspondence of Mr Justice Holmes and Harold J. Laski* (Cambridge, Mass: Harvard University Press, 1953), vol. 1, p. 115)

However, later realists expanded this behavioural analysis to see what sort of institutional response followed particular behaviour to cover not only a judicial response but the whole range of 'official' responses.

9.1.1.2 Karl Llewellyn

Llewellyn is often seen as the central figure in the American realist movement. His writings, spanning the most productive period of realism, not only contained within them the core themes for the movement, but also developed from being very critical of the judiciary to taking on a more constructive attitude. In 1931 he outlined the major themes of realism (K. N. Llewellyn, 'Some realism about realism: responding to Dean Pound' (1931) 44 *Harv L Rev* 1222).

He insisted upon the reality of judicial law-making and indeed saw it as essential in matching the law to the rapidity of social change. Law for Llewellyn was a means for the achievement of social ends and for this reason it should not be backward-looking for its development but should be forward-looking in terms of moulding the law to fit the current and future needs of society. Furthermore, realists should be concerned with the effects of law on society and he insisted that law should be evaluated principally in terms of its effects.

The realist's concern for the consequences of legal decisions was matched, according to Llewellyn, by their distrust of legal rules. Legal rules do not describe what the courts are purporting to do, nor do they describe how individuals concerned with the law behave. Legal rules as found in books and emphasised in judicial decisions do not accord with reality. Rules, as described in books and in judicial decisions, have essentially taken on a life of their own; they have in fact become 'reified' (see the approach of the critical legal studies movement, Chapter 12), and as such bear little resemblance to the actuality of the legal process. Legal rules are not the 'heavily operative factor' in producing the decisions of courts, although they appear to be so on the surface. The realist should be concerned with discovering those factors that really influence judges, and judges in turn should be more open about using them. It should be pointed out at once that while realists occasionally suggested that deciding cases was something of a game and that judges consciously manipulated legal rules, the claim was not generally made that judges routinely acted in bad faith, and that the writing of judgments in which legal rules were cited for justification was all done in bad faith. If there was a charge of bad faith, it lay against only those judges and scholars who denied that judging involved more than the formalist's mechanical application of uncontroversial rules.

Llewellyn also advocated a different approach to the study of law. He advocated that law be studied in far narrower categories than had been the practice in the past. He saw that the use of general rules to cover a vast array of different situations produced a distortion in the form of decisions that have adverse effects on the community. To apply the same rules to different situations is counter-productive because it ignores the fact that different considerations ought to apply. To apply the same principles of frustration in contract law to shipping cases involving the blockage of the Suez canal in 1956, and to employment contracts in the 1990s serves no useful purpose except to please those formalists who insist on a false uniformity in order to satisfy their desire to see law as a system isolated from the events it is purporting to control.

The requirement that law must be evaluated in terms of its consequences led to Llewellyn developing a sophisticated analysis of the purposes of law in his later works. Llewellyn described the basic functions of law as 'law-jobs' (K. N. Llewellyn, *My Philosophy of Law* (Boston, Mass: Boston Law Co., 1941), pp. 183–6). Law is an 'institution' which is necessary in society and which is comprised not only of rules but also an 'ideology and a body of pervasive and powerful ideals which are largely unspoken, largely implicit, and which pass unmentioned in the books'.

Jurisprudence should be concerned with looking at the whole, including the important ideals, instead of merely concentrating on the rules. 'The wider view of rules-in-their-setting yields rules both righter and more effective.' Law has jobs to do within a society. These are:

(1) The disposition of the trouble case: a wrong, a grievance, a dispute. This is the garage-repair work or the going concern of society, with (as case law shows) its continuous effect upon the remaking of the order of society.

(2) The preventive channelling of conduct and expectation so as to avoid trouble, and together with it, the effective reorientation of conduct and expectations in similar fashion. This does not mean merely, for instance, new legislation; it is instead, what new legislation (among other things) is about, and is for.

(3) The allocation of authority and the arrangement of procedures which mark action as being authoritative; which includes all of any constitution, and much more.

(4) The positive side of law's work, seen as such, and seen not in detail, but as a net whole: the net organization of society as a whole so as to provide integration, direction, and incentive.

(5) 'Juristic method' to use a single slogan to sum up the task of handling the legal materials and tools and people developed for the other jobs—to the end that those materials and tools and people are kept doing their law-jobs, and doing them better, until they become a source of revelation of new possibility and achievement.

(K. N. Llewellyn, *My Philosophy of Law* (Boston, Mass: Boston Law Co., 1941), pp. 186–7; see further K. N. Llewellyn, 'The normative, the legal and the law-jobs: the problem of juristic method' (1940) 49 *Yale LJ* 1355)

The first three jobs ensure society's survival and continuation, whilst the latter two increase efficiency and expectations. One may disagree with Llewellyn's list of the jobs of law but they do provide a more holistic approach to law-making and judicial activity than others. Llewellyn's law-jobs are not simply about making law open, accessible, and clear, they concern the pivotal role and function of law in society. Society, according to Llewellyn, will develop law institutions to perform these jobs. Is Llewellyn's list of tasks performed by law better than any other list? Is there any proof that the law actually does perform these jobs? His study of the Cheyenne Indians in the United States was an attempt to prove that even 'primitive' societies exhibit the first of his law-jobs (K. N. Llewellyn and E. A. Hoebel, *The Cheyenne Way* (Norman, Okla: University of Oklahoma Press, 1941)), and his contribution to and analysis of the American Uniform Commercial Code seemed to fit in with his second law-job (W. Twining, *Karl Llewellyn and the Realist Movement* (London: Weidenfeld & Nicolson, 1973), chs. 11 and 12). It seems better to view his list of law-jobs as both descriptive and prescriptive. If law is seen as a whole, as an integral and fundamental part of society, instead of looking at it in isolation simply as a set of rules to be pieced together like a legal jigsaw, then the true functions of law will be seen to be in line with his law-jobs.

9.1.1.3 Jerome Frank

Judge Jerome Frank, a federal judge in the United States, shared with all realists a scepticism of formalism but if anything his scepticism was much more fundamental. He saw that there were two categories of realists; first, the rule sceptics represented by Llewellyn, whose aim was in part to increase legal certainty or 'predictability'. Rule sceptics 'consider it socially desirable that lawyers should be able to predict to their clients the decisions in most lawsuits not yet commenced' (J. Frank, *Law and the Modern Mind* (Gloucester, Mass: Peter Smith, 1970), p. x). Rule sceptics were united in their belief that the paper rules, those formal rules found in judicial decisions and in books, were unreliable as guides in the prediction of decisions. If the real rules are discovered then a better description of uniformities in judicial decision-making is achieved and therefore reliance on the real rules will yield greater certainty.

While not disagreeing with this, Frank was dissatisfied with the narrowness of the rule sceptics' field of enquiry.

In this undertaking, the rule sceptics concentrate almost exclusively on upper-court opinions. They do not ask themselves whether their own or any other prediction device will render it possible for a lawyer or a layman to prophesy, before an ordinary suit is instituted or comes to trial in a trial court, how it will be decided. In other words, these rule sceptics seek means for making accurate guesses, not about decisions of trial courts,

> but about decisions of upper courts when trial-court decisions are appealed. These scep-
> tics cold-shoulder the trial courts. Yet, in most instances, these sceptics do not inform
> their readers that they are writing chiefly of upper courts.
>
> (*Law and the Modern Mind*, p. xi)

In other words rule sceptics, like many formalists, are concerned simply with the appeal
courts' decisions where legal rules and precedents take on a life of their own without much
regard to non-legal factors, or indeed to the question of whether the facts arrived at in the
lower court were actually the real facts. Appeal courts generally do not debate the facts,
and this, according to Frank, obscures a more fundamental problem. This led Frank to
discuss the second group of realists with which he identified, namely the 'fact sceptics'.

> Their primary interest is in the trial courts. No matter how precise or definite may be the
> formal legal rules, say these fact sceptics, no matter what the discoverable uniformities
> behind these formal rules, nevertheless it is impossible, and will always be impossible,
> because of the elusiveness of the facts on which decisions turn, to predict future deci-
> sions in most (not all) lawsuits, not yet begun or not yet tried.
>
> (*Law and the Modern Mind*, p. xi)

Frank was not alone in having a particular concern with the judicial response to the
facts of the case; this sensitivity is indeed one of the hallmarks of realist writing, to
which we now turn.

9.1.2 Sensitivity to facts and fact scepticism

In recent work, which both re-assesses realist writings and aims to develop legal realism
in a new direction, Brian Leiter states

> The Core Claim of Legal Realism consists of the following descriptive thesis about judi-
> cial decision-making: judges respond primarily to the stimulus of the facts. Put less
> formally—but also somewhat less accurately—the Core Claim of Realism is that judges
> reach decisions based on what they think would be fair on the facts of the case, rather
> than on the basis of the applicable rules of law.
>
> (Brian Leiter, 'Rethinking Legal Realism: Toward a Naturalized Jurisprudence' (1997) 76
> *Texas LR* 267 at p. 275)

However, the realist attention to the fact specificity of decisions played out in two quite
distinct ways: the first was a sort of 'fact scepticism', typified by the work of Frank,
which essentially claimed that the facts of cases were 'elusive' and therefore one could
never produce any theory which systematically mapped the facts of cases to the decisions of the court; thus the possibility of finding rules predicting judicial decisions on
the basis of the facts was essentially nil. The second response to fact specificity, typified
by the work of Llewellyn, was not that it was impossible to discern predictive rules, but
that such rules encompassed much more than the doctrinal rules of law.

9.1.2.1 Frank's fact scepticism

According to Frank, if we take the normal mode of judicial decision-making as the
application of legal rules to the facts of a case then, even if the rules are clear, such as not
parking on a double yellow line, or obeying the speed limit or driving on the left-hand

side of the road, it is still not possible to predict with certainty which way the trial court will decide simply because of the elusiveness of the facts. Frank points to two main groups of elusive factors which cannot be captured by any predictive theory based on observation of the behaviour of the courts.

> First, the trial judge in a non-jury trial or the jury in a jury trial must learn about the facts from the witnesses; and witnesses, being humanly fallible, frequently make mistakes in observation of what they saw and heard, or in their recollections of what they observed, or in their court-room reports of those recollections. Second, the trial judges or juries, also human, may have prejudices—often unconscious, unknown even to themselves—for or against some of the witnesses, or the parties to the suit, or the lawyers.
>
> (*Law and the Modern Mind*, pp. xii–xiii)

Rule sceptics with their predictive models assumed that there is an ascertainable set of facts, otherwise their attempts at predicting the results of court cases by looking at the 'real rules' would not have been possible. Frank denied that there is this certainty in the judicial process and claimed that if his model is followed there is no way in which predictions can be made. In addition, he denied that the rule sceptics could include within their real rules the second set of elusive elements he identified, which included the racial, religious, political, or economic prejudices of the judge and jury. Some of these prejudices may be uniform so that it is possible to say that such a judge does not favour women, or that a juror from such and such a background will not favour blacks, but it is impossible to include all the hidden, sometimes unconscious biases of judge and jurors. Such idiosyncratic biases cannot be factored into an analysis of behavioural patterns.

Furthermore, Frank argued that in a trial court the law and the facts become intertwined—there is not a simple application of the law to the facts; instead, the law emerges in an adversarial manner just as the facts do. When the jury comes to its verdict, they do not distinguish between law and fact, and in this state of confusion they decide the case on other grounds.

> Many juries in reaching their verdicts act on their emotional responses to the lawyers and witnesses; they like or dislike, not any legal rule, but they do like an artful lawyer for the plaintiff, the poor widow, the brunette with the soulful eyes, and they do dislike the big corporation, the Italian with a thick, foreign accent.
>
> (J. Frank, *Courts on Trial* (Princeton, NJ: Princeton University Press, 1949), p. 130)

These mistakes are simply compounded in the appeal court, which usually relies on the facts as adopted by the trial court. By concentrating on appeal court decisions, all lawyers, including the rule sceptics, appear to be accepting that there can be consistency and that the doctrines of precedent and stare decisis are important, or at least can be used to help to identify patterns of judicial behaviour. Frank denied this.

> This weakness [of the precedent doctrine] will also infect any substitute precedent system, based on 'real rules' which the rule sceptics may discover, by way of anthropology—i.e., the mores, customs, folkways—or psychology, or statistics, or studies of the political, economic, and social backgrounds of judges, or otherwise. For no rule can be hermetically sealed against the intrusion of false or inaccurate oral testimony which the trial judge or jury may believe.
>
> (*Law and the Modern Mind*, pp. xvi–xvii)

Although Frank's views were somewhat impressionistic, his own experience as a judge should not be discounted. To discover whether his views have value, the law student ought perhaps to spend more time observing trial court proceedings, rather than simply relying on reading appeal court judgments and their synthesis by academics, whether formalist or realist (rule sceptics). Even so, at the end of the day Frank's fact scepticism is implausible simply because it is wildly exaggerated. The problems of determining with a fair degree of accuracy and certainty what happened from the testimony of witnesses are well known, and we also know that one of the roles of the lawyer is to shape the telling of the facts to his client's advantage, and that lawyers do indeed do this. That does not mean that we have no critical faculties which we can bring to bear so that we can avoid, at the very least, wholesale errors in fact-finding and the worst influences of prejudice. The adversary trial was instituted for the very reason that it is believed that presenting the evidence and arguing the significance of it from two opposing perspectives enhances the likelihood that errors of fact and understanding of the facts will be minimised. To accept that the facts are so elusive, that there is simply no rhyme or reason to the judge's or jury's decision, seems to misdescribe and insult both at the same time.

It is also worth pointing out that one does not really find any argument that supports a genuine scepticism about facts. Rather, the scepticism lies in a scepticism about human rationality. Frank, no more than any other realist, denied that judges and juries responded to *something*; he was not denying that there was some reality, something that actually happened which led the parties to come before the court. His scepticism lay in a judge's or jury's ability to respond to that reality in any sort of rational way; his position ultimately amounts to the claim that judges and juries are unable to decide like cases alike and unlike cases differently, which is often seen as the most basic requirement of justice. Again, whether in fact judges and juries often fail to be rational in just this way is open to question; a claim that they are constitutively unable to do so seems exorbitant.

9.1.3 Rule scepticism

Formalism painted an ideal syllogistic picture of the judicial process, where the clearly established statutes or precedents are applied to the facts with little or no exercise of judgement on the part of the judges. Judges are portrayed in this formalist conception as machine-like and totally neutral. Rule sceptics were very critical of this established position and pointed to many fallacies in the traditional approach.

Realists first of all pointed to the vast panoply of precedents that had been built up in common law systems over the centuries. Realists argued that so many precedents could not be reconciled in any logical coherent way. Since precedents were inconsistent, there was no one right answer to a legal dispute, simply a variety of answers from which the judge had to choose one. Douglas wrote that 'there are usually plenty of precedents to go around; and with the accumulation of decisions, it is no great problem for a lawyer to find legal authority for most propositions' (W. O. Douglas, 'Stare decisis' in *Essays in Jurisprudence from the Columbia Law Review* (New York: Columbia University Press, 1963), p. 19).

Realists not only pointed to the fact that there are numerous precedents, they also insisted that there are numerous techniques for interpreting precedents. Throughout his works Llewellyn referred to the judicial ability to be able to avoid precedents that conflict with the judge's view. A judge may simply find a different ratio to the case in question or may distinguish on the grounds that the ratio is too wide or too narrow for the facts of the instant case. In this way judges downgrade unfavourable precedents whilst boosting those that favour their particular view. Llewellyn even went on to list 64 'available, impeccable precedent techniques' used by judges and academics alike for constructing their scheme of legal precedents and statutes. The fact that there are many methods of interpreting precedents increases the uncertainty of the law many-fold (K. N. Llewellyn, *The Common Law Tradition* (Boston, Mass: Little, Brown & Co., 1960), pp. 75–92).

Other realists pointed to the logical indeterminacy of established rules, in that no particular proposition could be said to generate a general proposition. This is a further development on Llewellyn's idea that a ratio of a prior case can easily be distinguished in a current case, the idea being that the ratio of that prior case is particular to that case and it cannot be used as a general rule in future cases with different facts. Of course it is easy to show that as a matter of simple logic, one can always 'get round' a rule by point-ing to some feature of the novel case which distinguishes it from the case where the precedent was laid down. As we shall see when we turn to Hart's discussion of rules and look at Wittgenstein's writings on rule following, the indeterminacy of rules is an issue with which any legal theory must contend, but the fact that logically one can always get around a rule is not a good argument for scepticism, because applying rules correctly is not an exercise in logic in the first place.

For the rule sceptic reliance on rules is a fallacy and judges either consciously or un-consciously continue to play the game by paying lip-service to rule formalism. Judges and lawyers do this because they are educated in that fashion. They are not prepared to make clear the real reasons for their decisions because it would be seen as a betrayal of the ideal of the rule of law, the idea that law is neutral and objective and not dependent upon any personal factors. For the realists it was quite clear that the ideal of a logical and coherent system is impossible to achieve and in fact the judge is not bound by any antecedent rules. It follows that for the realists a judge should not feel hidebound by established precedent because there is no logical reason that dictates a choice of one precedent over another; there is in fact only the political need to respect the ideal of the rule of law, so the judge, instead of being backward-looking, should look forwards and make policy-based decisions that are best for society. The fact that this amounted to an attack on the liberal ideal of the rule of law was not developed by the realists but has been taken on board by one of their successor movements—the critical legal scholars (see Chapter 13).

9.1.4 The prediction of decisions

The realists distrusted legal rules as giving the answers to disputes, but the rule sceptics at least denied that this meant that cases were unpredictable. They were concerned with discovering uniformities in judicial decision-making, so enabling the forecasting of future undecided cases as well as being concerned with making such predictions more accurate. 'The essential purpose behind the realist stress on predictivism was the pro-motion of certainty' (N. Duxbury, *Patterns of American Jurisprudence* (Oxford: Clarendon Press, 1995), p. 130). Formalists, of course, would explain judicial uniformity on the basis of the impact of pre-existing legal rules. The application by different judges of the same rule or principle to a similar set of facts is the main or sole reason for uniformity in judicial decision-making according to the traditional approach. Furthermore, tradi-tionalists would argue that the reason why, in a few cases, there seems to be doubt about the outcome of a particular undecided case is mainly due to a defect in the scheme of established rules they are concerned with identifying. They would argue that the law is not a perfect machine, that there are bound to be vague, inconsistent, and conflicting rules, and that the only way of improving the system is to tinker with the rules, to make them compatible and clear.

The realists argued that the existence of uniformities in judicial behaviour cannot be explained simply by the examination of rules but has to be explained by an analysis of the 'real rules', which includes legal and non-legal factors. Many of the rule sceptics agreed that there was some uniformity in judicial decision-making but it could only be explained successfully in terms of the real rules, and furthermore they played down the idea that simple intra-systemic modification of the paper rules would produce anything but a marginal improvement in judicial uniformity. Only an understanding of the real rules and more importantly a judicial recognition of, and more overt use of, these real rules would increase predictability of judicial decision-making in the future.

This concern with prediction shows that far from being radical, realism is quite a conservative approach to law. As Duxbury states

> ...predictivist-inspired realism treats as notionally desirable the facilitation of a for-mally certain, 'prediction-friendly' system of law. At the same time, the general pre-dictivist quest for legal certainty betrays an implicit fear of judicial discretion and incertitude. And it is thus that realism, certainly in its predictivist guise, appears to attempt to replace one formalist conception of law only to replace it with another.... The assumption that it may be possible to predict future legal decisions with consider-able, if not quite total, accuracy is hardly less formalist—is hardly less supportive of so-called slot machine justice—than the basic Langdellian belief that legal doctrine is reducible to a handful of common law principles which may be applied uncontrover-sially to future legal disputes.
>
> (*Patterns of American Jurisprudence*, p. 131)

The realists were essentially advocating a scientific or behavioural analysis of judicial decision-making rather along the lines of an anthropologist. However, although there were many attempts at providing predictive models, some of which are outlined in this section, it is right to say that they were somewhat crude and underdeveloped. As Beutel noted, the realists' 'scientific work' on law 'reached approximately the same stage as botany would, had its efforts been devoted wholly to counting leaves on trees' (F. K. Beutel, *Some Potentialities of Experimental Jurisprudence as a New Branch of Social Science* (Lincoln, Nebr: University of Nebraska Press, 1957), p. 112). The crudity of their analy-sis can be explained to a certain extent by the fact that the production of a predictive model was only part of their work; indeed, most spent their time on the critical aspect of realism, rule scepticism, rather than on the constructive job of forecasting and its improvement. Furthermore, those realists who did attempt a predictive model tended to concentrate on certain factors to the exclusion of others. For example, Rodell seem-ingly accurately predicted courts' decisions on the basis of an analysis of the personal views, characteristics, temperament, background, and political views of the judges involved in cases (F. Rodell, 'For every justice, judicial deference is a sometime thing' (1962) 50 *Geo LJ* 700).

However, a truly realist approach would have to identify all those non-legal factors such as morality, public opinion, judicial prejudice, and other personal factors, issues of public policy, governmental pressure, economic, sociological, and political factors, as well as the role of established rules if it was to present a totally rounded and accurate predictive model. Such a task would be mammoth, perhaps impossible. It is perhaps because of this that other realists tended to concentrate simply on judicial behaviour and eschewed any attempt to explain what the factors were that motivated judicial behaviour.

Herman Oliphant viewed patterns of regularity as characteristic of judicial decision-making but his rule scepticism meant that he could not put down such regularities to simple judicial reliance on stare decisis. Instead, he advocated a behaviouralist approach to forecasting. He argued that attention should not be focused on the judicial decision or the vocal behaviour of the judge as this simply contained the paper rules and obscured the real rules. Realists should ignore the judicial rationalisations and concentrate on judges' non-vocal behaviour. This simply means that legal analysis should be concerned with an examination of what judges actually do when 'stimulated' by the facts of the case before them, as a scientist may examine the effect of various stimulants such as light, heat, food, etc. on rats in a laboratory (H. Oliphant, 'A return to stare decisis' (1928) 14 *ABA* J 73).

Over a period of time the analyst can build up a picture of patterns of judicial behaviour not only in relation to particular disputes but also pointing to different approaches by different judges. He may find that judges are more likely to apply the rules of evidence in favour of those accused of white-collar crimes over those accused of joyriding, so that the chances of the latter being found not guilty are much less than the former. In addition, he may find that in those cases where both are found guilty, the likelihood is that the joyrider will be more severely punished than the white-collar criminal, even though the maximum sentence for each might be the same. Such conclusions will re-inforce the idea that the paper rules are simply manipulated by judges and that the real rules can only be discerned by ignoring them.

Throughout his long period of writing, Llewellyn was always of the opinion that court decisions were highly predictable. In his early works he denied that this predictability, or what he called 'reckonability', was primarily due to the impact of established rules and he advocated instead a behaviouralist approach along the lines of that developed by Rodell and Oliphant. However, in his later works Llewellyn moved towards a less radical model which, while not succumbing to the formalist obsession with rules, does appear to put more weight on judicial decision-making as containing all that is required for prediction of future decisions.

This change of direction in Llewellyn's writings emerges from his 'law-jobs' theory. Remember that the fifth law-job as identified by Llewellyn was the 'juristic method', namely the traditions of handling legal materials and tools for the other law-jobs he identifies. Those concerned with the law, or the 'men of law' as Llewellyn labelled them, develop legal 'crafts' by which he meant 'advocacy, counselling, judging, law-making, administering,...mediation, organisation, policing, teaching, scholarship' (K. N. Llewellyn, *My Philosophy of Law* (Boston, Mass: Boston Law Co., 1941), p. 188). In relation to the judicial craft, Llewellyn was at pains to point out that this is sometimes obscured by the end-product, namely, the judicial decision which contains within it legal rules. The formalist then becomes solely concerned with the rules and ignores the craft of the judge:

> [Rules] stand with such relative conspicuousness to observation, they accumulate so easily, they can be gathered so conveniently, and they are so easy to substitute for either thought or investigation, that they have drawn the attention of jurisprudes too largely to themselves; to the rules—as if the rules stood and could stand alone. A first evil has been the attribution to the rules of many results, e.g. of court decisions—which rest instead on the phases of judicial tradition. Not the least of that tradition is the ideal of

justice to be reached, an ideal equipped with a whole set of Janus-faced techniques for the handling of rules to keep them out of the way of justice. Reckonablity of result here lies only sometimes in the rules; it lies with some consistency in the tradition.

(*My Philosophy of Law*, pp. 188–9)

The reason for the predictability of decisions in the United States appellate courts lay, according to Llewellyn, not with the rules themselves but with the common-law tradition of the judges whose craft of decision-making ensures a conformance to a greater or lesser degree, depending on the 'period style' of the courts, of the legal rule with the needs of society.

Llewellyn saw reckonability in the appellate courts because of steadying factors in those courts as summarised by Rumble:

[Llewellyn attempts] to explain the patterns of uniformity in judicial decision-making by reference to 14 'major steadying factors in our appellate courts'. Supposedly, they furnish the basis upon which reliable predictions of future decisions can be made. The 14 are the existence of 'law-conditioned officials'; personnel who are 'all trained and in the main rather experienced lawyers'; the presence of 'legal doctrine' and 'known doctrinal techniques'; the responsibility of the judiciary for 'justice'; the tradition of 'one single right answer' for each case; the existence of written opinions 'which tell any interested person what the cause is and why the decision—under the authorities—is right, and perhaps why it is wise', and which may also 'show how like cases are properly to be decided in the future'; the existence of 'a frozen record from below' and the fact that the issues before the court are 'limited, sharpened, and phrased in advance'; the presentation, oral and written, of adversary argument by counsel; the practice of group decisions; the security for independent judgment which life tenure makes possible; a 'known bench'; the 'general period style and its promise'; and, finally, 'professional judicial office'.

(W. E. Rumble, *American Legal Realism* (Ithaca, NY: Cornell University Press, 1968), p. 151 summarising K. N. Llewellyn, *The Common Law Tradition* (Boston, Mass: Little, Brown & Co., 1960), pp. 19–51)

This summary of Llewellyn's later approach to judicial decision-making shows a greater respect for the legal system and the judicial office. Judicial certainty is neither a product of the simple application of rules, nor is it to be found by looking solely at extra-legal factors. It is to be discerned by understanding the tradition of the judges, and for Llewellyn this turned on judicial tradition or what he calls 'styles'.

One of the 'major steadying factors' which makes judicial decision-making predictable to a significant extent is the 'period style' of judicial reasoning. Llewellyn contrasted the 'grand style' of judicial law-making, which uses a mixture of principle and policy to keep the law relevant and predictable, with the dry mechanical application of old-fashioned rules characteristic of what he called the 'formal style'. Llewellyn quite clearly preferred the grand style of judicial reasoning, where the judge not only tests precedents against overarching principles which 'yield patent sense as well as order' but also against policy, namely the 'prospective consequences of the rule under consideration'. In this way the heritage of the law is constantly updated. The grand style leads to a 'functioning harmonisation of vision with tradition, of continuity with growth, of machinery with purpose, of measure with need' (*The Common Law Tradition*, p. 37). By looking to the future, judges adopting the grand style contribute to the

> ...on-going production and improvement of rules which make sense on their face, and which can be understood and reasonably well applied even by mediocre men. Such rules have a fair chance to get the same results out of different judges, and so in truth to hit close to the ancient target of 'laws and not men'.
>
> (*The Common Law Tradition*, p. 38)

Llewellyn's belief that only the grand style could produce reckonability of result is clear from this extract. The formal style, on the other hand, 'can yield reckonable results only when the rules of law are clear', which is not the case, according to Llewellyn, in the common law. He dismissed the formalistic notion that 'the rules of law decide the cases; policy is for the legislature, not for the courts, and so is change even in pure common law'. This narrow approach 'drives conscious creation all but underground' so that the law lags further and further behind the conditions and needs of society (*The Common Law Tradition*, pp. 35–45).

Llewellyn identified periods in American legal history when each style dominated, but his point was that only the grand style makes law work in the sense of fulfilling law-jobs. Not only should judges adopt the grand style but lawyers and academics as well should attempt to interpret law in a much more open way. He argued that lawyers needed to concentrate not on discovering the ratio of a case and fitting it into the rules relating to the area, but on examining the decision of a court for the flavour. In this way, even the average lawyer can increase his or her ability to predict decisions.

> I submit that the average lawyer has only to shift his focus for a few hours from 'what was held' in a series of opinions to what those opinions suggest or show about what was bothering and what was helping the court as it decided.
>
> (*The Common Law Tradition*, p. 178)

The move away from concentrating on the ratio of a case to looking at it in a wider social context works best when judges are open about their use of policy and wider issues of principle, rather than trying to hide them behind formal reasoning. Greater openness produces greater predictability.

9.1.5 Hart's argument against rule scepticism

The realist's rule scepticism must seem prima facie to be opposed to a rule-based theory of law such as Hart's. The opposite viewpoint of formalism, on the other hand, is seen as seeking to confer upon rules a certainty in application which they in many cases lack. Hart himself takes a view, suspicious of both types of approach, founded upon the proposition that

> Formalism and rule scepticism are the Scylla and Charybdis of juristic theory; they are great exaggerations, salutary where they correct each other, and the truth lies between them.
>
> (*The Concept of Law*, p. 144)

The starting point for Hart's analysis of this point is found in the 'open texture' of law.

Hart argues, incontrovertibly, that language, including legal language, is by its nature often uncertain and therefore leaves room for choices in interpretation and application. In a common law system, not only does statutory language demand the making of choices in its application but the application of case precedents involves a yet wider scope of choice. It is this factor which Hart treats as the 'open texture' of law.

Hart concedes that there is an area of judicial discretion in which judges do in effect have to make choices, but Hart also argues that these are 'fringe' instances and that, as for the scope of discretionary decision-making by a scorer, referee or umpire in a game, the overwhelming preponderance of cases will in practice be settled by and according to a rule. Thus

> We are able to distinguish a normal game from the game of 'scorer's discretion' simply because the scoring rule, though it has, like other rules, its area of open texture where the scorer has to exercise a choice, yet has a core of settled meaning.
>
> (*The Concept of Law*, p. 140)

Similarly, Hart argues, the application of law is normally settled by rules even if, in a few atypical cases, the matter falls to judicial discretion. It is important for Hart's theory that the uncertainty implied by judicial discretion should not be overstated, for otherwise it threatens to obscure the rule-based model which is being advanced. Thus, he states that

> ...at the fringe...we should welcome the rule sceptic...[whilst not being blinded] to the fact that what makes possible...striking developments by courts of the most fundamental rules is, in great measure, the prestige gathered by courts from their unquestionably rule-governed operations over the vast, central areas of the law.
>
> (*The Concept of Law*, p. 150)

Hart thus fully accepts, whilst at the same time restricting, the role of judicial discretion. It is important to understand that this acknowledgement of uncertainty at the fringe of judicial discretion does not amount to a concession to rule scepticism. For the rule sceptic, legal rules *never* really serve as guides to judges or anyone else. Hart no more conceded anything to rule sceptics by recognising that rules may have an uncertain fringe than he conceded anything to formalists when he recognised that rules work to provide certain solutions in the majority of cases, for the formalist claim is that rules *always* do so.

9.1.5.1 Hart's demolition of the predictive theory of rules

Unfortunately for the realists, or many of them, they linked their 'rule scepticism' with a hopeless conception of law, i.e. that the law is simply a prediction of what the courts will do, and Hart simply demolished this.

> ...if we look closely at the activity of the judge or official who punishes deviations from legal rules (or those private persons who reprove or criticise deviations from non-legal rules), we see that rules are involved in this activity in a way which [the] predictive account leaves quite unexplained. For the judge, in punishing, takes the rule as his guide and the breach of the rule as his reason and justification for punishing the offender. He does not look upon the rule as a statement that he and others are likely to

punish deviations, though a spectator might look upon the rule in just this way. The predictive aspect of the rule (though real enough) is irrelevant to its purposes, whereas its status as a guide and justification is essential.

(*The Concept of Law*, pp. 10–11)

This demolition of the predictive theory essentially sank American legal realism in philosophical circles. Leiter makes the point as follows:

Hart's devastating critique of the Realists in Chapter VII of The Concept of Law rendered Realism a philosophical joke in the English-speaking world. The realists, on Hart's reading, gave us a 'Predictive Theory' of law, according to which by the concept 'law', we just mean a prediction of what the court will do. Hart easily demolished this Predictive Theory of law. For example, according to the Predictive Theory, a judge who sets out to discover the 'law' on some issue upon which she must render a decision is really trying to discover what she will do, since the 'law' is equivalent to a prediction of what she will do! These, and other manifestly silly implications of the Predictive Theory, convinced most Anglo-American legal philosophers that realism was best forgotten.

(Brian Leiter, 'Rethinking Legal Realism: Toward a Naturalized Jurisprudence' (1997) 76 *Texas LR* 267 at p. 270)

9.1.6 **Wittgenstein on rule following**

In his most famous work, *Philosophical Investigations*, Ludwig Wittgenstein devoted an extensive passage to the nature of rule following. His views are open to many different interpretations and are controversial. The 'version' of the rule following considerations presented here draws extensively on the exegetical work of the two most prominent late twentieth and twenty-first century interpreters of Wittgenstein, Gordon Baker and Peter Hacker. According to their exegetical account, Wittgenstein was concerned to disabuse his readers of certain 'mythologies' philosophers had constructed about the nature of rules, mythologies, for example, (1) in which rules are kinds of entities which have a psychological force of some kind, pulling us to act in a particular way, that is, according to the rule, or (2) in which a picture of rule following depicts someone who understands a rule as following it by first interpreting the rule to himself, and then following the rule according to that interpretation, or (3), in which applying a rule is to logically extend the series of past applications of a rule. What Wittgenstein wished to reveal was that rule following, explaining a rule, and understanding a rule were essentially all of a piece, and rule following a kind of practical activity. We can get some way towards his view by considering these three 'mythologies' of rules (Wittgenstein identified others, but examining these three will do for our purposes).

As to the first, treating rules as having some sort of psychological force, pulling us to behave in a particular way, makes it appear that following a rule requires a kind of *passivity* on the part of the rule follower. But this is nonsense. *We* follow rules; they do not *lead* us. A road may serve as a guide to a destination, but it is the *traveller* who acts, *using* the road *for his own purposes*, not the road. The road does not *do* anything. Furthermore, there is no characteristic *feeling*, of pressure or compulsion, when one follows a rule. Indeed, would you not be following the rule if you did not have any attendant feelings of any particular kind? If you follow rules in anger for example—imagine you are a primary school student who is being unjustly punished by being made to write out lines—how could those feelings of anger alter what you were doing?

The second, the interpretative myth, begins with the truth that people who understand a rule are able to explain how the rule works, and this can be done in different ways. These explanations, or interpretations, can be misconceived as *directions given to the rule follower* for applying the rule, and this is the error. Taken to be directions, such interpretations would simply stand as rules for applying the first rule, and now the danger looms. If explanations of rules are treated as rules for following the rule in question, then one ends up with an infinite regress. For one can then posit interpretations of the rules for following the rule in question, and interpretations of them, and so on indefinitely. And if one buys into this myth one is led to a kind of rule scepticism, along the following line of argument; since there are myriad ways of explaining or interpreting a rule, there are myriad ways of seeing what it requires the rule follower to do; thus different rule followers will follow the rule in different ways according to their different interpretations of the rule, and so rules cannot really determine a single way of acting, a single way of applying the rule. Secondary interpretations of the primary interpretations cannot solve this problem, for just as there are myriad primary interpretations of the rule in question, there are myriad secondary interpretations of each of the primary interpretations. Therefore rule scepticism arises: rules do not guide behaviour in the way they are supposed to do; they are indeterminate. Wittgenstein, who was anything but a rule sceptic, showed this to be a kind of seductive nonsense. It begins by misunderstanding the nature of explanations of rules; to understand a rule is to be able to explain how it works. If I want to teach you the rule of addition, I might show you on a piece of paper using numerals, or by counting one stack of blocks and then a second stack of blocks and then putting one stack on top of the other and counting the resulting stack, or in any number of other ways. But these explanations are not instructions how to apply 'the rule of addition' conceived as something separate. Rather, explaining a rule (which might involve following the rule as part of a demonstration of how the rule works) is a different *activity* than following a rule; one does not have to frame an explanation or interpretation of a rule, and then follow it according to such an interpretation; in order to follow a rule one just follows the rule. As Wittgenstein put it

> ...there is a way of understanding a rule which is *not* an *interpretation* but which is exhibited in what we call 'obeying the rule' and 'going against it' in actual cases.
>
> (L. Wittgenstein, *Philosophical Investigations*, transl. G. E. M. Anscombe (Oxford: Basil Blackwell, 1958), para. 201.

The third mythology concerns the 'rule-ness' of rules, the way in which we perceive them to cause us to act consistently, *in the same way*, time after time. It is as if rules laid down rails which we follow in our various applications of rules, so that the different applications of our rules line up, pointing the way for us to apply the rule in the next case. This leads us to believe that by looking at our past applications of a rule, we can *extrapolate* from those past applications in a way which will logically entail what we must do in the next case where the rule has to be applied. The easiest way to show this is false is with an example. Imagine that, as a matter of fact, neither Paul nor you has ever added together any numbers larger than 1,000. You ask Paul to add 1,000 and 2 and he gives the answer 1,004. You ask him to show you his work, and he writes out '1,000 and 2 and 2 equals 1,004'. You then do the addition getting, of course, 1,002 and ask him to explain himself and he says, 'I don't understand; I thought the rule was that for numbers up to 1,000, one puts together the first and second numbers, and for numbers over 1,000, one puts in the second number twice'. How are you to respond to that? The point of the example is to show that there is nothing in the past applications of the rule that *logically* requires that it was your rule rather than Paul's rule that you were both following. As far as the past applications of the rule determine, it could just as well have been Paul's rule of 'addition' as yours that both of you were following. Again, the moral is not that you should collapse into a fit of rule scepticism. The moral is that this is the wrong way to go about trying to understand how following rules allows someone to act consistently, or go on in the same way.

The error here is to treat past applications of a rule as *evidence* for the rule follower of the rule he or she is following. If you regard your past applications as data points, from which you must extrapolate the rule you are to follow in the instant case, you will see (as in the example of Paul and you and 'addition') that the data points do not determine a single rule, but a multiplicity of rules. If you proceed in this manner, you will not know how to go on in the *same way* as before. But of course this is a nonsensical way of understanding rule following. Having added 24 and 36 to get 60 is not *evidence* for the correctness of the sum 2 + 1,000 = 1,002; rather, being able to do both these sums is a *criterion* for your possessing the rule of addition; if you do not get 1,002 from 1,000 + 2 then you simply have not mastered addition. For someone who understands the rule, there is no ground for uncertainty here.

This leads to Wittgenstein's basic insight about the nature of rule following. Understanding what a rule requires for its application is a matter of knowing *how*, or 'knowhow', not knowing *that*, that is, having learned a fact. Consult your own experience; learning to ride a bicycle, learning to swim, learning to talk, learning the rules of a game, are ways of learning to *do* something, not acquiring true beliefs. Learning of this kind requires *practice*, not memorisation. It is not memorising some fact or set of facts and regurgitating them on command. You should know this from your own legal study. You are given problem questions because these cause you actually to apply the rules, and it takes practice to become good at this kind of rule application, this legal analysis. You realise that you do not really understand the rules of, say, contract law if all you can do is recite all the 'rules' stated in a textbook but cannot correctly apply them to decide a case.

In exploring this practical aspect of rules, Wittgenstein used the example of measuring to emphasise these points. First of all, we normally think of ourselves as active, not passive, in taking measurements. Second, when we think about this familiar activity it seems absurd to think we might become embroiled in interpretations of the use of tape measures or scales or floored by trying to make sense of the pattern of our past measurements such that we would be paralysed by indecision as to how we could carry on measuring things.

Now, whilst it is fundamentally right to distinguish between knowing how and knowing that, it is not as if they cannot depend upon one another. Take an obvious example: applying a rule of the common law will require you know lots about the nature of the world, of human beings, of their history and culture. There is a huge background of facts that underpins our ability to create and then apply the rules of contract. The Wittgensteinian point is not that understanding a rule, which is to understand how to apply it and explain how it works to others, cannot depend upon having acquired 'knowledge that', having learned lots of facts; it is rather that the understanding of rules themselves is not this sort of knowledge. Another way of putting this is to say that it is not *propositional* knowledge; it does not consist in learning the truth of any factual propositions. Rules themselves are not true or false. Rules may be the *subject* of factual propositions, for example, 'the rule requiring consideration for the formation of contracts forms part of the common law', but a rule is not itself a factual proposition, but a standard of *behaviour*.

There are clear traces of the mythology of rules in the various rule-scepticisms of the legal realists we have looked at. And Wittgenstein's demolition of the idea that you can logically extrapolate a single rule from past applications of a rule would also seem to bury formalism, for formalism turns on the claim that a rule that must be applied in this case can be generated from past decisions by logical extension from those decisions. So, both rule scepticism and formalism sunk, a nice result. But the Wittgensteinian, practical perspective on rules also helps explain some other features of rules, in particular legal rules. Rules are practical devices, which are created to do things with a purpose in mind. Therefore, rules do not apply in every sort of circumstance that they may, at first glance, appear to apply. Rather, rules only serve a purpose in those situations in which it makes sense to follow them. As Hart and Raz have pointed out, rules have scope and are defeasible. Hart made a similar point when he talked about rules having a core area of application, and a penumbra of uncertainty. Thus a rule which states, 'No vehicles in the park', applies perfectly well to prohibit cars and lorries, which is the sort of traffic the makers of the rule had in mind when the rule was instituted. But it may not apply well or at all to other cases; the case of scooters, the case of emergency vehicles on the way to a rescue, the case of citizens who wish to mount a vintage car as a statue. Wittgenstein would say that it is part of the mistaken 'mythology' of rules that they should 'self-apply' in every possible circumstance. We apply rules, and we can see where their application is doubtful or problematic.

Finally, a frustrated reader might say, 'What you have said so far is all well and good but it is still not clear to me how different individuals apply the same rule in the same way. Might not Llewellyn be on to something when he suggests (9.1.4) that the predictability of court decisions lies in the 'steadying factors' which operate on judges, what we might today call the judges' 'social conditioning'? The answer from a Wittgensteinian perspective would be 'no'. All sorts of behaviour might be due to social conditioning, but if that thought is applied to rule following, it has to be considerably sharpened. Being taught rules, such as the rule of addition, or the rules of the English law of property, could in one sense be called socially conditioning. But the ability of one person to learn a rule from another person turns on something much more basic: our innate cognitive psychology. Having the same basic cognitive psychology provides us with what Wittgenstein called our ability to have 'agreement in judgments'. This is no more mysterious than learning to count and use a tape measure from another person. If we could not see parts of the world in terms of discrete individual objects, we could not learn to count them. If we could not conceive of one thing being longer than another, we could make no sense of the use of a tape measure. We can share rules because we share, to a great extent, a way of seeing the world. Whilst social and cultural factors no doubt come into play here, particularly, it might be thought, in the case of moral and legal rules, social and cultural factors themselves can only be factors because of our underlying common humanity, a common humanity that is nicely evoked by our ability to follow shared rules.

9.2 Legal interpretivism

Legal interpretivism is sometimes mistakenly taken to be a theory of adjudication. True, Dworkin's development of legal interpretivism was inspired in part by his criticism of Hart's central theoretical claim about adjudication as Dworkin saw it: that judges have a discretion to make law in cases where the law was unsettled. True also, Dworkin's typical starting point for introducing the theory is his alternative model of judicial decision-making in what Dworkin called 'hard cases', personified in Judge Hercules (6.3.1, 6.4.2, 6.4.3), and his characterisation of legal argument before the courts, in particular legal disagreement between lawyers and judges. But the theory is a theory of law, not a theory of adjudication. It is the interpretivist's claim that legal interpretivism is the best account of the nature of the law, and one of the payoffs of this theory is that it *explains* better than legal positivism the nature of legal disagreement and adjudication. In particular, it purports to explain the fact—if it is a fact; the claim is quite controversial (6.4.2, 6.4.3.1)—that judges and lawyers argue as if there is a correct legal answer to resolve any dispute before the courts, whatever the state of the law 'in the books', that is, whatever the relevant previous judicial decisions or statutes have to say (if anything) about the matter.

Legal interpretivism is a theory of law that claims the following: (1) that legal obligations are a type of moral obligation, and they are understood to be such by lawyers and judges and lay subjects of the law; (2) unlike non-legal moral obligations, legal obligations depend on the historical political practice of a society, in particular the practices of creating constitutions, legislating, and rendering decisions in courts of law; and (3) what legal obligations amount to, then, is determining *how* historical political practices contribute to what a subject of the jurisdiction is under a moral obligation to do; this is obviously a matter of political morality. For the interpretivist, therefore, to know what the law is, what legal obligations you actually have, is to have true beliefs about the moral significance of historical political decisions. (Legal interpretivists tend to be moral cognitivists, i.e., they believe that the question whether one is morally obliged to do *x* or refrain from doing *y* has a correct answer, and also that, despite much controversy over what morality requires of us, we can, at least in a significant number of cases, know what that is. This is tricky territory because some interpretivists appear to suggest that interpretivism is also a theory about what truth and knowledge in moral matters amounts to. Dworkin in particular seems to hold a view of this kind. We shall not explore that aspect of interpretive theory here. Suffice it to say that because intepretivists regard legal obligation to be a kind of moral obligation, their theory of legal obligation is part and parcel of whatever theory about moral obligation they hold, including what knowledge and truth in the domain of morality comes to.)

As we have seen (6.4.3), under Dworkin's brand of interpretivism, 'law as integrity', the task of determining what the law is that applies to any particular fact situation is determined in a 'Herculean' mode whereby two considerations, 'fit' with past political practice and 'substantive justice', are taken into account in order to produce a scheme of legal rights and duties which shows the legal practice of the political community in question in its best light, and then this scheme is applied to the instant case to generate the correct legal decision. But although legal interpretivism originated with Dworkin, the position has been adopted and developed by others, in particular Nicos Stavropoulos and Mark Greenberg. Legal interpretivism itself, not just Dworkin's version of it, now stands as the soi-disant 'anti-positivist' position in legal theory; it purports to show that positivism gives a false picture of law, while it gives the true one. It is useful then to say a few words about positivism to ensure that we have a fix on interpretivism's actual positivist target.

We must first dispense with what I shall call 'naïve positivism', a bad version of positivism that no theorist holds but which some critics of Hart drew from his discussion of judicial discretion in *The Concept of Law*, perhaps even Dworkin himself in his first critiques of Hart. Naïve positivism treats the law as a body of rules, like the rules of a game; in exceptional cases, however—for example, where the meaning of the words of a rule do not easily apply to the case in hand—the rules do not resolve the dispute; in such cases a legal official, a judge, who is modelled on a referee or an umpire in a game, has a discretion to decide the case one way or another based upon *non-legal* considerations. In common law systems a senior enough judge's exercise of this discretion is a means of creating new legal rules through the doctrine of stare decisis.

Why is this positivism 'naïve', and hence bad? The reason lies in its characterisation of the judicial duty to resolve cases and the impact the law has on that function. Judges (at least judges in the vast majority of extant legal systems) have an obligation to decide cases before them whether or not there is clear, settled law that more or less obviously determines the case. Especially in common law systems, the starting position is that judges are required to decide cases based upon all the good moral and other reasons which apply to give the just, fair, and otherwise sound result. From this positivist perspective, when there is a binding, relevant precedent or statute covering the case, the law in effect *takes away* the judge's right to decide, as he would otherwise be obliged to do on the balance of reasons as he understood it to be. As Green puts the point, following a discussion of 'permissive' sources of law, such as the judgments of foreign courts or scholarly works, which a judge may turn to in rendering a decision but is not legally bound to apply

> [A]bsent a source, a court is already permitted to act on any reasons that are relevant to the matter; in this way, too, judges are human. It is not as if we live in a world where judges have no reason to decide anything until law steps in and provides one. *The general function of sources in law is to block appeals to what would otherwise be good reasons for decisions.* The fact that someone feels uncomfortable around homosexuals is pro tanto a reason not to require him to associate with them—even if he is providing a service ordinarily available to the public. Anti-discrimination law steps in to provide a source that gives courts a new reason not to act on what would otherwise be a good reason for acting. Here, it does so in order to better secure conformity to reason overall and in the long run (for instance, by limiting the extent to which people can act on their typically overestimated predictions of discomfort, and their tendency to discount how that discomfort harms the autonomy of others or injures the public good) . (Italics added.)
>
> (L. Green, 'Law and the Causes of Judicial Decisions' (2009) Oxford Legal Studies Research Paper No. 14/2009, available at <http://papers.ssrn.com/sol3/papers.cfm?abstract_id=1374608>)

As this quotation emphasises, this positivist view of the way in which laws figure in adjudication is very much in line with Raz's coordination function of the law and the way in which the normal justification thesis justifies legal intervention (6.6, 8.2). There are often good reasons to decide a dispute both for the claimant and for the defendant. By imposing a rule, the law coordinates the behaviour of those who resolve disputes in areas where coordination is important for achieving socially valuable ends, such as a functioning law of property and contract. Notice also on this positivist perspective, the law does not just impose laws which prohibit judges from themselves balancing the reasons that apply to the case by giving a clear answer; the law may do less; it may simply narrow the range of reasons the judge may take into account by denying the availability of certain reasons. These constraints tend to receive less recognition, but they are just as vital. Where the common law does not point to a decision one way or another, and the judge is 'free to decide the point', as judges often put it, judges are still required to decide the case in a way which makes sense as a judgment *of the common law*, using common law concepts of property or contract or whatever. Whilst a judge is not barred from considering how German law deals with a similar point, a judge is not allowed to decide the case the way a German court would, justifying its decision on the basis of civil law concepts and doctrines. On this understanding of the positivist point of view it is very much the business of judges, in particular judges at the appeal level in common law jurisdictions, to use their brains to decide 'hard cases' as Dworkin calls them, cases in which the settled law does not give a clear answer, aiming to provide a reasonable, fair, and just result, though within the range of reasons that are available to them, which is typically not wide open.

Having this positivist characterisation of adjudication in hand, we can now sharpen our appreciation of the features of legal interpretivism that make it what it is, and distinguish it as an anti-positivist theory.

Trading on the common intuition that judges are there 'to apply the law', interpretivists begin with the thought that a legal theory which shows that judges can *always* decide a case on the basis of law that is already there is superior to one which says that judges are not always applying the law when they decide cases, as the positivist view just set out says. I leave it to the reader to consider whether that intuition is more or less the same as the idea that every case has one right *legal* answer, as the notion of the law is normally understood. A positivist might argue that the intuition is no more than that a judge must decide the case within the legal concepts and doctrine applying in the jurisdiction where he sits. In any case such an intuition leads interpretivists to the thought that decision-making according to law draws upon more considerations that count *as law* than what is recognised as law by positivists, i.e. only the rules generated by sources recognised by the rules of recognition of the jurisdiction. Another way of putting this is that for the interpretivist, the enterprise of determining what the law is is much more involved than the picture provided by positivists, of assembling the norms generated by the sources recognised by the rule of recognition.

As Stavropoulos has made clear, true legal interpretivism is often confused with two similar theories which are quite different. We can illustrate the differences using Dworkin's Hercules. A first variant might be called 'sources morally filtered'. On this view, Hercules first identifies the source-based, positive law on the basis of something like the rule of recognition; then he determines on the basis of considerations of political morality which theory of political morality provides the best justification of the source-based law—including the law which creates the institutions of the legal system, courts, legislatures, and so on, and their particular procedures—i.e. a justification which allows us to see that law in its best light, morally speaking; finally, this theory of justification provides a moral filter which excludes certain rules or certain applications of the rules of the source-based law because they are too far outside of, that is fit too poorly, the moral–political theory of justification identified in the second step. So, for example, the principle 'no man should profit from his own wrong', which formed part of the best justification of the law of New York state, ruled out the application of the statutory rules on testamentary succession which would otherwise have allowed a murderer to take under the will of the uncle he murdered.

The second variant we can call 'coherentism'. On this view, Hercules again works in steps. First, as above, he identifies the source-based law. Secondly, as above, he determines a theory of political morality which best justifies the source-based law. Third, Hercules will not only exclude those rules which do not make it through the moral filter as described in the last variant, but will hold to be law all those rules of law which do fit within the theory of justification, even if they are not part of the source-based law. On this view, when a judge develops the law by deciding a case even though there is no source-based law requiring the decision he can point to, he is applying a rule of law which is not source-based, but based upon the theory developed in stage two, this being the rule of law that comes from applying the stage-two theory. In this way, by excluding ill-fitting, 'outlier' rules, and incorporating the rules which derive from the application of the best moral–political theory of the law, the law is made more conceptually coherent from the standpoint of political morality.

True legal interpretivism is neither of these views. A true legal interpretivist denies that it is even *possible* to identify the so-called 'source-based' law without first engaging in a moral evaluation of the 'legal' practices of the relevant community. As Stavropoulos puts the point

> Interpretivism says that it is not political practice alone—such as the fact that Congress voted for a statute that says that gratuitous promises are not enforceable, that its power to enforce its decisions is recognized, or that it is treated as supreme law-maker by lawyers, or the fact that as a matter of settled practice courts do not enforce such promises—that makes legal propositions true, nor is it moral or other evaluative facts alone—e.g. that it is good that gratuitous promises should not be enforceable—that make them true either. Rather, legal propositions are made true by the best justification of political practice, i.e. the scheme of principle that underlies and governs political practice, including e.g. the fact that it is right that Congress should wield the power that it does or that courts' settled practice should have a large impact on our duties. Interpretivism therefore claims that legal requirements are sensitive to both the facts of the practice and the values served by it, but not fully determined by either.

Along similar lines, Dworkin now makes it explicit that fit with past political practice and substance are both theoretical values of political morality, both dimensions of evaluative interpretation, that interact.

> [In Law's Empire] I warned that 'fit' and 'justification' are only names for two rough dimensions of interpretation, and that further refinement would require a more clear analysis of other, discrete political values through which to understand these dimensions more thoroughly, so that we might see, for example, how to integrate them in an overall judgment of interpretive superiority when they pull in opposite directions. The key political concepts that must be explored in that way, it now seems to me, are those of procedural fairness, which is the nerve of the dimension of fit, and substantive justice, which is the nerve of political justification.
>
> (R. Dworkin, *Justice in Robes* (Cambridge, Mass.: Belknap Press, 2006), p. 171)

For the interpretivist, therefore, it is interpretation all the way down. What counts as a source of law is not a matter of historical fact alone; what counts as a source of law depends as well on moral considerations about what a good source of law is. What counts as a source of law is therefore controversial because there are controversies in political morality about how good a thing it is, morally speaking, for legislatures like ours, which operate in imperfect representative democracies, to make laws, and the extent to which they can make laws of any kind they want. Similarly, just because we recognise rules of precedent does not mean that any decision of the English Court of appeal *actually* binds its successors; that is a controversial issue in political morality attracting our thoughts about the power appellate courts ought to have in constraining future benches, and so on. The purported power of the legislature to pass such and such an act, or the purported obligation of a high court judge to follow the Court of Appeal are 'up for grabs' in the sense that a theorist interrogating the moral–political basis of

our legal institutions may convincingly persuade us that the best moral–political justification of the legal practices of our jurisdiction may indicate that it would be wrong
to treat, say, a particular piece of legislation as validly enacted, or a particular Court of
Appeal decision as binding; he might even convince us that Court of Appeal decisions
should never be treated as binding, but only ever persuasive. Furthermore, not only is
the 'source-based law' a matter for interpretative evaluation, the 'sources' themselves
are. Interpretivists accept that our legal discourse regards certain facts, 'political facts',
facts such as what a legislature or a court has done, as central to our understanding of
what the law is. But the category, 'political facts', is in itself a category subject to interpretative consideration in the sense that what we treat as a relevant political fact is a
matter of moral–political *evaluation*.

With this picture in mind, how do political facts generate the morally binding legal
obligations that citizens ought to comply with? The key word here is: *indirectly*. The fact
that the statutory highway code purports to impose a duty upon you to drive no more
than 70 mph on the motorway does not mean that it imposes a binding legal, that is,
moral–political, obligation upon you to do so; rather, that depends on the best justification of the powers of the legislature, the moral reasons you have to avoid injuring
others, the moral reason you have to coordinate your behaviour with them to achieve a
social goal, and so forth. The passing of the legislation providing for the highway code
itself is always only part of the picture in determining whether the law requires you to
follow what it actually says or does not say.

By contrast, the positivist view of law adopts a 'communicative' view of legislation.
For the positivist, what the law requires is what its recognised sources have said is
required. Whilst communications can be more or less precise, positivists accept that
courts and legislatures can express rules, rights, and duties, and by the very act of reading (or, less often now than in the past, listening to) the directive, the subject of the law
can know what his legal position is, that is, know what the rules are that he must follow,
what his rights and duties are. Of course, the law may be more or less complicated and
the lay subject of the law may need a lawyer's advice, but neither the lay subject nor
the lawyer is required to engage in a moral inquiry to figure out how to integrate the
directive within a scheme of moral–political justification of past political practice, and
thus to figure out how the court's order or the highway code changes the law. For the
positivist, of course, knowing what the law is does not resolve the question of whether
one is under a moral obligation to comply with it. Figuring that out may be more or less
difficult in the circumstances, but that is a different task from figuring out what the law
requires you to do. By contrast, for interpretivists, thinking that these tasks are separate
is the original positivist sin.

Which of interpretivism or positivism is more plausible?

First of all, it seems to be the case that a jurisdiction could, in principle, instanti-
ate a legal system which was either interpretivist or positivist in character. All parties
to the dispute are trying to explore the phenomenon of law as we experience it, and
though both cannot be right about say, the legal system of England and Wales, it is an
important part of understanding these theories to understand *what they think the law
is like*, and then consider that in light of your own sense of what the law, in your own
jurisdiction at least, is like.

Having said that however, whatever the failings of various theories we group under
the heading 'positivism', of which there are doubtless many, there seems to be a glar-
ing problem with interpretivism: it just seems very implausible. If interpretivism were
merely an account of the way that the law affects what we are morally bound to do, it
would be plausible enough, though a little too complicated for some people's tastes.

But as an account of what the *law* of any particular jurisdiction is, it seems to erase an important conceptual distinction which is generally held and seems to make perfect sense.

If interpretivism were merely an account of the way that the law affects our moral position, its claim would be that determining how the law changes its subjects' moral obligations is complicated because of all the interacting values of political theory that come into play, and that the best theoretical approach to determining how any subject of the law is morally bound to act is something like Hercules' approach. We would be required to try to integrate all the values in play, in particular the political values that would explain why we must take into account the actual past acts of legislatures and the courts, to come up with an over-arching scheme which would indicate the moral obligations each subject of the law had at any one time. As such, it would be an 'holistic' theory of those moral obligations which are generated, extinguished, or modified by the political practices of one's community, and how that generation, extinction, and modification works. A complex theory no doubt, but a perfectly intelligible one.

But interpretivism does not say that. It says that any norm which exists, or whose contours are determined, at least in part because of past acts in our community which in one way or another engage the values that give moral significance to our community practices *is* a legal norm. On a broad view of what counts as a 'community' practice that might engage the values of political morality, such as 'solidarity' or 'equality' or 'sociability' or 'communal flourishing', there would appear to be a distinct danger that the law would swallow up all of interpersonal morality and require us to treat willy nilly all sorts of organisations in our communities—schools, churches, universities, football clubs, charities, perhaps even business organisations—as institutions of law, parts of the legal system.

An interpretivist might reply that one test of success for any interpretivist theory of law is that it interprets the values underlying political morality so as not to generate this exorbitant account of what constitutes the law and the legal system, but it is not clear this way out is open to him. Indeed, the position may be quite the opposite. The scope within interpretivism for a radical revision of our understanding of the nature of law is obvious: it is as great as the latitude we see in political philosophy for controversy over the moral values that justify, or fail to justify, whatever institutions we have; the interpretivist must, I think, accept the theory's scope for radical departure from the common understanding of what counts as part of the law and legal system.

Interpretivism seems implausible on another ground. We generally accept that we may now be mistaken about what morality requires of us, given the history of our moral understanding: racist, sexist, and other views which were once more or less accepted as morally correct are now regarded as morally atrocious. We do not, however, seem to accept the same thing to be true of the law. That is, most of us would not accept the proposition that the participants in a legal system, its officials and subjects, could be systematically *wrong* or largely *ignorant* about what the laws of their jurisdiction actually were, any more than we would accept that French-speakers could be systematically wrong or largely ignorant of French grammar or vocabulary. But this is perfectly possible on the interpretivist view. To put this another way, since on the interpretivist view what the law is depends on what the true moral–political justification is of our past political practices, we may be ignorant now, and forever remain ignorant, of what the law governing restrictive covenants in English land law, or the speed limit on the motorway, ever was or is. An interpretivist might respond that whilst this is true in theory, it is unlikely in practice, but like the previous interpretivist reply, this does not seem to address the worry. For example, on the interpretivist view, it might, quite sensibly, be argued that, given the correct understanding of the moral values engaged by political practices and the actual history of those political practices in the United States, putting those practices into their best moral–political light entails that the law did *not* impose the binding legal obligations which provided for the system of slavery in the United States, at least by the time the 1860s rolled around. On this view, slavery was not legal, or rather, slavery was illegal, everywhere in the United States some time well before the civil war. But this seems a crazy thing to say. Conceptually, we want to say both that slavery was legal in the southern United States prior to the civil war *and* that it was inconsistent with any plausible moral reading of the past political practices in the United States, much less the reading that puts those practices in their best moral light. Furthermore, one of the *reasons* to abolish the laws permitting slavery was the fact that slavery was inconsistent with any plausible moral reading of the past political practices in the United States, much less the reading that puts those practices in their best moral light. To be clear about this point, interpretivists do not hold that an unjust law cannot be a genuine law that morally requires the subject's obedience. Even an unjust law, such as a tax law that unjustifiably favours the rich over the poor, can be a genuine law within a scheme of principle that makes best moral sense of our practices, for such a law could be justified on the grounds that it was laid down by a democratic legislature and that, even though the legislature misunderstood the substantive injustice it was perpetrating, on grounds of democratic procedural fairness citizens ought morally to comply with it. The present point is that we seem to be capable of thinking of odious rules as rules of the system, despite the fact that they are deeply inconsistent with the true values of the system, whereas an interpretivist, on any reasonable application of his theory, cannot.

There is a final point, where we may draw upon Wittgenstein's thoughts about rule-following (9.1.6) for some guidance. On the version of interpretivism presented so far, interpretivists do not have to doubt that a legislature can issue directives the *meaning* of which cannot be determined without moral investigation. Similarly, on this version, there is no difficulty understanding what the rule setting a 70 mph speed limit requires of drivers. On this version of interpretivism, the interpretivist believes only that the specific moral obligations the law creates, whether framed in terms of rules, rights or duties, are determined by engaging in the Herculean theoretical procedures set out above. However, occasionally interpretivists suggest that they hold a particular *semantic* thesis, along the lines that no rule of law can be understood, that is, one could not tell what a rule required of one, roughly, what the rule 'means', unless one engaged in a moral evaluation first; until you engaged in some sort of moral evaluation or interpretation of the rule, you would not know what a rule of law, such as a law requiring you to pay 5 per cent of the sale price of a house as stamp duty, required you to do. This seems plainly false. Understanding such a rule, like understanding what 'shut the door' means, or what addition requires you do with 5 + 6, requires no evaluation of the moral *merits* of the rule or command or procedure in some wider sense. All you have to know is what calculating a percentage and paying over money or shutting the door amounts to, or how to add. Many rules of law seem to be rules as simple as this, such as ones that set speed limits. Perhaps, however, some interpretivists believe that knowing what any *moral* rule or obligation requires of one—or *really* requires of one or *genuinely* requires of one—interpretivists are fond of this use of 'really'—requires moral evaluation. But this seems equally misguided for the same reasons. To the extent that what morality requires of one is framed in terms of rules—don't lie, for instance—then all one needs to know to follow the rule is to know what lying is. Having a moral rule like this can lead to two circumstances in which acting upon the rule may be problematic. One is the case where the rule is clear but it would seem wrong to follow it; Kant thought that we should not lie to John when, intent on murdering James, he pounds on the door and asks us where James is; most people, however, think this is a case when lying to John about where James is, is absolutely the right thing to do in the circumstances. Whether you are with Kant or with almost everyone else on this, there is no confusion here about what the rule would require; one would not be permitted to lie to John. There is no vagueness or uncertainty about that. The question is simply whether the rule which applies perfectly straightforwardly ought to be followed, and this requires moral evaluation of the circumstances, which may be difficult and lead to disagreement, such as that between Kant and almost everyone else. The second problematic case is the one where it is difficult to know whether or how the rule applies. Consider a more or less vague injunction such as 'be kind to everyone'; it may not be clear in many cases whether one should be kind, and moreover, what being kind would amount to. For Wittgenstein, in these cases we are no longer in the realm of working rules. Difficult borderline cases do *not* unsettle rules across their realm of application. Just because one can conceive of difficult cases where the application of a rule would be uncertain does not make the rule uncertain in cases where it clearly applies; the fact that I can conceive cases in which it is doubtful what I should do (say you were to ask me to pour you a cup of tea when we are in the weightlessness of outer space) does not mean that I am in doubt about what I should do right now (when you ask me for a cup of tea in my house here on Earth). But when a rule or other norm does not work, does not determine behaviour, it is not a guide to behaviour. Perhaps in such a case one should think about the rationale for the rule, for example, consider whether the rules of courtesy (to use a favourite interpretivist example) express respect, and then figure out how one might show respect in this instance even though one of the rules of courtesy may not clearly apply, or it would be difficult to know how to apply it, say saluting a superior officer when one's arms are full (nod one's head, perhaps?). The point of these two different cases where norms that work in some circumstances do not work in others (which may be true of all norms) is to make clear that it is not a plausible basis for interpretivism that it regards all moral rules (including of course legal rules on the theory) as requiring interpretations before those bound by them can know what to do. To adopt this view seriously would be tantamount to denying the existence of any general moral standards at all, as if morality required a first principles investigation on each occasion of acting. Such a view is not impossible to hold (act utilitarians hold such a view), but it seems particularly ill-suited as a foundation for a theory of law. In short, interpretivism can and should do without any 'interpretivist' semantic theory about norms. It has all the resources it needs to propose an interesting (if, I have argued, implausible) counter-theory to legal positivism in the way it relates the facts of political practice to moral obligation.

9.3 Adjudication and the rule of law

We have already encountered the basic idea behind the rule of law when we looked at Fuller's criteria of law-making and his claim that they constituted an 'inner morality of law' (2.5.2–2.5.3). The idea of the rule of law corresponds more or less to the idea that the function of the law is to guide the behaviour of its subjects, and this puts constraints on the creation, character, and application of law. Here is a typical list of those constraints: laws should be general, publicly proclaimed, prospective rather than retrospective, clear rather than vague and not overly complex, reasonably stable, possible to comply with, and applied consistently in accordance to their tenor (which usually entails the establishment of an independent judiciary). All of these criteria basically provided for the possibility of the *effectiveness* of the law's serving its guiding function; as we have seen in our examination of Fuller, none are absolute. Compliance with the rule of law is a matter of more or less. The moral character of the rule of law as a 'negative virtue' is elaborated by Raz.

> The rule of law is essentially a negative value. The law inevitably creates a danger of arbitrary power—the rule of law is designed to minimise the danger created by the law itself. Similarly, the law may be unstable, obscure, retrospective, etc., and thus infringe people's freedom and dignity. The rule of law is designed to prevent this danger as well. Thus the rule of law is a negative virtue in two senses: conformity to it does not cause good except through avoiding evil and the evil which is avoided is evil which could only have been caused by the law itself. It is somewhat analogous to honesty when this virtue is narrowly interpreted as the avoidance of deceit....The good of honesty does not include the good of communication between people, for honesty is consistent with a refusal to communicate. Its good is exclusively in the avoidance of the harm of deceit—and not deceit by others but by the honest person himself. Therefore, only a person who can deceive can be honest. A person who cannot communicate cannot claim any moral merit for being honest.
>
> (J. Raz, *The Authority of Law*, 2nd ed. (Oxford: Oxford University Press, 2009), p. 224)

Be all this as it may, why are we looking at the rule of law in a chapter on the law and adjudication? The reason is that recently, several scholars have noticed a different strand in the idea of the rule of law: the idea that certain areas of human endeavour *ought morally* to be organised *by law* rather than by other means of human organisation, for example, via administrative direction or political decision-making, and Waldron has persuasively argued that the role of the courts and adjudication is especially central to this vision of the rule of law. Furthermore, Waldron argues that this requires us to re-think the positivist's conception of law as a kind of instrument, a social technology; Waldron claims that from this perspective law is an *evaluative* concept; thus to say that some system of order is a legal system is to claim that it has moral worth.

Waldron points out that in popular invocations of the rule of law, the last criterion identified above, the consistent and correct application of the laws by an independent judiciary tends to get pride of place, and exploring this, one might see the rule of law as a more capacious idea with a greater moral significance than the one acknowledged by Raz above.

> The Rule of Law is an ideal designed to correct dangers of abuse that arise in general when political power is exercised, not dangers of abuse that arise from the law in particular. Indeed, the Rule of Law aims to correct abuses of power by insisting on a particular mode of exercise of political power: governance through law. That mode of governance is though more apt to protect us against abuse than, say, managerial governance or rule by decree. On this account, law itself seems to be prescribed as the remedy, rather than identified as the problem that a separate ideal—the rule of law—seeks to remedy....
>
> In my view, to describe an exercise of power as an instance of lawmaking or law-application is already to dignify it with a certain character; it is already to make a certain assessment or evaluation of what has happened.
>
> (J. Waldron, 'The Concept and the Rule of Law' (2008) 43 *Georgia Law Review* 1 at pp. 11, 12)

The anti-positivist direction of this is clear; the law is not just an instrument, but where we recognise a case of law, we recognise a morally good instrument of social ordering. Waldron calls the position he is attacking, under which wicked regimes we would not regard as morally good systems of social ordering are still counted as legal systems, 'casual positivism'. This is the positivist thesis about legal systems we identified at the beginning of Chapter 3.

Furthermore, the role of courts and adjudication have a special significance, which Waldron argues has received too little attention.

> [T]he operation of a court involves a way of proceeding that offers to those who are immediately concerned an opportunity to make submissions and present evidence, such evidence being presented in an orderly fashion according to strict rules of evidence.... The mode of presentation may vary, but the opportunity does not. Once presented, the evidence is then made available to be examined and confronted by the other party in open court. Each party has the opportunity to present arguments and submissions...Throughout the process, both sides are treated respectfully and above all listened to by a tribunal that is bound to attend to the evidence presented and respond to the submissions that are made in the reasons that are given for its eventual decision.
>
> These are abstract characteristics—and it would be a mistake to get too concrete given the variety of court-like institutions in the world—but they are not just arbitrary abstractions. They capture a deep and important sense associated foundationally with the idea of a legal system—that law is a mode of governing people that treats them with respect, as though they had a view of their own to present on the application of a given norm to their conduct or situation.
>
> ('The Concept and the Rule of Law', p. 23)

The special significance of courts leads Waldron to say the following about what the law of any legal system consists of: the law should include not only the decisions of the courts. But, argues Waldron,

> Once we do that, we are bound to feel some pressure to extend it to comprehend the basis upon which courts make their decision. If the courts seem to be establishing certain ways of understanding general norms, or if the courts seem to be articulating principles of decision that are intermediate between the enacted general norms and the decisions of particular cases, then it may be appropriate to describe such modes of interpretation and such intermediate principles as law, too.
>
> ('The Concept and the Rule of Law', p. 48)

Waldron concludes that these considerations strongly favour interpretivist accounts of law such as Dworkin's, which treat disagreements between lawyers and judges in particular cases as best explained by a conception of law that includes those norms which 'flow from' the best justifications of our past political decisions. This clearly opposes the second positivist thesis identified at the beginning of Chapter 3, i.e. that a norm belongs to a legal system on the basis of its sources, not its merits, that is, not on the basis that one could argue it would be justified to adopt such a norm.

We can consider Waldron's two anti-positivist theses in turn. As to the first, that 'casual positivism' is wrong and that law is an evaluative concept, it is not clear that Waldron makes his case. Consider the example of another kind of instrument, a knife (the example is Raz's).

Anyone who cooks or eats values knives; given what knives provide in the way of possibilities for cooking and eating, knives definitely contribute to human flourishing. Knives are great. But does this make the concept of a knife or the concept of 'knifework' *evaluative* concepts? It is hard to see how. What would appear to attract evaluations of knives would be the use of this concept in evaluative *contexts*, in particular when we are determining whether this instrument is the best or right instrument for the job. So, if we are comparing the knives to spoons or spanners as instruments for the preparation of beef tartare, knives win hands down. We will evaluate knives positively as the better, nay only option, for enabling the provision of this contribution to human flourishing. This sort of thing appears to be what Waldron has done by exploring the contexts in which the 'rule of law' is often employed. There are no doubt cases where governance through law, in particular through courts, may be the best, nay the only, option, say, for example, where the social ordering required is to organise the determination of a person's guilt for a serious crime. But it does not follow from this that courts are always the best, much less the only, option for governance. Courts would be rubbish tools for determining and implementing governmental economic policy. In this context, saying that the Chancellor of the Exchequer was acting like a high court judge would not be a compliment. It would nevertheless be *using* the concept of 'judge' correctly, in the same way that one might use the concept of 'legal system' correctly if one derogatively referred to a couple's treating their children as 'running their household like a legal system'. So it seems like 'law' and 'legal systems' are not evaluative concepts after all, though they may be used in an evaluative manner in certain contexts.

As to Waldron's second anti-positivist thesis, it falls prey to the worries that attend any form of interpretivism, as canvassed above. But it may fall at an earlier hurdle than that. One might simply deny that having accepted judicial decisions as part of the law the 'pressure to extend it to comprehend the basis upon which courts make their decision' leads to interpretivism of any kind. Rather, it should lead us to explore and comprehend as well as we can the distinction, which is conceptually clear but difficult to draw in practice, between the application of norms, which concerns certain aspects of the rule of law, and norm creation, which concerns others. Whilst if one is already a legal interpretivist, Waldron's move seems correct, Waldron gives no independent reason for denying that judges make law that would lead to his anti-positivist conclusion.

FURTHER READING

Allen, T., 'Law, justice and integrity: the paradox of wicked laws' (2009) 29 *Oxford Journal of Legal Studies* 705.

Baker, G., 'Following Wittgenstein: Some Signposts for *Philosophical Investigations* ss.143–242' in S Holtzman and C Leich (eds), *Wittgenstein: To Follow a Rule* (London: Routledge & Kegan Paul, 1981), p. 31.

Dagan, H., 'The Realist Conception of Law' (2007) 57 *University of Toronto Law Journal* 607.

Duxbury, N., *Patterns of American Jurisprudence* (Oxford: Clarendon Press, 1995).

Dworkin, R., *Justice in Robes* (Cambridge, Mass.: Belknap Press, 2006).

Fisher, W. W., Horowitz, M. J., and Reed T. A., *American Legal Realism* (Oxford: Oxford University Press, 1993).

Green, L., 'Law and the Causes of Judicial Decisions' (2009) Oxford Legal Studies Research Paper No. 14/2009, available at <http://papers.ssrn.com/sol3/papers.cfm?abstract_id=1374608>

Greenberg, M., 'The Standard Picture and its Discontents' in L. Green and B. Leiter (eds), *Oxford Studies in the Philosophy of Law* (Oxford: Oxford University Press, 2011), p. 39.

Leiter, B., *'Naturalising Jurisprudence: Essays on American Legal Realism and Naturalism in Legal Philosophy* (Oxford: Oxford University Press, 2007).

Leiter, B., 'Rethinking Legal Realism: Toward a Naturalized Jurisprudence' (1997) 76 *Texas LR* 267, 270.

Marmor, A., 'The Rule of Law and its Limits' (2004) 23 *Law and Philosophy* 1.

Penner, J., Schiff, D., and Nobles, R. (eds), *Jurisprudence and Legal Theory: Commentary and Materials* (Oxford: Oxford University Press, 2002), ch. 7.

Pound, R., 'Mechanical jurisprudence' (1908) 8 *Colum L Rev* 605.

Pound, R., 'The call for a realist jurisprudence' (1931) 44 *Harv L Rev* 697.

Raz, J., 'Dworkin: A New Link in the Chain' (1986) 74 *California Law Review* 1103.

Raz, J., *The Authority of Law*, 2nd ed. (Oxford: Oxford University Press, 2009), ch.11.

Rumble, W. E., *American Legal Realism: Skepticism, Reform and the Judicial Process* (New York: Cornell University Press, 1968).

Stavropoulos, N., 'Interpretivist Theories of Law', *Standford Encyclopedia of Philosophy*, available at <http://plato.stanford.edu/entries/law-interpretivist/>.

Twining, W., *Karl Llewellyn and the Realist Movement* (London: Weidenfeld & Nicolson, 1973).

Waldron, J., 'The Concept and the Rule of Law' (2008) 43 *Georgia Law Review* 1.

Wittgenstein, L., *Philosophical Investigations*, transl. G. E. M. Anscombe (Oxford: Basil Blackwell, 1958).

PART III

The Intellectual Foundations of the Liberal Social Contract Tradition

10

The Legal and Political
Philosophy of Thomas Hobbes

Introduction

Thomas Hobbes was born in 1588 in the English county of Wiltshire. He read classics at the University of Oxford. He worked as private tutor to wealthy families for a number of years while still working on history and classics—his first publication was a translation of the works of Thucydides. In 1640 he fled to Paris fearing for his life. The English civil war was in full swing and Hobbes had already expressed some royalist sentiments, although he did not fully identify himself as a royalist, which made him unpopular with that camp too. He returned to England in 1651 and in the same year he published *Leviathan*, his most celebrated work and main statement, along with *De Cive*, on political philosophy. Hobbes was undoubtedly influenced by and perhaps motivated by the dramatic political events of his time. However, his work should not be seen as historically indexed. His model of the State is as relevant as ever today and still influences not only political philosophers but also actual policy.

The task that Hobbes set for himself in his political philosophy was to work out a 'scientific' account of the State and its law. We should be careful not to misunderstand this. What Hobbes meant by 'scientific' is not 'descriptive' neither did he imply that principles and rules are a matter of predicting people's attitudes. For Hobbes 'science' is juxtaposed to 'prudence'. The latter refers to the experience we acquire from past experience, which may guide our behaviour in the future. The former is the product not of experience but reason.

> By this it appears that Reason is not as Sense, and Memory, borne with us; nor gotten by Experience onely; as Prudence is; but attayned by Industry; first in apt imposing of Names; and secondly by getting a good and orderly Method in proceeding from the Elements, which are Names, to Assertions made by Connexion of one of them to another; and so to syllogismes, which are the Connexions of one Assertion to another, till we come to a knowledge of all the Consequences of names appertaining to the subject in hand; and that is it, men call SCIENCE.
>
> (*Leviathan*, ch. V)

So, in Hobbesian terms a scientific account of the State is the formulation of foundational political principles on the basis of and as inescapably following from a set of assumptions, which are held as uncontroversial. In other words, if these foundational assumptions hold, then one way will emerge as the only effective and stable way of ordering our co-existence.

The first question then is what these assumptions are, on which Hobbes builds his political philosophy.

10.1 **Foundational assumptions**

A very large part of *Leviathan* is devoted to a detailed discussion of our constitution and capacities as human beings. Hobbes has something to say on a number of issues such as the will, emotions, speech, communication and much more. Not all of it is directly relevant to his political philosophy—in fact some commentators question what purpose much of that analysis serves—so let us focus on three points which are important for our understanding of the Hobbesian State.

10.1.1 **On the will**

For the philosophical tradition broadly based on Kant's teaching to one degree or another, the only constraints that the *free* will is subject to are constraints deriving from reason. We will look at this in the next chapter a little more closely but for now suffice it to say that the gist of the idea is that we freely make practical decisions (i.e. decisions as to what we ought to do or not) only when our decisions are not determined in the last instance by empirical factors such as our desires, impulses or external stimuli. Although we will of course have our own preferences and an interest in satisfying them, we must do so by subjecting our decisions to objective tests, which are set by reason alone. Whether we act freely and in accordance with the moral law will be determined by whether we pass those tests of reason.

Not so for Hobbes. The will, he tells us, is *nothing but* our reactions to stimuli.

> In Deliberation, the last Appetite, or Aversion, immediately adhaering to the action, or to the omission thereof, is that wee call the WILL; the Act, (not the faculty,) of Willing. And Beasts that have Deliberation must necessarily also have Will. The Definition of the Will, given commonly by the Schooles, that it is a Rationall Appetite, is not good. For if it were, then could there be no Voluntary Act against Reason. For a Voluntary Act is that, which proceedeth from the Will, and no other. But if in stead of a Rationall Appetite, we shall say an Appetite resulting from a precedent Deliberation, then the Definition is the same that I have given here. Will, therefore, Is The Last Appetite In Deliberating.
>
> (*Leviathan*, ch. VI)

The importance of this will be revealed soon and once we have considered the rest of the Hobbesian presuppositions.

10.1.2 **On freedom**

We said in the introduction that freedom and equality are fundamental points for liberal political philosophy but there is in-house disagreement as to what it means that we are free and equal. Hobbes regards freedom and equality in purely empirical terms.

First, for Hobbes freedom is nothing but a property of matter that is capable of motion. Freedom is not a pre-institutional right nor does Hobbes regard it in terms of the absence of impediments to our capacity of making choices for ourselves. Freedom is only the unimpeded ability to move in space.

> A FREE-MAN, is 'he, that in those things, which by his strength and wit he is able to do, is not hindred to doe what he has a will to.' But when the words Free, and Liberty,

> are applyed to any thing but Bodies, they are abused; for that which is not subject to Motion, is not subject to Impediment.
>
> (*Leviathan*, ch. XXI)

Now, take this conception of freedom in conjunction with his view on will. The upshot is that our freedom is not compromised when the range of our choices are limited by others or by external factors. Even when, through no fault of our own, we are faced with a dilemma between two choices, neither of which we are motivated to pursue, our decision is still a product of our will, since it is motivated by our appetite for the least bad option, and it is free because liberty has nothing to do with the conditions under which we make our practical choices. So, Hobbes tells us, even when we act out of fear, need or necessity, we nevertheless act deliberately and freely. It follows that it is not a compromise to our freedom or our capacity to deliberate and exercise our will for our acts to be circumscribed by a sovereign, the directives of whom we are under an obligation to obey out of necessity. And, as we will see a little later on, this is precisely how Hobbes conceives of the State.

10.1.3 On equality

Hobbes' conception of equality is also empirical. Once again he parts ways with the view of equality as a pre-political, natural right of all humans, a view underpinning other social contract theories. He describes equality in terms of our relative strengths. We are equal in the sense that no one can be stronger than all others in every way and therefore no one is guaranteed to dominate over others.

> Nature hath made men so equall, in the faculties of body, and mind; as that though there bee found one man sometimes manifestly stronger in body, or of quicker mind then another; yet when all is reckoned together, the difference between man, and man, is not so considerable, as that one man can thereupon claim to himselfe any benefit, to which another may not pretend, as well as he. For as to the strength of body, the weakest has strength enough to kill the strongest, either by secret machination, or by confederacy with others, that are in the same danger with himselfe.
>
> (*Leviathan*, ch. XIII)

This is fairly self-explanatory. Hobbes considers the concept of equality to be relevant only in relation to our physical capacities. Again, the full importance of the assumption will be revealed a little later but for now note that this conception of equality does not have any ramifications for the State and its law without further ado. Nothing follows merely from the fact that no one can outpower or outwit others. We need something further to tell us whether this is a state of affairs to which we ought to respond and how we ought to do so. It also does not follow that everyone is entitled to equal treatment by the State. The fact alone that we are roughly of equal strength does not have any such normative repercussions.

10.1.4 On the traits of human nature

The Hobbesian picture of humanity is completed with an account of three general human dispositions pertaining to our motivation, which are connected to our natural equality: competitiveness, diffidence or fear, and vainglory.

We are competitive not out of greed but because of the scarcity of resources available to us. We are rational enough to realise that not all of us can enjoy everything to the maximum degree. We in fact know that we cannot *all* enjoy *everything* that we may desire, because our desires over finite resources may clash. This makes us inclined to secure for ourselves all that we need in order to be able to survive and, if possible what is necessary for us to live our lives as well as possible.

We are also constantly wary, fearful of each other. Again, it is an instinct of self-preservation in combination with our rational faculties that explains this. We already know that we compete for the same goods and that there is no guarantee that we will be able to satisfy our needs or desires. We also know that others are in the same position as us. We therefore have no way of knowing whether others will not attack us in their effort to satisfy their needs and desires by obtaining what we have or what neither of us has but both of us want or need. In the absence of any mechanism that will standardise our expectations and fix our entitlements, we will be in a constant state of anxiety. The upshot of it is that conflict will very likely break out, because we will be inclined to strike pre-emptively so as to avoid the worst possible scenario.

Finally, our pride and vainglory make us want to be top of the heap and desire what others have. We are never content with what we have nor do we have any objective way of hierarchising our desires. But even when not motivated by vanity, we still want to be better than anyone else. We therefore covet the belongings or privileges of others.

10.2 'Man's natural condition' or the *state of nature*

Let us take stock. For Hobbes we are bearers of free will not because we are reasonable and we can subject our preferences to tests set by reason but because we have the capacity to form desires and act on them. These desires—and therefore our will and our actions—will very often be conditioned, if not altogether determined, by external factors, by circumstances that cause us fear or create a vital need. Hobbes also takes as given that we are naturally equal in terms of our strength and our chances of dominating over others. Finally, in light of that equality as well as the scarcity of resources, it is inevitable that we will be motivated to act out of competitiveness (in order to secure what we need or want), fear that others will strike first, and the pursuit of glory.

Left at that and in the absence of any normative or other constraints and assurances, our life-in-common will regress into the 'state of nature'. The state of nature is a state of uncertainty as to what belongs to whom or who may use what, as to the expectations and intentions of others, as to the future. In such conditions and motivated by our sense of self-preservation, we will be driven to war of all against all. Hobbes famously described the state of nature in the bleakest of colours. The following is arguably one of the most frequently cited passages in the history of political philosophy.

Whatsoever therefore is consequent to a time of war, where every man is enemy to every man, the same consequent to the time wherein men live without other security than what their own strength and their own invention shall furnish them withal. In such condition there is no place for industry, because the fruit thereof is uncertain: and consequently no culture of the earth; no navigation, nor use of the commodities that may be imported by sea; no commodious building; no instruments of moving and removing such things as require much force; no knowledge of the face of the earth; no account of

> time; no arts; no letters; no society; and which is worst of all, continual fear, and danger of violent death; and the life of man, solitary, poor, nasty, brutish, and short.
>
> (*Leviathan*, ch. XIII)

We have already mentioned this a few times but it is important to drive the point home, because it distinguishes Hobbes from much of the rest of the social contract tradition. In the state of nature there is no normative order capable of binding or motivating everyone. No one has an omnilaterally *justified* entitlement to anything. It is only political institutions that can govern our social co-existence by introducing norms, which are acceptable by and therefore binding for all. To quote Hobbes once again:

> To this warre of every man against every man, this also is consequent; that nothing can be Unjust. The notions of Right and Wrong, Justice and Injustice have there no place. Where there is no common Power, there is no Law: where no Law, no Injustice.
>
> (*Leviathan*, ch. XIII)

Note how this connects to and, indeed, underpins ideas that we have already encountered earlier on in this book. Recall the early empiricist legal positivism of Austin and Bentham as well as Hart's conventionalism. Much of that tradition rests, either implicitly or explicitly, on scepticism with regard to morality. This means that it rejects the idea that there can be an objective moral order, which we can intuit or discover with the use of our reason and which is able of governing our social co-existence. Therefore the contingent, man-made institution that is the law emerges as the only way of regulating our communities in a way that is recognisable and, in one sense or another, acceptable by all. The law becomes the only generally relevant yardstick of rightness or wrongness, justice or injustice. This basic framework of thinking about the law is traced back to Hobbes.

Now, the state of nature is largely a counterfactual, a hypothetical situation. Hobbes does not suggest that we did ever find ourselves in such a generalised state of lawlessness and war of all against all, although he did consider some historical cases as approximating this. At the same time though, it is not entirely a-historical neither is it impossible that it will ever materialise—in fact if it works as the basis of analysis it is precisely because it is possible. Any context in which people have to share space or resources but in which there is no central power capable of ordering their co-existence approximates the Hobbesian state of nature. The state of nature is a construction, the projection of the consequences of the lack of central government in light of the scarcity of resources, the natural traits of humans and our motivational disposition.

You should not be surprised to see Hobbes appealing to a hypothetical situation to make normative suggestions for the real world. Counterfactuals such as the state of nature are fairly frequently employed in the social contract political philosophical tradition. Their point is to paint an uncluttered picture of the world by singling out some basic and uncontroversial facts. These facts can then be used as the basis for the construction of foundational political principles by asking: 'if we were in this situation, what would be the best way of governing our social co-existence?'. This is not to say that those who employ such arguments subscribe to some sort of natural law idea to argue that norms will inexorably follow from facts. The idea is that, on the basis of the information available in the state of nature, everyone will have reasons to accept those foundational principles, and this will motivate a universal agreement on these principles and the institutions that they will support.

So, for Hobbes the state of nature is a possibility given the various facts about human nature. And, the state of nature being such as to make it impossible for anyone to satisfy any desires, the stake is how to exit that terrible situation and enter the peaceful civil condition.

10.3 Exit from the state of nature and entry into the civil condition

The civil condition is a governed state of affairs which will make it possible for us to satisfy our needs and desires without the constant fear and risk of being attacked by others, because we will know to some degree of certainty what is mine and what is thine and where the limits of our liberty and the liberty of others lie. How, then, to avoid entering the state of nature or how to exit it, should we be so unlucky as for things to come to this?

The solution to that predicament is to be found in nature itself. Hobbes singles out some 'laws of nature', to which we are subject and which will motivate us to seek entry into the civil condition. Once again, we should be careful here not to misunderstand Hobbes. These 'laws' of nature are not laws in the normative sense of the word. Hobbes does not quite argue that there are norms, which tell us what we ought to do and are somehow woven into the fabric of nature (although such an interpretation is not precluded by the text). The 'laws' of nature are dictates of reason, rational conclusions as to what we ought to do to avoid the misery of the state of nature. They do not themselves suffice to motivate us to want to avoid the state of nature. If we do though, and Hobbes takes it as given that we are generally inclined to pursue self-preservation and the satisfaction of our needs and desires, we must go about it in the way that these directives of reason instruct us to.

Hobbes lists 19 such 'eternal and immutable' laws of nature but we will only focus on the first three, because they are meant to provide the foundations of the civil condition. The first is the fundamental law of nature

> 'That every man, ought to endeavour Peace, as farre as he has hope of obtaining it; and when he cannot obtain it, that he may seek, and use, all helps, and advantages of Warre.' The first branch, of which Rule, containeth the first, and Fundamentall Law of Nature; which is, 'To seek Peace, and follow it.' The Second, the summe of the Right of Nature; which is, 'By all means we can, to defend our selves.'
>
> (*Leviathan*, ch. XIV)

So, according to the first leg of the fundamental law of nature, we should seek peace because we want to minimise the risks of the state of nature and make it possible for us to pursue our ideas of happiness and the good life. But reason also tells us that, when peace appears impossible, we must seek our self-preservation at all costs by defending ourselves and engaging in war with those who attack us.

Now, how do we go about seeking peace? Remember that in the state of nature there are no authorised entitlements, no mine and thine and everything is up for grabs by everyone. We know, however, that this is simply not viable and it clashes with our aim of pursuing peace in order for us to live a happy life. This is because, as we have seen, in the absence of any assurances that others will keep off our things, we are inclined to be competitive and fearful and therefore defensive. The only way out is that we all accept some limitations to this 'right' of ours to everything available in the world. And this is the second law of nature.

> That a man be willing, when others are so too, as farre-forth, as for Peace, and defence of himselfe he shall think it necessary, to lay down this right to all things; and be contented with so much liberty against other men, as he would allow other men against himselfe.
>
> (*Leviathan*, ch. XIV)

Let us not misunderstand Hobbes. He does not urge us to give up some of our entitlements and accept limitations to what will belong to us out of regard for others. We give up what could have been ours subject to the requirement of reciprocity, i.e. only to the extent that others will be prepared to make similar concessions. Absent reciprocity, we would still be stranded in the state of nature, in which everyone owns nothing and everything at the same time. So, we make these concessions by striking agreements with others, by entering into contracts, 'covenants' to use Hobbesian vocabulary. We promise others that we will accept some restrictions to our entitlements on the condition that they make similar promises to us.

This second law is complemented by the third law of nature

> That Men Perform Their Covenants Made: without which, Covenants are in vain, and but Empty words; and the Right of all men to all things remaining, wee are still in the condition of Warre.
>
> (*Leviathan*, ch. XV)

The requirement that promises be kept is a conceptual necessity. It is part of the very sense of promising that the pledge be truthful and that the promisor intends to honour his word to the promisee. In turn, the intention to honour does not suffice but must be acted upon by taking steps towards honouring one's promise. To look at it from a different angle, it would be a performative contradiction, though not a logical one, for one to say 'I promise to φ but do not intend to φ'. The third law of nature therefore guarantees that covenants will not remain vacuous words but that they will have a purchase in the real world and that they will be capable of performing the purpose which makes them necessary in the first place, i.e. the achievement of a civil, peaceful condition.

So, to summarise. We generally want to satisfy our desires and our sense of self-preservation urges us to satisfy our needs. That same rational sense tells us that we can only do so in a peaceful condition, in which we will have some assurance that others will refrain from coveting what we consider to be ours. This can be achieved by setting clear boundaries between 'mine' and 'thine'. In the absence of any other normative constraints in the state of nature, the only way of doing so is by mutual agreements on the basis of reciprocity, agreements which bind us as a matter of conceptual necessity.

10.4 **The social contract**

The next step in establishing the civil condition is the setting up of the State. But first we should ask why we need a State to begin with. If we can strike mutually binding agreements with others in order to live in conditions of peace, why does this not suffice to guarantee a relatively secure environment?

The answer is in the motivational force of the laws of nature and the promises we exchange. They bind us internally, *in foro interno* to use Hobbes' language, and when it is safe to act upon. This commitment is however hypothetical, in that we are bound to abide by the laws of nature and keep our promises to the extent that others will do so too. When others do fulfil their obligations, we are under an obligation to honour ours as well. Our external acts are therefore not governed by the laws of nature without further ado, because we can always fail to act on those laws when it is safe to do so. After all, let us not forget the second leg of the fundamental law of nature: 'and when he cannot obtain it, that he may seek, and use, all helps, and advantages of Warre'. For it to be possible for us to be committed *in foro externo*, we need further assurance that others will act on the laws of nature and the promises they have made. Once a further level of obligation is in place, we will be relatively certain that others will act accordingly and not disappoint our expectations because it will not be safe for them to do so. And this further level is provided by the State and its law.

So there are good reasons and we are sufficiently motivated to set up a State that will formalise rules in a manner that is objective and binding for all. We go about this by entering into a contract with one another, the social contract. All citizens agree with each other to authorise the sovereign to issue commands, by which all will be bound. They also promise to the sovereign to accept as binding the laws that she will enact. The sovereign herself, however, makes no promises to her subjects. She is the beneficiary of the social contract and not a party to it. The upshot of this is that she is under no obligation towards citizens.

Let us clarify these basic terms of the social contract a little further. First of all, why a contract? Well, Hobbes, and many other social contract theorists, assumes that one can take on an obligation only if one accepts that obligation. Promising is the clearest way of assuming such duties. Recall once again the legal positivist tradition that we considered earlier on in the book, and the distinction between moral and social normativity. For Hobbes only the latter is possible or, at the very least, of relevance in the political sphere.

We should draw a distinction here, which will help us better to understand what situations Hobbes has in mind. He imagines two ways of a sovereign coming into power: by acquisition and by institution. In both these cases, sovereignty is the product of acts of promising. Sovereignty is typically *acquired* at the end of a war when one side emerges victorious and the other side pledges obedience to the new sovereign. Sovereignty is conferred by institution, when the members of the community exchange promises of obeying the sovereign with each other. So, in sovereignty by acquisition, it seems that there are two parties rather than three: victors and losers. In sovereignty by institution there are multiple parties: each citizen separately and the sovereign. If this is so, then the two social contracts are apparently radically different. In the former, one party pledges obedience to the other but, in order for there to be a covenant at all, the other party must make some promises too. But this would test the consistency of the Hobbesian scheme not least because it would undermine the unconditional nature of sovereign authority. In the latter case, a third party becomes the beneficiary of the social contract, a party that is not bound by any promise. Nevertheless, Hobbes insists that the two cases may differ contingently but not essentially; the social contract and its terms remain the same. One way of making sense of this is by rethinking the situation that generates sovereignty by acquisition. Although at first sight it is a case of victors versus losers, if we consider the situation in Hobbesian terms, we will see that even those who fought on the side of the victors also have good reason to pledge obedience to the leader-cum-sovereign, because even they can never be certain that allegiances and the balance of power will remain stable, that they will always be on the sovereign's right side or that a new war will not eventually break out. They may, of course, benefit in the short term compared to the losers, because the sovereign may favour them. This, however, is a substantive matter having to do with the content of the commands of the sovereign rather than how she acquires her authority. Both victors and losers have an interest in seeking peace in a way that will be stable in the long run, therefore they strike an agreement very much like the agreement that confers authority to the sovereign by institution.

Now, does Hobbes believe that there can be no legitimate State if the citizens do not explicitly promise to each other that they will obey the sovereign come what may? Not quite. This is not unimaginable in cases of sovereignty by acquisition, where agreements are made and treaties are signed. But we would be hard pressed to find anything of the sort in most other contexts. In the vast majority of cases, we are born into a State and remain its citizens until our death without ever having explicitly to pledge obedience to the sovereign, although we implicitly do so by not actively resisting. One possible response to this is that the social contract is not actual but hypothetical. Although we were never given the opportunity explicitly to agree to submit ourselves to the authority of the sovereign, we are held to have done so by living as members of the political community and accepting its terms by omission.

This invites the objection that Ronald Dworkin has raised against the very idea of a social contract. If the contract is hypothetical, then it cannot be binding. If the parties do not exchange promises and agree to perform certain tasks, then they cannot be held to have taken on any obligations. Even if we accept that the participants in the hypothetical state of nature are idealised reflections of ourselves, the fact that *they* accept the terms of the social contract has no binding effect on *us* in the actual world. The answer typically given by social contractarian theorists to this is that the device of the social contract should not be taken literally as an exchange of promises between concrete individuals. It is rather a counterfactual construction of the reasons of rational persons, who exercise their rational capacities in their co-existence with each other. Once one recognises what rationality requires, then one will also recognise the obligations that this generates.

Now, if that is what the original contract is, a theoretical construction of the reasons we may have for agreeing to some terms of social cooperation in light of certain uncontested facts about human nature and society, then it must eventually be actualised for it to be able to serve as a stable foundation for real political communities. In other words, there must be some mechanisms, some procedures, through which citizens will be able to express their consent to the basic terms. Hobbes does not really provide for any such mechanisms, he does not tell us how the promise to each other and to the sovereign is to be actualised or reconfirmed by each generation. This should not surprise us, however. Recall that, for Hobbes, fear and necessity are not incompatible with freedom of will. Even if we decide under pressure and fear for our lives, our decisions are a genuine expression of our will. Actually subjecting our will to the commands of the sovereign is therefore a sufficient indication that we have accepted the original contract, even though this acceptance is not fully autonomously motivated.

10.5 The sovereign's powers and the form and content of government and law

So, let us accept that a social contract is necessary and that we are bound by it. In the next step we must ask what its terms are. We have already alluded to Hobbes' very straightforward answer: we agree to submit our external freedom to the sovereign altogether.

To put it simply, we agree blindly to obey the sovereign's commands and only the sovereign's commands. Note the implications of this. The sovereign's law emerges as the *only* objective normative order that is capable of binding us all and providing normative foundations for our political communities. As we pointed out earlier, the sovereign's commands are the only universal standards of justice and injustice, of right and wrong. It also follows that *the content* of these commands has no bearing on our obligation to obey them. We are under a duty to follow the sovereign's laws even though we consider them morally wrong or even if they fail to promote our interests. This is because, even though we may find ourselves substantively short-changed, we would be far worse off if there were no law to standardise everyone's expectations and set *some* boundaries between the spheres of control of each citizen.

A third implication of the foundational term of the social contract is that it sets no limits to what the sovereign may legitimately demand of us. This does not mean that the sovereign will not be subject to other constraints, say from God, her personal morality or indeed prudential considerations regarding the best way of governing. But her authority will be absolute in that it will not be subject to any legal or constitutional such constraints. Recall Austin here, who viewed the sovereign as *legally* illimitable and notice how this view reflected the Hobbesian image of sovereignty.

In fact, Hobbes goes even further. Because having a central source of authoritative directives as enjoying priority in relation to other values or interests, the unity and exclusivity of that authority must be maintained. This has a direct implication regarding the separation of powers. The sovereign is under a duty to maintain all three state powers, i.e. the legislative, executive and judicial powers. Give one of these powers away, Hobbes tells us, and you will not be able to exercise the others because they are so closely interlinked. This, of course, does not mean that it is imperative that the same person or group of people acts as legislators, executive and judges—although this would be desirable. It means that the powers ought not to be separated and be held and exercised independently. Although this is probably rather unpalatable to most of us, because the separation of powers is so entrenched in contemporary political and legal cultures, it makes sense in Hobbesian terms. Recall that the only measure of justice and rightness are the sovereign's commands and no norm is pre-institutionally omnilaterally binding. It therefore follows that the sovereign can do no injustice. This already lifts the need for a mechanism of checks and balances. There is no standard other than the sovereign's commands against which, say, an independent judiciary can assess the law. And, in cases of ambiguity or inconsistency between laws, it is imperative that conflicts are authoritatively resolved by the sovereign or else there is a risk of her authority being undermined because it is fragmented.

It is for largely the same reasons that Hobbes rejects democracy as a system of government too. It follows from the fact that the state of nature is a normative void that citizens have no pre-existing right of participation in the process of public norm determination. Neither is their liberty undermined by the fact that they are subject to rules, which they have not co-decided or which they are under an obligation to obey out of fear or necessity. At the same time, as we have already seen, the sovereign is under a duty to not fragment her authority. Not only this but it would also be imprudent of her to do so. Hobbes draws on historical experience of democratic regimes, which collapsed under the pressure of conflict and uncertainty—this is for him too much of a risk to take. Therefore citizens' liberty is safeguarded more effectively in the context of absolute sovereignty than in a democratic regime. This does not mean that the sovereign will not and should not receive advice on how to rule, it is in fact the most prudent thing for her to do. But taking advice is one thing and deferring the power to make final decisions to a group of people is another.

Although the Hobbesian sovereign is largely absolute, there are *some* limits to her powers. First there are some formal ones, which follow from the very rationale of having a central law-enacting authority, which is to enable citizens to know the limits of their external freedom and that of others. Laws ought to be promulgated and be knowable and accessible in advance; they should be intelligible; they should be applied impartially and consistently with their meaning (which precludes, for example, that the innocent be punished). In other words, laws must be enacted and enforced in such a way as to make it possible for citizens to follow them.

Let us make a brief detour, since we are on the point of the form of law. Hobbes is held to be the original command theorist of law. Although he did not explicitly talk about the nature of law, in the same way as Austin or Hart did, he clearly conceptually reduces law to the commands of the sovereign. At the same time, though, he recognises that these commands may take different forms. Unlike Austin, who famously included sanctions (presumably in the narrower sense) in the conceptual core of law, Hobbes saw that some laws will be penal and some will be distributive. He saw what Hart did too, that some laws coerce us into acting in a certain way and some enable us to act in a certain way. And, despite their different form, they both count as laws, because they are pronouncements of the sovereign's will and they are accepted by the people as such on the basis of the social contract.

To turn to law's content, are there any substantive limits to the sovereign's power? From the absence of any substantive, constitutional or legal, constraints to what the sovereign can demand of us it should also follow that citizens are under an unconditional obligation to obey the sovereign's commands. If we take on an obligation to obey everything the sovereign commands us to do, then we are under a duty to obey anything she commands us to do. And, indeed we largely are and, when we fail to abide by the law, then it is within the sovereign's legitimate powers to punish us for our failure. An implication of this is that we do not have a right to resist the sovereign. We may disagree with her laws but we are not justified to disobey them, let alone rebel against them. But what if the sovereign asks us to do something that will undermine our very self-preservation? What if her commands go against the very rationale of having a sovereign issuing commands in the first place?

On an empirical level and to some extent, this is perhaps a moot point. First of all, a law which remains completely quiet on issues of distribution and so on, will not even be recognised and accepted as a legal system by the members of the community, who are looking for solutions to the problem of the clash of external freedoms. But it is also not likely that a sovereign will provide solutions to these problems, but solutions which lead to the self-destruction of the whole community. She will be prudent enough to want, if not the well-being of citizens, at least the preservation and stability of the political community. But this does not rule out the possibility of the sovereign requiring *individuals* to accept what may be contrary to their sense of self-preservation, say the death penalty or long term incarceration. Once again, the parallels between Hobbes and contemporary legal positivism are obvious here. Recall Hart and his 'minimum content of natural law'. If we were giant land crabs, Hart told us, fully self-sufficient and independent, we would not require certain laws. But, alas, we are a lot more vulnerable than supercrabs and we need laws, which will address these facts, 'truisms' for Hart, about human nature.

In any case, even if it is hard to imagine such a legal system, it cannot be theoretically ruled out, because there is nothing in the social contract stopping the sovereign from making such unreasonable demands. Hobbes does not deny that individuals are justified to resist and try to secure their self-preservation, as long as they do not enlist others in organised rebellion. (Note how this is arguably inconsistent because it may turn out that the most appropriate way of striving for self-preservation is collective rebellion). Now, most people will no doubt find it unpalatable that the right to resist is restricted to so few cases and that the right to collective resistance is ruled out. And what makes all this even more difficult to accept is Hobbes' rejection of democracy as a form of governance, which means that people may never be given the chance to express their view on the law. Nevertheless, we should make sure we see his argument in the right perspective. We are under a political and legal obligation to obey the sovereign come what may. We are, at the same time, at liberty to try to influence the decisions of the sovereign. But, should these decisions go against us, then we do not have a political or legal right to rebel. When the sovereign's commands threaten our self-preservation, we are faced with a dilemma that cannot be solved from within politics or law, both of which are made possible precisely *because* there is a sovereign and a State no matter how iniquitous it may be. The terms of the social contract cannot provide solutions to such conflicts without being renegotiated. If we decide to resist, we enter a realm of conflict that cannot be governed by law. And in order for it not to regress into the state of nature, we are under an obligation not to encourage others to follow us down that road.

10.6 Is Hobbes' political philosophy liberal? Is it suitable for our times?

In the introduction we said that liberalism's main concern is to reconcile freedom and equality in a diverse social world. Now we have seen that, for Hobbes, the only political arrangement that can work is a state of absolute power in the hands of one person or a group of people. There is no room for democracy, no separation of powers. Nor is the sovereign under any obligation to distribute resources among citizens in accordance with any pre-institutional standards of fairness. You will be justified in thinking that none of this looks particularly liberal.

This is true but one has to think about it in the right perspective, i.e. juxtaposed to its opposite. In Hobbesian thought, the alternative to the all-powerful sovereign is the state of nature in which nothing is possible, let alone the actualisation of our freedom. For Hobbes, we are free when we are relatively secure and this is all that can be guaranteed at the constitutional level of setting up a State. We can certainly hope and strive for more freedom. We could try to influence State policies, although there is still no guarantee that we will be able to achieve our aims. But all this is only possible from within a constituted State under an absolute sovereign.

The question then should be rephrased. Is the Hobbesian scheme *liberal enough*? Well, liberal enough *for whom*? Who is the subject of political philosophy? Is it an idealised conception of humans with certain universal and diachronic characteristics? If so, then the question is, first, whether it is possible to construct such an idealised and generally acceptable conception of humanity that can serve as the foundation for the construction of a State. Many think it impossible. They believe that conceptions of the essence of human nature are never context-independent, that even if we can single out some regularly recurring characteristics, they are determined by historical circumstance and using them as the foundation for the political and law only serves to perpetuate this historical circumstance.

But let us accept as a working hypothesis that it is possible to say with some degree of certainty what human nature is. We should then ask whether Hobbes' version of it is correct. Are the characteristics that he imputes to us genuinely immutable and universal features of humanity? Many would disagree. Why, for example, should we only rely on instrumental rationality and exclude our passions or our emotions from the foundations of politics? Such disagreements are plausible and reasonable. The fact that they emerge raises the second level question of how they can be resolved. How are we even to begin to decide what counts as human nature that can support our normative practices?

Alternatively, political philosophy may be much more modest than this. Perhaps all it can tell us is how the State and its law ought to be set up in the here and now, in contexts in which there can be sufficiently general agreement over certain foundational facts. And, it may indeed be the case that this is the only claim that Hobbes meant to raise. Perhaps his aim was to construct a political system suitable for England in the aftermath of a traumatic and deeply divisive civil war. Perhaps he only meant to convince his contemporaries, and maybe this would explain his rich rhetorical flare too, that they must avoid the horrors of another civil war at all costs and that the only way of so doing would be by submitting to the power of the sovereign.

In that case, the question is whether the Hobbesian state is still relevant today. To answer this, we should ask whether Hobbes proceeds from an accurate description of our conditions of existence, of the ways in which we understand ourselves and others. And this must be a relatively uncontroversial description, one that everyone should be able to accept. We will come back to this point when we discuss John Rawls' political liberalism but for now let us just raise the suspicion that it is questionable whether Hobbes offers such a starting point. At this stage of the development of our societies, perhaps not all societies but at least some, we regard ourselves as capable of more than simply striking a compromise, a *modus vivendi*. We want a State that does not liberate us by repressing us but one that will respect our ideas about a happy life and will allow us the space to pursue these ideas.

FURTHER READING

Hobbes, T., *Leviathan: or, The matter, forme and power of a commonwealth, ecclesiasticall and civill* (1651).

Hobbes, T., *De Cive* (1642), published in English as *Philosophical Rudiments Concerning Government and Society* (1651).

Hobbes, T., *Dialogue Between a Philosopher and a Student of the Common Laws of England* (1681).

Curran, E., *Reclaiming the Rights of Hobbesian Subjects* (Hampshire: Palgrave Macmillan, 2007).

Finkelstein, C., *Hobbes on Law* (Aldershot: Ashgate, 2005).

Foisneau, L. and Sorell, T. (eds.), *Leviathan after 350 years* (Oxford: Oxford University Press, 2004).

Gauthier, D., *The Logic of 'Leviathan': the Moral and political Theory of Thomas Hobbes* (Oxford: Clarendon Press, 1969).

Hampton, J., *Hobbes and the Social Contract Tradition* (Cambridge: Cambridge University Press, 1986).

Hoekstra, K., 'Hobbes on Law, Nature and Reason' (2003) *Journal of the History of Philosophy* 41(1): 111–20.

Martinich, A. P., *Hobbes* (New York: Routledge, 2005).

Nagel, T., 'Hobbes's Concept of Obligation' (1959) *Philosophical Review* 68 (1), 68–83.

Sorell, T. (ed.), *The Cambridge Companion to Hobbes* (Cambridge: Cambridge University Press, 1996).

Springboard, P. (ed.), *The Cambridge Companion to Hobbes's Leviathan* (Cambridge: Cambridge University Press, 2007).

Warrender, H., *The Political Philosophy of Hobbes: his Theory of Obligation* (Oxford: Oxford University Press, 1957).

11

The Legal and Political Philosophy of Immanuel Kant

Introduction

Immanuel Kant was born in 1724 in Königsberg, then part of Prussia and now called Kaliningrad and part of Russia, and died in 1804. He is considered one of the most important, and is certainly one of the most influential, philosophers in history. He is also one of the most important representatives of the Enlightenment. His oeuvre covers an impressive range of subjects from metaphysics to astronomy. Some of his most important works on metaphysics, morality, and politics include the *Critique of Pure Reason*, the *Critique of Practical Reason*, and the *Metaphysics of Morals*. If there is one thing that underpins all of Kant's work, is his belief in the primacy of reason. Very much epitomising what the Enlightenment was all about, Kant believed that with the use of our reason we can master the truth about the world and harness our capacity to know and understand it but also arrive at conclusions as to the right thing to do in morality, politics, and law. Kant's aim was to connect reason and experience in a seamless whole.

11.1 A background note on Kant's moral philosophy

Kant's moral theory is arguably more influential, and certainly more widely known, than his political and legal philosophy. Although it is the latter that is of interest to us in this chapter, we will give a very brief and rough outline of his moral theory so that we can later ask in what relation his moral and political philosophies stand, a question which is not only of philological but also of philosophical significance.

The starting point in Kant's moral philosophy is the 'factum of reason'. What factum means here is open to interpretation. Some interpret it as 'fact', some as 'deed', while others regard it as meaning more or less 'premise'. The precise meaning will have serious repercussions for the plausibility of Kantian moral philosophy but this is not our concern here. What we need to know is that the factum of reason is our *consciousness of the moral law*. Kant means this: we customarily find ourselves in practical dilemmas, in which we are called to make decisions as to what we ought to do. We also hold ourselves and others responsible for actions or omissions. What all this suggests is that we have the capacity to make practical decisions *freely*, decisions which are not determined by anything but our will. So the will is free only when it is subject to pure constraints of reason and not to external, empirical imperatives or pressures such as our desires. Perhaps it is helpful to juxtapose this to Hobbes' understanding of the will and freedom. As you will recall, the will is never free in this sense for Hobbes. It is always subject to other factors from the desires that we develop independently to the fear or necessity caused by factors external to us.

In order for us to be able to exercise our will fully, freely, and autonomously, and to act in a morally correct manner, we must grasp the conditions of the moral law and subject our decisions to that moral law. Let us unpack this. We always act on the basis of an imperative, a 'maxim' to use Kant's terminology. Most of these maxims are hypothetical, i.e. they point to means of achieving certain goals. For example, when deciding what one wants to do as a job, one may think along these lines: 'I want to become a lawyer, therefore I ought to do a law degree for me to be able to qualify', and so on. Being guided in the last instance by such instrumental considerations, acting on hypothetical maxims, implies that our will is subject to contingent constraints bound to experience and is therefore not free. Kant of course does not deny that we will more often than not act on our preferences. After all, life would be intolerable if we were never allowed to pursue our ideas of happiness. What he does tell us is that these contingent preferences cannot have the last word, they cannot determine our actions in the final instance.

So, as we have already said, we ensure that our actions are free and right when we subject them to tests predicated on practical reason alone. These tests form the moral law, which is revealed to us as the *categorical imperative* (CI). Note that whereas hypothetical imperatives are conditional on our goals, the moral law is *categorical* because it applies to us simply by virtue of our being practically reasoning beings. The CI requires that we 'act only in accordance with that maxim through which you can at the same time will that it become universal law' (4:421). This basic imperative is analysed into three distinct but unified formulations:

The universal law of nature formula

'Act as if the maxim of your action were to become by your will a universal law of nature'. (4:421)

The humanity formula

'So act that you use humanity, whether in your own person or in the person of any other, always at the same time as an end, never merely as a means'. (4:429)

The autonomy formula

'Supreme condition of [the will's] harmony with universal practical reason [is] the idea of the will of every rational being as a will giving universal law'. (4:432)

There is another formulation, the 'kingdom of ends' one, which some view as part of the autonomy formula and others as self-standing. According to this, we should:

'act in accordance with the maxims of a member giving universal laws for a merely possible kingdom of ends' (4:439)

Since our purposes here are different, we will only give a brief explanation of how the CI works. The humanity formula requires that you imagine your reason for your action, as if it were binding on all as a matter of natural law. Then you must ask yourself whether that maxim will be possible in a world in which it is held as a universal law. This sounds paradoxical but a kind of paradox is exactly what Kant is driving at. The standard example is giving a promise without intending to keep it. Say you select that as your maxim. You should then think of a world in which promising without any intention of keeping that promise is a natural, universal law. If that were the case, then promises would be meaningless. This, though, is a contradiction in conception. You are therefore under a 'perfect' duty to abstain from promising without the intention of honouring your promise. Now, if your maxim does not lead to such a conceptual contradiction, then you should ask yourself whether you would *will* to act on that maxim in a world in which it holds as universal law. If that contradicts your will, then you are under an 'imperfect' duty to not act on that maxim.

The humanity formula requires that we respect others as individuals and not for their instrumental value for our goals. This is not to say that we may not try to obtain and enjoy services that others can provide to us. It is inevitable, and indeed desirable, that labour be divided in such a way that all of us be treated by others, in this restricted sense, as means to their ends some of the time. What Kant means is that we should not treat others as *mere* means. This centrally entails that we ought to show respect for the humanity in others, with 'humanity' entailing the capacities of rationality and reasonableness as well as the capacity to develop our talents and skills.

The autonomy formula requires that, when acting, we regard ourselves not as *subjects* of the moral law but as *legislators* of universal laws. The moral law does not exist in nature in some form or another waiting for us to intuit or somehow discover it. Our actions are validated as morally right to the extent that we have autonomously decided them and not with reference to some ideal removed from us as reasoning beings. But note also that autonomy does not simply mean freedom of choice, which is perhaps the currently prevalent meaning of the term. In its Kantian conception, autonomy is our capacity to set constraints on our choices ourselves, to harmonise our decisions with the rest of humanity. And the kingdom of ends formulation spells out the social dimension of the CI. It requires that we legislate for a community of moral agents who are bearers of free will.

As you can see, the CI does not tell us *what* we ought to do. It does not prescribe the content of our actions nor does it hierarchise values or goods. It tells us *how* we ought to decide when acting. It sets the procedure, which we should follow to ensure that our actions will be right in the sense that they will be respectful of us and others as members of humanity. This, however, does not make this conception of morality uncontroversial. It relies on a very specific and contested description of agency in terms of pure practical reason in direct competition with prudential or communitarian conceptions of morality. This is important for our purposes because, as we will see a little later on, if Kant's political philosophy is reducible to the CI, then its acceptability will depend on whether one accepts the moral philosophy in which it is anchored.

11.2 The foundations of Kant's political and legal philosophy

Kant's theory of the State and law is mainly offered in the part of his *Metaphysics of Morals* entitled 'Doctrine of Right' as well as in his essay (1793) *On the common saying: that may be correct in theory, but it is of no use in practice* (commonly referred to as *Theory and Practice*). Note that what Kant means by 'Right' is not the narrower sense of the word, to which we are generally used and which connotes an entitlement of some sort. What is translated as Right (or sometimes as Justice or Law) is '*Recht*', the general idea of justice or political right, that is a system of laws which will govern our external behaviour and make it possible for all of us peacefully to co-exist in a civil condition.

Kant's main concern is the same as that of Hobbes: to offer a way out of the state of nature and into a civil, rightful condition. The way that he pursues this aim is, however, rather different to Hobbes'. As we saw, Hobbes' starting point is human nature and our characteristics of competitiveness, fear and pride in combination with the laws of nature, chief amongst them our rational drive for self-preservation. The upshot of this is an absolute sovereign, who is authorised by the parties in the original social contract to enact public norms, which will be binding for all citizens quite independently of their content. As we would expect now that we are a little more familiar with his moral philosophy, Kant cannot subscribe to the same ideas. The Hobbesian sovereign is at liberty to impose any conception of the good she sees fit to her subjects. For Kant, being subjected to the conceptions of the good of others is an unjustifiable limitation of our freedom. 'No one can coerce me to be happy in his way', he tells us (8:291). So the main question still remains unanswered. How can we all live together, in the same space, having to share the same resources without giving up any of our liberty?

Kant's starting point is the Universal Principle of Right (UPR), according to which

Any action is right if it can coexist with everyone's freedom in accordance with a universal law, or if on its maxim the freedom of choice of each can coexist with everyone's freedom in accordance with a universal law (6:231).

This UPR is instantiated for every individual as 'innate right'. We have the right to be free with freedom being independence from the choices of others.

Freedom (independence from being constrained by another's choice), insofar as it can coexist with the freedom of every other in accordance with a universal law, is the only original right belonging to every man by virtue of his humanity. (6:237)

The UPR and innate right are the cornerstones of Kant's political philosophy. Everything else flows from the right to be independent of the choices of others. Before we go on to discuss what it is exactly that follows, however, we should ask a prior question. Where do the UPR and innate right come from? How are they grounded? You will be perhaps disappointed, but possibly not surprised, to hear that there is no definitive answer to the question. Let us however rehearse some possible solutions to the riddle.

The most obvious way of grounding the UPR would be by reducing it to the Categorical Imperative. Indeed, many Kant commentators regard the UPR as *derived* from the CI and therefore as an instantiation of the latter in the context of the State and its law. To put it simply, the CI tells us what we ought to do as moral agents and the UPR tells us how we ought to behave and what the law may demand of us as political agents, as citizens. Such a relationship of derivation would at first sight neatly bring together these two aspects of Kant's practical philosophy. But, on closer inspection, it will become apparent that it also causes some difficult substantive problems. Recall that the CI procedure is meant to generate maxims that not only bind us but also motivate us. In other words, it is the process of internally imposing laws unto ourselves, of legislating for ourselves. Should the UPR be entailed by and derived from the CI, it would follow that the laws of the State must morally motivate us and that our claims must be morally mutually recognised. Political and moral duties would therefore be indistinguishable in content so that the former would be reduced to merely institutionalised instances of the latter.

There are two central and interconnected problems with this. First, it is not clear how having a central authority setting and enforcing CI/UPR-derived duties would be justified at all. We would of course be under such privately owed duties and they would be a lot more extensive than most liberals would be prepared to accept. But a justification of the State does not seamlessly follow from that.

Secondly, the legitimacy of the State would depend entirely on moral reasons and the extent to which the law lives up to the CI and is therefore capable of motivating us. Now this is not necessarily a problem in the sense that it is not inconceivable, although it is rather improbable, that we all become enlightened enough to act morally at all times on the guidance of the CI without fail. It becomes a problem, however, when one considers that, as we have already hinted, understanding morality in terms of autonomy and the CI is not the only option available. There is an enormously wide and dynamic range of conceptions of morality available. For some to act morally may be to act in accordance with the CI but for others it may be to act in a way that will maximise happiness for oneself and for others. And not only are these two conceptions incompatible but it is also not immediately apparent how the tension between them can be resolved. This is what John Rawls has described as the 'fact of reasonable pluralism' and we will return to this in the next chapter. For now, however, let us emphasise this. If the UPR is derived from the CI, then it, and subsequently all law, is predicated on morality *qua* autonomous action quite obviously at the expense of all other conceptions of morality. It would therefore be justifiable only if one subscribes to Kantian ethics. Absent some supplementary account of law's authority independently of morality, non-Kantians would have neither a reason nor an obligation to obey the law. The only way of making non-Kantians comply would be by force, which already amounts to failing to achieve the original goal of setting the conditions of peaceful social co-existence.

However, such a strong link between the UPR and CI is heavily contested both on textual and substantive grounds. Kant explicitly tells us that the UPR is a 'postulate incapable of further proof', which seems to suggest that it is distinct to the CI and that it therefore establishes freestanding political obligations and justifies the institutional structure of the State. Moreover, Kant also clearly argues that we are under two distinct sets of duties: duties of virtue and duties of right or justice. The former flow from morality understood in terms of the CI. The latter are imposed on us by State law. Duties of virtue motivate us and govern our behaviour as a matter of 'internal legislation'. Duties of right on the other hand bind us whether we endorse them and are motivated by them or not. They are duties, which pertain to our external freedom, that is our interactions with the material world. Very importantly, duties of right are enforceable by the State. In fact, the very point of Kant's political philosophy is to set the conditions under which the State is justified to exercise coercion on citizens.

The problem is that if the UPR is independent of the CI, then it is rather unclear how it is grounded at all. This is important because, as we shall see a little later, the UPR generates a host of duties, chief amongst which is the duty to leave the state of nature and establish a rightful, juridical condition. One possibility is that the UPR is analytically necessary in contexts in which a large number of people must live together as independent beings while having to occupy the same, finite space. The UPR must hold for such co-existence to be possible. And once we have captured it as a presupposition, it can then govern our external behaviour, the ways in which we may or may not interact with the world so as not to interfere with the independent choices of others. On this reading the UPR seems similar to the CI but parallel to it; they are distinct manifestations of our autonomy in two different and distinct realms. This is still not entirely convincing. Analytically deriving a requirement of freedom does not suffice. The UPR still relies on a substantive account of freedom as independence, which does not follow analytically but needs to be substantively grounded. And the only way of doing this available to Kant is by recourse to the requirements of pure practical reason and the CI. But this establishes anew too strong a connection between his moral and political philosophy. The latter becomes an externally imposed normative system worked out for subjects with the moral characteristics grounded on reason.

So, to summarise the problem with the relationship between Kant's moral and political philosophy. On one level, it is a philological problem of concern mainly to Kant scholars. Is Kant's practical philosophy unified or broken down into two fragments? On another level, it is a philosophical puzzle of great practical significance. If Kant's political philosophy is grounded in his moral philosophy, then serious questions are raised concerning the State's very justification as well as its suitability in a pluralistic context, in which not everyone is compelled to accept the CI as the ultimate moral law. If, on the other hand, they are separate, then it is unclear how the UPR is grounded in the first place.

11.3 From innate right to private right and public right

So this is where we left things before we discussed the relationship between Kant's moral and political philosophy: We are all bearers of one innate right. This consists in our right to be independent of the choices of others. This pertains first and foremost to our external freedom but innate right also has an internal implication, which we have not mentioned yet. This is 'rightful honour', which imposes constraints on what we can do with ourselves. Not only ought we not to interfere with the independence of others but we are also under an obligation not to allow others to use us as means to their ends. For example, we ought not to sell ourselves to others as slaves. As we will see later, such obligations from rightful honour have a bearing on the content of the law and what it can demand of us. So, let us turn to the question of what the practical upshot of this right to independence is.

A way of working that out is by exploring the ways in which we interact with each other and in which we can subsequently interfere with the independence of others. Kant singles out three such contexts: property and self; contract; status. This list, as Arthur Ripstein argues, is supposed to be exhaustive (Ripstein, A., *Force and Freedom*: *Kant's Legal and Political Philosophy* (Cambridge, MA: Harvard University Press, 2009). Every instance in which we interact with others and in which our private spheres may therefore clash can be reduced to and understood as a manifestation of one of these three categories.

It is easy to see how we wrong others by violating their independence, if we interfere with their physical or psychological integrity in an unauthorised and unwarranted manner. Interferences with others' property is equally a violation of others' independence. This is so quite independently of any harm caused properly understood. Say I drink a bottle of wine that belongs to you and then replace it with a much more expensive wine. Imagine also that you are not particularly attached to the original bottle—it is just a wine that you happened to have. It should be uncontroversial that I will not have caused any harm in any meaningful sense. Nevertheless, I will still have wronged the other because I will have subjected you and your property to my choices and limited your ability to pursue your own ends.

We can similarly interfere with the independence of others by overstepping the authority granted to us by the terms of a contract, which all the parties have consented to. Our consent will authorise others to make use of us in some way. It thus renders rightful what would otherwise have been wrongful because unauthorised. All this, however, only to the extent of our consent. If the other party to the contract transgresses the contractual authorisation, then their action is wrongful.

What distinguishes status relationships from contractual ones is that the former are not fully consensual. The most central example is that of parents and children. We are, quite obviously, born into a family without our consent. And yet the fact that we are located in that context and we are dependent on our parents generates some mutual obligations and entitlements. When these normative boundaries are overstepped, we wrong the other party by forcing them to pursue ends which they have not freely selected. So, when parents require their children to act in ways which are not in their best interest, they wrong them.

In their combination, duties generated in these three contexts constitute what Kant calls 'private right'. Private right generates norms, which govern our interactions as individuals. Recall Hobbes here and notice the parallel. For Hobbes, we can normatively restrict our ability to interfere with the world by entering into covenants with each other as individuals. Although Kant's list of instances of interaction may be more extensive and complete, the idea is the same. We do interact as individuals and there are some restrictions as to what we may or may not do, restrictions which, unlike in Hobbes, follow from innate right.

But privately made covenants are not sufficient. For Hobbes this is because of the problem of assurance: if there are no guarantees that others will honour their contractual obligations, then I am under no obligation towards them either. Kant singles out three central defects with private right, which render it incomplete as a way of governing our political co-existence. These defects are: private right's inability omnilaterally to authorise unilateral choices; its indeterminacy; and the insufficient assurance that it provides.

Kant illustrates the first problem with the example of initial acquisition. Imagine that we are in the state of nature, where everything 'belongs' to everyone and therefore no one, a State in which no one has any *entitlement* to anything in the world, although everything is physically available to everyone. If I lay my hands on, say, a piece of driftwood and therefore put it under my control, I unilaterally choose to make it mine. This choice, however, cannot bind anyone else. Others may have prudential reasons for steering clear of my driftwood, they may have no use for it or they may fear me because I am stronger than them, but no such *normative* restrictions are in place. I cannot create any obligations on the part of others simply by acting on a preference of mine. More is required for my choice to have omnilaterally binding force.

Kant's way of understanding the problem of determinacy is not altogether different to standard ways of thinking about norm-application. The idea is that norms do not fully prescribe the conditions of their own application. For example, we may have general principles of private right regarding property but these will not apply themselves to facts so as to be able to tell us with any specificity what belongs to whom. This indeterminacy will inevitably generate disputes regarding the boundaries of our entitlements, which need to be resolved.

Finally, Kant views the problem of assurance in much the same way as Hobbes. In his own words

> I am therefore not under obligation to leave external objects belonging to others untouched unless everyone else provides me assurance that he will behave in accordance with the same principle with regard to what is mine. This assurance does not require a special act to establish a right, but is already contained in the concept of an obligation corresponding to an external right, since the universality, and with it the reciprocity, of obligation arises from a universal rule. (6:256)

A solution to these three problems is provided by *'public right'*, that is a set of public norms and procedures, which bind everyone equally. And this is the moment at which the State is instituted. Public right requires a central authority enacting norms and introducing duties and rights that no single individual has the authority to introduce. Therefore public right is more than the expression of the will of some individuals. It is the expression of the 'general will', an expression borrowed from Jean-Jacques Rousseau, which captures the crux of the Kantian version of the social contract. Public right is predicated on a general agreement that universal legislation is necessary to govern our external relations.

> Public *right is therefore a system of laws for a people, that is, a multitude of human beings, or for a multitude of peoples, which because they affect one another, need a rightful condition under a will uniting them, a constitution (constitutio), so that they may enjoy what is laid down as right. (6:312).*

We will now turn to the terms of that original contract, the conditions of institution of the State and the constraints to its powers and, subsequently, its law.

11.4 The original contract, the State and law

Again the parallel to Hobbes is striking but so are the differences. For Hobbes too, it is impossible for us to enjoy anything without a central authority providing normative assurance. For Hobbes, we are motivated to enter the civil condition on our rational sense of self-preservation, which compels us to accept some restrictions to what we would otherwise have been able to enjoy. For Kant, we are *required* to enter the rightful condition, a requirement that follows from the UPR. We are under *a duty of right* to accept being governed by a juridical State ('the postulate of public law'). The Kantian original contract therefore does not depend on an *actual* exchange of promises between citizens. It is not necessary for us to meet in general assemblies and agree on the terms of the contract nor does Kant need to surmise from our not resisting the sovereign that we accept her authority. For Kant, failing to accept the terms of the original contract would amount to our unilaterally imposing our choices on others and interfering with their external freedoms. Now, this follows from the UPR but it also begs the question that we have already touched upon. If our failure to agree to the original contract makes us responsible for violating a foundational duty of right, we must then ask how that duty is established. As we have already seen, this is not entirely clear. If it is an extension of the CI and a manifestation of autonomy in a different context, then the problems that we highlighted earlier are opened up. If that duty is freestanding, then it appears to be a little *too* freestanding. Be that as it may, it is important to emphasise that the Kantian original contract is a matter of obligation which binds us independently of our agreement to it.

You will also recall that for Hobbes each citizen severally is a party to the social contract while the sovereign is the beneficiary of the contract. Individuals therefore have duties towards each other and towards the sovereign while the sovereign is not answerable to any of the parties. Kant distinguishes between individuals on the one hand and the State as the manifestation of the corporate body political on the other. The latter is constituted by the original contract and supervenes on the multitude of individuals without it being identical with the aggregate of these individuals. Individuals subject themselves to the State, which enjoys superior authority. But the State may not be *any* kind of State, *any* kind of civil condition. It must be a *juridical* State, a *rightful* condition. This is central to the character, form and content of the Kantian State. It is no longer the expression of the will of the sovereign, *contra* Hobbes, but it is rather the authorisation of public personnel to enact, execute and enforce laws, which will give effect to people's right to independence from the choices of others. Another expression of the same idea of the original contract in combination with the idea of innate right is that the State may not impose on people laws *that people cannot give themselves*. Self-legislation is central to Kantian political philosophy and has some important repercussions for the form and content of law.

The first such repercussion has to do with the separation of powers. Unlike the Hobbesian scheme, which, as we have seen, requires that State powers remain unified, the Kantian original contract requires that the three powers of the State—i.e. legislative, executive, and judicial—be kept separate. We have seen that public right is a necessary response to the defects of private right: unilateral choices must be omnilaterally authorised; general principles must be determined so as to be able to resolve disputes over the content of our entitlements; and to provide assurance that everyone will be under the same duties. These three defects are to be addressed in three distinct ways. It is necessary to have a legislative body, which will enact omnilaterally binding norms; an executive, which will implement and enforce these norms to achieve the necessary assurance; and a judicature to determine the meaning of law and apply it. Take away one of these powers and it will be impossible for one safely to exercise one's external freedom. At the same time, merge the three branches of government and it will not be possible for the three separate tasks to be performed.

To understand why each State power is necessary as a distinct authority, consider the parallel that Kant draws between them and the three stages of a practical syllogism, that is the process of applying a general rule (major premise) to concrete circumstances (minor premise) in order to arrive at a decision (conclusion). The legislative authority provides the major premise by enacting legislation applicable to all. The executive provides the minor premise by issuing those necessary acts, which make the citizen subject to the universal law enacted by the legislature. And the judicature is there to secure the citizen's recognised entitlement and resolve any disputes surrounding it. This may seem a little counter-intuitive to us, as it does not quite resonate with our understanding of legal syllogisms. We are used to understanding the major premise as the applicable law, the minor premise as the facts of the case and the conclusion as the subsumption of the facts under the law. For Kant this subsumption happens in the minor premise with the help of the executive. In cases of dispute the judiciary is called to give peremptory force to the application of the law to concrete circumstances. All this will make better sense in cases in which an administrative act is required for an institutional fact to come about. To illustrate with an example by Byrd and Hruschka (Byrd, S. B. and Hruschka, J., *Kant's Doctrine of Right: A Commentary* (Cambridge: Cambridge University Press, 2010), Parliament introduces a law on how property over land may be acquired; the executive issues a land registry act; in cases of contestation, a court will assess how the concrete circumstances have been subsumed under the universal rule. Each of these stages are necessary for the syllogism to be possible and each State power is necessary for our independence in our external freedom from the choices of others to be guaranteed.

Although the three State powers—and for Kant there can only be three—are separate, the legislative authority is supreme amongst them. This is because it belongs directly to the united will of the people. For the same reason it cannot wrong people—one may be wronged only by the acts of others and not by one's own acts. You may think that this again echoes Hobbes, who regarded us as giving *carte blanche* to the sovereign, who can therefore not wrong us because she sets the very criteria of rightness and wrongness. This, however, would not be accurate. For Kant the legitimacy of the legislature depends on whether it does express the general will.

We will return to this but, first, let us pause to highlight something rather strange in Kant's thought. He tells us that the members of the 'society who are united for giving law', i.e. those who participate in the legislature, are those properly called citizens. Now, from everything we have said so far, one would expect that everyone should be entitled to be part of that legislature with no remainder; that every human being is entitled to be a citizen by virtue of his or her humanity alone. And yet, Kant narrows down the criteria of inclusion in citizenship rather radically. He tells us that

> The only qualification for being a citizen is being fit to vote. But being fit to vote presupposes the independence of someone who, as one of the people, wants to be not just part of the commonwealth but also a member of it, that is, part of the commonwealth acting from his own choice in community with others. This quality of being independent, however, requires a distinction between *active* and *passive* citizens, though the concept of a passive citizen seems to contradict the concept of a citizen as such. (6:315)

And he then goes on indicatively to list those who are passive citizens and therefore not capable of full citizenship rights: apprentices, domestic servants, all women. All these non-citizens are still 'associates' in the State and they are still entitled to be treated equally and have their independence secured. However, they are not entitled actively to participate in legislation. Now, this is clearly unpalatable by our standards. It is, however, consistent with Kant's thought. As we have seen, the general will of the people is independent of their actual desires or beliefs. It can therefore be constructed on their behalf by any other party. Accordingly, those passive members of society are not shortchanged, to the extent that the State does its job well in safeguarding their external freedom against external interferences. The question, though, is what the criterion of their exclusion is. Why is it that these people and not others are not considered active citizens? Kant's answer seems to be that these people are not propertied and are therefore dependent 'upon the will of others'. Is this sufficient explanation? Not really. If anything, one would expect that Kant would have good reasons to require the State to redistribute wealth in such ways as everyone would become an 'active' citizen. He, however, opts for the exact opposite solution. Most Kant commentators reject this as an aberration or as an attempt on Kant's part to not be too controversial in a political context where not everyone was actually considered equal. Nevertheless, it is a telling implication of the way in which Kant views legitimacy, namely as contingent on the freedom of citizens but independent of the self-understanding of citizens.

Although the original contract and the postulate of public right have direct implications on the *character* of government—including the separation of powers—they do not tell us anything about the *form* of government. Since legislation is meant to embody and give effect to the general will, one would expect that a democratic regime would be necessary according to Kant. But it is not. A variety of systems of government may equally well serve the aim of protecting the external freedom of citizens against interferences from others. The only necessary requirement is that government be representative of the general will. As we have seen though, such representation can take place independently of the views of those who are being represented. It is therefore not theoretically impossible for an absolute sovereign perfectly to capture the general will—although such a sovereign will still have to respect the republican minimum of keeping the three State powers separate. Therefore, the factor deciding what kind of regime is preferable is empirical and has to do with how the general can best be represented in light of actual circumstances. Kant, in fact, shows extreme scepticism towards models of direct democracy, because he fears it may make the general will prey to the will of the actual majority. He instead favours a representative democracy with an aristocratic elite exercising the task of government.

We have so far seen what the terms of the original contract mean in relation to the form of the State. Let us now see what exactly their repercussions are for the form and content of law.

First of all, it follows from the fact that authority resides with law rather than the personnel of the State that the laws of the State must be of such form that they are able to govern people's interactions in a way that safeguards their freedom *qua* independence from each other. In other words, the requirements of the rule of law must be observed. Laws must be properly promulgated and easily accessible by its subjects, principles of due process and natural justice should be in place, and so on. Otherwise, the State would cease to be a juridical condition but would rather be a collection of arbitrarily issued and enforced commands by some over others. And this is clearly not to exit the state of nature, which is what the original contract is all about.

The original contract also has a central implication for the content of law, an implication which reflects the crux of liberal thought. When Kant says that it follows from the original contract that the State cannot give laws, which the people cannot give to themselves, he sets the limits of the reach of the State, the limits between the public and the private. Contrast with Hobbes again. His liberalism is minimal in that it consists in the minimum requirement that there is some external authority, which sets the framework of our liberty. How narrow or wide that framework is cannot be determined *a priori* and necessarily depends on the predisposition of the sovereign and other factors external to the social contract itself. For Kant, however, the State cannot overstep the boundary between the public and the private. Kant's example is religion. The State cannot impose a religion onto the citizens—although whether it is permissible for there to be an official religion is another matter. The Hobbesian sovereign may not do so because it is imprudent and will cause uproar but the Kantian sovereign is under a duty to not do so, because she is not justified to take any measures other than those necessary to safeguard people's external freedom. Similarly, the Kantian sovereign may not force her subjects to be motivated by justice. This would amount to interfering with people's internal freedom, when the State's purpose is to regulate external freedoms and establish corresponding duties irrespective of citizens' motivation.

The original contract has further substantive ramifications for the content of law, of which we will only mention a few. It grounds the presumption of innocence, as it would be a direct violation of our independence if we were to be held responsible and be punished without any proof of fault

...a human [is] *beyond reproach* since before he performs any act affecting rights he has done no wrong to anyone'. (6:238)

Freedom of expression also follows directly from innate right. To the extent that we do not violate the independence of others (for example, by lying in order to defraud them), we are at liberty to communicate anything we like even though we may be insincere. Innate right authorises one

> to do to others anything that does not in itself diminish what is theirs, so long as they do not want to accept it—such things as merely communicating his thoughts to them, telling or promising them something, whether what he says is true and sincere or untrue and insincere; for it is entirely up to them whether they want to believe him or not.

It also compels the institution of a criminal law, which will ensure that the effects of wrongdoing will be redressed and the state of rightfulness restored. It permits the State to tax its people so as to maintain the rightful condition by funding public services and so on. As we mentioned earlier, it follows from the rightful honour extension of innate right that there must be external restriction to some of our internal freedom too. The State is permitted not to allow us to do things with ourselves that would place ourselves as mere means to the goals of others. There should, for example, be restrictions to the freedom of contract such that we are not allowed to sell ourselves in slavery.

There is a host of permissions and requirements, both positive and negative, that follow from the original contract, which we are not listing here. The important thing to remember is that in the Kantian scheme, the foundations of the State are not purely formal but they have substantive ramifications for the form and content of the State and law.

11.5 Kant on revolution

Recall Hobbes again: the sovereign has the right to demand anything of us and, so long as the social contract has been accepted, we do not have a right to resist, although we may be justified to do so when our lives are at stake. You would expect Kant's position on revolution to be different. Since the State is all about laws that we can give ourselves so as to safeguard our independence from others, then you would expect that when the State fails to live up to that task, we have the right to resist. And yet, this is not so.

Clearly, there may be cases in which there is no juridical State at all. Despotic regimes, in which the sovereign maintains all powers to herself and rules by force rather than law, do not count as Kantian States. In such instances it is also irrelevant to ask whether citizens are granted the right to revolt. Properly to speak of a right only makes sense within a constituted juridical State.

So what happens when such a juridical State is indeed in place but still fails properly or fully to perform its tasks? After all, it is not inconceivable, in fact it is more probable than not, that no actual State will meet all the requirements of justice set by Kant. Even then, Kant tells us, revolution is not justified. This follows from the very foundations of the State. Remember that the point of constituting a State is to exit the state of nature and establish the rightful condition. By revolting against a juridical State and trying to overthrow the government, the revolutionaries do not try to improve the State but to return to the state of nature and this cannot be sanctioned by the State itself. To be clear, this does not mean that it is not possible that people will *in fact* revolt against the State or that they may not consider their actions justified by some other standards.

It means that they will not be *legally* justified, because it is paradoxical for a legal system to allow its own demise. But, and more importantly, they will also not be *politically* justified because revolution is in direct violation of the terms of the original contract and the duty imposed by the UPR. Revolutionaries will be trying to impose their unilateral choices onto others and this, as we have seen, cannot be done in a rightful manner from outwith a juridical State.

So what are we supposed to do in States which are borderline legitimate or borderline just? Use the freedom of expression, Kant tells us

> Thus freedom of the pen—kept within the limits of esteem and love for the constitution within which one lives by the subjects' liberal way of thinking, which the constitution itself instils in them...is the sole palladium of the people's rights. (8:304)

We should do our best to try to improve the State by letting the sovereign know what is wrong and trying to instigate reforms to improve our position under universal law.

These views are of course not uncontroversial. In fact they were even controversial at the time and Kant himself changed his view on the justification of resistance and revolution over the years. Many thinkers of the Enlightenment had defended at least a qualified right to revolt but also the big civic revolutions of the time, such as the American and French revolutions, were largely legitimised on the right to revolt grounded on natural rights borne by all humans. Today, a number of constitutions around the world recognise the right and indeed the duty of citizens to resist a government which violates fundamental freedoms and rights. And most people would think that in the face of generalised injustice, the people have the right, and not just the capacity, to resist and revolt even when the State meets some minimum requirements of legitimacy.

Let us highlight three implications of Kant's view on revolution and legitimacy. First, it clearly presupposes that we can tell where the threshold of legitimacy lies. He tells us which basic formal and substantive requirements an ideal legitimate State must meet but it is not all that clear when an *actual* State ceases to be despotic and becomes juridical, a *Rechstaat*. Consequently, we are in the dark as to when revolution is justified. Moreover, given that Kant introduces very few, if any (there is disagreement on this), substantive requirements as to how wealth should be distributed and his approach is far from egalitarian, it follows that in a Kantian State those who are significantly worse-off and who do not have *actual* access to the press or other fora of political dialogue, will have no actual legitimate way of protesting about their position and will therefore remain disenfranchised.

Finally, it seems that for Kant the metamorphosis of actual States through revolution will always and inescapably be a moment of violence. Say that an actual State is legitimate but unjust and that this injustice triggers a revolution, which overthrows the government and therefore, in Kantian terms, drags the whole society back into the state of nature. And say that the revolutionaries then go on to set up a juridical State anew. This new State will always be haunted by the wrongful act upon which it was founded. It will be founded on the unresolved, and indeed irresolvable, conflict between the *ancien regime* and the new government. This, one may object, is not a problem if we conceive of the Kantian State in historical isolation as a static and self-contained entity; if, in other words, we think of Kant's political philosophy as setting out the ideal towards which an already constituted *Rechstaat* should be striving. Nevertheless, it reveals the latter's inability to account for the legitimacy of political transition and therefore to ground the new regime on justified and stable foundations.

FURTHER READING

Beiner, R. and Booth, W. J. (eds.), *Kant and Political Philosophy: The Contemporary Legacy* (New Haven: Yale University Press, 1993).

Byrd, S. B. and Hruschka, J., *Kant's Doctrine of Right: A Commentary* (Cambridge: Cambridge University Press, 2010).

Byrd, S. B. and Hruschka, J., *Kant and Law* (Aldershot, UK ; Burlington, VT: Ashgate, 2006).

Flikschuh, K., *Kant and Modern Political Philosophy* (Cambridge: Cambridge University Press, 2000).

Guyer, P., *The Cambridge Companion to Kant and Modern Philosophy* (Cambridge, New York: Cambridge University Press, 2006).

Hill, T., 'Questions About Kant's Opposition to Revolution' (2002) *The Journal of Value Inquiry*, Vol. 36, Nos 2–3, pp. 283–98.

Hruschka, J., 'The permissive law of practical reason in Kant's Metaphysics of Morals' (2004) *Law and Philosophy* 23/1, pp.45–72.

Kant, I., *Practical Philosophy*, transl. and ed., Mary J. Gregor, the Cambridge ed of the Works of Immanuel Kant (Cambridge: Cambridge University Press, 1996) (especially *An Answer to the Question: What is Enlightenment?; Metaphysics of Morals; On the common saying: that may be correct in theory, but it is of no use in practice*).

O'Neill, O., 'The public use of reason' (1986) *Political Theory* 14/4, pp. 523–51.

Pogge, T., 'Is Kant's Rechtslehre Comprehensive?' (1998) *The Southern Journal of Philosophy*, Vol. 36, Issue S1, pp. 161–87.

Rawls, J., *Lectures on the History of Moral Philosophy*, ed. B. Herman (Cambridge, MA: Harvard University Press, 1999).

Ripstein, A., *Force and Freedom: Kant's Legal and Political Philosophy* (Cambridge, MA: Harvard University Press, 2009).

Rosen, A., *Kant's Theory of Justice* (Ithaca: Cornell University Press, 1993).

Timmermann, J., *Kant's Groundwork of the metaphysics of morals: a commentary* (Cambridge, New York: Cambridge University Press, 2007).

Timmons, M., *Kant's Metaphysics of Morals: Interpretative Essays* (Oxford: Oxford University Press, 2002).

Williams, H., *Kant's Critique of Hobbes* (Cardiff: University of Wales Press, 2003).

12

John Rawls' Political Liberalism

Introduction

The aim of this Part of the book is to explore three important steps in the development of the liberal social contract tradition of justifying the State and its law. In the previous two chapters we discussed two early representatives of that tradition, Thomas Hobbes and Immanuel Kant. We saw that Hobbes' account of the legitimacy of the State revolves largely around the rational sense of self-preservation motivating us to form congruent communities governed by a central source of authority. Kant's aim is the same but he arrives at it on the basis of the foundational thesis that all are free in the sense that we all have the right to be independent from the choices of others. He then works through the ideal and actual implications of this freedom. Thus, for Kant the original contract is not the product of an actual or assumed agreement between citizens but rather a theoretical construction of the general will of the people, which is itself premised on reason and is therefore independent of our individual attitudes.

We will now turn to a contemporary reworking of the idea of the social contract, one which straddles the boundary between Hobbesian rationality and Kantian reasonableness, namely John Rawls' political liberalism. First, a background note to place things in context.

John Rawls (1921–2002), an American who taught at Harvard University, is often credited with reviving political philosophy. His 1971 seminal book, *A Theory of Justice* departed from the philosophical current of the time of engaging in conceptual analysis or metaphysics but also the tendency of political philosophers before him to simply apply moral philosophical doctrines to political contexts. His aim was to work out a theory of justice, underpinned by a theory of State legitimacy, by being attentive to the specificities of the political, that is the realm of social co-existence and public institutions, and the peculiarities of the modern condition.

A Theory of Justice very quickly became the most central reference in political philosophical literature. For most liberals it was an inspiration. For non-liberals it was *the* theory to defeat. It therefore inevitably became the subject of a great deal of criticism. A lot of it missed its target but much of it did not and that urged Rawls to rethink and reformulate some basic ideas. This led to *Political Liberalism*, which is our focus in this chapter. In particular we will concentrate on the theory of State legitimacy offered in *Political Liberalism*, rather then the accompanying theory of justice; point out the instances in which Rawls has changed direction since *Theory of Justice*, and highlight the extensions and implications of political liberalism in relation to law. Note that, although Rawls had much to say on international politics and law, we will focus on his account of the legitimacy of States and their law.

12.1 **The 'fact of reasonable pluralism'**

We said in the introduction that the central task of liberal political philosophy is to work out a way of governing the social co-existence of people with different preferences, desires, impulses, beliefs. This is Rawls' starting premise too. But, unlike most thinkers before and after him, he takes it a lot more seriously and places it in a narrower historical context.

Our societies, Rawls tells us, are more than ever characterised by the diversity and proliferation of conceptions of the good and the right. People are committed to a dynamic variety of 'comprehensive doctrines', both moral and metaphysical. 'Comprehensive' doctrines are those systems of beliefs on what gives life its meaning and value. Religions are perhaps the most typical examples of such doctrines but they are not the only ones. Philosophical doctrines, for example, utilitarianism or Kantian moral philosophy, serve the same types of purposes. They rely on distinctive metaphysical conceptions of the person, i.e. on what it means for one to be an individual and what it means to be a moral agent, and on views as to how we ought to live our lives, treat each other, assess and hierarchise our desires, and so on.

Importantly, these doctrines are largely incompatible with each other. They conflict on matters of central importance. A utilitarian will not see eye to eye with a Kantian on moral duties and rights neither will a Marxist agree with a libertarian on the conception of the person that should underpin political organisation. Now, you will think, it is inevitable that there will be such differences between strongly held beliefs on such important issues. This is right but what makes things even more difficult, according to Rawls, is that such differences are insurmountable, that there is no immediately discoverable way of resolving the controversy on metaphysical and moral questions. We should be cautious here: Rawls does not suggest that there can be no such thing as truth in morality or metaphysics. His political philosophy remains quiet on this matter— and this is the only consistent thing for Rawls to do, as we shall see later. He makes the much more modest argument that we do not *currently* have the capacity and means to arbitrate between such controversial views. We cannot assume the point of view from nowhere, from which we will be able to judge who is right and who is wrong. There is no objective way available to us of for proving to others that their idea of happiness is mistaken. Some day perhaps we will be able to achieve this kind of objective knowledge but currently we simply cannot. And this is not because we are too opinionated and stubborn. Some people will of course be so and refuse to recognise the strength of others' arguments. But on many other occasions, even when people are presented with the same data and arguments, they draw different conclusions and place more emphasis on different evidence without there being any way of proving some of them wrong and others right.

This fact of disagreement and conflict between sets of beliefs about truth and morality is what Rawls terms the 'fact of reasonable pluralism'. We have already begun to explain what is reasonable about this pluralism but it is worth insisting a little more on this point. As we will see later, Rawls uses the idea of reasonableness in a variety of senses throughout his work. In this context, reasonable pluralism is the plurality of reasonable comprehensive doctrines. A doctrine is reasonable when it relies on the employment of practical and theoretical reason and, crucially, when it is conscious of its fallibility and open to the possibility of change. And if it is open to the possibility of its falsification, then it will be open to the possibility of verification of other, competing doctrines. Note that this is still a rather loose conception of reasonableness and it is not meant to serve as a stringent threshold criterion of assessment of doctrines in political dialogue. It is also quite inclusive because, viewed in the long run at least, most doctrines will display the flexibility to respond to reasonable criticism and adapt accordingly. What is crucial at this stage is to register as relevant the fact that there are comprehensive doctrines out there, which are not rigidly dogmatic and yet may be impossible for them to agree on fundamental issues, to realise the full importance of the 'burdens of judgement', i.e that

> ...many of our most important judgments are made under conditions where it is not expected that conscientious persons with full powers of reason, even after full discussion, will all arrive at the same conclusion. Some conflicting reasonable judgments (especially important belonging under peoples' comprehensive doctrines) may be true, others false; conceivably, all may be false. These burdens of judgment are of first significance for a democratic idea of toleration.
>
> (J. Rawls, *Political Liberalism* (New York: Columbia University Press, 2005 (expanded edition; first published 1993), p. 58)

You may wonder, why is this of any importance to a theory of the legitimacy of the State and law? It is, because the point of any such theory is uncontroversially to justify foundational principles and a corresponding institutional structure. It follows from the unprovability of the truth or falsity of reasonable views regarding truth, the good and the right, that there is no way of grounding the superiority of any one of these doctrines. Therefore, imposing the demands of one such doctrine onto those who do not accept its premises and conclusions, is already an act of coercion rather than justified use of authority. Why, for example, should a social democrat accept the legitimacy of a State based on free-market principles *on the basis of* the moral and metaphysical assumptions that underpin free-market libertarianism? Or why would a polytheist regard as legitimate a State organised around the principles of a monotheistic religion, if this entails accepting the foundational principles of that religion?

All this begs a prior question: why should the foundations of the State be justified to everyone in the first place? What if the reasons underpinning the State and law are independent of the acceptance of those, to whom they apply? An advocate of a certain strand of natural law, for example, would argue that one's failure to accept the requirements identified by reason in light of the actual conditions of our existence, is simply and precisely a failure, which has nothing to do with the validity and strength of objectively intuited reasons for action. And recall how Ronald Dworkin would argue something similar. We may disagree on what the right thing to do is but only one of the many possible conceptions will be right and the methodological tools of integrity allow us to arrive at that objectively correct answer. Whether all endorse that right answer or not is of no relevance to its rightness.

Rawls gives a two-pronged answer to this and we will discuss it later in more detail. For now, let us only hint at it. First, the need for justification *to* others follows from the fact that we recognise each other as cooperating agents in society with similar capacities of control over our lives. Secondly, it is a matter of stability. If the State is not convincingly grounded in a way that no one will have any justified grievances, then its foundations will be shaky.

The upshot of all this is that the justification of the modern State ought not to be anchored in any one comprehensive doctrine but should remain neutral between such doctrines. It ought to be purely political, i.e. nonmoral, and freestanding, independent of any controversial doctrine. At the same time, it also ought to be able to be accepted by everyone in the political community not only despite their beliefs to which each subscribes but also *on the basis* of these beliefs. In other words, the political justification of the State must be such that it will cohere with and be accommodated within each citizen's comprehensive doctrine so that everyone will be able to accept it albeit for different reasons. In what follows we will try to clarify this political conception of State legitimacy and justice and explain how Rawls suggests that it may be achieved.

12.2 The 'original position' and Rawls' political constructivism

When discussing Hobbes we said that counterfactual constructions such as the state of nature are quite common in political and legal philosophy. Such constructions provide the description of a situation, which everyone will be compelled to accept and then one works through that situation's normative implications for political organisation. Rawls starts from a similar counterfactual situation, which he terms the 'original position'. In a nutshell, in the original position we are unaware of the actual circumstances of our existence. Thus, we are symmetrically situated and aim at agreeing on terms of social cooperation. Let us unpack this in more detail.

First of all, what does it mean for us to be symmetrically situated and why should we be so? Remember that the stake is to agree on basic terms of social cooperation, which will not be rooted in any comprehensive doctrine or serve a specific conception of the good and which will therefore be acceptable by all. For Rawls, the only way of achieving this is by ensuring that this agreement is made under conditions of *impartiality*. We must make sure that we are not influenced by contingent interests, which are determined by our actual, and in most cases unstable and temporary, situation in the real world. This entails putting aside such contingencies, bracketing them off so as to ensure to the greatest degree possible that our conclusions will be of universal validity and applicability. The upshot of this should be that our agreement does not simply perpetuate already existing conditions but sets foundational principles, which serve as normative criteria allowing us to rethink and revise those conditions.

How then do we achieve this? By placing ourselves behind the 'veil of ignorance'. The veil excludes all contingent facts about ourselves and our societies from the original position. We must leave out all knowledge of our income and social standing, our gender, our religious beliefs, our ethnic background, and so on. If we are fully unaware of what we actually have or who we actually are, we will be relieved of the pressure exercised on our reason and will by the incentives or disincentives that our situation gives us. To put it simply, we will not be guided by our interest in securing our fortune or position of power or our interest in exiting the position of disadvantage that we may actually find ourselves in.

Not all knowledge is excluded from the original position—this would debilitate participants altogether. But the allowed information pertains to every participant equally and is not tied to the circumstances of anyone in particular. In particular, participants in the original position know that they are *free* and *equal* and they carry with them their *rationality* and *reasonableness*. Rawls uses each of these ideas in slightly peculiar ways so we must be careful not to misunderstand them. We are free not in the sense that we enjoy a pre-political right to freedom by virtue of our humanity. Rawls understands freedom in a rather formal sense. We are free in that we regard ourselves and others as capable of developing conceptions of the good. Freedom is therefore not tied to any specific conception of the good but only to our ability to form views as to what makes for a happy and fulfilled life.

We are also free in that we regard ourselves and others as 'self-authenticating sources of valid claims'. This means that citizens

> ... [r]egard themselves as being entitled to make claims on their institutions so as to advance their conceptions of the good... These claims citizens regard as having weight of their own apart from being derived from duties and obligations specified by a political conception of justice, for example, from duties and obligations owed to society.
>
> *(Political Liberalism,* p. 32)

We are *equal* in the sense that we regard ourselves and each other as having the moral power of freedom, the power to form conceptions of the good independently of the requirements of society and political institutions, to the same degree requisite for us to be participants in a political society governed by terms of social cooperation, on which all participants have agreed.

Notice the difference between Rawls' conception of freedom to that of Hobbes and Kant. Hobbes spoke of freedom in terms of our ability to move unimpeded in the world. Kant's political conception of freedom was connected to the external manifestation of our independence. Rawls does not reject either of these understandings of freedom, indeed his conception of the State and justice largely secure freedom in these senses, but it is a different, formal sense of freedom as a capacity of the modern subject that plays a foundational part.

The moral powers of freedom and equality are our capacities of rationality and reasonableness. We are rational in a largely instrumental sense: we have the ability to correlate means and ends. This is not to say that we are self-interested. We may have ends, which are to our benefit narrowly speaking. But we are still capable of choosing means suitable for the achievement of these ends. We are reasonable, first, in a sense that is already familiar to us from the previous section, namely in that we acknowledge the burdens of judgement, the tensions between beliefs and doctrines which constitute the fact of pluralism. But we are also reasonable in the sense that we want to cooperate with others rather than imposing our will on them. We are therefore prepared to propose terms of cooperation, which will be acceptable by all other participants in society, although we should be careful to note that this does not necessarily mean that we are altruistic, and motivated by the well-being of others.

Before we move on to discuss what participants in the original position will do, let us pause to consider a possible objection. We said earlier that, in light of the fact of pluralism, Rawls is keen to justify the State in a way that will not be anchored in any metaphysical or moral doctrine. And yet we now see that at the very foundation of the original position, therefore at the basis of the whole theory, lies a certain conception of the person as free, equal, rational, reasonable. How can then Rawls coherently maintain both arguments?

It is true that in the initial formulation of the original position in *A Theory of Justice*, the original position appeared to rely on a description of metaphysically necessary characteristics of humans. This attracted a great deal of criticism. Communitarian thinkers, for example, argued that the abstraction of the original position is deeply controversial and, indeed, incorrect. Why should one accept, the objection goes, that we are individuals bearing these characteristics and therefore so radically separated from our communities rather than regard us as an integral *part* of and in a relation of mutual constitution with these communities? Or why should the conception of persons as free and equal be preferred over other alternatives, say *homo faber* or *homo laborans* or *homo oeconomicus*?

These are justified objections. Not because Rawls got the metaphysics of personhood wrong, if anything it seems more accurate and intuitively attractive than the communitarian account, but because he did rely on such metaphysics in the first place thus clearly contradicting his claim to neutrality. Rawls took the criticism on board and this motivated the change of direction and the recasting of his liberalism as *political*. For this recasting to work, he also clarified the moral powers of freedom and equality. They are not, he explains, universal and diachronic metaphysical traits of humans. They are characteristics of the modern subject in specific contexts, namely modern constitutional democracies. In these contexts, *we have come to see* ourselves and each other as capable of forming conceptions of the good and as agents with an interest in cooperation with each other. Rawls therefore provides a description not of an ideal or a-historical subject but of the typical political subject in specific, contemporary contexts.

Now, say that we accept that it is possible to reduce the political subject in modern constitutional democracies to some basic characteristics. This still does not make the problem disappear altogether, because it does not tell us how this can be done in a non-arbitrary manner. The question can be asked although this time slightly reformulated: why pick these characteristics of the modern subject over so many others? The answer lies in the institutions that we have already developed in such modern constitutional democracies. What emerges from these democratic State institutions is that in our political lives, in our lives as citizens, we have developed this specific outlook of ourselves and others as capable of having and pursuing conceptions of the good to an equal degree.

With the metaphysical burden of the description of the subject removed, the character of the original position is clarified too. It can no longer be misunderstood as an account of necessary implications of some universal and diachronic characteristics of humans. Neither is the claim that the agreement reached in the original position is *true* and therefore binding a-historically. The original position is a 'device of representation'

> ... it describes the parties, each of whom is responsible for the essential interests of a free and equal citizen, as fairly situated and as reaching an agreement subject to conditions that appropriately limit what they can put forward as good reasons.
>
> (*Political Liberalism*, p. 25)

As a device of representation, it paints an uncluttered, neutral picture of the social world allowing us to work out the foundational principles of social cooperation suitable for subjects who display a certain attitude, i.e. subjects who regard themselves and others as free and equal in the specific sense that we have already outlined.

The political turn in Rawls' liberalism has another central implication. Since it is a theory of State legitimacy and justice worked out for specific subjects and contexts, its range of application is significantly narrowed down. It does not apply to societies in which people do *not* regard themselves and others as free and equal in the political realm, i.e. to non-democratic constitutional societies. Rawls' political liberalism does not presume to tell other people how to organise their political co-existence. It is an account of how we can make the most of what we already value in liberal democracies. Some may think that this is circular—if we already value freedom and equality, then what can a new theory of political liberalism add? The answer is that it can assist us in seeing clearly what the common denominator of our societies is and how we can consistently and fairly organise our political co-existence on the basis of these attainments.

So, to summarise the story so far, the original position is a counterfactual situation, in which representatives of actual people as trustees of these people's interests place themselves behind the veil of ignorance. The veil excludes knowledge of the actual circumstances of each participant and only allows knowledge of the moral powers of freedom and equality of the modern subject in constitutional democracies, i.e. our capacity of forming conceptions of the good to the requisite degree as to be coopera- ting agents in society, and our traits of rationality and reasonableness, i.e. our ability to set ends and pursue them with suitable means and our ability to have and act on a sense of justice. Moreover, the participants also know some basic and inescapable facts about human societies, chief amongst which is the relative scarcity of resources and some scientifically proven facts about the world (note that scientific doctrine is not a comprehensive moral doctrine for Rawls, unless of course it is given moral or political texture). The stake, then, in the original position is for these symmetrically situated participants to reach a universal agreement on terms of social cooperation, to agree on a social contract. The question is not all that different than the one Hobbes tries to ask, although the substantive differences are of course significant: if placed in the circum- stances of the original position, how would we organise our political co-existence?

Now, why would the participants in the original position be motivated to reach an agreement? Rawls' answer is again in the same vein as Hobbes' but substantively dif- ferent. Participants will have a higher order interest in developing and exercising their moral powers of freedom and equality.

> To say that these interests are 'higher-order' interests means that, as the fundamental idea of the person is specified, these interests are viewed as basic and hence as nor- mally regulative and effective. Someone who has not developed and cannot exercise the moral powers to the minimum requisite degree cannot be a normal and fully cooperat- ing member of society over a complete life.
>
> (*Political Liberalism*, p. 74)

So, this higher order interest both motivates the parties to reach an agreement and determines the content of that agreement, namely to set up a framework enabling all citizens to exercise their freedom and equality.

Crucially, the decisions of the participants in the original position will apply only to the political realm, to use Rawls' nomenclature, to the basic structure of society. This draws a clear and rigid distinction between the public and the private. The basic struc- ture comprises those basic institutions, which distribute rights, duties, resources, and so on. The precise content of the basic structure, that is the precise range and character of institutions that it will include, is open. In fact, it cannot be determined in advance, because, as we will see in a little while, much of it depends on actual conditions in a given society. What can be said at this stage, however, is that it will have to include constitutional essentials, institutions pertaining to (some conception of) property, the legal process, and so forth. Be that as it may, what is important for now is to point out the clear distinction between the public/political, which is institutionally manifested as the basic structure, and the private. The social contract agreed on in the original posi- tion only binds citizens *as citizens*. Therefore, it cannot determine people's moral rela- tions and moral motivation, it may not govern private associations and so forth. Now, where exactly the boundary between the private and the public lies is far from easy to determine. Rawls himself was ambivalent on this over the course of the development of his theory of the State and justice. The family is perhaps the most controversial and difficult such example. While some would not hesitate to classify familial relations under the private realm, some, for instance feminists, would disagree and place domestic relations firmly within the political. Everyday economic activity is another such example. It is contested whether the basic structure should impose duties and constraints, other than tax-related or some basic anti-exploitation ones for example, on how one ought to behave in one's economic relations with others. Nevertheless, the claim is that there is such a boundary, wherever it may be, between the private and the public and the social contract only pertains to the latter.

This already sets out the basic parameters of Rawls' version of the social contract. The original position sets the conditions of impartiality and reciprocity, which will lead to an agreement amongst all rational and reasonable members of the political community on the terms of social cooperation and the foundations of a well-ordered, fair society. Recall here Ronald Dworkin's objection to the social contract tradition, which we discussed in relation to Hobbes. The original position is a hypothetical situation. But a hypothetical agreement has no binding force on any of the parties. Rawls' response is that the original position specifies a public perspective shared by all participants. Its results are therefore constructed on that basis in a way that all participants will be compelled to accept. And they will accept them not as morally or metaphysically true but as reasonable and appropriate for our political communities. And this is the crux of Rawls' methodology of *political constructivism*.

12.3 The principles of justice

So what will the participants in the original position decide? Which terms of social cooperation will they opt for? Although the answers to these questions are of great significance, and have indeed attracted an enormous amount of attention over the years, we will not insist on them a great deal, because our main focus are the conditions of liberal legitimacy rather than the substantive extensions of Rawls' theory. Nevertheless, we will give a brief outline of Rawls' account of justice narrowly conceived for two main reasons: first, to give as complete an outline as possible of Rawls' political thought and, secondly, to explore the relation between justice and legitimacy in a Rawlsian State.

In view of the conditions in the original position, Rawls argues that the participants will agree on the following fundamental principles of justice:

(1) Each person has an equal claim to a fully adequate scheme of equal basic rights and liberties, which scheme is compatible with a similar scheme for all.

(2) Social and economic inequalities are permissible only to the extent that they satisfy two conditions:

first, they must be attached to offices and positions, which must be open to all under conditions of fair equality of opportunity;

second, they are to be to the greatest benefit of the least-advantaged members of society (the difference principle).

The first principle, the 'liberty principle', refers largely to basic rights that every citizen ought to be granted by the constitution. It guarantees that everyone enjoys those liberties, which are basic because necessary for one to be a free and equal participant in the political community. They are also *inalienable* liberties. Neither the State may curtail them nor may their bearer, i.e. each citizen, forsake them. The liberty principle enjoys 'lexical priority' in relation to the second principle and basic liberties enjoy priority over any other liberty. This means that for any pattern of distribution of goods and resources to be established, everyone must be afforded this protection of their basic liberties. Their priority also means that basic liberties may not be curtailed to satisfy economic imperatives or for the sake of other goods. This is not to say that the basic liberties cannot be restricted at all, they can. But they may only be restricted to satisfy other basic liberties and to the extent that these restrictions apply equally to everyone. To use one of Rawls' examples, during the Vietnam war, American college students were exempted from the draft. Given that the latter is a restriction of basic liberties, the exemption is unjustifiable even if there are good pragmatic reasons for it (for example, college graduates contributing more to the national economy).

Now, which are these liberties? How do we distinguish between basic and non-basic rights? Rawls singles out five sets: liberty of conscience and thought; freedom of association; political liberties such as the rights to vote and to stand for office; the integrity and freedom of the person; and liberties flowing from the rule of law. These are not singled out because they enjoy some sort of metaphysical or moral priority but rather because they are linked to the moral powers of freedom of equality, which are, as we have seen, powers of the modern subject in the here and now. So if, say, our freedom of conscience were curtailed, we would not be able to develop and pursue to the requisite degree a conception of the good. To use a concrete example, if citizens were not allowed to form and exercise religious beliefs or if they were coerced into endorsing a specific religious doctrine, their freedom, i.e. their capacity to choose and pursue a conception of the good and their character as self-authenticating sources of valid claims, would be undermined.

All this, however, would be pointless, if citizens did not enjoy at least a minimum of material equality too. It is all very well to say that we all enjoy the same liberties but if the actual conditions which will allow us to make the most of those liberties are not in place, then we may as well not be afforded these rights in the first place. This brings us to the second principle of justice, which has two legs: the equality of opportunity principle and the difference principle. This, and especially the difference principle, is where Rawls parts ways with a great deal of liberal theory, because he grounds a requirement of redistribution of wealth as a matter of justice, rather say as a matter of beneficence and charity.

The principle of equality of opportunity ensures that randomly acquired privileges do not advantage one or disadvantage others when bidding for positions. At the very least, this implies that no one may be discriminated against on grounds of gender, ethnic background, and so forth. But it also imposes substantive and positive obligations not to exclude anyone from the job market, this is the primary context of application of the principle, because they do not meet conditions unrelated to talent or skills. For instance, companies ought not to be allowed to make jobs available only to, say, graduates of private schools. Equality of opportunity also serves to correct structural inequalities. For example, it establishes a duty on the part of the State to enable everyone to try to acquire those minimum skills and qualifications necessary for one to be able to pursue one's ideas of happiness and do well in society.

The difference principle has proved to be perhaps the most controversial of Rawls' claims. The basic idea is that some inequalities are permissible but only to the extent that they benefit the worse-off members of society. Rawls departs from blanket egalitarianism, as he does not claim that inequalities in income distribution are an affront to freedom or equality. At the same time, he departs from the libertarian idea that any non-market restrictions to what one may do with resources which one has lawfully acquired is a restriction of one's liberty. Rawls' position is somewhere in between. The starting point is still the original position. The participants there, rational and reasonable as they are, will not want to take any chances upon exiting the original position. They will not want to find themselves short-changed, should they argue behind the veil of ignorance that, say, those with lower income should shoulder the financial burden of public services. Participants in the original position will want to achieve the maximum of the minimum (the so-called 'maximin' principle). At the same time, they are not motivated by pure altruism and want to know that, should they work hard and do everything within their abilities, they will be able to enjoy the fruits of their labour without any excessive restrictions being imposed by the State.

Now, what does all this mean in practice? It means that the State—do not forget that the principles of justice apply, at least directly, only to the basic structure—must establish such institutions as to ensure that wealth will be redistributed in such ways as to guarantee that no one falls beneath certain minimum standards of living. The most obvious way of doing this is by taxation and using that income to guarantee free essential public services and goods such as health, education and so forth but also to take measures that will redress unjustified inequalities. This may sound pretty obvious to many of us but it is not really. Many liberal theories, or at least self-styled 'liberal' theories (Rawls in fact vehemently argues that there is nothing liberal about such theories), have no interest in redressing inequalities. In fact, they consider any such State intervention an affront to liberty. The Rawlsian State proactively ensures that everyone will enjoy the same liberties and opportunities not only normatively, formally but also actually, by redistributing wealth. This is often misunderstood as a defence of the welfare state, as we know it, so we should be cautious. Rawls does not suggest that the State ought to make the worse-off dependent on it by handing out one-off benefits or anything of the sort. A State based on justice as fairness is under an obligation to create the necessary conditions, which will enable the worse-off to improve their situation by being trained, finding a job and developing further.

12.4 **The stability of the liberal State**

We saw in the chapters on Hobbes and Kant that it does not suffice for a State to be based on legitimate principles, it must remain stable in the long run as well. And the conditions of stability must be at least in-line with the conditions of legitimacy. Hobbes, for example, considered the same rational motivation, which necessitates the State in the first place, to be the guarantor of stability too. Rawls, then, will have to somehow account for stability on the same grounds as those of the legitimacy of the State but this time outside the original position and with citizens fully aware of their actual circumstances.

There are two main mechanisms of ensuring the stability of the terms of social cooperation: overlapping consensus and public reason. Let us explain them in turn.

Upon exiting the original position, we no longer deal with ideal representations of ourselves but with actual citizens with flesh and bones, with conceptions of the good, beliefs and interests. How, then, are these to be reconciled? Impartiality and neutrality are once again the answer. This time, however, impartiality will be achieved by embedding the political conception of justice in the comprehensive moral and meta-physical doctrines of each citizen. To put it simply, this means that everyone should be able to accept the political conception of justice and the institutions that it justifies *on the basis of* the doctrines, to which each subscribes. This does not require citizens to sign up to an alternative moral doctrine or to adapt their doctrines to the political conception of justice, which serves as a type of superior regulative doctrine. Neither does it mean that each citizen must accept the political conception of justice *for the same reasons*. An overlapping consensus also does not amount to a majoritarian view of rightness, as there is no guarantee that the majority will act on public reasons, which are acceptable by all. It means that that conception of justice must be such that it fits in, that it coheres with all citizens' comprehensive doctrines and not just the majority's. A Christian and a Marxist, for example, may not accept and place it within their doctrines in the same way. They may do so from their own perspective and in their own terms so long as they do. Once the political conception of justice cuts across all comprehensive doctrines, then overlapping consensus will have been achieved. And this will mean that the State will be stable *for the right reasons* and not as a result of coercing citizens nor as a matter of a *modus vivendi* à la Hobbes.

You may wonder why a liberal State should try to accommodate all comprehensive doctrines available out there. Why should the rest of us go out of our way to take seri-ously and count as participants in the political community, say, racists or fundamen-talists or shameless plutocrats? The answer is to be found in the Rawlsian sense of reasonableness. We have encountered this idea already when setting out the fact of reasonable pluralism. Once again, it is overlapping consensus between *reasonable* doc-trines that a liberal, democratic State ought to try to achieve and there are good reasons to exclude unreasonable views from it.

But what counts as 'unreasonable', you will ask. Unreasonable doctrines or people are those who refuse to recognise in others the basic moral powers of freedom and equal-ity. This makes them unreasonable not because they fail to accept a universal moral truth or anything of the sort—it cannot be overemphasised that Rawlsian political liberalism is precisely about steering clear of such conceptions of truth about morality. The idea of reasonableness is itself political and unreasonable doctrines are discounted because they purport to be participants in a well-ordered society while, at the same time, refusing to accept the very presuppositions underpinning a well-ordered society. In contradicting themselves so, they exclude themselves from the process of justifying terms of social cooperation and from guaranteeing their stability. However, we should also emphasise that this conception of reasonableness excludes very few views, some of which we have already mentioned. It is not very likely that a great number of people will harbour views which refute the very foundations of modern societies.

There are of course all sorts of pragmatic problems with overlapping consensus, chief amongst which is how to actualise it (we will say a litle more on this later) and, prior to this, whether it is even possible to construct a political conception of justice, which can be accommodated in every moral doctrine and still be substantive enough to be able to govern our co-existence. Rawls does not harbour any such high hopes. He fully recognises that achieving overlapping consensus is extremely difficult. At the same time, though, it is undoubtedly not impossible. And it becomes more likely, when one considers how political dialogue and mutual understanding have been facilitated by new forms of direct communication.

There is, however, another issue of a philosophical nature, which poses more of a challenge to Rawls. If the political conception of justice requires overlapping consensus to be achieved, then it seems that the original position does little or no work at all. It seems that the very *justification* of the conception of justice is not done from an impartial perspective any longer but from the point of view of actual, situated citizens. But if this is so and there is no objective perspective of justification, then Rawlsian constructivism does not look all that different from the Hobbesian State, in which self-interested agents get together to strike a compromise, a *modus vivendi* (for this objection see J Habermas, 'Reconciliation through the public use of reason: Remarks on John Rawls's political liberalism' (1995) *The Journal of Philosophy* 92/3, pp. 109–31).

Rawls responds to this objection by distinguishing between three stages and types of justification. In the first stage, the political conception of justice is justified *pro tanto*, that is tentatively, by examining whether such a conception can provide reasonable answers with regard to political values alone. In the next stage, each citizen must justify the political conception of justice by embedding it in his or her comprehensive doctrine (although this does not entail a requirement that each and every citizen does in fact subscribe to a comprehensive doctrine—some may well go through life without developing a coherent set of moral beliefs). Some citizens will accommodate the political conception of justice into their doctrines as *true*, if it overlaps with such claims to truth that these doctrines raise. Others may only embed it as reasonable. Either way, the conception of justice remains freestanding and political and the reasons for which each citizen accepts it do not alter its very character. In the final stage, the political conception of justice is publicly justified by political society.

> In this case, reasonable citizens take one another into account as having reasonable comprehensive doctrines that endorse that political conception and this mutual accounting shapes the moral quality of the public culture of political society. A crucial point here is that while the public justification of the political conception for political society depends on reasonable comprehensive doctrines, this justification does so only in an indirect way. That is, the express contents of these doctrines have no normative role in public justification; citizens do not look into the content of others' doctrines, and so remain within the bounds of the political. (*Political Liberalism*, p. 387)

Public justification is complemented by the requirement of the use of *public reason*. In a liberal State citizens are under a 'duty of civility' only to resort to public values and standards when deciding on fundamental political issues. This is not a legal duty, therefore there may not be any legal consequences should a citizen invoke controversial moral reasons in political discourse—this would, after all, be an unwarranted curtailement of citizens' freedom of speech. The duty of civility stems from citizens' sense of justice, their reasonableness in the sense of their willingness to cooperate with others in society on fair, commonly accepted terms. Similarly, public values and standards are only those that can be accepted by citizens without their having to make any concessions to their moral or metaphysical doctrines. In other words, public, political standards are those standards that are derived either directly or indirectly from the freedom and equality of citizens. Public reason would therefore include commonly accepted rules of logic and canons of reasoning as well as scientific doctrines but would preclude controversial moral arguments and epistemological methods.

It is very important to note that the requirement of public reason only applies to the public and not the private or social spheres. Public reason does not stop people from trying to convince others of the rightness of their beliefs neither is it meant to replace these beliefs (although we should note that Rawls hopes that eventually these moral beliefs will be aligned with the political conception of justice). It is only meant to be exercised in public, political contexts, where decisions on basic liberties and constitutional essentials are made. The most typical such context, indeed one used by Rawls to illustrate the point, are supreme courts—especially those which are given the task of interpreting the constitution—and the reasoning rules, which they must follow. Supreme court judges may not follow their own morality or the religious or philosophical doctrines of others.

> They must be, and appear to be, interpreting the same constitution in view of what they see as the relevant parts of the political conception and in good faith believe it can be defended as such.
>
> (*Political Liberalism*, p. 237)

In doing so, the supreme court will protect the law against assaults by majorities, which may want to impose their own views. It will ensure that the law remains properly justified on the basis of public, political standards, which everyone can accept.

12.5 The stages of application of the political conception of justice

So far, we have discussed the basics of Rawlsian political constructivism, namely how a political conception of justice can be properly justified, which conception of justice emerges as the constructive upshot of the original position and, finally, how the liberal State will remain stable in the long term. Let us now see how the principles of justice will be applied and underpin an institutional structure.

Rawls sets out a 'four-stage sequence' for the attainment of a just society. The stages, of which the first is the original position, are all hypothetical constructs designed to facilitate consideration of the questions arising in the creation of a just society. The four stages in sequence are:

(a) The enunciation of the principles of justice from the original position, which we have already discussed.

(b) A partial lifting of the veil of ignorance so far as the general circumstances of the society but not the individual circumstances of the actors are concerned and the devising of a constitutional system dealing with powers of government and the rights of citizens. This process must, amongst other factors, cope with different and possibly opposed political viewpoints. Granted the priority of liberty, the outcome is assumed to be some form of constitutional democracy.

(c) Having established a constitution, the next step is legislation in accordance with the principles of justice, as well as the constitutional procedures. The legislators are intended to act in the light of general interest rather than to their personal advantage. It is admitted that judging whether or not a law is just may be difficult, especially in the context of the inequalities of the difference principle, and that it may be easier simply to determine whether a law is not unjust.

(d) The final stage is that of application of the laws and rules by judges and administrators and their working in the actions of people generally, at which point, of course, the veil of ignorance is wholly removed.

As you can see, through the four stages the veil of ignorance is gradually removed. This implies that at the earlier stages, it is not possible to determine how constitutional essentials will be applied once the veil of ignorance has been wholly lifted. Another way of putting the same point is that an institutional structure cannot be designed from a philosophical perspective. This can only be done in view of actual conditions in a society, including actual comprehensive doctrines. This does not only pertain to humdrum regulation of minor matters but also to basic institutions. For example, the conditions of legitimacy of the State and the principles of justice will not necessitate any particular way of divvying up resources and regulating property relations. Justice as fairness may be served equally well by institutions of private or collective property. Similarly, a representative parliamentary democratic system such as the ones with which we are familiar, is not necessitated by the foundations of the liberal State. What the latter do require is a political system, which will facilitate the expression of citizens' views so as to actualise overlapping consensus, public reason and so forth but how exactly this will be organised is another matter. Indeed, whole areas of law may prove to be unnecessary. For instance, there is nothing in the foundations of the liberal State that necessitates criminalisation and punishment. If a better way is available with which to deal with violations of the law, then this may be preferable to punishing.

Rawls himself believed that a representative democratic system based on private property (which is, though, subject to non-market restrictions, as we have seen) is the best possible system in current circumstances. What is important to highlight, however, is that very little will be determined from a philosophical perspective. Citizens will be under some unconditional duties flowing directly from the original position, such as the duty to respect the physical, psychological and sexual integrity of others. The State will also be under an obligation to enact and protect some constitutional essentials, such as the freedom of expression and participation, and so forth. But, save for such rather minimal and rather thin (freedom of expression, for instance, does not determine how the press ought to be regulated) requirements, nothing else can be determined from a philosophical standpoint.

12.6 Justice and liberal legitimacy

Throughout this chapter, we have been drawing on two themes: the legitimacy of the liberal State and the requirements of justice as fairness. The former depends on whether the State is anchored in political, freestanding principles and on the condition that an overlapping consensus is achieved amongst comprehensive doctrines available in society. And when a State is legitimate, it is authoritative and citizens are therefore under an obligation to abide by its laws. Whether a State is fair depends on whether it takes these measures, which will guarantee that everyone enjoys the same amount of basic liberties as well as the minimum of welfare, enabling everyone to be an equal participant in the political community. Legitimacy and justice are relatively independent but, nevertheless, related. But in what relation exactly do they stand?

This interrelation is not a worry in ideal conditions. Ideal Rawlsian States will be both fully legitimate and just. However, actual States may not be so. A just State will not necessarily also be legitimate. A policy may have just results but it will not be legitimate if it is arbitrarily imposed on citizens, say, by violating the rule of law or by-passing democratic procedures. At the same time, a legitimate State may not always be just. It is not unimaginable that a policy will have been passed with all the democratic procedures fully observed but, at the same time, it will be unjust. In fact, we do not have to look far from home for such examples. Many of today's States meet, to a sufficient degree, the conditions of liberal legitimacy but, at the same time, they often sanction striking inequalities, which blatantly do not meet the conditions of justice as fairness. The question then is what demands a legitimate but unjust or a just but illegitimate State can make of its citizens. Are we under an obligation to obey the laws of such a State?

Even in actual conditions, there must largely be a balance between legitimacy and justice. This is because to some extent they depend on one another. A grossly unjust State is likely not to meet the conditions of legitimacy either. Imagine, for instance, a State which altogether excludes from income redistribution or fails to grant some basic liberties to a class of people. Such a State will be unjust and illegitimate, because it fails to treat the members of that class of people as free and equal. Observing basic standards of justice is therefore a condition of legitimacy too. Where exactly the threshold lies may of course be difficult to quantify. Nevertheless, the important point is that such a boundary in principle exists.

So, a State ought to be both procedurally *and* substantively just at least to a minimum degree. Problems occur, however, when a State is partially unjust, that is when it meets the conditions of legitimacy and the basic conditions of justice such as the distribution of basic liberties but still fails to treat some citizens fairly. Imagine, for instance, a class of people, say a professional group, who are afforded basic rights and so forth but, at the same time, they are short-changed by an unfair State policy of social insurance. In such cases, we are still under a duty to obey unjust laws. Neither the members of that group nor any other citizen is authorised to disregard those unjust laws. The State, though, is under an obligation to redress the injustice. And it is within citizens' rights to try to instigate reform.

In fact, in a nearly just society and when all else fails, citizens are entitled to engage in civil disobedience, in order to communicate both to the institutions of the State and to the rest of the citizens the injustice and the need for reform. They are justified to do so under certain conditions, which we will only mention very briefly: they ought not to engage in violence; they ought publicly and openly to communicate their demands; in doing so they ought to appeal to public reasons (even when using moral language one may still be appealing to public reasons, for example, Martin Luther King or Archbishop Desmod Tutu); when deciding which course of action to take, they ought to consider the interests of others.

FURTHER READING

Cohen, G. A., *Rescuing Justice and Equality* (Cambridge, MA: Harvard University Press, 2008).

Davion, V. and Wolf, C. (eds), *The Idea of a Political Liberalism: Essays on Rawls* (Lanham, MD: Rowman and Littlefield, 1999).

Fleming, J. and Cordaro, S. (eds), 'Rawls and the Law', Symposium, (2004) *Fordham Law Review* 72: 1380–2175.

Freeman, S., *Justice and the Social Contract: Essays on Rawlsian Political Philosophy* (Oxford: Oxford University Press, 2006).

Freeman, S., *The Cambridge Companion to Rawls* (Cambridge: Cambridge University Press, 2003).

Freeman, S., *Rawls* (London: Routledge, 2007).

Griffin, S., and Solum, L. (eds), 'Symposium of John Rawls's Political Liberalism' (1994) *Chicago Kent Law Review* 69: 549–842.

Habermas, J., 'Reconciliation through the public use of reason: Remarks on John Rawls's political liberalism' (1995) *The Journal of Philosophy* 92/3, pp. 109–31.

Pogge, T., *John Rawls: His Life and Theory of Justice* (Oxford: Oxford University Press, 2007).

Rawls, J., *A Theory of Justice* (Cambridge, MA: Harvard University Press, 1971).

Rawls, J., *Political Liberalism* (New York: Columbia University Press, 2005 (expanded edition; first published 1993)).

Raz, J., 'Disagreement in Politics' (1998) 43 *American Journal of Jurisprudence* 25, p. 42.

Sandel, M., 'The Procedural Republic and the Unencumbered Self' (1984) 12 *Political Theory* 81.

PART IV

Against and Beyond Liberalism

13

Marxist and Post-Marxist Theories of Law

Introduction

Karl Marx (1818–83) and Friedrich Engels (1820–95), Marx's long term and close collaborator, aimed at accounting for historical and social development and at formulating a theory of emancipation. Although Marx dealt incidentally with law, he never formulated a distinctive legal theory. Nevertheless, law, a central means of social integration and control in modernity, cannot be absent from such a theory.

In this chapter, we will first go over some fundamental tenets of Marxist social and political theory. We will then outline some of the ways in which the place of law has been conceptualised in Marxist theory. In the second part of the chapter we will discuss an account of law, which is heavily, although not exclusively, influenced by Marx, namely the critical legal studies movement. One caveat: the topics covered in this chapter are immensely complex and their practical significance extremely wide and a brief exposition can hardly capture this complexity. The analysis here should therefore be treated as a very brief introduction, which aims at guiding you through some fundamental ideas.

13.1 The groundwork of Marxist social and political theory

Marx and Engels rejected the idealism that marked much of contemporary European thought. At the time they wrote, German philosophy in particular was typically 'idealist' in orientation, by which is meant that reality lay in 'ideas' or forms of understanding, and what was considered important for human progress and development was a greater grasp or appreciation of such ideas. Thus a more and more sophisticated understanding of the ideas framing our understanding of the natural world led to scientific achievement; a more sophisticated understanding of ideas of the nature of man and his social relations led to political progress, and so on. Marx and Engels advanced an alternative understanding of human progress, which rather than being a form of idealism, was a form of 'materialism'. It was not humans' greater sophistication in ideas which explained historical social change, but rather our material conditions, in particular the means of economic production. Social and political structure reflected the ownership of resources and the division of labour at any one period in history.

Marx's and Engels' materialism incorporated a 'dialectical' theory of progress derived from the work of G. W. F. Hegel. Hegel (1770–1831) proceeded from Immanuel Kant's proposition that every thesis has an antithesis to argue that the contradiction between thesis and antithesis can be resolved to reveal a higher reality termed a 'synthesis'. As an idealist, Hegel argued that man's understanding of any phenomenon developed in stages as one imperfect idea (thesis) was revealed to be only a partial understanding of reality; that aspect of reality which it failed to capture (antithesis) worked in opposition to it, generating a kind of crisis of understanding. The crisis of understanding was resolved as the tension or battle between thesis and antithesis was overcome by the realisation of a synthesis. The synthesis both overcame the tension and preserved the truth that lay in the prior, partial grasp of reality. The new synthesis would then serve as a new thesis, whose partiality would again be revealed by a new antithesis, the tension to be resolved once more by a new synthesis. This 'dialectic' then was conceived as a continuing process resolving contradictions in the attainment of higher states of knowledge until a condition of absolute understanding would be reached. According to this Hegelian dialectic social development is also seen as a continuing resolution of contradictions leading to a final synthesis in the achievement of the optimum conditions of human life. For Hegel the primary vehicle for this process of development was the State which, consequently, he emphasised as an entity greater than the sum of its parts and having an importance which transcends the interests of its individual members. In the Hegelian State the individual finds fulfilment in playing a proper role in the State. This view conformed neatly with the State ideology of Prussia and, after 1870, of Imperial Germany, and underlay much political thought of the period.

Marx did not accept the statism of the Hegelian dialectic but advanced a varied form of the dialectical analysis, dialectical materialism, which emphasised not an unfolding of more and more sophisticated states of knowledge but changes in economic relations as the engine of social development. In classical Marxist thought the starting point is the economic base and all other social and political phenomena are seen as a 'superstructure' which rests upon it and takes its form at any given time from the nature of the developing economic relations within the base. It is in this sense that Marxist thought is said to be 'materialist'. It claims to be founded upon 'real' economic relations in the processes of production, rather than upon 'ideal' states of human understanding about society. The following extract encapsulates the crux of Marxist theory.

> In the social production of their life, men enter into definite relations that are indispensable and independent of their will, relations of production which correspond to a definite stage of the development of their material productive forces. The sum total of these relations of production constitutes the economic structure of society, the real foundation, on which rises a legal and political superstructure and to which correspond definite forms of social consciousness. The mode of production of material life conditions the social, political and intellectual life process in general. It is not the consciousness of men that determines their being, but, on the contrary, their social being that determines their consciousness. At a certain stage of their development, the material productive forces of society come in conflict with the existing relations of production or –what is but a legal expression for the same thing– with the property relations within which they have been at work hitherto. From forms of development of the productive forces these relations turn into their fetters. Then begins an epoch of social revolution. With the change of the economic foundations the entire immense superstructure is more or less rapidly transformed.
>
> (K. Marx, *Preface to a Contribution to the Critique of Political Economy* [1859] in D. McLellan (ed.), *Karl Marx: Selected Writings*, 2nd ed. (Oxford: Oxford University Press, 2000), p. 425)

The economic base comprises means and relations of production and the superstructure every other epiphenomenon, including religion, politics and, indeed, law. The former always shapes and determines the latter in ways, which depend on the form that production takes. To illustrate very roughly with an example, in small-scale agrarian societies, which depend a great deal on the physical environment, we should not be surprised to see the elements deified. But accepting that the base determines the super-structure still does not tell us *how* this relation exactly works. We will discuss this in relation to law a little later on. First, though, we will give a brief outline of the Marxist take on capitalism.

13.1.1 Capitalism and what is wrong about it

Capitalism is only one of a variety of modes of production. It has, however, been the dominant one in large parts of the world (and is rapidly spreading) roughly since the end of the nineteenth century. Its main characteristic is that *use value* is transformed into *exchange value*. The worth of pretty much everything in the world is reduced not to what it is or its function in our lives but to its relation to other things, with which it can be exchanged. Now, in order for exchange to work, a universal standard of value must be invented and that is money. Everything is therefore monetarised, placed in the 'cash nexus' and thus becomes capable of being bought and sold. Everything becomes a commodity.

Combine this fundamental idea of commodification with the fact that, in capital-ism, the means of production as well as the end products themselves are not owned by the workers any longer. To envisage this, think of the early stages of the Industrial Revolution with the archetypical image of the assembly line (remember Charlie Chaplin in *Modern Times* and you will get the idea). A series of workers each performs a task in the process, at the end of which something new is produced. The machines and the end product belong to the industrialist. All that the workers have to sell in these relations of exchange is their labour, their capacity to work. Once the product has made it to the market, it is sold at a premium, at a price higher than the workers' salaries or the cost of production. And this 'surplus value' is pocketed by the owner of the means of produc-tion, whose wealth is therefore increased disproportionately to the wealth of the work-ers, who, do not forget, if they want to enjoy the product of their own labour, will have to buy it and spend the extra money which goes to the industrialist.

This discrepancy creates two distinct classes. On the one hand, there is the ruling class of the bourgeoisie, which owns the means of production. On the other, there are the proletarians, whose work is commodified and who find themselves in an increas-ingly worse position in relation to the bourgeoisie and are subordinated to the latter. The driving force of change in capitalism is the conflict between these two classes. The impoverished proletariat will eventually rebel to better its position and reclaim the means of production, overthrowing capitalism. Capitalism is haunted by this inherent contradiction, which will lead to its demise. It therefore needs something further, in order to temper this tension. As we will see later on, the superstructure provides one such way.

Now, so far, we have a rough description of a specific mode of production in moder-nity. And the whole of the Marxist oeuvre could, on one level, be seen as a descriptive teleological account of the transition from one mode of production to the next with it all culminating in a cooperative, communist society. But there seems to be more to it. The view is rather clear in Marx, and all the more so in Marxist literature and pol-itical practice post-Marx, that there is something *wrong* with capitalism. The point is not only that capitalism is unsustainable and that it will eventually collapse under the weight of its own contradictions but that *its collapse ought to be forced*. After all,

Marx aims openly at emancipation and he insists that 'the philosophers have only interpreted the world, in various ways; the point is to change it' (K. Marx, *Theses on Feuerbach* [1845] in D. McLellan (ed.), *Karl Marx: Selected Writings*, 2nd ed. (Oxford: Oxford University Press, 2000) p. 173). In fact, Marx's aim was not only political emancipation, by which we mean the establishment of institutions, which will guarantee the public freedoms of citizens and will allow for a free private sphere. This is partial emancipation for Marx because it is still based on competition between people and not on cooperation, it views freedom negatively and in terms of the opposition and conflict between people and their interests. Marx was interested in *human* emancipation too, in our liberation as human beings through cooperation in our communities (K. Marx, *On the Jewish Question* [1844] in D. McLellan (ed.), *Karl Marx: Selected Writings*, 2nd ed. (Oxford: Oxford University Press, 2000), pp. 46ff).

But how do we make the transition from the description of a mode of production to the normative statement that under capitalism we are not free and it is only in a cooperative, communist society that we will be truly emancipated? In order for such an argument to be made, there needs to be a fixed starting point, a standard against which different modes of social and political organisation will be judged. A moral such standpoint is not available to Marx. Morality is rejected as being part and parcel with the idealist misrepresentation of the world as independent of our material conditions of existence. At the same time, an account of human nature as universal and timeless must be rejected too for the same reasons. For Marx, to say that we are competitive or selfish (recall Hobbes) or whatever else of the sort is an arbitrary abstraction which selectively and therefore falsely represents real conditions and social relations. So what *is* the problem with capitalism?

The answer seems to lie in something like, but not quite, a view of human nature. Let us explain this. It is *something like* an account of human nature because it is a statement about humanity at a high degree of generality. For Marx we are *productive* beings. We are a 'species-being' reproducing our own conditions of existence through our interaction with our environment. We can only produce and reproduce our environment and ourselves in cooperation with others. We are always in such relations of interdependence. This is not *quite* an account of human nature in that it does not rely on some abstraction that supervenes on material reality. It does not falsely universalise contingent characteristics.

As we have seen, capitalism rests on our separation from our environment and from the product of our labour, in that it takes them away from our control and places them within the control of the ruling class. In doing so, it 'alienates' us from our species-being in a variety of ways. It alienates us from the product of our work, which belongs to the owner of the means of production. It alienates us from our very work, because it commodifies it, it turns it into an exchange value thus putting it too under the control of the employer. It also estranges us from each other, because we cease to view ourselves and others as cooperating agents and are forced into relations of exchange and competition. Capitalism therefore distorts the conditions of our existence. A communist society, in which workers own the means of production and live cooperatively rather than in opposition to and competition with each other, is the only one that can align political and human emancipation, because it is the only society in which we can live harmoniously without drawing sharp distinctions between individual and community, the public and the private (which, remember, are the staples of liberal political theory).

Admittedly, this is a descriptive account, and a very powerful one at that, of which mode of production will guarantee peaceful coexistence, and therefore a better life for everyone, because it will be in-line with our species being. It may also explain that people will want emancipation and strive for it. However, it still does not really give us any reasons for which to prefer communism to capitalism. For that to be possible we need a further premise according to which it is *good* that we live by realising our species-being. But such moral arguments do not cohere with Marxist thought, although this is contested, not least because abstractions such as good or bad, right or wrong have no place in a communist society. But we will leave this at that and move on to discuss the place of law in Marxist thought.

13.1.2 Law as an element of the superstructure

This is what we have said so far. In Marxist thought, material relations of production constitute the base, which determines the superstructure of epiphenomena such as politics, religion, education, culture and, crucially for our purposes, law. Capitalism is inconsistent with our species-being, because it alienates us from our labour, our production and from each other. The class conflict, to which this leads, will eventually lead to the demise of capitalism. To avoid this, capitalist relations of production need to be stabilised. This is the main task of the superstructure so let us now focus on law and see how it serves that purpose.

One way of viewing the relationship between the economic base and law as an element of the superstructure is instrumentalist. Simply put, according to this view the law is a means of oppression and domination of the proletariat by the ruling class. The latter has a stranglehold on the State and its law and uses it in order to advance its interests. It is argued by this strand of Marxism that law is present in all phases of class domination prior to the proletarian revolution but not to carry equal emphasis in all stages of development. Thus, law is perceived as having a relatively minor role in the phase of feudal domination but as coming into its own during the bourgeois phase, not least because of its close relationship with institutions of private property. The bourgeois State is seen as expressing itself through legal forms, typified by ideas such as a Diceyan 'rule of law', which Marxists perceive as a deceptive cover for the operation of bourgeois economic and industrial power. Engels expressed this view clearly in remarking that

> ...law is sacred to the bourgeois, for it is...enacted...for his benefit.... Because the English bourgeois finds himself reproduced in his law...the policeman's truncheon...has for him a...soothing power. But...[t]he working man knows...that the law is a rod which the bourgeois has prepared for him; and when he is not compelled to do so he never appeals to the law.
>
> (F. Engels, 'The condition of the working class in England' [1842] in K. Marx and F. Engels, *Collected Works* (London: Lawrence and Wishart, 1975), p. 514)

And in the words of Lenin

> According to Marx, the state could neither arise nor endure if it were possible to reconcile classes. According to Marx, the state is an organ of class rule, an organ for the *oppression* of one class by another; it is the creation of 'order', legalizing and perpetuating this oppression by moderating the clashes among the classes.
>
> (V.I. Lenin, *The State and Revolution* [1917] (London: Penguin, 1992), p. 9)

There is of course *some* truth in this crude instrumentalism. We need only to look around us to see that there is a very strong affinity between the representatives of big capital (hedge-fund managers, bank executives, corporate magnates, press moguls) and a large part of the political classes and other elites. It is probably also true that this affinity is translated into mutual favours, the upshot of which is the perpetuation of the bourgeois-proletarian divide and the disempowerment of the larger part of the population, the participation of which is at best exhausted in elections. But, true as this may be, it cannot serve as a general theory of law in capitalist society. First of all, for such a conspiracy theory to be true, it requires an implausibly cohesive view on the part of a dominant class. This argument is made by Hugh Collins, who also suggests that the law in general does not display the basic discontinuities, which the shifting demands of such a class-instrumentalist model would seem to suggest. Collins suggests that it may rather be the case that legal reasoning is, internally, a coherent exercise but one conducted in a context which is shaped by the currently dominant ideology. Thus

> Instead of lawyers and judges serving as the lackeys of the dominant class…, doctrinal development is…an anxious search for rules which correspond to common-sense ideas of right and wrong based upon the dominant ideology…. but our understanding of those phenomena no longer coincides with…the thesis of the autonomy of law.
>
> (H. Collins, *Marxism and Law* (Oxford: Clarendon Press, 1982), p. 73)

This point is corroborated by empirical facts. Think of actual capitalist laws, such as labour-friendly ones, human rights, laws on consumer protection, which seem to protect the proletarians rather than oppress them. Take the early example of the Victorian Factory Acts, which Marx himself discusses in the *Capital* (K. Marx, *Capital*, Ch. 15 'Machinery and Modern Industry'). Among other things, those Acts included clauses regulating the hours of work, protecting the health of workers and interests of underage labourers, and obligating employers to provide education to workers. In our days all this is considered basic, indeed sub-standard, but at the time it was unprecedented. On one level, these may be dismissed as designed simply to maintain the larger interests of the dominant class by staving off the discontent of subordinate classes through marginal concessions or as a compromise between branches of capital. But not all of it can be rejected out of hand in such a crude way and, in fact, Marx himself refrained from so doing.

So, there must be a different way of explaining the link between the capitalist economic base and law as an element of the superstructure. One such way is by recourse to the concept of ideology. Ideology in Marxist thought is the misrepresentation of our real conditions of existence. It can work in a variety of ways. On a very basic level, legal ideology masks real inequalities by misrepresenting actual conditions as normatively irrelevant. For instance, when entering into an employment contract, the worker and the industrialist are considered free and equal in law and their agreement is validated by precisely those normative characteristics imputed to them. But this blatantly disregards the real discrepancies in wealth and bargaining power between the parties, the crippling inequalities, which deprive workers of choice and those real forces which *in fact*, though not in law, make them enter these contracts in order to secure a livelihood. Similarly, when big corporations aggressively sell their products to the worse-off (think of the sub-prime mortgages, which led to the 2008 financial crash), the latter are considered to be buying of their own free will as bearers of the freedoms of all legal subjects, without any regard to the *actual* ways, in which needs, both real and false, are created by the market itself. Lenin again:

> 'Equal right' says Marx, we indeed have here; but it is *still* a 'bourgeois right' which, like every right, *presupposes inequality*. Every right is an application of a *uniform* standard to *different* people who in fact are not identical, are not equal to one another; and therefore 'equal right' is really a violation of equality and an injustice. Indeed every person, having performed as much social labour as another, receives an equal share of the social product [...].
>
> People, however, are not equal; one is strong, another is weak; one is married, another is not; one has more children, another has fewer, and so on.

> (V.I. Lenin, *The State and Revolution* [1917] (London : Penguin, 1992), p. 83)

So, legal ideology mystifies social relations and screens actual, substantive inequalities with the rhetoric of formal equality. But it works in subtler ways too. Louis Althusser (1918–90), a structuralist Marxist thinker, distinguishes between repressive (RSA) and ideological state apparatuses (ISA), which are mutually complementary. RSAs are those agencies of the State which openly exercise force to dominate the subordinate class and advance the interests of the ruling class. The police, the army, and so forth belong here. ISAs are those practices and institutions, which reproduce relations of production, therefore the class division, by naturalising the categories that underpin capitalism embedding them in real, material practices. The school, the church, culture, are all real institutions, which reproduce and reinforce our understanding as subjects of a certain sort, which allocate roles in society in-line with the roles necessary for the reproduction of the capitalist relations of production. And the more we partake in these practices, the more we *become* such subjects. Ideology generally and legal ideology more specifically thus serve to legitimate capitalism, to create the illusion in the sphere of ideas that there is something necessary about the current state of the world.

Ideology shapes the 'false consciousness' of the proletariat, though not only the proletariat; it forces the internalisation of the idea that capitalist social relations are necessary. Some may object: if we are always in the grip of false consciousness, how can we ever be sure that we are free even after a revolution? This would be a silly objection. The fact that we are constantly subject to ideological mechanisms does not mean that we cannot break away from them. But we will fully be rid of them only when the relations of production are such that the representation of our social relations in abstract categories is not necessary any longer. This will be the case in a communist society, in which means of production will be owned by all equally and our mutual understanding will not rely on exchange and opposition but on cooperation. We will return to the concept of ideology later on, when we turn our attention to the critical legal studies movement.

All this does not mean that there is nothing to be won through law. In fact, Althusser considered the superstructure as relatively autonomous from, although determined in the last instance by, the economic base. This means that the struggle for emancipation can take place through superstructural elements too. To put it roughly, we can bring about changes to the law (remember the non-repressive legislation that we have already talked about), which will then change the social relations determined by the mode of production. Indeed, some Marxist writers show even more faith in the rule of law. E. P. Thomson, a historian, examined the Black Act 1723, which made a capital offence of poaching in the Royal Forests of Windsor. Without denying that this story can be told in standard Marxist terms (only those who needed to poach, because they were propertyless, would actually poach and be hanged for it), he also concludes that the Act was considered equitable and applicable to all irrespective of social or economic standing. And this means that we should not throw the baby out with the bath water. The working class can achieve victories politically, which can then be protected by the law and the rule of law. In Thompson's words

> I am insisting only upon the obvious point, which some modern Marxists have overlooked, that there is a difference between arbitrary power and the rule of law. We ought to expose the shams and inequities which may be concealed beneath this law. But the rule of law itself seems to me to be an unqualified human good. To deny or belittle this good is a desperate error of intellectual abstraction.
>
> (E.P. Thompson, *Whigs and Hunters: The Origin of the Black Act* (London: Penguin, 1975), p. 266)

Nevertheless, the consistent Marxist position is that the law can only serve in the interim period on the way to a socialist society, in which both political and human emancipation will be realised. For example, Bankowski and Mungham focus upon, and strongly criticise, social welfare law and other forms of law purporting to assist the materially disadvantaged in modern society (see Z. Bankowski and G. Mungham, *Images of Law* (London: Routledge & Kegan Paul, 1976)). They suggest that such laws deceive people into believing that a transformation of the capitalist condition can be achieved by law, a view which any Marxist would reject. They also suggest that the proliferation of such forms of law in the late twentieth century actually represents the self-interest of lawyers, i.e., it creates more profitable work for them. Ultimately, they consider that the law will indeed wither away along with the capitalist conditions, which it reflects. They also suggest, however, that in the new and consensual ordering of things some new form of legality will develop in order to resolve 'clashing diversities' in a free but still complicated society (see *Images of Law*, p. 31).

The claim that law will wither away in socialist society is most powerfully made by arguably the greatest theorist of law and Marxism, Evgeny Pashukanis (1891–1937). Pashukanis accounts for capitalist law in a non-instrumentalist way but also without resorting to an account of ideology merely as a mechanism of psychological manipulation. He tells that

> ...the task is by no means to recognize or deny the existence of legal ideology (or psychology), but rather to show that legal categories have no other significance than the ideological.
>
> (E. Pashukanis, *The General Theory of Law and Marxism* in P. Beirne and R. Sharlet (eds.), *Pashukanis: Selected Writings on Marxism and Law* (London: Academic Press, 1980), p. 54).

Instead Pashukanis aimed at teasing out a necessary relationship between law and capitalism by viewing law in terms of social relations. To do this, he considered carefully Marx's account of capitalism in terms of exchange relations.

Capitalist society is above all a society of commodity owners. This means that in the process of production the social relationships of people assume an objectified form in the products of labour and are related to each other as values. Commodities are objects whose concrete multiplicity of useful qualities becomes merely a simple physical covering of the abstract quality of value, and which appears as the ability to be exchanged for other commodities in a definite ratio. This quality appears as something inherent in the objects themselves, by force of a type of natural law which acts behind people's backs entirely independent of their will.

But if a commodity acquires value independently of the will of the subject producing it, then the realisation of value in the process of exchange assumes a conscious volitional act on the part of the owner of the commodity. Or, as Marx says, 'commodities cannot send themselves to a market and exchange themselves with one another. Accordingly, we must turn to their custodian, to the commodity owner. Commodities are objects and therefore defenceless before man. If they do not go of their own will, he will use force, i.e., appropriate them'. (E. Pashukanis, *The General Theory of Law and Marxism* in P. Beirne and R. Sharlet (eds.), *Pashukanis: Selected Writings on Marxism and Law* (London: Academic Press, 1980), p. 75).

What this means is that for the exchange relations, the cornerstone of capitalism, to be possible at all, legal categories are required, which will establish the necessary abstract relations between people and objects, the categories of property, contract, and so on. These allow people to lay claims over things as well as over others. But, and *contra* Kant whose basic idea about what necessitates law is very similar, they do not predate exchange relations, they are not universal categories somehow woven into the fabric of nature. They are mutually constitutive with capitalism. All this obviously applies to private law but, and this may seem counter-intuitive, it is equally applicable to criminal law too. Again, not because criminal law and the criminal justice system are instruments of oppression in the hands of the ruling class, which they often are, but because they are based on the abstraction of our social relations, on the mediation of abstract normative categories, which separate us from our social environment and represent us as isolated individuals in opposition to each other. And this is in fact reflected in the very form of criminal procedure, in which responsibility is a method of payment for a good or a right that one has usurped.

> An understanding of the true meaning of the punitive activity of the class State is possible only by perceiving its antagonistic nature. So-called theories of criminal law which derive the principle of punitive policy from the interest of society as a whole are occupied with the conscious or unconscious distortion of reality. 'Society as a whole' exists only in the imagination of these jurists. In fact, we are faced with classes with contradictory, conflicting interests. Every historical system of punitive policy bears the imprint of the class interest of that class which realised it. The feudal lord executed disobedient peasants and city dwellers who rose against his power. The unified cities hanged the robber-knights and destroyed their castles. In the Middle Ages, a man was considered a lawbreaker if he wanted to engage in a trade without joining a guild; the capitalist bourgeoisie, which had barely succeeded in emerging, declared that the desire of workers to join unions was criminal.
>
> (E. Pashukanis, *The General Theory of Law and Marxism* in P. Beirne and R. Sharlet (eds.), *Pashukanis: Selected Writings on Marxism and Law* (London: Academic Press, 1980), pp. 116).

It follows from this strong connection between modern law and capitalism that, once relations of production are no longer exchange relations but relations of cooperation and interdependence, the abstractions of modern capitalist law will gradually (Pashukanis does not believe that it will happen overnight) wither away. There will, at least in the interim, still be a need for some technical-administrative regulation. But the important point is that this will be less and less dependent on the abstraction of the legal subject and its consequences.

Such a view was completely in conformity with the ideas of 'war communism', the 'new economic policy' and, to a somewhat lesser extent, the first two 'five-year plans', the first three phases of Soviet political development, covering the period of Lenin's rule from 1917 to 1923 and the first part of Stalin's rule from 1923 until 1937. It was, however, wholly incompatible with the ideas of the later Stalin dictatorship, and for this reason both the theory and its author were eliminated. Pashukanis' ideas were never re-adopted in the Soviet Union, although after the fall of Stalin the injustice of his personal fate was recognised. In Western Marxist debate upon law, however, Pashukanis continues to exert a significant influence.

13.2 The critical legal studies movement

The critical legal studies (CLS) movement initially emerged in the United States in the 1970s. It would be a mistake genealogically to connect it exclusively to Marxism. There are of course unmistakeable Marxist influences to it, although CLS departs from the crude instrumentalism of early Marxism and views law as a relatively autonomous domain and places special emphasis on its ideological function too, but it was also shaped by American legal realism as well as post-structuralist thought. It offers a radical alternative to established legal theories. Its main aim is to tease out the contradictions of liberal legal thought and to debunk the myth that law and legal reasoning is a way of achieving objective, politically neutral right answers.

> While traditional jurisprudence claims to be able to reveal through pure reason a picture of an unchanging and universal unity beneath the manifest changeability and historical variability of laws, legal institutions and practices, and thus to establish a foundation in reason for actual legal systems, critical legal theory not only denies the possibility of discovering a universal foundation for law through pure reason, but sees the whole enterprise of jurisprudence...as operating to confer a spurious legitimacy on law and legal systems.
>
> (A. Thomson, 'Critical approaches to law: who needs legal theory?' in I. Grigg-Spall, and P. Ireland, *The Critical Lawyers' Handbook* (London: Pluto Press, 1992), p. 2)

> ...law cannot be usefully understood as...'superstructural'. Legal rules the State enforces and legal concepts that permeate all aspects of social thought constitute capitalism as well as responding to the interests that operate within it. Law is an aspect of the social totality, not just the tail of the dog.
>
> (D. Kennedy, 'Legal education as training for hierarchy' in D. Kairys (ed.), *The Politics of Law. A Progressive Critique*, rev. ed. (New York: Pantheon Books, 1990), pp. 38–58 at p. 47)

In what follows we will outline some basic theses of CLS and focus especially on its account of legal ideology. We will then refer specifically to the work of one of the movement's most influential representatives, Roberto Mangabeira Unger, who tried to harness the force of law to achieve social change.

13.2.1 A critique of liberalism, formalism, and objectivism: teasing out law's immanent contradictions

As with American legal realism, the critical legal scholars form part of a movement in jurisprudence, rather than offering a unified theory. The unifying feature of the realists was their attack on formalist modes of reasoning. This is indeed one of the features of the critical legal studies movement and one that links them to early realism tradition, but it is not the common bond that unites it. Rather, the uniting feature is a profound disenchantment with liberal legalism as a whole. This encompasses not only a fundamental disbelief that the law has objective content and is neutral in its operation, but also a belief that the liberal legal tradition has used this portrayal of the legal system to mask the fundamental contradictions inherent in the law. The law is portrayed as rational, coherent, necessary, and just by liberal legal scholarship, when in fact, according to the critical legal scholars, it is arbitrary, contingent, unnecessary, and profoundly unjust. This constitutes a direct attack on the ideal found embedded in Western legal and political thought, the rule of law.

Furthermore, critical legal studies is an attack on Western liberal concepts of basic civil and political rights which purportedly guarantee, in a legal sense, the individual's freedom of speech, assembly, and religion, and in a political sense that liberal democracies are based on the concept of the freedom of the individual. These rights and freedoms are portrayed in the Western tradition as being the only true way to self-realisation and freedom of the individual. The critical legal scholars' aim is to show that these rights and freedoms, although put forward as essential to an individual's fulfilment, actually serve the political and economic requirements of liberalism. For instance, the concept of freedom of contract, though not a civil and political right in the recognised sense, is not a liberating concept but one that ties individuals to the market-place and serves the basic aims of capitalism. Contract law, along with all other bodies of law in a liberal society, serves political ends. Indeed, for the critical scholars they are simply politics in disguise. Why then do people accept the liberal traditions of the law?

> People do not hold to theories of the kinds I have been criticising [liberal legal theories] simply because they serve conservative ends. At least some people believe in them because they think they're true, even though it seems to them too bad that they are true.... For a lot of people, legitimating theories, theories that show the rationality, necessity, and (often) efficiency of things as they are, serve as a kind of defence mechanism. These theories are a way of denying, of avoiding, of closing one's eyes to the horribleness of things as they are.
>
> (D. Kennedy, 'Cost-reduction theory as legitimation' (1981) 90 *Yale LJ* 1275 at p. 1283)

The CLS attack on formalism goes beyond the claim made by the American legal realists, that deductive reasoning is impossible in law and that law alone cannot determine the outcome of its application. In the words of Unger

> By formalism I do not mean what the term is usually taken to describe: belief in the availability of a deductive or quasi-deductive method capable of giving determinate solutions to particular problems of legal choice. What I mean by formalism in this context is a commitment to, and therefore also a belief in the possibility of, a method of legal justification that can clearly be contrasted to open-ended disputes about the basic terms of social life, disputes that people call ideological, philosophical, or visionary.
>
> (R. Unger, 'The critical legal studies movement' (1983) 96 *Harv L Rev* 563 at p. 564)

The corollary of the critique of formalism is the critique of objectivism. Unger again:

> Objectivism is the belief that the authoritative legal materials—the system of statutes, cases, and accepted legal ideas—embody and sustain a defensible scheme of human association. They display, though always imperfectly, an intelligible moral order. Alternatively they show the results of practical constraints upon social life—constraints such as those of economic efficiency—that, taken together with constant human desires, have a normative force. The laws are not merely the outcome of contingent power struggles or of practical pressures lacking in rightful authority.
>
> ('The critical legal studies movement' , p. 565)

Formalism and objectivism are interconnected. In order for one to believe it possible that one can reason in law independently of political debate, one must also subscribe to the belief that legal material constitutes a coherent and universally acceptable whole.

CLS aim to debunk both these ideas and to

> demonstrate that a doctrinal practice that puts its hope in the contrast of legal reasoning to ideology, philosophy, and political prophecy ends up as a collection of makeshift apologies'
>
> ('The critical legal studies movement', p. 573)

One central way of disclosing the faults of liberalism, formalism and objectivism is by teasing out contradictions inherent in the law. It is the critical lawyers' view that liberal legalism represents the *status quo* in society and that it seeks to mask the injustice of the system. They attempt to seek out the conflict-ridden substance that is hidden beneath that apparently smooth surface.

> The descriptive portrait of mainstream liberal thought...is a picture of a system of thought that is simultaneously beset by internal *contradiction* (not by 'competing concerns' artfully balanced until a wise equilibrium is reached, but by irreducible, irremediable, irresolvable conflict) and by systematic *repression* of the presence of these contradictions.
>
> (M. Kelman, *A Guide to Critical Legal Studies* (Cambridge, Mass: Harvard University Press, 1987), p. 3)

Kelman proceeds to identify the central contradictions in liberal thought that have been identified by the critical lawyers. First he identifies

> ...the contradiction between a commitment to mechanically applicable rules as the appropriate form for resolving disputes (thought to be associated in complex ways with the political tradition of self-reliance and individualism) and a commitment to situation-sensitive, ad hoc standards (thought to correspond to a commitment to sharing and altruism);...
>
> (*A Guide to Critical Legal Studies*, p. 3)

The contradiction between rules and standards is one that Kelman identifies with the writings of Duncan Kennedy. Kennedy contrasts the individualism present in the dominant liberal legal thinking, in the form of the application of rigid and precise rules, with the notion of altruism or collectivism.

> Altruism denies the judge the right to apply rules without looking over his shoulder at the results. Altruism also denies that the only alternative to the passive stance is the claim of total discretion as creator of the legal universe. It asserts that we can gain an understanding of the values people have woven into their particular relationships, and of the moral tendency of their acts. These sometimes permit the judge to reach a decision, after the fact, on the basis of all the circumstances, as a person-in-society rather than as an individual.
>
> (D. Kennedy, 'Form and substance in private law adjudication' (1976) 89 *Harv L Rev* 1685 at p. 1773)

Kennedy goes further than the American legal realist argument that justice cannot be done in each case because there is insufficient certainty and objectivity in the legal process on which to build a sustainable doctrine of precedent. The fundamental contradiction between individualism and altruism is a problem not only for a judge but is symptomatic of society in general. 'The fundamental contradiction—that relations with others are both necessary to and incompatible with our freedom...is not only an aspect but the very essence of the problem' (D. Kennedy, 'The structure of Blackstone's Commentaries' (1979) 28 *Buffalo L Rev* 205 at p. 213). In the law, this fundamental contradiction can be seen in the competing and contrasting legal terminology found present, for example, in the debate between subjectivity and objectivity in such diverse areas as criminal law and international law (see further M. Tushnet, 'Legal scholarship: its causes and cures' (1981) 90 *Yale LJ* 1205). More specifically, in the law of contract, for example, there is a clear dichotomy between those concepts which favour individualism, for example, freedom of contract which may result in a defenceless individual being taken advantage of by a more powerful individual or company, and those concepts which favour altruism, such as duress and undue influence. Within the capitalist legal order with its liberal philosophy, contract law is dominated by the former.

The second contradiction Kelman identifies in the critical lawyers' critique of liberalism is

> ...the contradiction between a commitment to the traditional liberal notion that values or desires are arbitrary, subjective, individual, and individuating while facts or reason are objective and universal *and* a commitment to the ideal that we can 'know' social and ethical truths objectively (through objective knowledge of true human nature) or to the hope that one can transcend the usual distinction between subjective and objective in seeking moral truth.
>
> (*A Guide to Critical Legal Studies*, p. 3. Kelman identifies a third contradiction between intentionalism and determinism, see *A Guide to Critical Legal Studies*, pp. 86–113)

The second contradiction is pointed at one of the central tenets of positivism—the separation of law from value judgements. Nevertheless, as with the first contradiction between individualism and altruism, this aspect goes further than simply a critique of writers such as Kelsen. The main thrust is that both everyday culture and the liberal theory that supports and legitimates it downgrade values and beliefs to the extent that they are simply seen as matters of taste, peculiar to the individual, whereas reasoned analysis of facts and laws yields universal maxims which can guide any individual's behaviour.

The aim of the critical scholars is to show that these contradictions are to be found in all legal concepts and rules, even in so-called clear cases where the contradiction has simply been successfully repressed over a period of time. The assumption behind this is that within each contradiction one set of values is paramount in liberal legal theory, namely individualism over altruism and objectivism over subjectivism.

13.2.2 The method of critique: trashing, delegitimation, and dereification

These are the various techniques the critical lawyers use to reveal the underlying contradictions in the law and the deep-rooted hierarchies of power that are also hidden beneath the neutral exterior of the law. The political motivations behind these techniques are made clear in the following extract.

> There is little systematic work on law and power despite the fact that a defining feature of law is that it operates to facilitate exploitation and discrimination.... We therefore need to explain how this concept of 'law' is used to justify the political order of modern society.... The pervasiveness of law in modern society means that law must be challenged from within by means of what we call legal insurgency. It is not enough to be critical of law and its underlying political structures; we need to move beyond mere criticism to critique and thereby expose the contradictions underpinning the principles, policies and doctrines of bourgeois law. The material effects of law and the ideological bases upon which it is manufactured must be analysed and deconstructed in order to comprehend the power of modern legal discourse as a dominant intellectual paradigm.
>
> (S. Adelman and K. Foster, 'Critical legal theory: the power of law' in I. Grigg-Spall and P. Ireland (eds), *The Critical Lawyers' Handbook* (London: Pluto Press, 1992), p. 39)

Deconstruction of law and legal language takes three main forms. 'Trashing' is essentially aimed at revealing the illegitimate hierarchies (power structures) that exist within the law and society in general. The task of the critical lawyers is to reveal those hierarchies and undermine them. The hierarchy of power is not the simple one envisaged by Marxists, who see it in terms of classes, but is much more complex and found at every level, including universities, where there is a power relationship between lecturer and student (see A. Freeman, 'Truth and mystification in legal scholarship' (1981) 90 *Yale LJ* 1229).

Indeed, trashing or debunking the traditional methods of teaching law is an important element in critical legal studies and has led to some universities in the United States and the United Kingdom actively pursuing a critical agenda. The following extract from Kelman explains the purpose of trashing or debunking.

> We are also engaged in an active, transformative anarcho-syndicalist political project.... At the workplace level, debunking is one part of an explicit effort to level, to reintegrate the communities we live in along explicitly egalitarian lines rather than along the rationalised hierarchical lines that currently integrate them. We are saying: Here's what your teacher did (at you, to you) in contracts or torts. Here's what it was really about. Stripped of the mumbo-jumbo, here's a set of problems we all face, as equals in dealing with work, with politics, and with the world.
>
> (M. G. Kelman, 'Trashing' (1984) 36 *Stanf L Rev* 293 at p. 326)

'Delegitimation' appears from the writings of the critical scholars to be a slightly different aspect of the deconstruction process. It is aimed at exposing what the scholars see as one of the most important functions of law in a liberal society, namely the legitimation of the socio-economic system of that society. To delegitimate law the scholars attempt to strip away the veneer of legitimacy to reveal the ideological underpinnings of the legal system. To many scholars the legitimacy conferred on the social system by the law is vitally important to the continuance of that system with all its unfairness and exploitation.

> The law's perceived legitimacy confers a broader legitimacy on a social system and ideology that...are most fairly characterised by domination by a very small, mainly corporatised elite. This perceived legitimacy of the law is primarily based on notions of technical expertise and objectivity and the idealised model of the legal process.... But it is also greatly enhanced by the reality that the law is, on some occasions just and sometimes serves to restrain the exercise of power.
>
> (D. Kairys, 'Introduction' in D. Kairys (ed.), *The Politics of Law. A Progressive Critique*, rev. ed. (New York: Pantheon Books, 1990), p. 7)

Generally speaking the law serves to mask exploitation by using the imagery of fairness, equality, and justice. The summary of the critical approach to contract law given below (see 13.2.3) will illustrate this.

Finally, an aspect of the deconstruction process which is firmly linked to trashing and delegitimation is 'dereification'. For critical scholars like Gabel, the law is characterised by reification, which involves a gradual process whereby abstractions, originally tied to concrete situations, are then themselves used, and operate, instead of the concrete situations. Simply put, the abstraction or concept takes on the form of a thing (P. Gabel, 'Reification in legal reasoning' (1980) 3 *Research in Law and Sociology* 1 at p. 2). This process can be seen in the law, which over the centuries of its development gradually becomes divorced from the actual human relations it is attempting to regulate. The process is not obvious but is clouded in legal mystification so that people both within the law, and outside the law but subject to it, mistake the abstraction for the concrete. Concepts like mortgages, consideration, trusts, wills, take on a life of their own and become totally divorced from their original conception. In so doing the purpose behind the concept becomes disguised. In the case of the legal terms listed, the purpose behind these was the facilitation of monetary exchange in a society built on the control and movement of capital. 'Legal reification is more than just distortion: it is also a form of coercion in the guise of passive acceptance of the existing world within the framework of capitalism' (J. S. Russell, 'The critical legal studies challenge to contemporary mainstream legal philosophy' (1986) 18 *Ottawa L Rev* 1 at p. 19). Dereification is simply the recognition and exposure of such fallacies, to reveal the law as it really is.

13.2.3 A specific example of the critical approach: The critical approach to contract

So far we have outlined some central themes and methods employed by CLS. In this section, the critical scholars' approach to individual legal subjects will be analysed by relating their analysis of the law of contract. As well as deconstructing contract law, it will be seen that the critical scholars advocate a new critical method of teaching the subject. This is part of the critical scholars' wider analysis of legal education as a whole, which is beyond the purview of this chapter (see generally A. Thomson, 'Critical legal education in Britain' (1987) 14 *J Law & Soc* 183; D. Kennedy, 'Legal education as training for hierarchy' in D. Kairys (ed.), *The Politics of Law. A Progressive Critique,* rev. ed. (New York: Pantheon Books, 1990), p. 38).

Contract has been chosen to illustrate the critical approach to a specific legal subject area not only for the reason that all students of law have been subjected to contract in one form or another, but also because of the related reason that the critical writings in contract law are well developed since the subject is seen as central to the liberal legal edifice. Most other areas of law receive a similar, though sometimes less convincing, treatment, and the reader should sample these in an area of interest (good collections are to be found in D. Kairys (ed.), *The Politics of Law. A Progressive Critique,* rev. ed. (New York: Pantheon Books, 1990); and I. Grigg-Spall and P. Ireland (eds), *The Critical Lawyers' Handbook* (London: Pluto Press, 1992)).

Alan Thomson provides a useful introduction to the critical approach to contract law, particularly the teaching and exposition of the subject (A. Thomson, 'The law of contract' in I. Grigg-Spall and P. Ireland (eds), *The Critical Lawyers' Handbook* (London: Pluto Press, 1992), pp. 69–76). He starts by examining the assumptions behind the traditional approach to contract law found in many textbooks and courses. These usually start by making students aware of how many contracts they had made that day, suggesting that the course will not only be practical but help to explain a central aspect of the social order (all the quotes below are from Thomson, 'The law of contract').

> Yet what follows in courses based on the standard textbooks dramatically fails to ful-fil...these expectations. Although in the student imagination the law of contract tends to become the lasting model and the measure of 'real' law, its practical relevance is extremely limited, and as for going to the heart of the social order, this is denied from the moment in those first examples when it is assumed that contract is the 'natural' form of social relations, and the only issue becomes how they are to be regulated.

Contract introduces students into the lore and mystery of the law so that they accept from the outset that proper law does not have a social or political dimension.

> Like the reality constructed in our primary socialisation as children, the reality of law which the law of contract first constructs tends to retain for ever its massive power over us.

The whole of the traditional contract course excludes any element which might under-mine the concept of the rules as being not only neutral but natural for any social order, not just the liberal legal order. This is done in a variety of ways, for example, by attempt-ing to construct a seamless web of precedents all logically bound together. The dif-ficulty of applying this to practical examples of contractual situations is avoided by applying the principles to purified sets of facts which are either the hypothetical fact situations found on tutorial sheets or in exams or are the simplified set of facts to be found in leading textbooks.

> Questions of social and distributive justice, which relate to consequences and which threaten the orderly world of rules and principles, are simply outlawed from the toy-town world of the contract class....
>
> In this way the liberal individualist conception of injustice (which restricts justice to general rules of just conduct and ignores the fact that different people and different groups have different access to the resources of wealth, education and power), remains

unchallenged as the silent underpinning of the law of contract. Just rules are conveniently conflicted with a just world. Indeed one of the features of the law of contract which appeals to students is that since it is comprehensible without any knowledge of the real world, a simple idea of justice as the-same-rules-all suffices. It is important to recognise that this apparent comprehensibility is only possible if one excludes from sight the unequal world to which the law of contract applies.

This neutral and natural approach to contract downplays the importance of such features as undue influence, duress and unfair contract terms, which if fully understood and put in a central position in the contract curriculum would undermine the edifice by revealing contract to be an instrument of power. If this truth is revealed then it will be seen 'how contract merely serves to provide a cloak of legitimacy to the underlying structural inequalities of power in society, such as those of class, gender and race'.

Contract law thus serves the ideological function of reinforcing the conception that law is neutral, self-contained, that it cannot be challenged, and that it is the product of reasoned analysis. In addition, it projects an image of the law that teaches students and purveyors of the traditional approach three lessons.

The law of contract creates a master-image of the well-ordered society; a society in which law appears as the 'haven of justice', divorced from the dirtiness of business, politics, power and the conflict of interests and values; a society which rises above the uncertainties and incoherences of political and moral argument. This is the first and most general lesson which the law of contract teaches. However, it teaches two more particular ideological lessons.

First, it serves to make the contingent fact of capitalism, the appearance of social relations as market-exchange relations, look like the necessary facts of life, by concealing that the conceptualisation of social relations as contractual is not outside history but *has* a history. Secondly by creating the appearance that, through the law of contract, such relations are, or can be made, subject to universal principles of common-sense and justice, it serves to put the justice of the market-based social order beyond question.

Once the student has almost inevitably accepted the legitimacy of these lessons, the continuity of the dominant liberal legal ideology is assured. Those students as lawyers, academics, or judges will perpetuate the ideology with which they have been imbued.

To undermine this reinforcement of the *status quo*, Thomson suggests that a critical contract course should diverge as much as possible from standard texts and examine the primary materials themselves to reveal the uncertainty of contract law. This means not only examining cases from the Court of Appeal, but also cases at first instance, as well as looking at the formation of contracts in practice, a method which will reveal the power relationships to be found in nearly every contract. Like Karl Llewellyn (see Chapter 9), Thomson advocates an examination of the law of *contracts* not the law of contract, to reveal how it is impossible to bring employment contracts and consumer contracts under the same reasoned principles and to show that it is only by abstracting from reality that the law of contract can be maintained as a coherent whole. Cases should be viewed in terms of consequences and in terms of the moral and political attitudes which drive the judge.

By drawing out the dominant liberal individualism and the very occasional glimpse of other views informing contract cases, one cannot avoid confronting the fact that contract law is not outside politics but part of it.

By revealing the indeterminacies and incoherence in contract, the subject is revealed not as a universal set of principles that are natural and timeless but as a product of history. It is to that history that the analysis will now turn, but before doing so it is useful to state Thomson's conclusion.

> ...most importantly, by opening up contract law in these ways, exploring it in terms of its consequences, drawing out the political ideologies it silently expresses, revealing the historical circumstances of its development, and demonstrating the potential openness of the cases, one brings into sight exactly what the textbooks suppress, namely ideas about the expression of social relations in terms which give voice to quite different ways of conceiving living together. Thus while contract gives legal expression to society as a collection of isolated distrustful strangers, submitting only to general rules out of enlightened self-interest, to challenge contract is to struggle to conceive of and express other ways of living together, based on altruism, ideas of solidarity or on constructing norms through engaging in genuine conversation and discussion.

As Thomson states, once the superficial veneer of universality and timelessness is stripped away from the façade of contract law, what is revealed is that contract law is a product of history and has been shaped by a combination of politics and economics to create the apparently self-sufficient set of principles that is the law of contract today. Peter Gabel and Jay Feinman provide a useful historical analysis of contract law as ideology (J. M. Feinman and P. Gabel, 'Contract law as ideology' in D. Kairys (ed.), *The Politics of Law. A Progressive Critique*, rev. ed. (New York: Pantheon Books, 1990), pp. 373–86).

They start with a brief historical survey of contract law in the eighteenth century, the pre-capitalist era, painting a picture of socio-economic 'reality' which appears somewhat simplistic and idyllic. The system is composed of traditional hierarchies based on ownership of land and inherited position. The ideology of contract law reflected this in that it was hostile to commercial enterprise, which would threaten this system. Contract law struck down unconscionable bargains in this period and imposed contracts where justice required, for instance when there was reliance on a promise.

The nineteenth century or the era of capitalism witnessed a fundamental change. People were divided into classes and the working class was exploited. Society was subordinated to the market and to monetary exchange. This was accompanied by a move from an emphasis on community to individuality, with individuals being isolated and alienated.

> Within a short stretch of historical time, people experienced and were forced to adapt to the appearance of the factory and the slum, the rise of the industrial city, and a violent rupture of group life and feeling that crushed traditional forms of moral and community identity....[This transformation] created that blend of aggression, paranoia, and profound emotional isolation and anguish that is known romantically as the rugged individual.
>
> ('Contract law as ideology')

How could people be persuaded to accept such conditions?

> One vehicle of persuasion was the law of contracts, which generated a new ideological imagery that sought to give legitimacy to the new order. Contract law was one of many such forms of imagery in law, politics, religion, and other representations of social experience that concealed and denied the oppressive and alienating aspects of the new

social and economic relations. Contract law denied the nature of the system by creating an imagery that made the oppression and alienation appear to be the consequences of what the people themselves desired.

('Contract law as ideology')

Because judges and lawyers were in a privileged position in the system they naturally expressed the legitimacy of the system. Contractual legal concepts thus became reified and supposedly autonomous and objective. For example, the imagery of 'freedom of contract' developed an exterior that concealed the reality that such freedom was conditional upon that person's status, whilst the concept of consideration idealised and reified the grubby world of competition and bargaining. In other words, the imagery of the law served to deny the oppressive character of the market-place and the lack of real, personal liberty experienced by people in their private lives, as well as in their workplaces.

During the twentieth century capital became concentrated in fewer companies leading to monopolies which, combined with the development of trade unions, led to the limited protection of workers and consumers from such great collections of capital and power, so that modern capitalism became characterised by varying amounts of State intervention. Law helps to maintain such a system by supplementing its previous preference for market individualism with principles based on collective welfare, which results in some efforts towards redistributive justice. The ideology of law is again seeking to obscure the essentially oppressive nature of the socio-economic system. The people are still isolated and alienated. Despite the development of doctrines of duress and undue influence and wider doctrines of unconscionability of bargains, unfairness is still rampant in the market-place. The ideology of the individual and freedom of contract are still dominant.

13.2.4 The role of Roberto Unger

Much of the critical legal endeavour is concerned with the identification of defects and concealed agendas in law; the identification of the sources of marginalisation and alienation may be seen as at least an important stage in a process of response. It is to these feelings of isolation and disenchantment with society, that are often felt but misunderstood by individuals, that Roberto Unger's often highly abstract and sometimes impenetrable analysis of law and society turns.

13.2.4.1 Contextuality

Whereas traditional perspectives on law and society view the present system found in Western liberal societies as the only one capable of marrying individual freedom with social order, Unger views a legal system that does not have any profound understanding of *personality* and society as simply being a 'brutal and amoral conflict' that only benefits the rich and powerful operating under the benevolent cloak of the rule of law (R. M. Unger, *Passion: An Essay on Personality* (New York: Free Press, 1984), p. 47).

Unger shares with the rest of the critical legal studies movement a desire to deconstruct, dereify, and trash the liberal legal order. For him legal adjudication is purely arbitrary and used for political purposes to further the needs of the powerful and the persuasive in society *(Passion: An Essay on Personality,* p. 47). In addition, the legal process, with its surface of neutrality and fairness, serves to slow down any process of change that there may be in society. In other words, the legal system with its inherent backward-looking nature simply reinforces the *status quo* and stymies any type of revolution, whether violent or not, within society. Unger is of the opinion that such a blanketing effect is bad for society because it is against human nature. As well as advocating that adjudication in legal decisions should be concerned with an open-ended debate about values instead of a narrow doctrinal discussion of precedent, he goes much further by arguing that the whole concept of fixity in society, embodied in the legal system by the concept of *stare decisis,* is contrary to fundamental human needs (R. M. Unger, 'The critical legal studies movement' (1983) 96 *Harv L Rev* 561 at pp. 564–76).

Unger's very complex analysis of human nature (clearly greatly simplified here) leads him to discern a fundamental contradiction between, on the one hand, our longing for other people, and on the other, our fear of other people. Individuals need each other in order to become fulfilled, but in so doing they are made vulnerable to those others, who, if they are so minded, can make use of this vulnerability to exploit them. This contradiction not only goes to personal and family relationships but is as important when individuals interact to gain the necessities of life, when other people may seize the opportunity to use the exchange of goods or labour to subjugate the individual in 'an entrenched hierarchy of power and wealth' *(Passion: An Essay on Personality,* p. 96).

Unger then analyses the contradiction between our altruistic and individualistic desires using the modernist approach to 'contexts'. He shares the belief that both our mental and social lives are shaped by 'institutional and imaginative assumptions' known as 'contexts'. He further believes that it is impossible to think or act in a way that is completely free from all conceptual or social contexts. He expresses the view that all conceptual or social contexts can be broken or revised. In this way new contexts may be created which in turn will be broken or revised. This allows for change in society and for the individuals in it. The more rigid a context is then the more difficult it is to change or to revise it. On the other hand, the more 'plastic' a context is the greater the flexibility and potential for change.

The point appears to be that rigid contexts lead to individuals being categorised in terms of the *roles* they play in society, rather than as individuals, who, if they choose, may decide to play a variety of roles and feel free to move between them. Rigid contexts, in part produced by the pseudo-fixity of the legal system, lead to people being categorised *only* or at least *mainly* in terms of the role they play such as spouse, employee, woman, or lawyer. The self-perpetuating rigidity of the system entrenches people in these roles and prevents them from attempting any form of self-assertion by trying any context-breaking or context-changing acts which might upset the social order and the *status quo.* Furthermore, once individuals are fully programmed into their roles they can then be exploited.

It follows that individuals are more likely to be treated as persons rather than as roles in a society that is comprised of plastic contexts rather than rigid ones. Plastic societies are more amenable to self-assertion and to reconciling the apparent contradiction between a person's altruistic and individualistic desires by preventing exploitation. To make society more plastic, individuals must reject rigid contexts, which in the case of law involves a rejection of rigid hierarchies of rigid rules which lead to exploitation of individuals in their assigned roles, and instead enter into an open-ended debate about politics *(Passion: An Essay on Personality,* pp. 7–27). Unger also suggests other methods involving a change in the structure of society whereby an individual's narrow functional role in that society can be changed for the better.

13.2.4.2 Empowered democracy

Hugh Collins gives us a simple example of the problem that Unger's critical societal theory attempts to surmount. He asks the reader to imagine that he or she wants to be a creative writer. The problems facing such a person are virtually insurmountable, even in a developed Western country. The need to survive and to look after any dependants stifles such an ambition, primarily because that choice is not a free one but is dependent on the prospective writer finding a *market* for his or her work. Faced with this unforgiving and rigid context so prevalent in liberal societies, and maintained by their legal systems, namely the primacy of the market-place, the writer's ambitions become thwarted and instead he or she opts for a second-best career or job.

> In the spirit of critical social theory, Unger argues for the possibility of establishing social conditions more suitable for satisfying this quest for self-fulfilment. Not everyone could become a creative writer, of course, but then probably few would find this option attractive. The point is not to establish a community of literati, but rather social conditions which empower individuals to explore successfully the myriad ways in which they may imagine their lives will flourish and have meaning or purpose.
>
> (H. Collins, 'Roberto Unger and the critical legal studies movement' (1987) 14 J *Law & Soc* 387 at p. 389)

Unger argues from the basis of contextuality for the need to establish a super-liberal society within the terms of the 'programme of empowered democracy' (R. M. Unger, *Politics, a Work in Constructive Social Theory*, vol. 2, *False Necessity. Anti-Necessitarian Social Theory in the Service of Radical Democracy* (Cambridge: Cambridge University Press, 1987), p. 341). This programme contains Unger's vision of society and has three main elements, namely a new and radically different system of legal rights, a reorganisation of the constitution and government, and finally a reconstruction of the economy.

Unger's system of rights differs greatly from the established system of civil and political rights found in Western liberal democracies. He proposes to replace that system, which simply serves the strictures of the market economy, with four types of super-liberal rights, namely 'market rights', 'immunity rights', 'destabilisation rights', and 'solidarity rights', all designed to produce a plastic society, where individuals will be able to seek and achieve self-fulfilment. Market rights are 'the rights employed for economic exchange in the trading sector of society' and are dependent on his vision of a radically reconstructed economy. Immunity rights 'protect the individual against oppression by concentrations of public or private power, against exclusion from the important collective decisions that influence his life, and against the extremes of economic and cultural deprivation'. If individuals are to be encouraged to engage in the transformation of society, they must have not only negative freedom from interference but also positive freedom from want. The third group of rights identified by Unger allows the individual to venture further in his or her attempts to transform society. Destabilisation rights 'protect the citizen's interest in breaking open the large-scale organisations or the extended areas of social practice that remain closed to the destabilising effects of ordinary conflict and thereby sustain insulated hierarchies of power and advantage'. Finally, solidarity rights 'give legal form to relations of reliance and trust...Solidarity rights form part of a set of social relations enabling people to enact a more defensible version of the communal ideal than any version currently available to them' (*Politics, a Work in Constructive Social Theory*, vol. 2, pp. 520–36).

Unger is somewhat unclear about the exact nature, extent, and protection of these rights. What is clear is that they are dependent on the second and third elements of his programme for empowered democracy.

Unger's programme for the remodelling of government is based on the premise that the present variety of constitutional structures within societies are far too rigid, so promoting confrontation and alienation. His basic argument is that instead of having an entrenched 'stifling and perverse institutional logic' there should be a 'multiplication of overlapping powers and functions'. A multiplication of the number of branches of government with greater decentralisation leads to the diffusion of power to all individuals instead of to a class of powerful individuals at the top of the existing hierarchies within society. This in turn will increase the opportunities for individuals to engage in transformative activities and so change society from being based on individuality to being based on community. The reorganisation of government would further involve the abolition of the traditional doctrine of separation of powers into the executive, the judiciary, and the legislature. These would not only overlap but would be virtually unrecognisable when compared to the existing institutions. For example, Unger suggests that the judiciary 'may forge complex interventionist remedies allowing for the destabilisation and reorganisation of large-scale institutions or major areas of social practice, even though such remedies may be irreconcilable with the received view about the appropriate institutional role of the judiciary (or of any other branch of government)'.

Unger does propose a system of priority with his scheme based on the principle of 'the absolute restraint one power may impose on another'. In the case of a constitutional deadlock he proposes a system of referenda and elections and in particular he proposes immediate elections when the government is not receiving popular support. The legitimately elected government would be supervised by the 'decisional centre' encompassing the roles traditionally allocated to the judiciary and the legislature. Further principles in Unger's complex vision of society (greatly simplified here) include the concepts of 'miniconstitutions' 'for limited contexts and aims'; 'subsidiarity' requiring that 'power to set rules and policies be transferred from a lower and closer authority to a higher and more distant one only when the former cannot adequately perform the responsibility in question'; and 'antigovernment' such as trade unions and neighbourhood organisations to form 'restraining social counterweights', which will diminish 'the risk of despotic perversion' *(Politics, a Work in Constructive Social Theory,* vol. 2, pp. 444–80, p. 551).

Central to Unger's proposals for the reconstruction of the economy in his post-modernist society is the rejection of the current 'private-rights complex of the advanced Western countries', in particular the central concept of 'the consolidated property right: a more or less absolute entitlement to a divisible portion of social capital'. Inequalities are inherent in such a system and any attempts at reforming the present system will be inadequate, since they will still be based on the concept of the 'consolidated property right'. Instead of this present iniquitous system, Unger proposes 'a perpetual innovation machine', the primary example of which is a 'rotating capital fund' *(Politics, a Work in Constructive Social Theory,* vol. 2, pp. 480–508). Collins gives a useful summary of this element and the way that it fits into Unger's wider theory.

Unger claims that contemporary politics possesses a disabled institutional imagination. In other words, it fails to recognise that markets and democracies can be organised in a huge variety of ways. For example, liberalism (and, for that matter, Marxism) has always assumed that exclusive ownership of the means of production must constitute a cornerstone of market economy. Unger suggests, however, that instead of the means of production being owned either by the State or individuals, it should be possible to create a rotating capital fund through which the State would make loans of capital to entrepreneurs for a fixed period of time, and then, having permitted the entrepreneur to reap sufficient profit to provide the necessary incentive for efficient production, the State should reclaim the balance of the funds in order to make fresh loans. This scheme of a rotating capital fund avoids the excesses of domination involved in either communism or capitalism through control over the means of production, yet preserves incentives for efficient production. Unger offers further illustrations of the [current] disabled institutional imagination.... In each case, by a recombination of familiar ideas into novel institutional arrangements, Unger seeks to demonstrate how practical reforms could enable us to transcend the formative context of our society.

(H. Collins, 'Roberto Unger and the critical legal studies movement' (1987) 14 *J Law & Soc* 387 at p. 401)

An attempt has been made to give the reader a flavour of Unger's alternative society. The summary by its nature tends to exaggerate the flaws in his scheme, such as the exact nature and protection of his new legal rights, the danger that his system may create an over-elaborate and ever-changing bureaucracy that may not necessarily transform society, and finally the fact that his rotating capital fund, for instance, will not remove domination, only reduce it. An attempt by the reader to analyse the detail of his proposals will offset many of these criticisms. Furthermore, what Unger is doing above all is making the reader think of a different society which will overcome the contradictions and unfairness of current Western society. He is offering *an* alternative, not necessarily *the* alternative to current structures in society and in philosophy (for a liberal philosophical critique of Unger's philosophy see W. Ewald, 'Unger's philosophy: a critical legal study' (1988) 97 *Yale LJ* 665). He is in many ways attempting to introduce into philosophy and politics an open debate about society by offering a vision of there being much wider choices than the ones offered in so-called liberal democracies.

FURTHER READING

Althusser, L., *On Ideology* (London, New York: Verso, 2008).

Althusser, L., 'Ideology and Ideological State Apparatuses' in *Lenin and Philosophy and other Essays*, transl. Ben Brewster (New York and London: Monthly Review Press, 1971), pp. 121–76.

Anderson, P., 'Roberto Unger and the Politics of Empowerment' (1989) 173 *New Left Review* 93.

Beirne, P. and Sharlet, R. (eds), *Pashukanis: Selected Writings on Marxism and Law* (London: Academic Press, 1980).

Boyle, J., *Critical Legal Studies* (Aldershot: Dartmouth, 1992).

Cain, M. and Hunt, A., *Marx and Engels on Law* (London: Academic Press, 1979).

Collins, H., *Marxism and Law* (Oxford: Clarendon Press, 1982).

Collins, H., 'The Decline of Privacy in Private Law' (1987) 14 *Journal of Law and Society* 91.

Douzinas, C., Goodrich, P., and Hachamovitch, Y., *Politics, Postmodernity and Critical Legal Studies* (London: Routledge, 1994).

Finnis, J., 'On the Critical Legal Studies Movement' in J. Eekelaar and J. Bell (eds), *Oxford Essays in Jurisprudence 3rd Series* (Oxford: Clarendon Press, 1987), ch. 7.

Fitzpatrick, P., and Hunt, A. (eds), *Critical Legal Studies* (Oxford: Basil Blackwell, 1987).

Goodrich, P., *Reading the Law* (Oxford: Basil Blackwell, 1986).

Grigg-Spall, I. and Ireland, P., *The Critical Lawyers' Handbook* (London: Pluto, 1992).

Harris, J. W., 'Unger's critique of formalism in legal reasoning: Hero, Hercules, and Humdrum' (1989) 52 *Modern LR* 42.

Head, M., *Evgeny Pashukanis: A Critical Reappraisal* (Abingdon: Routledge-Cavendish, 2008).

Hirst, P.Q., *On Law and Ideology* (Basingstoke: Macmillan, 1979).

Horwitz, M., 'The Rule of Law: An Unqualified Human Good?' (1977) 86 *Yale LJ* 561.

Hunt, A., 'The theory of critical legal studies' (1986) 6 *Oxford J Legal Studies* 1.

Hutchinson, A. (ed.), *Critical Legal Studies* (New Jersey: Rowman & Littlefield, 1989).

Marx, K. and Engels, F., *Collected Works* (New York and London: Lawrence and Wishart, 1975).

McLellan, D. (ed.), *Marx: Selected Writings* (Oxford: Oxford University Press, 1977).

Phillips, P., *Marx and Engels on Law and Laws* (Oxford: Martin Robertson, 1980).

Price, D. A., 'Taking rights cynically: a review of critical legal studies' [1989] *CLJ* 271.

Simmonds, N., 'Pashukanis and Liberal Jurisprudence' (1985) 12 *Journal of Law and Society* 2 135–151.

Thompson, E. P., *Whigs and Hunters: The Origin of the Black Act* (London: Penguin, 1975), pp. 258–69.

Unger, R., 'The Critical Legal Studies Movement' (1983) 96 *Harv LR* 561.

Žižek, S., *Mapping Ideology* (London: Verso, 1994).

14

Feminist Legal Theory

Introduction

Feminist legal theory addresses the connections between sexism and law. As we have seen in Chapter 13 the law is not immune from sweeping criticisms which cast it as more an agent of injustice than justice, and feminist legal theory makes just this sort of criticism.

14.1 Sexism and law

Like racism, sexism is not easy to define satisfactorily. One might begin by saying that sexism in outlook is the belief that women are (in some ways at least) inferior to men, whilst sexism in practice or deed is the treatment of women less favourably than men for no other reason than that they are women. There are different ways in which the law and sexism might be connected.

In a sexist society, i.e. in a society where sexist attitudes are the norm or at least widespread, the law, being a social institution that reflects the mores of society, will reflect those sexist attitudes in the various rules it contains. This is trivially easy to show in the legal history of any society. Until the reforms of the nineteenth century, the legal status of married women in England was regarded as being submerged in that of their husband's; in consequence, they were, for example, unable to hold legal title to property. It was not until the early twentieth century that women were legally entitled to vote, and not until the last decades of the twentieth century that laws were enacted to address discrimination on the basis of sex in employment. Many other examples could be mentioned, and feminist legal scholars have certainly drawn attention to the various ways that the 'law on the books' is sexist. But the law might be connected to the existence of sexism in other, more profound ways. Following in the footsteps of the critical legal scholars, feminist theorists may likewise deny that legal doctrine is objective, neutral, and coherent in the way that law is often presented to be; if it is not, what holds the law together may be an outlook reflective not only of the privileged and powerful economic and political classes, but also of the dominant sex. Or, to consider one more possible connection, the basic structural concepts of the law, such as rights, and the way in which legal disputes are resolved, may represent a 'masculine' conception of justice and injustice, and 'masculine' techniques for the resolution of disputes. If this sort of criticism can be made out then obviously the entire legal enterprise may be seen to be discriminatory against women.

As any reader of this book will know, while few people would be happy to say 'I'm a sexist', for that would normally amount to admitting one was a certain kind of a bigot, there is much disagreement, both amongst women and between women and men, as to what counts as a 'sexist' attitude. For example, it is not at all uncommon for people to believe that, in certain ways, women and men *just are* different, for example with respect to their biological reproductive capabilities, and that this requires them to be treated differently. The first maxim of justice is 'treat like cases alike, and different cases differently', and so if men and women differ in significant ways, this must justify different treatment. Assuming that these differences are genuinely matters of fact, and genuinely significant, then it would seem inappropriate to call their proper appreciation 'sexist'. As we shall see, there are a number of different feminist legal theories. One of the things that the different feminist legal theories attend to is the appropriate way of determining whether a distinction or attitude is genuinely sexist.

14.1.1 Sex and gender

While the word we give to illegitimately discriminatory practices against women is 'sexism', it might more appropriately be called 'genderism'. Feminist legal theorists typically distinguish between sex and gender. Sex refers to the biological attribute of being female or male (although the actual biological categories of female and male are not entirely precise). Gender, on the other hand, refers to the much broader conceptual distinction between the feminine and the masculine; gender is what gives us female and male stereotypes. While all women are female, women are not equally feminine. Feminine characteristics are those which women typically, and more to the point, 'appropriately' display: characteristics such as sensitivity, emotion, and modesty. Similarly, all men are male, but some men are more 'masculine' than others, displaying strength, leadership, stolidness, rationality, and so on. It is, of course, not the project of feminist theory to affirm these stereotypes and perpetuate the idea that women should be feminine, men masculine. Rather, the distinction is there to point out that many of the ideas that underlie sexism operate to make it seem that there is a 'natural', 'objective', connection between femaleness and femininity, maleness and masculinity. If our attitudes about gender are such that a woman who is a strong leader is, in our perception, to that extent 'less a real woman', some sort of anomaly or freak, then we will not perceive it as sexist to marginalise or ignore such a woman: how could it be an offence against women to give short shrift to someone who really is not one, or at least who is not really acting like one? In this way, examining the social construction of gender allows the theorist to reveal the 'hidden' sexism embodied in ideas of what is 'natural' to women and men. Furthermore, recognising gender allows feminists to recognise, and show solidarity with, others who are treated unfavourably because they fail to meet the stereotypical behaviour expected of them: non-athletic or passive men, tomboys, or other girls or women who have 'masculine' characteristics, but in particular, gay, lesbian, bisexual, and transgender individuals.

14.1.2 Feminist legal theory and practice

In keeping with other critical legal theoretical movements, feminist theory of law is concerned with a kind of oppression: the oppression of women, obviously. It is therefore not surprising that feminist legal theorists typically refuse to maintain any sharp distinction between 'theory' and 'practice'; particular legal issues, such as the law's treatment of rape victims and offenders, the resolution of custody disputes, the regulation of pornography, the employment law treatment of pregnancy and other aspects of reproduction affected by the law, are not just examined to glean theoretical insights. Feminist work which reveals oppressive regulation must, at the same time, suggest an agenda for legal reform, for the simple reason that pointing out an injustice is the same thing as pointing out something that needs to be rectified. Indeed, one of the greatest successes in feminist legal theory has been in the way that by 'naming' behaviours from a feminist theoretical perspective, attitudes towards those behaviours have significantly altered within the law and more broadly in society.

The introduction of terms such as 'date rape', 'domestic violence', and 'sexual harassment', for example, might seem rather simple and obvious linguistic ploys, but in some ways they have been remarkably effective.... Not only have these new terms put a name to existing, but dimly perceived, wrongs to women, but they have also brought them into the broader public consciousness. That is, the terms have effectively brought the named phenomena into being for those parts of the community for which they were either invisible or unthinkable.

(N. Naffine, 'In Praise of Legal Feminism' (2002) 22 *Legal Studies* 1 at p. 75)

While it would be wrong to say that, as a matter of logic, there is a necessary conflict between theory and practice, a common tension arises between what might be called practical or strategic goals and cognitive or theoretical goals. Pointing out an injustice is not the same thing as remedying it, even though the former is necessary for the latter. But we also know that *how* we frame an injustice is often instrumentally or strategically important, i.e. in regard to the prospects for its reform. As the passage from Naffine just quoted indicates, feminists have achieved success with certain ways of naming injustice. But consider the slogan, 'There's no such thing as consensual sex', which is associated with Andrea Dworkin and Catharine MacKinnon, and which pithily summarises the claim that male–female sexual intercourse *has meaning* for both men and women as a manifestation of masculine power and female submission in which the *idea of consent* is inessential—a rather difficult, but by no means absurd, theoretical point. Nevertheless, in terms of feminist practice, that slogan may have been a *strategic* disaster, as it allowed opponents of feminism to claim that feminists are crazy man-haters who believe all men are rapists. In light of this sort of experience, an understandable concern with success at reforming the law can, then, work to blunt the pursuit of ideas which are promising or inhibit the frank statement of ideas which are otherwise theoretically strong in order not to undermine the climate for reform. From the opposite perspective, it is possible to become mired in arid theoretical disputes which waste energy better spent on pursuing change, and theoretical disputation can undermine political solidarity and commitment.

14.1.2.1 Consciousness raising

'Consciousness raising' was a form of feminist political practice which arose in the late 1960s in the United States. It was founded on the idea that women were isolated from each other politically, and because of the domination of men over women in any mixed-sex setting, women were often silenced by the conventions of discourse. By allowing women to speak to each other in all-women discussion groups about their own experiences, without their speaking being cut short or re-interpreted by men, women's consciousness of their own circumstances would be raised. They would be able to recognise in the stories of others a more general pattern to the ways in which their lives were unfulfilled, and they would become conscious of how sexism affected them personally. Individual women would then become capable of analysing how society oppressed women, identifying occasions where sexist attitudes shaped people's behaviour. In this way consciousness raising became the most distinctive and successful aspect of feminist practice.

14.2 The varieties of feminist legal theory

The problem of sexism can be approached in a variety of ways, as feminist legal theory fully reveals. The classification of feminist legal theories into liberal, radical, cultural/difference, and postmodern feminists below is undoubtedly crude, but the divisions are, it is submitted, illuminating, for it connects the feminist theories to the broader political philosophical currents and traditions which they draw upon. It is, however, necessary not to 'shoehorn' any particular theorist into a particular category just for the sake of categorisation. It is no more the case in feminist legal theory than anywhere else that an individual theorist is just the reflection of the tradition in which he or she works.

14.2.1 Liberal feminism

Liberal feminism can claim to be the 'original' feminism. The basic premise of liberal feminism, drawing upon the Enlightenment's rejection of tradition as a sound basis for moral understanding, and embracing the Enlightenment's humanistic ideas of equality and universality, is that women and men are equal. Equal how? Most profoundly, women, just as men, have lives which are of value; women just like men deserve equal concern and respect; each woman's life *counts* just as much as each man's life, and women are to be treated as ends, not means, just as men are to be so treated. Therefore, as a matter of principle, it is wrong to deny women the chance to be autonomous 'authors of their own lives' just as it would be to deny men that chance, and in particular, it is wrong to discriminate against women in life opportunities, restricting them, for example, to lives as wives or mothers in the home and placing barriers to their entering various careers. Nor is it acceptable to deny them a role in the public life of their communities or nations; in particular, denying them the right to vote or hold office is completely unacceptable.

Liberalism is the dominant political outlook of the Western world in the modern age. It should not be confused with the use of the word 'liberal' when 'liberals' are contrasted with 'conservatives' in mainstream political debate. The vast majority of citizens in Western democracies are liberals in the sense that they accept, and indeed normally strongly endorse, the equality of citizens, a more or less regulated market economy (as opposed to State economic planning), the rule of law, and democratic government. Of course, there are many contrasting perspectives on the liberal outlook. At the core of liberalism, however, is the picture of the individual as a *rights-bearer*, i.e. as someone who has certain inalienable and inviolable rights, such as the right to life, to freedom of expression, to freedom of association, to property, and so on, which reflects the idea that the lives of individuals are the only genuine object of value, which the law and state must respect.

Of course, if you are seen not to measure up as fully human, then there is no need to extend all of these rights to you. It is one of the greatest of tragedies that the intellectual tools provided by the Enlightenment were very unevenly applied; white men alone were considered to be fully capable of being rights-bearers. In consequence, it is not surprising that much of the energy of liberal feminists over the last couple of centuries has been expended on the project of simply destroying various myths about women's inadequacies. The good news, however, is that this project has been enormously successful. As regards the legal rights and life opportunities for women in the Western democracies, the world of 60 years ago is simply unrecognisable. All feminist theorists recognise the genuine importance of these gains, but, at the same time, many have questioned whether a theoretical approach to feminism drawing mostly, or exclusively, on liberal political theory, is ultimately sufficient to meet the challenge of sexism; indeed, perhaps the majority of feminist theorists would agree that liberalism has worked to entrench, not eradicate, if not sexism *simpliciter*, then at least certain elements of contemporary sexism.

14.2.1.1 The critique of liberal feminism

The critique of liberal feminism can be put in this way: liberalism is individualistic, essentialist, and universalist, and these characteristics of liberalism undermine its effectiveness in addressing sexism.

Liberalism is founded upon the equality of individuals, on each person's right to equal treatment under the law and by the State. Liberalism requires laws, therefore, to be sex-blind. 'Affirmative action' programmes, for example, which positively discriminate in favour of historically disadvantaged groups, are difficult to justify on liberal grounds however praiseworthy the motive behind them, because any form of discrimination along these lines violates the right of every individual to be treated as an individual, not just a representative of a group. But feminists understandably argue that this simply takes for granted that people are equally situated, equally capable of exercising their rights, and this is false.

Another aspect of liberal individualism which is troubling for feminism is the way in which liberalism regards human social relationships as a matter of choice, of the exercise of the freedom of association. Under liberalism, each individual is autonomous, free from constraints imposed by others in being the 'author' of his own life. By contrast, many feminists and other legal theorists insist that social connections within the family and the community are *constitutive* of a person's identity, not simply a matter of 'consumer choice'. But liberalism is blind to this, and so it cannot take account of the way in which sexism might be embedded in our social relationships and which might profoundly affect a woman's ability to exercise the rights a liberal State confers upon her. Perhaps the most trenchant aspect of this criticism is feminism's critique of the 'public–private distinction'. Liberals typically distinguish a public realm, which comprises the arena of employment, trade, and politics, in which a person deals with other individuals protected by his or her legal rights, from the private realm, of love, family, friendship, which operates according to a different logic, and where it would be inappropriate for the law or the State to intrude. So, for example, 'domestic' violence was for a long time regarded as something which was not really the business of the police or the law. But as feminists point out, this outlook simply fails to appreciate the way in which deeply ingrained sexism in private affairs, such as roles in the family, can significantly impair the exercise of rights in the public realm. Love, family, friendship, rather than being a 'haven in a heartless world', may be a large part of the problem, being the arena where everyone can act at their most sexist.

The charge of essentialism concerns the rationalist roots of liberalism. Liberalism is founded upon a picture of the individual as a rational chooser, and this picture is justified on an *a priori* conception of the nature of the human being. Individuals are *essentially* rational choosers, whose freedom is freedom from irrational preferences and desires. But this picture can be challenged. In particular, it can be argued that individuals can never be free—when they act 'freely'—from the influence social and political institutions have over the content of their preferences and desires. This is particularly important for understanding the legitimacy of the way individuals treat each other. Treating someone as an end rather than a means requires being able to distinguish these different ways of treating someone in a particular social and historical context. Feminists can strongly argue that history shows that attitudes about the 'nature of women' and what they 'really want', i.e. what it is to treat them as ends, is extremely malleable, and socially constructed.

The problem with liberalism's universalism may be captured in the idea that for liberals, equality means sameness. To treat men and women equally is to treat them the same. If women deserve equal rights with men, that is because they are, at the appropriate level of abstraction, the same as men, i.e. as rational, autonomous, choosers. But, argues the critic, liberalism gives women equal rights only so long as they act like men; they can be seen to compete equally on the level playing field of the market-place only so long as the differences between men and women are ignored. To take the obvious case of reproductive capability, a woman's choice to 'have children' means something vastly different from a man's 'choice' to do 'the same' in the context of employment. For the critic of legal liberalism, in view of this difference, the only fair and just thing to do would be not to treat men and women in exactly the same way. But though it is certainly a reason to treat them *differently*, it is not a ground for treating men and women *unequally*. In other words, in order to achieve genuine equality we have to move beyond the simplistic, universalist assumption that equal treatment, under the law in particular, means identical treatment.

14.2.2 **Radical feminism**

As the term implies, 'radical' feminism claims that in order for sexism to be eradicated, there has to be a root and branch abolition of the current relations between the sexes. Radical feminists see the sexual division as the foundational division at the heart of social life, in the same way, for example, as Marxists see class divisions as the central organising feature of economic and political life. The most well-known radical feminist theory is that of Catharine MacKinnon, whose work we shall look at in some detail below. MacKinnon's theory is typical of radical feminism in focussing in particular on sex, sexuality, and reproduction, the more 'biological' rather than 'gender/cultural' aspects of the situation of women. In general, radical feminists regard the oppression of women to be primarily located in men's domination over women in terms of sex and reproductive rights, and it therefore makes perfect sense for radical feminists to concentrate their theoretical and practical energies on issues such as the regulation of pornography, the law of rape, the law of marriage, and abortion rights. The legal regulation of each of these areas in its own way has traditionally disempowered women and empowered men. The work of radical feminists can be seen as the 'sexual turn' in feminist legal theory, and its effect has been profound. Indeed, for many law students, radical feminist legal theory *is* feminist legal theory because of the way that radical feminists have systematically exposed male dominant perspectives in the general law.

The examples are legion, from the reconceptualisation of the defence of provocation to murder to the law regulating abortion. It was radical feminists who championed abortion rights, arguing that the denial of the right to abortion was a facet of male control of reproduction. It was radical feminists who argued that pornography was the graphic depiction of sexualised violence against women that normalised the rapist's conception of sexual desire, and that the protection of pornography by the right to freedom of expression revealed the law to privilege the monetary interest of the pornographer over the lives and health of women.

14.2.2.1 The critique of radical feminism

Radical feminism is typically criticised for being essentialist, oppositional, and utopian.

The charge of essentialism is different here from the charge as laid against liberal feminists. Here the charge is that radical feminists have betrayed their own former allegiance to consciousness raising, the practice of listening to women's real stories and accepting their understanding of their own experiences, and insisted on a sexism–sexuality connection which many women do not feel as real in their own lives. Radical feminists, so the criticism goes, emphasise sex above all else, whereas the causes and effects of sexism are much more varied. This characterisation of sexism 'essentialises' women as the submissive sex partner; to be a woman is just to be subjected to sexual violence, but this reduces women to the very sexual stereotype that feminism seeks to overcome.

Radical feminism is criticised as being oppositional because, it is argued, it cannot make allies with other oppressed groups, such as those who are oppressed because of their race, and it cannot reach out to those men who are willing to work to end sexist oppression. As to making common cause with other oppressed groups, radical feminists, it is said, regard sexist oppression as more basic and more greatly implicated in the structure of social and political relations than other forms of oppression. For the radical feminist, it is easier to be 'colour-blind' than 'sex-blind'. In consequence, it is difficult for the radical feminist to devote energy to eradicating less basic forms of oppression, and so it is difficult to act with others to the extent that this makes it seem that sexism is just another 'ism'. As to reaching out to men some, though by no means all, radical feminists draw a separatist conclusion from the realisation of how deeply sexism is ingrained in male–female sexual and reproductive relations.

In terms of radical feminism's utopian character, Frug puts the point well.

> Only when sex means more than male or female, only when the word 'woman' cannot be coherently understood, will oppression by sex be fatally undermined.
>
> (M. J. Frug, 'A Postmodern Feminist Manifesto (An Unfinished Draft)' (1992) 105 *Harv L Rev* 1045 at p. 1075)

For many people, it is difficult in the extreme to envisage a world in which no real significance would attach to the distinction between men and women, and surely, it is felt, it is utopian to pursue that which we cannot even comprehend.

It is difficult to weigh the strength of these criticisms in the abstract, for their force is very much dependent upon the truth of radical feminist claims. If, upon examination, radical feminists do a better job than other feminist theories of explaining the shape and the source of sexism, and in particular its persistence, then it would appear (1) that it has established something more or less essential about what it means to be a woman; (2) that sexism, as radical feminists perceive, is profound in a way that other forms of oppression are not; and (3), that if we are committed to the cause of justice, eradicating sexism will not be utopian even if the changes required are profound, and difficult to fully grasp in advance.

14.2.3 **Cultural/difference feminism**

The cultural/difference feminist outlook can be captured in the idea that there are no *persons*, just men and women. Liberalism's embrace of the abstract person, the autonomous individual chooser, is profoundly misguided. One simply cannot strip the femaleness away from a woman to find the liberal person beneath. Radical feminism is right to see that sexism operates primarily in the way it deals with the difference, especially sexual and reproductive differences between men and women, but it over-problematises these differences, regarding differences as being conceivable only as sites of oppression: according to the cultural/difference feminist, the recognition of difference is not *per se* an act of, and a prelude to further oppression.

The motto of cultural/difference feminism could be 'Equality does not mean sameness'; indeed, if we are ever to have political equality, it cannot, for it would be impossible to simply eradicate the differences between men and women, adults and children, between people of different genetic, cultural, religious, and ethnic backgrounds. We had better learn to live with difference, and the principal way in which this is to be done is not to ignore, marginalise, or positively undermine the perspective of non-dominant individuals or groups. In the case of law, cultural/difference feminists argue that the law has failed to take into account the woman's point of view.

Cultural/difference feminism has been heavily shaped in one direction by the work of Carol Gilligan, and in another by Robin West. Gilligan is a psychologist who, in her 1982 book, *In a Different Voice*, argued that boys and girls reason differently to resolve moral dilemmas. Boys tend to emphasise people's individual entitlements, and generate rules to resolve conflicts. The boys' approach to moral realising is captured by Gilligan with the phrase 'an ethic of rights'. Girls, on the other hand, seek to resolve moral dilemmas by emphasising the personal relationships involved, and seek compromises so that everyone's interests are taken into account; this reflects an 'ethic of care'. Feminist legal theorists see in this work an implicit critique of the legal system. The legal system clearly adopts an ethic of rights, and attention can be drawn as well to competitive/adversarial 'winner takes all' court proceedings that discourage compromise. In this way, the law can be seen to take a masculine approach in its very reasoning. Not only does this negatively affect the prospects of female lawyers, who more naturally cleave to a different way of moral reasoning, but it also privileges men generally, as they are more likely to resolve social conflicts in daily life in a way the law can effectively cognise and thus are more likely to be suited to playing by the law's rules.

Robin West's characterisation of this strand of feminism can be summed up in her connection thesis.

> The connection thesis is simply this: Women are actually or potentially materially connected to other human life. Men aren't.
>
> (R. West, 'Jurisprudence and Gender' (1988) 55 *Univ. of Chicago LR* 1 at p. 14)

For West, the cultural feminists emphasise or celebrate the positive possibilities of these connections, in particular the mother–child bond and the source of identity and understanding it gives to women. And she regards the radical feminist as one who dwells upon the negative aspects of such a connection, the way that sex and pregnancy are like invasions, forging connections which can imperil a woman's autonomy and sense of individual identity. According to West, the project of a feminist jurisprudence is to make it clear to legal culture that the masculine understanding of individuals as basically separate and unconnected simply does not reflect the world as seen by women, and that in areas of law in which women are most primarily affected, such as reproductive rights, the woman's perspective must be made to be heard.

14.2.3.1 The critique of cultural/difference feminism

Cultural/difference feminism draws some of the critiques of both radical and liberal feminism. In keeping with the critiques of radical feminism, cultural/difference feminism is equally open to the claim that it 'essentialises' women as the 'connected' sex. It can also be viewed as politically conservative, as liberal feminism is sometimes accused of being; but with the opposite twist: if liberal feminism is conservative because it allows women equal rights on the basis that they will act like men, then cultural/difference feminism may appear to consign women to those traditional roles of the caring professions, teachers, nurses, and so on, and motherhood. Most profoundly, however, it may simply not be the case that for most women, let alone all, the 'ethic of care' best describes the way they morally reason, nor that women's connectedness is so prominently a feature of their sense of identity and relation to others.

14.2.4 Different perspectives on gender

It is worth pausing here to consider how liberal, radical, and cultural/difference feminists address the idea of gender. Olsen sets out a series of dualisms, with qualities or characteristics associated with masculinity on the left, with their feminine counterparts on the right:

> rational/irrational
>
> active/passive
>
> thought/feeling
>
> reason/emotion
>
> culture/nature
>
> power/sensitivity
>
> objective/subjective
>
> abstract/contextualised
>
> principled/personalised
>
> (F. Olsen, 'Feminism and Critical Legal Theory: An American Perspective' (1990) 18 *International Journal of the Sociology of Law* 199 at p. 200)

The reader can surely add other binary distinctions which are prevalent in distinguishing the masculine from the feminine. Like Olsen, feminist theorists in general regard these dualisms as both sexualised—the ones on the left are masculine—and hierarchised—the ones on the left are also better, more valued by society. How ought feminists to deal with this? We will get a different answer depending upon whether the theorist is liberal, radical, or cultural/difference in outlook.

The liberal theorist is prone to accept the hierarchy (though perhaps in not all of its details), but reject its sexualisation. Thus, a liberal feminist would deny that the traits on the left are necessarily masculine any more than those on the right are necessarily feminine. People are individuals, and as individuals they may reflect traits or qualities from either side of the division. On the other hand, it is another question entirely whether we should value activity over passivity, or thought over feeling, and so on. So long as women are seen to be just as capable as men of being objective, for instance, it is not an issue for feminists whether we prize the former over the latter.

The cultural/difference feminist, on the other hand, is likely to accept the sexualisation (though perhaps in not all of its details), but reject the hierarchy. That is, the cultural/difference feminist regards men and women as different, with different traits and typical characteristics, but does not accept that these different traits and characteristics should be valued differently. Rather, the goal of the cultural/difference feminist is to ensure that society revalues the right hand side of the division, so that passivity is valued as equally as activity, and so on.

The radical feminist will have none of either approach. So long as the categories 'male' and 'female' have meaning, they will be understood in terms of various traits and characteristics, and whatever characteristics are associated with the male, they will be more highly valued. Take, for example, the dualism principled/personalised. The radical feminist can imagine the order being reversed, so that the masculine outlook was personalised, the female principled. It would be easy to see how the valuation of the characteristics would change. The personalised outlook would reflect the man who knows his own mind, is able to absorb arguments, but still knows that the ultimate decision always lies in one's gut. Whereas 'principle' is really just what comes out of whiny talking shops from people who never shut up, from women and 'girly' men like egghead philosophers. And notice that those dualisms which do not seem likely to be able to be shifted in this way, such as power/sensitivity, are just those dualisms that express male domination.

14.2.5 Postmodern feminism

Postmodern feminism can be seen as a response to the perceived failures of liberal, radical, and cultural/difference feminisms. Like other postmodernists, postmodern feminism is concerned with the violence of classification and the way that language and theory are not merely ways of expressing truth but are also ways of suppressing other ways of seeing things. Thus postmodern feminists subscribe to the postmodern injunction to listen to all the *different* voices, voices which are unlikely to express identical experience or reveal their speakers as finding the same meanings in our various social interactions.

In particular, postmodern theory shares postmodernism's general suspicion of grand theory, its emphasis on the fragmentation of truth and meaning and the harm or wrong that occurs when we try to capture truth and meaning in representational systems like language, and its emphasis on the multiplicity of people's perspectives.

Radical feminism is most likely to attract the charge of 'grand theorising'. In particular, MacKinnon's claims regarding the connection between the inequality of women and male domination in sex and sexuality is the sort of tight and foundational connection of which postmodernists would be suspicious. By purporting to explain so much it must necessarily abstract away from all nuance and subtlety. Furthermore, its suggestion that the unequal treatment of women can be understood on the basis of this 'one, big truth' which must be addressed in feminist practice is the sort of theoretical and practical claim which, for the postmodernist, is uncongenial, as it displaces other ways of understanding and combatting sexism.

Like other postmodernists, postmodern feminists also emphasise (as they see it) the fragmented nature of our grasp on reality; in the case of sexism, our understanding of it is always provisional and is best informed by a continual juggling and revision of those elements which seem most informative at the moment. We must always bear in mind the way in which ways of seeing and speaking 'fix' our ideas and can inhibit openness to different perspectives, perspectives which might undermine the theoretical *status quo* by, at the least, revealing received ideas to be partial in both senses of the word.

Finally, as the debate between the liberal, radical, and cultural/difference feminists reveals, the lived experience of sexist ill-treatment is likely to generate and has generated a multiplicity of different 'takes' on the problem. The postmodernist insists on the validity of contrasting, even conflicting perspectives. As Frug puts it

> In their most vulgar, bootlegged versions, both radical and cultural legal feminisms depict male and female sexual identities as anatomically determined and psychologically predictable. This is inconsistent with the semiotic character of sex differences and the impact that historical specificity has on any individual identity. In postmodern jargon, this treatment of sexual identity is inconsistent with a decentered, polymorphous, contingent understanding of the subject.
>
> Because sex differences are semiotic—that is, constituted by a system of signs that we produce and interpret—each of us inescapably produces herself within the gender meaning system, although the meaning of gender is indeterminate or undecidable. The dilemma of difference, which the liberal equality guarantee seeks to avoid through neutrality, is unavoidable.
>
> (M. J. Frug, 'A Postmodern Feminist Manifesto (An Unfinished Draft)' (1992) 105 *Harv L Rev* 1045 at p. 1046)

14.2.5.1 The critique of postmodern feminism

One can criticise postmodern feminism in the same way that postmodernism has typically been criticised, as providing no basis for valid critical scrutiny. If every perspective is (equally) valid, then none is. Whether this criticism bites turns, one might suggest, on the work of the theorist in question. The recognition of the contingency in social relations and a respect for the provisional character of truth claims need not undermine one's critical faculties. Postmodernism is also often criticised for leading to political impotence, for in refusing to endorse the possibility of truth, it refuses to endorse the truth of claims of oppression. This is probably a misreading, however, for postmodernism's anxiety is with the concept of non-perspectival truth, 'Truth with a capital T', not the idea that certain things are the case. To be a postmodernist is not to deny that things happen, that a woman may have been sexually harassed at work, nor that such a thing was a wrong done to her, but to deny that such events are best understood through the lens of a grand theory about sexism or the nature of morality.

14.2.6 Feminist legal theory and the interaction between sexism and racism

Feminist legal theorists have faced the charge that their views are reflective not of all women, but of white, economically privileged women. Feminists in general accept that sexism is far from the only problem many women face, and that feminist theory should be sensitive to other sources of oppression. The question is whether a theoretical endeavour to bring anti-sexist and anti-racist theory together will bear fruit, or whether it is more productive to recognise the instance of the other, but not confuse the different projects of each. Collins' work (Collins, P., *Black Feminist Thought: Knowledge,*

Consciousness, and the Politics of Empowerment (London: Routledge, 1991)) is an example of an analysis which seems to demonstrate that the oppression of black women in the United States can only properly be seen when both racism and sexism are taken into account. The stereotypes of the black woman as the 'welfare mother', the 'Jezebel' (the sexually aggressive woman), or the 'mammy' (the surrogate mother to white children) are all stereotypes, the production of which seems to have required sexist and racist attitudes to have worked 'synergistically'.

14.3 The work of Catharine MacKinnon

Of all feminist legal theories, Catharine MacKinnon's work is possibly the best known, and contains a number of important ideas. Probably the most central idea in her work is the claim that our understanding of the difference between the sexes is through and through saturated with the acceptance of male domination. Furthermore, this idea of male domination is sexualised, which is to say that men's power over women is conceived of as a kind of sexual power.

> [Feminism] has a theory of power: sexuality is gendered as gender is sexualised. Male and female are created through the erotization of dominance and submission.
>
> (C. MacKinnon, 'Feminism, Marxism, Method and the State: Toward a Feminist Jurisprudence' (1983) 8 *Signs* 635 at p. 635)

The arena where sexism is most evident because most 'true to itself' is that of sex and reproduction, for it is there that men are most clearly seen to be 'on top'—the pun is intended, and MacKinnon herself argues that sexism is embedded in our language, in particular in language which deals with sex. MacKinnon has famously said

> [M]an fucks woman: subject verb object.
>
> (C. MacKinnon, *Feminism Unmodified* (Cambridge, Mass: Harvard University Press, 1987), p. 124)

Our language of sex reveals that our conception of the relation of men to women in sex is that of the man as active subject, of woman as passive object; he 'does it' to her, and not vice versa. The point is meant to be taken both epistemologically as well as politically. MacKinnon's claim is that feminism is not simply the political movement whose purpose is to eradicate sexism, but that feminism is a theory of knowledge as well. Specifically, feminism claims that the categories of male and female are known to us through what she calls the 'male point of view', which is the sexist point of view of male domination. The male point of view, however, is not generally perceived as a point of view, much less a male one. Rather, it is perceived as the 'objective' view; men are men and women are women and their differences are perfectly natural, as anyone viewing the situation 'objectively' can see. In consequence of this unconscious bias which shapes our very concept of sex, the goal of feminism cannot simply be to oppose the oppression of women, but it must do so in the knowledge that this will involve overthrowing the categories 'man' and 'woman', 'male' and 'female' as we presently understand them.

14.3.1 **The feminist theory of the State**

According to MacKinnon, unlike other political theories which may be applied to the situation of women (liberalism applied to address the unequal rights of women, Marxism applied to address the economic exploitation of women), feminism must see the State as male. The State and the law reflect the male point of view and the law does so especially when it purports to be acting at its most neutral. This is so because the State and the law are the supreme manifestation of power relations in a society, and as regards men and women, men have the power. As a reflection of male power, the law confers and enforces rights which authorise the male experience of the world. For a woman then, the State simply cannot be trusted. This is particularly evident, claims MacKinnon, in the case of the law's regulation of pornography and rape.

14.3.2 **The legal regulation of pornography and rape**

According to MacKinnon, pornography violates women's civil rights by interfering with their right to freedom of expression. Rather than being primarily a form of freedom of expression itself, the main function of pornography, which is not the same thing as sexually explicit art or literature but is the depiction of the sexualised degradation of women, is to silence women. It silences them because it fosters a climate of incomprehension of women's own experience of sex and sexuality, making it difficult or impossible to speak about that experience, and may lead to the under-reporting of sexualised criminal behaviour such as rape. It may also silence them in the sense that their words may be misunderstood. The eroticisation of violence and submission in pornography helps create an environment in which women are understood to find male force sexually attractive, and in which 'no' means 'yes'. The main effect, then, of pornography is that it harms women by taking away their freedom of expression, and in consequence the battle between pornographers and women, the victims of pornography, is a battle in which both sides can claim that they are enforcing their right to freedom of expression.

The central feature of MacKinnon's analysis of rape law is that the law, adopting the male point of view and unable to draw on women's perspective, is completely incapable of accommodating women's experience of rape. In particular, the law attempts to draw a line between 'rape' and normal, permissible, heterosexual sex, making the former illegal and the latter perfectly acceptable.

> Feminists have reconceived rape as central to women's condition in two ways. Some see rape as an act of violence, not sexuality, the threat of which intimidates all women. Others see rape, including its violence, as an expression of male sexuality, the social imperatives of which define all women....
>
> The point of defining rape as 'violence not sex' or 'violence against women' has been to separate sexuality from gender in order to affirm sex (heterosexuality) while rejecting violence (rape). The problem remains what it has always been: telling the difference. The convergence of sexuality with violence, long used at law to deny the reality of women's violation, is recognised by rape survivors, with a difference: where the legal system has seen the intercourse in rape, victims see the rape in intercourse. The uncoerced context for sexual expression becomes as elusive as the physical acts come to feel indistinguishable. Instead of asking, what is the violation of rape, what if we ask, what is the nonviolation of intercourse? To tell what is wrong with rape, explain what is right about sex. If this, in turn, is difficult, the difficulty is as instructive as the difficulty

> men have in telling the difference when women see one. Perhaps the wrong of rape has proven so difficult to articulate because the unquestionable starting point has been that rape is definable as distinct from intercourse, when for women it is difficult to distinguish them under conditions of male dominance. (C. MacKinnon, 'Feminism, Marxism, Method and the State: Toward a Feminist Jurisprudence' (1983) 8 *Signs* 635 at pp. 646–47)

From this perspective MacKinnon and Dworkin's claim that consent is immaterial to rape makes sense: consent is simply not a constitutive feature of the concept of (non-rape) permitted sex; it therefore cannot be the thing whose absence distinguishes sexual intercourse that amounts to rape.

14.3.3 MacKinnon's impact

It is difficult to overestimate MacKinnon's impact on the course of feminist legal theory. Even those feminists who disagree profoundly with her views would acknowledge that MacKinnon's analysis has probed the relationship between sexism and sexuality in ways which have been very illuminating. The standard criticism of MacKinnon's work is that it takes the part for the whole, and regards the sex/power connection as the essential foundation for the male sexist hegemony over women. Whatever else must be brought into the picture to give a fuller account of women's oppression, however, the greatest strength of MacKinnon's analysis is surely its contribution to explaining the persistence of sexism. Long after most men and women have abandoned much of the old sexist outlook concerning women's inferior intelligence and much else, most people today still strongly believe that men and women have different sexual natures, often along the very lines of dominance and submission that MacKinnon reveals.

14.4 A liberal feminist revival?

In recent years, the philosopher Martha Nussbaum has led something of a revival of liberal feminism. Nussbaum argues that the liberal tradition is one of equal concern and respect for each individual. It need not be understood to be egoistic, nor need it emphasise the separateness of persons rather than their connectedness. And liberalism's great strength, which other political traditions do not have the conceptual tools to fully embrace, is its concern that the purpose for which the State and the law are instituted is to contribute to the flourishing of each individual, individuals whose lives are considered 'one by one' and not merely as members of a group, and as individual, distinct ends, so that no individual's well-being can be sacrificed in the interests of others. To the extent that feminism's primary task is to address the oppression of women, liberalism has the virtue of requiring that the oppression of every single woman is addressed. Furthermore, liberalism's embrace of freedom can be seen as not only compatible with but also emblematic of feminism's fight against female oppression, for what sexist oppression does, at its worst, is remove from women the birthright belonging to every human, the joy individuals have in using their own minds and bodies free from coercion.

FURTHER READING

Bartlett, K. T., 'Feminist Legal Method' (1970) 103 *Harv L Rev* 829.

Frug, M. J., 'A Postmodern Feminist Manifesto (An Unfinished Draft)' (1992) 105 *Harvard L Rev* 1045.

Gilligan, C., *In a Different Voice* (Cambridge, Mass.: Harvard University Press, 1982).

Lacey, N., *Unspeakable Subjects* (Oxford: Hart Publishing, 1998).

MacKinnon, C., 'Feminism, Marxism, Method and the State: Toward a Feminist Jurisprudence' (1983) 8 *Signs* 635.

MacKinnon, C., *Towards a Feminist Theory of the State* (Cambridge, Mass.: Harvard University Press, 1989).

Naffine, N., 'In Praise of Legal Feminism', (2002) 22 *Legal Studies* 71.

Nussbaum, M., *Sex and Social Justice* (Oxford: Oxford University Press, 1999).

Patterson, D., 'Postmodernism/Feminism/Law' (1992) 77 *Cornell Law Review* 254.

Penner, J., Schiff, D., and Nobles, R., (eds), *Jurisprudence and Legal Theory: Commentary and Materials* (Oxford: Oxford University Press, 2002), ch. 16.

Smart, C., *Feminism and the Power of Law* (London: Routledge, 1989).

West, R., 'Jurisprudence and Gender' (1988) 55 *Univ. of Chicago LR* 1.

15

Postmodern Legal Theory

Introduction

Apart from the grand narratives of the classical legal theories, such as positivism, natural law, interpretivism, or political philosophies such as the social contract tradition that we have explored, there is another way of telling the story of the State and law. It is this alternative, which is customarily referred to as poststructuralism or postmodernism that we shall discuss in this chapter. This reading is alternative in that, on one level, it understands itself in and through its difference to the 'jurisprudence of totality', associated with grand narratives of legal theory. As a by-product of the Enlightenment and modernity, the 'jurisprudence of totality' claims to be arriving at right and unique answers regarding law and justice with the use of rational and purportedly flawless methodology. Postmodern jurisprudence does not treat the law as a whole with a concrete history that can be reconstructed and interpreted as a seamless web. On the contrary, it explores the law as fragments, whether these fragments are texts or practices. It introduces new methodologies, which turn from the universal to the local, from the construction of self-contained structures to the reasons for the collapse of such edifices. On another level, this 'other' jurisprudence is always other to itself. It is never fulfilled but rather exists and reproduces itself through a constant deferment of the possibility of justice but also the possibility of theory. Suspicious of totalities, it is fearful of becoming a totality itself. What often ensues is its apparent inability to offer concrete answers to concrete problems or to discuss the problem of the relationship between law and justice in a coherent and practically significant way.

Before we go on to decipher as much of the above as there is time and space for, a few introductory remarks are called for. First, despite the fact that in this context various theorists and theories are examined together and the focus is on their common ground, postmodern jurisprudence is not homogeneous. There are as many differences between its strands as there are commonalities. Secondly, this kind of philosophy resists hagiographies. Precisely because it shifts focus from the author to the text and from the subject to the context, there is always something paradoxical about organising its exposition around authors. However, to the extent that some authors have produced seminal, groundbreaking works, this cannot be avoided. Therefore this chapter cannot but try and balance references to authors and ideas hoping to minimise the undermining force of the paradox.

In the first section, we shall introduce the distinction between the modern and the postmodern conditions or eras with reference to the work by Jean François Lyotard. We will then discuss two fundamental ideas underpinning modern law and legal theory, namely, the rational and autonomous subject, and the clarity and objectivity of meaning of the legal text. With reference to Michel Foucault and Jacques Derrida we will show how postmodern thought questions these foundations of modernity. Finally, we will discuss the practical significance of postmodern jurisprudence, its ability to provide answers to pressing questions of law and justice.

15.1 A critique of the project of modernity

What is implied by the prefix 'post' in poststructuralism and postmodernism is a temporal but, more importantly, a substantive transcendence of systems of thought that are deemed to have lost their explanatory value in view of historical developments towards the end of the twentieth century.

The definition of modernity, and subsequently the clarification of the content of postmodernity, is not merely a chronological question. On the contrary, it is the most central, substantive problem in the debate between postmodern philosophy and those theories that deny that there has been a paradigmatic change and that maintain that we still experience the project of modernity. Therefore, this question will permeate the whole of this chapter and will surface at various stages of the discussion in one way or another. It is useful, however, to give a very general and brief introduction to the problem as a first impression of what postmodernism tries to transcend.

There are many contradictory opinions on the matter but, for the purposes of understanding postmodernism, it is helpful to place the starting point of modernity in or immediately after the Enlightenment of the eighteenth century. That period bears witness to the establishment of the reign of reason. As the Western world emerged from what might be termed the 'theological terrorism' of the Middle Ages, a new, secular faith emerged, a faith in the unity of the world and the ability of humankind to discover and describe it with the use of reason. This new intellectual endeavour was based on and revolved around the formulation of cross-temporal, universal valid principles. Thus a new kind of metaphysics emerged and permeated all forms of human activity from art to politics. This new metaphysics was accompanied by a moral theory that revolved around the idea of the autonomous, timeless, universal rational subject and the existence of transcendental principles of truth and justice.

In the words of Jean-François Lyotard

> I will use the term modern to designate any science that legitimates itself with reference to a metadiscourse of this kind making an explicit appeal to some grand narrative, such as the dialectics of Spirit, the hermeneutics of meaning, the emancipation of the rational or working subject, or the creation of wealth. (J. F. Lyotard, *The Postmodern Condition: A Report on Knowledge*, transl. G. Bennington and B. Massumi (Manchester: Manchester University Press, 1984), p. xxiii)

Modern thought turns from the local to the universal, from the particular to the abstract, in order to draw from the latter principles that will explain and/or justify the former. Kantian transcendental moral philosophy, Marxist social and political theory, liberalism, both economic and political, to mention but a few obvious examples, attempt to discover and formulate those unique elements that either explain social evolution or set the normative standards against which practical reason should develop.

Law and legal philosophy became integral parts of the project of modernity. A cursory glance at the major political and legal theories up until the second part of the twentieth century reveals the robust faith in the possibility of the world as a coherent totality governed by a law, which in turn conforms with a normative metadiscourse. Consider, as examples: Austin's jurisprudence of the sovereign as a singular and unique normative source; Kelsen's self-contained and self-legitimising system of norms; Hart's reliance on unequivocal (and univocal) semantics underpinning the law's justice; the legal realist critique of legal practice that reveals a principled faith in the law as such; Finnis' reworking of natural law theory on grounds of the seven 'self-evident' goods that are common to all; Dworkin's moral cognitivism and his theory of law as interpretive integrity, which leads unmistakably to the one right answer. Although undoubtedly contradictory in their particularities, all these distinct theories are based on the same premise: truth, justice and the law are discoverable in an objective, rationalistic way. They try to portray law as a unified whole, and posit the rule of law as the method of 'neutral, non-subjectivist resolution of value disagreement and social conflict' (C. Douzinas, and R. Warrington, *Postmodern Jurisprudence: The Law of Text in the Texts of Law* (London: Routledge, 1991), p. 14).

The history of modernity continued uninterrupted until the twentieth century, when several momentous changes took place in all areas of human activity and self-understanding: the rapid technological development and the changes in the mode of production and the new forms of communication it brought about; the emergence of psychoanalysis and the new perspectives it introduced for the understanding of human motivation and action; the shift of scientific focus from the visible—the phenomenon— to the unseen micro-basis of everything that exists (for example, quantum physics that reveal the randomness and contingency of reality); the relativisation of the truth about space and time; the proliferation of emancipatory movements especially by disenfranchised groups which reclaimed their voice; in art, the emergence of schools that moved from representation to the abstract visualisation of space, time, and human nature. It soon became apparent to many writers that a re-thinking and re-conceptualisation of the conditions of our existence was called for.

15.2 The transition from the modern to the postmodern

A seminal work that often serves as a starting point in accounts of poststructural and postmodern theory is Jean-François Lyotard's *The Postmodern Condition*, which gives a philosophical account of the transition from the modern to the postmodern. The book's subtitle *A Report on Knowledge* reveals his main aim, which is to record and make sense of the passage from the epistemological paradigm of the Enlightenment to the technologisation or computerisation of all forms of knowledge.

Lyotard starts from the premise that computerisation and the miniaturisation and dispersion of technology are bound to radically change the nature of knowledge. The validity of modern scientific knowledge rests on the possibility of referring to normative meta-orders that provide the criteria, against which the scientific nature of statements will be judged. Some of those requirements are that scientific statements must be provable in the sense that the referent—i.e. the idea or thing that the statement refers to or symbolises—must exist in the world; the addressee must be able to bring herself in the position of the addressor, that is she must be able to assent and reproduce the statement with the same claim to validity and truth; the statement must have a unique referent, otherwise it would stand defenceless to the critique on grounds of its inconsistency; by the same token, as long as proof can be produced to support the statement, reality is the way the statement describes it. Scientific knowledge is being expressed and transmitted in one specific linguistic form, in a specific 'language game', to use the Wittgensteinian term borrowed by Lyotard (see L. Wittgenstein, *Philosophical Investigations*, transl. G. E. M. Anscombe (Oxford: Blackwell, 1953). Language games are forms of communication bound to specific contexts or forms of life. Apart from being bound to the context, a crucial aspect of language games is that they always abide by rules that are unique to them. The language game of the acquisition and transmission of scientific knowledge relies on constative utterances—i.e., denotative statements of fact that raise a claim to truth—to the extent that they are verifiable or falsifiable by reference to a reality external to them.

In contrast to scientific knowledge 'narrative knowledge' is not based on proof but rather on the customary ways of acquiring, testing and reproducing information. This kind of knowledge can be transmitted with a variety of speech acts. Deontic, i.e. normative, or interrogative statements sit as comfortably in narratives as constative utterances. Moreover, narratives embody the rules, which permeate and regulate them rendering reference to a normative meta-order unnecessary. Lyotard illustrates his point with the example of the Cashinahua storytellers. The Cashinahua are an indigenous people of south-eastern Peru speaking their own Cashinahua language, which is also spoken in parts of Brazil. Their storytellers start their narrations by stating that they were once told the story themselves and, when they conclude the story, they give the name they bear to their audience. It is those statements that legitimate them in telling the story and also account for its truth. The source of legitimacy and truth is therefore the particular itself and not its classification under universal categories nor its correspondence to some objective reality.

Let us leave the difference between scientific and narrative knowledge to one side for a moment and make a short detour to give an account of Lyotard's analysis of language games or genres of discourse and their incommensurability. Although the idea is present in *The Postmodern Condition*, it is in another work, *The Différend*, that he offers a more elaborate analysis (J. F. Lyotard, *The Différend: Phrases in Dispute*, transl. G. Van Den Abbeele (Manchester: Manchester University Press, 1988). Lyotard starts by promoting *the phrase* as the only indubitable and indivisible object of analysis. Everything can be understood as a phrase. Even the denial of the phrase must be included in a phrase. What is it that makes possible the transition between one phrase to another in the course of a dialogue, debate or any other instance of use of language? A phrase must be followed by and linked to another phrase. But the content of the follow-up phrase is contingent in that there is nothing inherent in the phrase that predicts or dictates its extension. For instance, there are an infinite number of phrases that can follow from the phrase: 'I'll come over to your house'. However, only one of the possible candidates can be actualised and its actualisation will happen by way of exclusion of the other alternatives. This does not mean that the selected alternative is more correct than the excluded ones. Its selection is dictated by some pre-existing rules that are bound to the specific genre of discourse and not by reference to some external reality.

Therefore, genres of discourse determine which links to other phrases are pertinent but they also set the ultimate communicative goals, the *stakes*, in Lyotard's terminology. Each genre sets its own stakes and the latter is achieved again by way of exclusion of the stakes of other genres. It is at this level that the incommensurability of genres of discourse is revealed. Incommensurability here means that there can be no meaningful communication between different genres of discourse. They do not and indeed cannot have a shared way of making sense of referents and, moreover, they cannot be classified under the same metanarrative, which would unify all the rules of legitimation. They are not permeated by the same rules and they cannot be reduced to a common indivisible element, such as the word, precisely because meaning is bound to the context and it is not the product of the synthesis of some inherent and *a priori* content of the words. Lyotard terms this instance of contact and conflict between incommensurable genres of discourse *'différend'*.

Let us now go back to the tension between scientific and narrative knowledge. Science has prevailed as the ultimate and unique metadiscourse, claiming to be able to provide justificatory rules for all language games. Thus, legitimation became conceivable only in terms of reference to principles or universal truths about the world. Therefore, it involves the application of pre-existing, familiar categories in order to judge the truth, validity or rightness of statements. Lyotard refers to the scientific metadiscourse in the following way:

> Reality is not what is 'given' to this or that 'subject', it is a state of the referent (that about which one speaks) which results from the effectuation of establishment procedures defined by a unanimously agreed-upon protocol, and from the possibility offered to anyone to recommence this effectuation as often as he or she wants. (J. F. Lyotard, *The Postmodern Condition*, p. 4)

The legitimation of scientific statements is strongly interconnected with the justification of axiological or prescriptive statements, i.e., statements concerning the rightness of actions. Despite the fundamental, essential differences between those two language games and despite the fact that prescriptions cannot be deduced from descriptions, in other words what *is* the case can never lead us to conclusions as to what *ought* to be the case, judgements of truth and rightness seem to collapse into each other. In Lyotard's words

> The question of the legitimacy of science has been indissociably linked to that of the legitimation of the legislator since the time of Plato. From this point of view, the right to decide what is true is not independent of the right to decide what is just, even if the statements consigned by these two authorities differ in nature. The point is that there is a strict interlinkage between the kinds of language called science and the kind called ethics and politics: they both stem from the same perspective—the choice called the Occident.
>
> (*The Postmodern Condition*, p. 31)

In a nutshell, Lyotard reports the postmodern condition as the new situation—still inextricably linked to modernity and, indeed, stemming from it—which witnesses the proliferation of genres of discourse to such an extent that it is impossible for metadiscourses such as science to claim to be able to provide homogeneous justifications for all language games. He defines postmodernism negatively as 'incredulity towards metanarratives', the loss of faith in the possibility of regulating all the co-existing language games or genres of discourse in a way that will do justice to all of them.

The discussion of *différends* can now be transposed from the level of language to the realm of the political. In politics, the occurrence of *différends* means that some forms of life, some social groups, which share a language game that does not coincide with the dominant political system of meaning, will be silenced and disenfranchised. Instead of focusing on the fruitless task of imposing normative supra-orders, we are called to try and acknowledge the instances of *différend*, instances of conflict between genres of discourses leading to the violent imposition of one language game and way of life onto others.

The relevance of Lyotard's analysis for the law should be clear by now. Modern law seeks to become an all-regulating metanarrative. It claims to be able to regulate all social discourses with reference to rules and principles, which are objective and, as such, accepted by everyone. A great deal relies on this ideal of objectivity as acceptance or acceptability. All modern legal theories revolve around it to a certain degree. Instead, the postmodern perspective highlights that objectivity is achieved by silencing all alternatives. It is important to understand that this is not a contingent critique of the law nor is it a version of American legal realism. It is a critique that reveals the inherent inability of the law to make sense of and communicate with other discursive genres that it comes in contact with.

> ...the panglossia of statutes, delegated legislation, administrative legislation and adjudication, judicial and quasi-judicial decision-making; the multiform institutions and personnel; and the plural non-formal methods of dispute avoidance and resolution cannot be seen any longer as a coherent, closed ensemble of rules or values
>
> (C. Douzinas, and R. Warrington, *Postmodern Jurisprudence: The Law of Text in the Texts of Law* (London: Routledge, 1991), p. 27)

So, postmodernist thought mainly aims at teasing out these contradictions of modernity the way a painter or an author must always put to the question the rules and methods of their art.

> If they do not wish to become supporters (of minor importance) of what exists, the painter and the writer must refuse to lend themselves to such therapeutic uses. They must question the rules of the art of painting or of narrative as they have learned and received them from their predecessors. Soon those rules must appear to them as a means to deceive, to seduce, and to reassure, which makes it impossible for them to be 'true'. Under the common name of painting and literature, an unprecedented split is taking place. Those who refuse to reexamine the rules of art pursue successful careers in mass conformism by communicating, by means of the 'correct rules', the endemic desire for reality with objects and situations capable of gratifying it.
>
> (J. F. Lyotard, *The Postmodern Condition*, pp. 74–5)

Nevertheless, and despite most people's view that postmodern thought is practically inert, there is the possibility that postmodernism, by rejecting many aspects of modern society, does have a positive agenda.

> The Enlightenment sought to free humanity from the chains of unthinking tradition and religious bigotry. It sought to master the world through science and remake the world according to the dictates of reason. It sought to understand and recast society in rational and scientific terms, and it was confident about the ability of the human intellect to do this. Two centuries later, humanity is imprisoned by new chains that the Enlightenment forged for us. These are the chains created by science, technology, and rationality, which in the course of liberating us subjected us to new forms of control, bureaucracy, mediaization, suburbanization, and surveillance. We still need liberation, we still need emancipation, but now it is from the products of our previous emancipation—from computer data bases, sound bites, political action committees, voodoo economics, electronic surveillance, commodified video images, and the industrialization of professional culture. The emancipation we now require cannot be on the same terms

as those proposed by the Enlightenment. It must, at least in part, be a rejection of the terms by which we freed ourselves from pre-Enlightenment thinking.

(J. M. Balkin, 'What is Postmodern Constitutionalism?' (1992) 90 *Michigan Law Review* 1966 at p. 1989)

15.3 Two pillars of modern jurisprudence challenged: the subject and meaning

We may now turn to consider—from the postmodern perspective—two fundamental ideas underpinning modern law and legal theory: the rational and autonomous subject, and the clarity and objectivity of meaning of the legal text.

15.3.1 The modern subject and power

The paradigm of modernity is epitomised in the Cartesian dictum *Cogito ergo sum* ('I think therefore I am'). Descartes promotes the human subject and her reason as the most fundamental explanatory tool and normative principle.

The subject is *autonomous* and *free*. Her autonomy consists in her not depending on her environment for her existence. This, of course, is meant in a metaphysical sense. It does not mean that we are self-sufficient in the sense that we do not need our environment for our subsistence but rather that we *interact* with it rather than being *mutually constituted*. *Inter*action presupposes a dichotomy, a radical separation between the two parties interacting. The subject is thus severed from her surroundings but also from other subjects, which become autonomous, complete, self-contained units. This isolation accounts for the subject's freedom as well, her freedom to make choices and to act accordingly. Precisely because she is free to decide and act, the subject is accountable for her actions. To be more precise, this accountability is to be seen as a result of the combination of the freedom of the subject and her rationality.

The subject is *rational*. There are two sides to this. One is epistemological: the rational subject pre-dates the world and it is presupposed by it. Therefore, the use of reason becomes the only way of experiencing the physical world as well as the only criterion for the truth of propositions about the world. The other is moral: it is only if there are exceptional circumstances impeding the use of reason that we are not held accountable for our actions.

The Cartesian subject is also *universal* and *diachronic*. The abstraction that is the subject knows no spatial or temporal limits. We all experience the world in the same way and every deviation is precisely that: a deviation due to extraordinary circumstances. The cross-temporality of the subject is what makes it possible to reconstruct past histories, reasons, intentions, aims, thoughts. It is also because of this cross-temporality that we can project the way we think to the patterns of others. Our subjectivity enables us to express normative views and judgements regarding the lives of others, irrespective of how different our context is from theirs.

The law, as we know it, is nothing but a reflection of isolated subjects and the ways in which they freely enter and exit associations and communities. The system of human rights, which constitutes the cornerstone of Western legal cultures, safeguards and, at the same time, is justified by the perpetual subject, her inviolable personal sphere and her ability to define the boundaries of this sphere. Even group rights that seemingly transcend the individual do not go as far as to cancel the significance of the latter. Groups are still unions of free individuals and they are simply granted some rights of self-determination, in order to define themselves in opposition to other groups or, more importantly, the State as a whole. So, in a way, groups are subjectified, they are given the same rights as individuals and they are perceived in isolation from and in contradistinction to their environment. (For a postmodern critique of human rights, see C. Douzinas, *The End of Human Rights* (Oxford: Hart Publishing, 2000).

Private law is the apotheosis of the fetishism of the subject. For example, it presupposes free individuals entering contractual relationships and accepting responsibility for non-observance of the terms. Criminal law also reserves a central place for the subject. Personal responsibility, the ascription of guilt or innocence to individuals or to groups of individuals, the concept as well as the forms of punishment—these are but a few principles and practices of criminal law that presuppose and are underpinned by the notion of the universal, rational, autonomous subject.

But the fact that this perception of the subject has prevailed in theory (and has therefore determined political and legal practice to a very large extent) does not mean that it is the only way of understanding ourselves in the world. One theorist offering an alternative is Michel Foucault (1926–84). Foucault was one of the most important and influential thinkers of the twentieth century. His long and distinguished, albeit not ordinary, academic career culminated with his election in 1970 as Professor of the History of Systems of Thought at the College de France, a title that he chose and which already reveals a lot about the intellectual task he had set himself. (For a very accessible introduction to Foucault see G. Danaher, T. Schirato, and J. Webb, *Understanding Foucault* (London: SAGE, 2000). Also very useful is *The Cambridge Companion to Foucault*, G. Gutting, ed. (Cambridge: Cambridge University Press, 1994)). He questions the Cartesian subject and understands the person as constituted by the discourses, practices and institutions in which she partakes.

Foucault's methodology revolves around two central ideas: *archaeology* and *genealogy*. Foucault spelt out the archaeological method in his *Archaeology of Knowledge* in an attempt to systematise the methodology he had used in *Madness and Civilisation: A History of Insanity in the Age of Reason*, transl. R. Howard (New York: Pantheon, 1965), *The Birth of the Clinic: An Archaeology of Medical Perception* (London: Tavistock Publications, 1973), and *The Order of Things, An Archaeology of the Human Sciences* (London: Tavistock Publications, 1970). Archaeology consists in shifting the focus from the subject to rules and relations underlying what he terms *epistemes* or discursive formations. Thus it goes beyond the consciousness of individuals, trying to discover the way discourses develop the conditions of their development independently of agents and actors. This displacement makes possible a historiography of the unconscious that highlights the differences between the ways similar phenomena were perceived in different eras. For example, the discourse on madness and the emergence of the Great Incarceration in the seventeenth and eighteenth centuries provided a case study demonstrating the differences between discourses concerning insanity.

If archaeology accounts for the inner workings of discourses, genealogy accounts for the possibility of transition from one discourse to another. Without forming grand historical narratives or principles of historical development, genealogy shows the essentially contingent origins of historical development. Contrary to Marxist historical analysis, which privileges the material over anything else in the historical process, but also contrary to all epistemologies that try to formulate principles permeating historical evolution and single out recurring patterns, genealogy turns to the apparently small and insignificant and to connections between historical phenomena that cannot be accounted for with recourse to principles of universal and diachronic validity.

Apart from these methodological tools, there is also a substantive thread running through much of Foucault's intellectual production. In a nutshell, it could be said that his main aim was to establish and explain the relationship between knowledge and power in terms of the subjectification of human beings.

> [My goal] has not been to analyze the phenomena of power, nor to elaborate the foundations of such an analysis ... My objective, instead, has been to create a history of the different modes by which, in our culture, human beings are made subjects.
>
> (Michel Foucault, in H.L. Dreyfus and P. Rabinow (eds) *Beyond Structuralism and Hermeneutics / With an Afterword by Michel Foucault* (Chicago: University of Chicago Press, 1982), p. 208)

Foucault understands power very broadly as an unstructured complex of discourses, practices, institutions, structures, systems of rules, and so on. Therefore, power refers to more than relations of forceful domination of one party over another. As such its function is not simply destructive but also enabling in the sense that power relations shape subjectivities, i.e. they construct subjects. How is this possible? In Foucauldian terms power and knowledge are intertwined to the extent that they constitute one another thus losing their conceptual independence. To know something is to control it and to control it is to know it. When controlling something, however, one does not get a knowledge and understanding of the hidden, universal essence of what one controls. In other words, controlling does not provide access to the Cartesian subject that exists beyond the instance of exercise of power. The subject is constructed *through* the exercise of power. For instance, the incarceration of the mad forms a knowledge (a discourse, an *episteme*) of madness and also constructs the category of 'the mad', the subject of the insane.

Let us now bring together all of the above and explain them in their combination with reference to one of Foucault's books that is more closely associated with the law than any other of his works, namely *Discipline and Punish* (M. Foucault, *Discipline and Punish: The Birth of the Prison*, transl. A. M. Sheridan (New York: Pantheon, 1977)). In this work Foucault examines the evolution of punitive institutions and practices. He employs the genealogical method to explain the transition from the inhumane, vindictive corporal punishment of the Middle Ages to the civility of incarceration, which reveals a move from power as outright violence to power as knowledge and discipline. An idea epitomising this new conception of power as observation is Jeremy Bentham's *Panopticon*. Etymologically, the *Panopticon* suggests the possibility of watching everything at all times and that was Bentham's aim precisely: the creation of a circular prison with a watchtower in the middle, from which guards would have visual access to all the cells, while they would remain invisible to the prisoners. Thus not only would it be possible for the inmates to be watched always but it would also be impossible for them to know whether they were being observed or not. In that way their behaviour would be controlled not forcefully but through the terror of observation. The genealogical method allows us to draw connections between the emergence of prisons with other institutions and discourses. These other institutions and discourses might seem to be basing their operations on completely different principles but it is soon revealed that they too operate as disciplinary mechanisms: schools, factories, offices (think of open-plan workplaces), and so on. In the later stages of his work Foucault focused on the sexual subject, the way sexual identity is constructed, the rules that govern the discourse of sexuality and the (self-)understanding of the person on grounds of his or her sexual orientation (M. Foucault, *History of Sexuality, Volume I: An Introduction* (New York: Pantheon, 1978); *Use of Pleasure* (New York: Pantheon, 1985); *The Care of the Self* (New York: Pantheon, 1985).

In the light of the Foucauldian analysis, the modern myth of the free, autonomous, universal subject collapses. The social person is fragmented and the multiplicity of her social roles is determined by the discourses in which she partakes. Thus the law's claim that it treats the subject as unencumbered and transcendental is proven to be false. The law is a discourse of power that constructs the subjects in a way that will serve and perpetuate its own operations. It must settle and delineate the identity of the parties in a meaningful way, which will be translatable and intelligible in the vocabulary of legal rules and the legal institution.

The law of the sovereign State, which is justified and authorised by the freedom and universality of the subject but also governs that subject through the latter's freedom and autonomy, which allow law to be endorsed ceases to be the only source of power. It is in fact secondary to disciplinary power, which governs embodied beings by normalising their behaviour in a way that is both physical and internalized.

> ...power is not to be taken as a phenomenon of one individual's consolidated and homogenous domination over others, or that of one group or class over others. What, by contrast, should always be kept in mind is that power, if we do not take too distant a view of it, is not that which makes the difference between those who exclusively possess it and retain it, and those who do not have it and submit to it. Power must be analysed as something which circulates, or rather something which only functions in the form of a chain. It is never localised here or there, never in anybody's hands, never appropriated as a commodity or a piece of wealth. Power is employed and exercised through a net-like organisation. And not only do individuals circulate between its threads; they are always in the position of simultaneously undergoing and exercising this power. They are not only its inert or consenting target; they are also the elements of its articulation. In other words, individuals are the vehicles of power not the points of application.
>
> (M. Foucault, 'Two Lectures' in C. Gordon (ed.), *Power/Knowledge* (New York: Harvester, 1980), p. 96)

15.3.2 Meaning, deconstruction, and law

Apart from the idea of the Cartesian subject and the sovereign power that it authorises, modern philosophy relies very heavily on the possibility of discovering the one, objective and clear meaning of utterances, whether they be spoken or written. In jurisprudence this confidence is manifested as the belief in the intelligibility of rules. The hugely influential legal theory of H. L. A. Hart, for example, is based by and large on the clarity of the legal text. Hart's central thesis is that words have a semantic core and a penumbra of doubt. Hard cases arise only when facts cannot be subsumed under the semantic core but seem to constitute borderline cases falling under the penumbra. After we have discovered the meaning of the rule and it turns out that deduction is impossible, i.e., if it is revealed that there are no available rules that would regulate the instant case, then judges must exercise their discretion. Ronald Dworkin might disagree with Hart on the particulars, and especially the problems of judicial activism and gaps in the law, but his theory of law-as-interpretation revolves around the same central axis: the legal text and the unity of its meaning. To be sure, 'legal text' is understood in its broadest possible sense, embracing statutes and court rulings as well as other sources of legal principles, but it is still a text, as the chain novel analogy suggests.

Postmodern jurisprudence does not share that faith in the legal text. Where traditional, modern legal theories see intelligibility and certainty, postmodern jurisprudence sees openness, inconclusiveness and indeterminacy. Traditional, modern jurisprudence relies on the text as objectively accessible and independent of its context. Thus, the problems that might arise because of the fact that the text must be interpreted by specific people in specific historical instances is addressed and reduced to a contingent problem of application. Postmodern jurisprudence sheds a different light on the legal text and its meaning. Instead of treating the legal text as a safety mechanism that can lead to objective, substantive fairness and justice despite the inevitable constraints that the real context imposes, postmodern legal thought sees the meaning of the text as *always* contingent on and bound to a context; instead of hoping to discover the one, true, right meaning of the law, the famous Dworkinian right answer, or instead of rejoicing or bragging for having indeed discovered it in specific instances, it recognises that meaning is always deferred and so is the question of justice; instead of interpreting, it 'deconstructs'.

Much of the postmodern critique of the law on grounds of the constant unattainability of the meaning of the text derives from or rests on the idea of deconstruction, as developed by Jacques Derrida. It is notoriously difficult to summarise the theory of deconstruction, not least because of the perplexing nature of a lot of Derrida's works. Moreover, to the extent that deconstruction is about the deferment of meaning, it would be paradoxical to try and grasp the one definite meaning of deconstructive texts. However, it is possible to single out a few key points.

Derrida questions the diachronic philosophical tendency to understand the spoken word as prior and superior to the written word. Traditional philosophy holds speech to be giving us direct access to the truth about ourselves and the world, because it embodies thought in an unmediated manner. It can therefore represent thought in the present. What follows from this is that alphabetical, phonetic writing, i.e., writing that corresponds to sounds and their word-forming combinations instead of representing concepts or ideas, is the most precise and therefore best kind of writing. Or at least it is the best one possible. This is so because all writing is inevitably inferior to speech as a means of representation, for it is twice removed from consciousness and reality. Insofar as writing is the representation of speech, which is a representation in itself, and given that it also takes place in the absence of the speaker as well as the referent, it is artificial and parasitic and distorts meaning.

Derrida sees this privileging of speech over writing, this *logocentrism* or *phonocentrism*, as indicative of a specific metaphysics, the *metaphysics of the presence* (J. Derrida, *Of Grammatology*, transl. G. C. Spivak (Baltimore: Johns Hopkins University Press, 1976). The metaphysics of presence relies on the possibility and ability of knowing and describing the state of the world at any given time. Deconstruction rejects this hierarchisation of speech and writing. No language can correspond fully and purely to thought, because it will always rely on symbols, signifiers that are iterable, i.e. repeatable. So, speech suffers from exactly the same problem as writing. (On the question of textual meaning, see J. Derrida, *Positions* (Chicago: University of Chicago Press, 1981).) Deconstruction reveals the impossibility of this project and draws our attention to the constant deferment of meaning, which can only be extracted in relation to another, with reference to what is absent and is never immanent in the symbol, whether that be a word or anything else. Derrida refers to this idea that combines difference and deference with the neological term *différance*.

As a text that by and large seeks to provide answers as to the truth or falsity of propositions but also as to the rightness or wrongness of actions in the present, the law would be an obvious target for the project of deconstruction. However, it was not until 1989 that Derrida spoke explicitly about law and justice in a symposium entitled 'Deconstruction and the Possibility of Justice' at the Cardozo Law School. His paper was entitled 'Force of Law: The "Mystical Foundation of Authority"' and has since dominated the discussions on deconstruction, law, and justice. As with the rest of Derrida's work, it is an impossible task to give a summary that would do justice to what is a very complex text full of detours, parentheses and subtle or explicit allusions to other texts. But then again, giving a summary is hardly the point.

Following Montaigne and Pascal, Derrida draws a sharp distinction between justice and the law: justice can never be actualised, it is always to come. Justice is the experience of *aporias,* an irresolvable paradox. The law, on the other hand, cannot give in to paradoxes, it cannot forfeit its duty to provide enforceable reasons for action in particular circumstances.

The first *aporia* is what Derrida calls the '*épokhè* of the rule'. (In its Greek etymology, *aporia* signifies a lack of resources but also the lack of a passage.) Justice demands that rules be not merely followed but reconfirmed at each instance of decision. A judge must reinvent the law for each particular case, for each new decision. Passing a just judgment presupposes freedom, independence from any kind of normative constraint. If judging is only an act of rule-following then it can at best be legal, but it will never be just. Although a decision is guided by the pre-existing rule, it calls for an act of re-interpretation. The law must be reset and judicial decisions must

> conserve the law and also destroy it or suspend it enough to have to reinvent it in any case, rejustify it, at least reinvent it in the reaffirmation and the new and free confirmation of its principle.
>
> (J. Derrida, 'Force of Law: The "Mystical Foundation of Authority"' in *Deconstruction and the Possibility of Justice* (D. Cornell, M. Rosenfeld, and D.G. Carlson (eds) (London: Routledge, 1992), p. 23)

Derrida detects a paradox in this need for simultaneous destruction and creation of the law: no decision can be just in the present tense.

> For in the founding of law in its institution, the same problem of justice will have been posed and violently resolved, that is to say buried, dissimulated, repressed.
>
> ('Force of Law', p. 23)

The second *aporia* of the law concerns the 'undecidable':

> The undecidable is not merely the oscillation or the tension between two decisions; it is the experience of that which, though heterogeneous, foreign to the order of the calculable and the rule, is still obliged—it is of obligation that we must speak—to give itelf up to the impossible decision, while taking account of law and rules.
>
> ('Force of Law', p. 23)

The law suffers yet another *aporia*: the spatial and temporal constraints, which dictate the need to make a decision, impose the urgency of a judgment. The amount of information that can be brought into legal discourse is and must be finite, because the instance of deciding interrupts the discourse, marks the end of communication. That moment of urgency can be understood in terms of speech acts. Constative utterances can only have a truth-value. They can only be correct but never just. Justice remains exclusive to performative speech acts under the condition that they rest on other prior conventions and subsequently performative acts. Because every constative act relies on a performative one, the truth of the former depends on the justice of the latter. Justice can never be achieved by decision in the present. The instant of precipitation will always play its destructive role. Nevertheless justice is immanent in the law as *à venir*, it is always *yet to come*.

15.4 The practical significance of postmodern thinking about law

You will be wondering what the practical significance of all this is. How does it help us to reach decisions in legal questions? To affirm rights and say with any degree of certainty that we have made a correct decision? Indeed, does recognising the poly-centricity of power or the open-endedness of meaning provide us with any normative sense of rightness or wrongness, any normative tools against domination? Asks Nancy Fraser of Foucault

> Why is struggle preferable to submission? Why ought domination to be resisted? Only with the introduction of normative notions of some kind could Foucault begin to answer such questions. Only with the introduction of normative notions could he begin to tell us what is wrong with the modern power/knowledge regime and why we ought to oppose it.
>
> (N. Fraser, 'Foucault on Modern Power: Empirical Insights and Normative Confusions' *Praxis International* 1 (October 1981): 272–87 at p. 283)

And Binder poses the same pressing questions of deconstruction:

> First because deconstruction shows every argument to contain its opposite, it seems nihilistic. Second because deconstruction is said to 'annihilate the subject'—to deny the individual identities of authors and of characters—it seems to deny individual responsibility for evil. Third, because it exposes the futility of efforts to deny loss, contradiction and violence, deconstruction seems to urge acceptance of their necessity. Perhaps an 'antihumanist' philosophy that attempts to annihilate the subject sees no great loss in the annihilation of subjects.
>
> (G. Binder, 'Representing Nazism: Advocacy and Identity at the Trial of Klaus Barbie' (1989) 98 *Yale Law Journal* 1321 at p. 1377)

At the same time, the postmodern, and especially the deconstructionist, outlook on law, seems to harbour a messianic undertone. If justice is always to come, if it is divorced from our practices (recall how justice is a civic virtue bound to the here and now for liberal social contract thinkers), then it inhabits a domain that exists somewhere and somehow inaccessible by us and yet exists. But what good is that? It does not only make us aware of the fallibility of our normative judgments and it is always wise to be modest in that way, it in fact makes it impossible for us to aspire to treating each other justly under *any* circumstances.

Balkin makes a greater effort to analyse the relationship between deconstruction and justice. He recognises the problem 'that deconstructive techniques do not seem to support any particular vision of justice; indeed they appear to preclude the possibility of any stable conception of the just or the good that could provide the basis for political belief or the authority for political action' (J. M. Balkin, 'Being Just with Deconstruction' (1994) 3(3) *Social and Legal Studies* 393 at p. 393).

However, Balkin clearly believes that deconstruction, if it is to have any purpose or value, must be capable of being used to reveal injustice. Deconstruction, in a strict Derridian sense, seems to be engaging in an endless round of word play, the purpose of which is to reveal various alternative meanings and 'truths', leaving it up to the interpreter to choose on the basis of that individual's own moral convictions. This might be sufficient in the world of literary criticism, and it is perfectly acceptable at one level to treat legal texts in the same way. Nevertheless, 'if deconstruction merely discovers instability and incoherence in all texts, then it cannot help us decide that one interpretation is better than another, or that one conceptual scheme is more just than another' (Balkin, 'Being Just with Deconstruction', p. 395). Derridian deconstruction lacks relevance when turning to the legal and social order, where it is essential to take the debate a step further.

> Why might anyone want to deconstruct law or legal doctrine? One reason has to do with the pursuit of justice. We might want to demonstrate that the law or some part of the law is unjust. Alternatively, we might want to show that the law or some part of the law conceals aspects of social life we believe to be important, and that its failure adequately to deal with these aspects leads to injustice. This is a 'critical' use of deconstruction in a very ordinary sense of that word—it involves pointing out that something is wrong and arguing that it could and should be made better or done better.
>
> ('Being Just with Deconstruction', p. 394)

However, it is not sufficient simply to assume that deconstruction can be used to reveal injustice: it must be justified. The answer lies in the reason why individuals (including Derrida) undertake deconstruction. They do so because they believe that 'there is a better way of looking at things, even if this is in turn subject to further deconstruction' (Balkin, 'Being Just with Deconstruction', p. 395).

For Balkin, deconstruction is not simply to reverse the hierarchy between conceptual opposites such as 'racial equality' and 'apartheid'; rather the deconstructive argument becomes the 'careful and patient analysis of the grounds of similarity and difference between conceptual opposition in shifting historical and practical contexts of judgment'. Balkin argues that 'one deconstructs a conceptual opposition by showing that it is really a nested opposition. A nested opposition is a conceptual opposition in which the two terms "contain" each other; that is they possess simultaneous relationships of difference and similarity which are manifested as we consider them in different contexts of judgment.' 'To analyze this opposition as a nested opposition, we might ask whether there are certain features of apartheid that have unexpected commonalities with particular theories of racial equality, and whether discovery of these similarities can assist in our legal and social critiques' (Balkin, 'Being Just with Deconstruction', p. 398. See further J. M. Balkin, 'Nested Oppositions' (1990) 99 *Yale Law Journal* 1669).

For instance, if apartheid is defined, initially, by governmental distinctions based on race, it has similarities with one conception of racial equality which, for example through programmes of positive discrimination, is also based on similar governmental decisions. Thus this forces the interpreter to look for a better distinction between these two 'opposites', for example, one based on 'the presence of racial subordination, or the state's decision to replicate or foster beliefs about white supremacy and black inferiority'. 'The goal of this analysis is to change our view of the real issues involved, by discovering relevant grounds of similarity and difference. Such an analysis, in turn, will lead to new concepts, categories and distinctions that can be further deconstructed.' '[D]o some conceptions of racial equality produce or maintain racial subordination by other means? If so, then they have important similarities to systems of apartheid, and these similarities can serve as the basis of a critique' (Balkin, 'Being Just with Deconstruction', pp. 398–9). Thus the process of deconstruction continues, seeking a better explanation or conception of 'racial equality' by looking at what is supposed to be its conceptual opposite. Each reinterpretation brings a better understanding, though each in turn can be deconstructed. There is no absolute truth, though there are relative truths. Nevertheless, the process of deconstruction is not a scientific one—'it is informed by the values and commitments of the individual deconstructor, and the directions she chooses to investigate'. Thus although theoretically deconstruction is 'potentially endless, our own deconstructive arguments must come to an end at some point', unless our underlying political and moral values are themselves deconstructed (Balkin, 'Being Just with Deconstruction', p. 399). Balkin thus concludes at this point that although deconstructive argument will not lead 'inexorably to justice', it can 'used rightly... assist us in our critical endeavors' (Balkin, 'Being Just with Deconstruction', p. 400).

This does not really seem to take the argument any further in establishing a firm link between deconstruction and justice. Clearly with these inadequacies in mind, Balkin attempts to make a link between deconstructive argument and the 'transcendental value of justice', by positing law and justice as conceptual opposites:

> We deconstruct law for critical purposes because of a perceived inadequation between law and justice—because we seek a justice yet unrealized in law. Thus our deconstruction of law assumes a conceptual opposition between law and justice. However, deconstruction asks us to reconceptualize every conceptual opposition as a nested opposition. When we reconceptualize the opposition between law and justice as a nested opposition, we discover that there is in fact a complex relationship of mutual dependence and differentiation between the two.
>
> ('Being Just with Deconstruction', pp. 400–1)

'Law is always, to some extent and to some degree, unjust.' However, the only way of articulating a person's conceptions of justice is through imperfect laws. Such laws will be inadequate, leading to a deconstruction and a modified law, and so the process continues. Balkin states that

> [W]e must think of our value of justice as an insatiable demand that can never be fulfilled by human law. In short, we must postulate a human value of justice which transcends each and every example of justice in human law, culture and convention. In this way our deconstructive argument brings us to a transcendental value of justice. Thus the normative use of deconstruction becomes what I call 'transcendental' deconstruction, because it must presume the existence of transcendental human values articulated in culture but never adequately captured by culture.
>
> ('Being Just with Deconstruction', p. 402)

Nevertheless, Balkin is not approaching Plato's transcendental values, simply 'the insatiable yearning or longing for justice lodged in the human heart'. 'Hence, our laws are imperfect not because they are bad copies of a determinate Form of justice, but because we must articulate our insatiable longing for justice in concrete institutions, and our constructions can never be identical with the longings that inspire them' (Balkin, 'Being Just with Deconstruction', p. 402; see further J. M. Balkin, 'Transcendental Deconstruction, Transcendent Justice' (1994) 92 *Michigan Law Review* 1131). Despite Balkin's valiant attempt to drag deconstruction away 'from the abyss of normative nihilism' (Balkin, 'Being Just with Deconstruction', p. 403), towards the pursuit of justice, the interpreter of Balkin is still left with the sense that since justice lacks any definable content, the analysis has taken us no further than justice simply being an individual's (including Balkin's) assertions or convictions. Having aligned themselves with scepticism postmodernists cannot accept any notion of there being 'basic goods' or a 'minimum content of natural law', as posited by modernists in the 'opposing' traditions of naturalism and positivism.

15.4.1 Deconstruction and the liberal constitution

The application of the deconstructive technique to the liberal constitution is not only a useful illustration of how postmodernism is applied to legal texts, or more accurately legal concepts, but also how postmodernists use this technique to dejustify or delegitimate the liberal constitution. Indeed, many modernist legal theories are forms of constitutionalism, in that they reinforce the idea of a society governed by the rule of law with the supreme law or the constitution at the top of the pyramid of laws. Mention need only be made of Hart, Kelsen, or Rawls. The recognition of law as the key to the exercise of power facilitates the legitimation of the exercise of such political power. Thus constitutional jurisprudence is one of the 'grand narrative[s] of modernity' (Douzinas and Warrington, *Postmodern Jurisprudence*, p. 28) which, when deconstructed, will reveal the inadequacy of its claim to the truth. Clear links can be seen here between postmodernism and critical legal studies in this respect.

Schlag looks at the practice of liberal justification, which he sees as premised upon a 'popular constitutional mythology' (P. Schlag, 'The Empty Circles of Liberal Justification' (1997) 96(1) *Michigan Law Review* 1 at p. 3).

> The popular narrative recounts the story of a sovereign people who in a foundational moment established their own state by setting forth in a written constitution the powers and limitations of their government. The very identity, content, and character of this government is established by the Constitution itself. In turn, the authority of this Constitution stems from the consent of the governed—their acquiescence in a limited surrender of their sovereign power in return for the benefits of a limited, representative government.
>
> ('The Empty Circles', p. 3)

The key concepts for liberal constitutionalists are 'The Constitution', 'The Founding', 'The People' and 'The Consent of the People'. The Constitution is the 'authoritative paramount norm' which is invoked in a variety of ways 'as icon, symbol, plan, rule, argument, text, spirit—to perform a variety of actions—constitute, organize, control, regulate, inspire, justify'. The Founding is 'an origin that signals a discontinuity between all that has happened before and all that will happen after that moment'. 'The People also occupy a special place in the popular constitutional mythology. From the high school civics classroom to the most intellectualized law school seminar, the people is held to be Sovereign'. 'Flowing from this is that the legitimacy of the

Constitution depends upon the Consent of the People' (Schlag, 'The Empty Circles', pp. 3–5).

These concepts are so deeply embedded in American culture that it rarely seems to be an issue of what gave the generation of 1787 the authority to delimit freedom for all subsequent generations, who in reality have not been consulted, despite the mythology of consent. Liberal jurists tend to obscure these problems by 'rendering the key ontological identities and narratives more capacious and appealing than the historical originals'. Rawls' principles of justice, Hart's rule of recognition, or Dworkin's principle of integrity give us 'the kind of norm that will allow each of us to read into it whatever we wish to find there. The more abstract, mystical, or capacious the paramount norm, the less it will exhibit concrete features that might trigger the objection of any particular reader.' The problems of the founding moment being simply a point in history is removed by Rawls' 'timeless' original position or Hart's mythical transition from pre-legal to legal world (a step from the pre-modern to the modern). The problem of lack of consultation with the real subjects of the constitution is removed by the invention of 'grand supra-individual subjects', such as Dworkin's Hercules or Rawls' persons in the original position, who clearly give their consent to the constitution (Schlag, 'The Empty Circles', pp. 12–17).

Schlag is concerned not simply to reveal the myths of liberal constitutionalism, for myths by themselves are perhaps inherent in any conception of society. He believes that it is necessary to take the deconstruction further. The overall myth of liberalism offers the individual (interpreter) a stark choice:

> Choose the myth or face perdition. Within the circle there is something good, appealing, admirable, necessary, sensible, reasonable (this is liberalism), while on the outside there is something bad, unappealing, contemptible, unavoidable, senseless, and unreasonable (this is the antithesis of liberalism and goes by names such as chaos, tyranny, totalitarianism, and so on).
>
> ('The Empty Circles', pp. 24–5)

The individual has to choose the whole system or nothing else. Once consent to the paramount norm is established this 'necessarily entails consent to a whole series of institutions and practices that are authorized by the paramount norm. Once the paramount norm is accepted, it is as if the entire liberal pinball machine lights up' (Schlag, 'The Empty Circles', p. 25). Despite liberal myths of rational free choice in the original contract between State and government, individuals in reality choose liberalism for emotional reasons such as fear of dictatorship or anarchy (see Hobbes at 10.4). In reality, the element of choice is not available to the liberal consumer, given that they live within a political world 'already mapped out in liberal categories'. The only benchmarks given to the individual within such a world are liberal ones and these benchmarks themselves are not subject to criticism—'the liberal thinker approaches a category such as "rights" with the same degree of credulity that a medieval scholar approaches the category of "angels", or a communist apparatchik the category of "bourgeoisie"' (Schlag, 'The Empty Circles', pp. 32–4).

What Schlag is pointing to is that liberalism is not a rational choice, it is an emotional one, and thus does not have a superior claim to acceptance than other visions of society. Schlag reveals this by deconstructing the language of liberal constitutionalism, revealing it simply to be a legitimation of a political choice that was made by certain individuals centuries ago. The use of 'metalanguage' such as the 'rule of recognition' (Hart) or the 'original position' (Rawls), is an abstraction from the US constitution of

1787 and the founding fathers (Madison, Hamilton, etc.) in order to represent liberal-ism as timeless and rational. Furthermore, the system is self-perpetuating, in that inter-pretation of law within the liberal system, according to liberal jurists (see, for example, Dworkin, Chapter 6), is undertaken by reference to these meta-narratives. The point of deconstruction though is that those meta-narratives themselves, as Schlag has shown, are themselves deconstructible revealing a clearer, less mythological, interpretation. Thus the 'Constitution' is represented as the 'Paramount Norm' or words to that effect by liberal thinkers, but further deconstruction will reveal it to be 'Ultimate Authority' and so on (Schlag, 'The Empty Circles', pp. 43–6).

15.4.2 Postmodern constitutional theory

Postmodernism may be successful in deconstructing the rigid, arbitrary norma-tive structure of the liberal legal system but, as with critical legal studies, the issue is whether it can offer an alternative without falling into the trap of constructing another legal leviathan. Postmodernists recognise the importance of the constitution to the liberal legal order, but would they retain it within a postmodern society? Ladeur offers a postmodern constitutional theory, based on what he calls a 'self-organising society' (K. H. Ladeur, 'Post-Modern Constitutional Theory: A Prospect for the Self-Organising Society' (1997) 60 *Modern Law Review* 617).

As with those visions offered by Unger (see 13.2.4), the propositions are essentially based on an improvement of liberalism. Liberalism based on a rigid and illegitimate constitution, though, is clearly inadequate. There needs to be a transformation of the system because of the 'growth of complexity', namely the recognition that there is uncertainty and indeterminacy in every aspect of law and life. This forces the 'legal sys-tem to reintroduce more flexibility, more capacity for self-description and more learn-ing capability into the range of its operations' (Ladeur, 'Post-Modern Constitutional Theory', p. 620). However, an 'experimenting society' is still linked to 'the liberal prin-ciple that a constitution must always be based on a kind of pre-constituted order', for without it there lies the path towards chaos. Despite this attempted reconciliation of the old order with the new flexibility, it is difficult to see any justification beyond the pragmatic for the retention of the old order as the following extract illustrates.

> A post-modern society cannot be integrated by common shared beliefs but rather by overlapping networks of practical differentiated political and social interactions. These generate a kind of implicit knowledge which functions as the raw material for setting up explicit conventions. Civilised society should be based on the possibility of the pursuit of self-interest, a strategy from which much more learning capability and universality can be generated than by an abstract discourse of justice which is not adapted to the description of constraints imposed on networks of collective actors, and, at the same time, this permits it to take advantage of its inherent productive potential to permit greater differentiation and innovation. This approach could introduce new life into the a-centric distributed order of rights and competencies of the liberal system.
>
> ('Post-Modern Constitutional Theory', pp. 626–7)

A possible deconstruction of this language suggests that the vision is a depressing one where, because of the lack of accepted values, pragmatics dominate, where individu-alism no longer predominates but fluctuating 'organisational networks of relationships' are built on self-interest. The collapse of any distinctions upon which modern liberal so-ciety is built—particularly the distinction between 'public' and 'private' sectors—results in an unstructured, self-regulating society, where liberal justice discourse may form a background but has little relevance. 'The stress of this conception is laid on a paradoxical eternal determination of internal self-determination of organisational networks of interrelationships, leading towards a new legal order of a "self-organising" society which is distinguished from the primary liberal society of individuals by its characteristic that its self-modification comprises of its own rules.' Rather than substantive rights, a postmodern society would be based more squarely on 'procedural rules stressing flexibility, innovation, experimentation'. Although a rights-based individualistic society has been relatively successful in managing indeterminacy, the constitutional system now needs to be remodelled to take account of indeterminacy leading to a 'more complex, more rapidly self-modifying and self-organising society' (Ladeur, 'Post-Modern Constitutional Theory', pp. 627–9).

15.5 **Reconstruction**

While Ladeur perhaps shows that postmodernism can be allied to capitalism, the more natural bent of postmodernism is left-leaning. Capitalism is equated with liberalism and modernity and only continues its domination through a combination of inertia and hegemony. Bonaventura de Sousa Santos has provided a vision of a postmodernist transition to a new alternative. As with all postmodernism, Santos recognises the 'increasingly complex network of subjectivities' enmeshing each individual. Correspondingly there is a 'proliferation of political and legal interpretive communities' whose activities will result in a decanonisation and trivialisation of the law. While recognising that 'modern men and women are configurations or networks of different subjectivities', Santos depicts four, later six, prevalent 'structural subjectivities' arising out of the four dominant 'structural places' found in contemporary capitalist society: 'the household-place', 'the workplace', 'the citizen place', the 'world place' (B. de Sousa Santos, 'The Postmodern Transition: Law and Politics' in A. Sarat and T. R. Kearns (eds.), *The Fate of the Law* (Ann Arbor: Michigan University Press, 1991), 79 at pp. 105–7), and later the 'market-place' and 'communityplace' (B. de Sousa Santos, *Towards a New Common Sense* (New York: Routledge, 1995), p. 485).

While providing for more focus on particular subjectivities than is normal in postmodernism, de Sousa Santos also narrows down the dominant forms of power in capitalist society, thus distinguishing himself from Foucault:

> But again I think, and now contrary to Foucault, that we cannot go to the extreme of giving up the task of structuring and grading forms and power relations. If power is everywhere, it is nowhere. In my view, the four structural places...are the loci of four major power forms circulating in our society. These power forms are: Patriarchy, corresponding to the householdplace; exploitation corresponding to the workplace; domination, corresponding to the citizenplace; and unequal exchange, corresponding to the worldplace. There are other forms of power but these are the basic ones...Of all four forms of power, only one, domination, is democratic, and even so in a limited degree and in a small group of countries in which the advanced capitalist societies are included. *The political aim of postmodern critical theory is to extend the democratic ideal to all other forms of power.*
>
> ('The Postmodern Transition', p. 108 emphasis added)

Thus in the householdplace, the contradiction and competition is between the dominant paradigm of the 'patriarchal family' and the emergent paradigm of the 'cooperative domestic community', which includes 'all alternative forms of domestic sociability and sexuality'. In the workplace the competition is between the dominant paradigm of 'capitalist expansionism, and the emergent paradigm of eco-socialist sustainability' which involves 'free associations of producers, geared towards the democratic production of use-values, without degrading nature'. In the market-place the contradiction is between the paradigm of 'individualistic consumerism', and the paradigm of 'human needs' in which 'the satisfiers are at the service of needs' and the 'market is but one of many forms of consumption'. In de Sousa Santos's other additional structure, the communityplace, the competition is between 'fortress-communities' and 'amoeba-communities'. Within the latter 'identity is always multiple, unfinished, undergoing a process of reconstruction and reinvention that is, in fact, a process of ongoing identification'. In the citzenplace, where the competition is between 'authoritarian democracy' and 'radical democracy' with the latter as the emergent paradigm, 'the democratic process is furthered by the transformation of relations of power into relations of shared authority, despotic law into democratic law, regulatory common sense into emancipatory common sense'. In the worldplace, the transition is away from unequal development and exclusive sovereignty towards 'democratically sustainable development and reciprocally permeable sovereignty'. The latter will abolish the North–South hierarchy and thus will result in the emergence of a 'new system of international and transnational relations guided by the principles of cosmopolitanism and common heritage of mankind' (de Sousa Santos, *Towards a New Common Sense*, pp. 484–9).

As with Roberto Unger in the field of critical legal studies, de Sousa Santos is prepared to make presumptions, to offer structure, although of an intensely flexible nature. De Sousa Santos does this by looking at the established paradigms on which capitalist societies are built and then offering opposites or rather alternatives. The technique is typically postmodern, though the willingness to make choices from multiple subjectivities is not.

De Sousa Santos' distillation of the basic structures in society flows down into the law. For instance, domestic law reflects the householdplace and so on. The undemocratic and rigid nature of these laws is under attack as there emerge 'forms of law that are explicitly liquid, ephemeral, ever negotiable, and renegotiable, in sum disposable'. It is perhaps controversial that de Sousa Santos gives EC legislation as an example of the new law. The new law is an 'antiauratic law, an interstitial, almost colloquial law, which repeats social relations instead of modelling them, and in such a way that the distinction between professional and non-professional legal knowledge (as much as the discrepancy between the law in books and the law in action) ceases to make sense' (de Sousa Santos, 'The Postmodern Transition', pp. 112–13).

De Sousa Santos recognises that for postmodernism to move away from mere deconstruction towards reconstruction it is necessary 'to reinvent the future by opening up new horizons of possibility mapped out by radical new alternatives. Merely to criticize the dominant paradigm, though crucial, is not enough. We must also define the emergent paradigm, this being the really important and difficult task.' De Sousa Santos urges a return to utopian thinking on the basis that modernity is generally hostile to such thinking. He is arguing against the alternatives offered by liberalism of either 'modernity or barbarity'. The seeds of the utopian alternatives are found within the margins and within the 'other' of modernity (de Sousa Santos, *Towards a New Common Sense*, pp. 479–82). For inspiration de Sousa Santos looks to innovative, somewhat chaotic, 'frontier' societies, where authority and power have not been channelled and centralised, as well as baroque subjectivity which 'lives comfortably with the temporary suspension of order and canons' investing instead in 'the local, the particular, the momentary, the ephemeral and the transitory'; and above all 'The South', which 'signifies the form of human suffering caused by capitalist modernity'. Praising the notions of community and solidarity which draw on all three inspirations of frontier, baroque, and the South, and found clearly expressed in the writings and thoughts of Chomsky and Gandhi, de Sousa Santos's methods of paradigmatic contradiction and competition between the structures of modernity and the emerging radical paradigms are powerful and compelling. As with Unger this is not 'the blueprint of a new order', but evidence that the 'collapse of the existing order...does not entail barbarism at all'. 'It means, rather, an opportunity to reinvent a commitment to authentic emancipation, a commitment, moreover, which, rather than being a product of enlightened vanguardist thought, unfolds as sheer common sense' (de Sousa Santos, *Towards a New Common Sense*, pp. 491–519).

FURTHER READING

Balkin, J. M., 'Understanding Legal Understanding: The Legal Subject and the Problem of Legal Coherence' (1993) 103 *Yale Law Journal* 105.

Boyle, J., 'Is Subjectivity Possible?: The Postmodern Subject in Legal Theory' (1991) 62 *University of Colorado Law Review* 489.

Burchell, G., Gordon, C., and Miller, P. (eds.), *The Foucault Effect: Studies in Governmentality* (London: Harvester Wheatsheaf, 1991).

Carty, A. (ed.), *Post-Modern Law* (Edinburgh: Edinburgh University Press, 1994).

Culler, J., *On Deconstruction : Theory and Criticism after Structuralism* (London: Routledge & Kegan Paul, 1983).

Davies, M., *Delimiting the Law: 'Postmodernism' and the Politics of Law* (London: Pluto Press, 1996).

Doherty T., (ed.), *Postmodernism: A Reader* (London: Harvester Wheatsheaf, 1993).

Douzinas, C., Goodrich P., and Hachamovitch, Y., *Politics, Postmodernity and Critical Legal Studies* (London: Routledge, 1994).

Golder B. and Fitzpatrick P., *Foucault's Law* (London: Routledge, 2009).

Gutting, G., *Michel Foucault's Archaeology of Scientific Reason* (Cambridge: Cambridge University Press, 1989).

Howells, C., *Derrida: Deconstruction from Phenomenology to Ethics* (Cambridge: Polity Press, 1998).

Hunt, A. and Wickham, G., *Foucault and Law: Towards a Sociology of Law as Governance* (London: Pluto, 1994).

McGowan, J., *Postmodernism and its Critics* (London: Cornell University Press, 1991).

Mootz, F. J., 'Is the Rule of Law Possible in a Postmodern World?' (1993) 68 *Washington Law Review* 249.

Norris, C., *What's Wrong with Postmodernism: Critical Theory and the Ends of Philosophy* (Hemel Hempstead: Harvester Wheatsheaf, 1990).

Patterson, D., *Postmodernism and Law* (Aldershot: Dartmouth, 1994).

Penner, J., Schiff, D., and Nobles, R., (eds.), *Jurisprudence and Legal Theory: Commentary and Materials* (Oxford: Oxford University Press, 2002), chs 19 and 20.

Schlag, P., 'Normativity and the Politics of Form' (1991) 139 *University of Pennsylvania Law Review* 801.

Silverman, H. J., *Derrida and Deconstruction* (London: Routledge, 1989).

Weed, E., 'Reading at the Limit' (1994) 15 *Cardozo Law Review* 1671.

Wickham, G. and Pavlich, G. (eds.), *Rethinking Law, Society and Governance: Foucault's Bequest* (Oxford: Hart Publishing, 2001).

Williams, J., *Lyotard : Towards a Postmodern Philosophy* (Cambridge: Polity Press, 1998).

INDEX